Prime Minister Boris …

… and other things that never happened

PRIME MINISTER BORIS ...

... AND OTHER THINGS THAT NEVER HAPPENED

edited by

DUNCAN BRACK

and

IAIN DALE

Biteback Publishing

First published in Great Britain in 2011

This edition published by
Biteback Publishing Ltd
Westminster Tower
3 Albert Embankment
London SE1 7SP

ISBN 978-1-84954-362-0

10 9 8 7 6 5 4 3 2 1

A CIP catalogue record for this book is available from the British Library.

Typeset in Bembo by Duncan Brack.

Printed and bound in Great Britain by
CPI Group (UK) Ltd, Croydon, CR0 4YY.

Contents

Introduction

Duncan Brack and Iain Dale

> People make their own history but they do not make it just as they
> please; they do not make it under circumstances chosen by themselves,
> but under circumstances directly encountered, given, and transmitted
> from the past.
>
> *Karl Marx*

Here in this book you will find twenty-two examinations of things
that never happened, from John Maynard Keynes being drowned at
sea in 1916, to Richard Nixon being elected President of the United States
instead of John F. Kennedy, to the United Kingdom staying out of war in
Iraq in 2003, to the Liberal Democrat–Conservative coalition government
not being formed in 2010. And you will also find two things that haven't
happened yet …

This is the third in the series of books of political counterfactuals one or
both of us has produced, the others being *Prime Minister Portillo and Other
Things That Never Happened* (2003) and *President Gore and Other Things That
Never Happened* (2007). Although 'serious' historians tend to look down
their noses at at the study of counterfactuals, they have a distinguished
record. Winston Churchill contributed a chapter (on what if Robert E.
Lee had won the battle of Gettysburg) to a 1931 collection called *If It Had
Happened Otherwise*, and other counterfactual analyses have been published
by historians and sociologists such as Robert Fogel, Geoffrey Hawthorn
and Niall Ferguson. Earlier in 2011, Biteback published Francis Beckett's
collection *The Prime Ministers Who Never Were*.

We believe that counterfactual history does have value. It can reinforce the analysis of what actually happened by identifying the points at which things could have happened differently, and the relevance at each of these key points both of individual choices and of broader socio-economic forces. It can help in analysing the causes underlying particular events; arguably, as Fogel pointed out, in making claims for causes of any kind, historians are always implicitly considering and discarding potential counterfactuals.

Ferguson used his volume *Virtual Hisory: Alternatives and Counterfactuals* to illustrate his objections to deterministic theories of history such as Marxism, and to put forward the case for the importance of contingency in history. But counterfactuals can also illustrate the limits on contingency and the constraints on individual choice. As Marx himself argued, in the quotation at the head of this introduction, it is the interaction between individual choices and historical context which governs the events of the past.

To achieve these aims, the counterfactuals must of course be plausible. Start to change one decision or happening or event in history, and it can be difficult to justify not changing others. There have to be boundaries, and the more rigorously these are policed the more convincing – and the more analytically useful – the results become. So the chapters in this book are limited to occasions where very little needed to have happened differently for the ultimate outcome to have been transformed – and, mostly, to changed individual choices or actions set against unchanged economic and social backgrounds.

Three of the chapters, for example, deal with deaths (of Lloyd George and Keynes in 1916), an illness (or, rather, the lack of it, in the case of Macmillan in 1963), and a succesful coup (rather than the failed one against Gorbachev in 1991). Each, and particularly the first, could have had profound consequences for the modern world – yet each needs no great adjustment in political, social or economic circumstances to be plausible.

Other chapters focus on individual choices: of Attlee's decisions over cabinet posts in 1945, of Blair's over his resignation in 2007, and of Brown's over the calling of an election in the same year. All these decisions are the sole preserve of the Prime Minister, and these counterfactuals require no assumptions other than over one man's choices. Others look at collective decisions which could have turned out differently: over British membership of the European Economic Community in 1972 (a neat counterpoint to the chapter on 'What if the Britain had entered the Common Market in 1957?' in *President Gore*), of the government's handling of the miners' strike in 1984, and over the UK's participation in the war in Iraq in 2003. One chapter looks at the outcome of a commercial decision taken differently, if Rupert Murdoch had failed to buy *The Times* in 1981 – an intriguing possibility with a very up-to-date resonance.

Since, like its predecessors, this is a book of political counterfactuals, several chapters examine possible alternative election outcomes, including those of the US presidential election of 1960 (in reality, Nixon almost won) and of the 2010 general election here in the UK. That result was so close that if a mere 3,000 Conservatives had voted differently, no fewer than sixteen seats would have changed hands. Possibly, however, as is argued here, the outcome in terms of the government would have been the same – at least to start with …

The 2010 result and the actual outcome of the election – the Liberal Democrat–Conservative coalition – took almost everyone by surprise; at the start of the negotiations, this was seen as a highly unlikely conclusion. Another chapter examines the consequences of what was seen then as a more probable arrangement, a 'confidence and supply' agreement between the two parties. Maintaining the 'coalition' theme, another chapter analyses a possible alternative outcome to the formation of the National Government from the political crisis of 1931.

General elections having been rather thoroughly dealt with in this book's two predecessors, several chapters here look at different outcomes of internal party elections, including Mrs Thatcher winning the Conservative leadership contest in 1990, Gordon Brown standing for the Labour leadership in 1994, David Davis being elected Conservative leader in 2005, and Hillary Clinton securing the Democratic presidential nomination in 2008.

One more chapter analyses not just one different election result, but a whole host of them, following the introduction of proportional representation in Britain in 1918 (as, in reality, almost happened). This would represent a profound change in terms of elections, but, as our contributor argues, maybe not all that much in terms of government outcomes.

As in the previous two books, the authors have adopted a variety of approaches, including scholarly analyses of the possibilities and causalities of different outcomes, and fictional accounts of alternate political histories – and sometimes both. One chapter is written as a thriller, envisaging the assassination of a Pope, while the final two in the book revolve around the political career of Boris Johnson: one concerns the recent past and the escond addresses a question on eveyone's lips ...

If any reader has ideas for topics, or authors, for a potential further volume, we would be very pleased to hear them; send us your ideas via email at duncan@dbrack.org.uk and/or iain@iaindale.com. In the meantime, we hope you are stimulated, provoked and entertained by *Prime Minister Boris and Other Things That Never Happened* – but could have.

Authors

David Bean is currently completing a master's degree in ancient history at the University of St Andrews, where he also holds a degree in international relations and philosophy. A former project manager with the Co-operative Group, he is also an active member of the Conservative Party.

David Boyle is a fellow of the New Economics Foundation and the co-author of *Eminent Corporations* (Constable, 2010) and other books.

Duncan Brack is the Editor of the *Journal of Liberal History*, and has co-edited and contributed to two previous volumes of political counterfactuals, *Prime Minister Portillo and Other Things That Never Happened* (Politico's, 2003) and *President Gore and Other Things That Never Happened* (Politico's, 2006). He is currently special adviser to Chris Huhne MP, Secretary of State for Energy and Climate Change.

Richard Briand is a freelance writer and political commentator. He wrote a chapter in *President Gore and Other Things That Never Happened*, published by Politico's in 2006. He reviews books for the *Political Quarterly* and *The Spectator*.

Simon Buckby was a journalist for the BBC and the *Financial Times*, then Campaign Director of Britain in Europe. **Sam Cannicott** was a media and policy adviser to the Liberal Democrats, and worked as a press officer for the party during the 2010 election campaign. They now both work for Champollion, an independent communications consultancy specialising in public policy issues.

Matt Cole is a Visiting Fellow of the Hansard Society and Head of Modern History and Politics at King Edward VI College in Stourbridge. He is the author of *Democracy in Britain* (EUP, 2006) and *Richard Wainwright, the Liberals and Liberal Democrats* (MUP, 2011), and at the last five general elections he has been a political analyst for BBC radio.

Philip Cowley is Professor of Parliamentary Government at the University of Nottingham. His other publications include *The British General Election of 2010* (with Dennis Kavanagh) and *The Rebels*. He also wrote (with Matthew Bailey) 'What if Ted Heath had stepped down in 1974?' in Iain Dale and Duncan Brack's *Prime Minister Portillo and Other Things That Never Happened*.

Iain Dale is Managing Director of Biteback Publishing and *Total Politics* magazine. He presents a weekday radio show on LBC 97.3 and is a contributing editor to *GQ* magazine.

Jane Griffiths is a writer who is very keen on politics, or a political person who is very keen on writing, as you prefer. She was born in London but lived for a long time in Reading, where she was Labour MP for Reading East from 1997 to 2005, when she stood down after being deselected by the local party. She lives now in Strasbourg, France, where she works as a legal editor and is currently trying, without much success, not to be a socialist ...

Graham Kirby is a regular contributor to *Tribune* magazine as a theatre and arts critic. His translation work for theatre include Euripides' *Medea* and *Bacchae* as well as Aeschylus' *Agamemnon*. He is also a director of the Iris Project, an educational charity.

Andy Mayer is the Deputy Director of Liberal Vision and has been a liberal campaigner for twenty years. He is the secular humanist representative on Southwark's Standing Advisory Council for Religious Education.

Tony McNulty was Labour MP for Harrow East from 1997 to 2010. He was a minister variously for housing, planning and regeneration (ODPM), transport, immigration, police and security, employment and London (attending cabinet). He continues to be active in Labour politics – and in writing, broadcasting and reflecting.

Sam Macrory is political editor of *The House Magazine* and also writes for ePolitix.com.

David Mills was a special adviser to Liam Byrne as Minister for the Cabinet Office and Chief Secretary to the Treasury. Before that, he was deputy editor of the *GMTV Sunday Programme*. He currently works for Guardian News and Media.

Ted Morris works in financial services, and is a keen student of modern political history.

Adrian Moss is an award-winning screenwriter, based in Gloucestershire, who runs a small production company producing educational films for UK publishers, charities and universities. He was at university during the miners' strike in 1984, and has a deep affection for coal.

Mark Munro lives in London and follows the politics of the capital closely. He is madly devoted to his wife.

Jaime Reynolds works for the European Commission on international environmental policy. He has written extensively on Liberal history (including contributions to the previous collections of counterfactuals edited by Duncan Brack and Iain Dale) and on Eastern European politics.

Peter Riddell is a Senior Fellow of the Institute for Government and was a political journalist for over thirty years, until July 2010 as chief political commentator of *The Times*. He has written seven books on British politics, most recently *In Defence of Politicians – in spite of themselves*.

Neil Stockley is a director of a public affairs consultancy and a former policy director for the Liberal Democrats.

Mark Stuart is a Research Associate at both Nottingham and Hull Universities, where he teaches British politics and helps to run the revolts website (www.revolts.co.uk). He has written biographies of Douglas Hurd and John Smith, and is a regular political columnist with the *Yorkshire Post*.

Christian Walker is a recent graduate in international relations, and is currently completing his masters degree in international relations (security) at the University of Birmingham. He has a long-standing interest in counterfactual history, founded on his interest in international politics and history, and fuelled by that 1990s' staple of early evening television, *Sliders*.

Dr Robert Waller has been the author of eight editions of *The Almanac of British Politics* (Routledge) between 1983 and 2007, and is a former Fellow and Lecturer in History and Politics at Magdalen, Trinity and Wadham Colleges, Oxford.

Chapter 1

What if Lloyd George and Keynes had gone to Russia in 1916?

David Boyle

It was a horrible shock to hear of the *Hampshire* disaster and to know that you missed it by so little. I could hardly breathe when I realised it at first … and it was your birthday!

Letter to Keynes from his mother, 6 June 1916

It is 5 June 1916. The Grand Fleet has returned to its North Sea bases days ago, battered but unbowed after its ordeal at the Battle of Jutland. In France, the final preparations are being made for the British offensive on the Somme. At the fleet anchorage at Scapa Flow in the Orkney Isles, a senior government delegation heading for Russia is on board a small drifter, battling against the wind to board the cruiser HMS *Hampshire*.

It is an undignified business. The sea is too rough for the cruiser to dock and too violent to climb a gangway from a boat in the usual way. It requires a hoist. First up the grey sides is Lord Kitchener, the Minister for War, not just a great man but also, as the Prime Minister's wife puts it, 'a great poster'. Prince Felix Yusupov, the future murderer of Rasputin, has been impressed by his grasp of Russian affairs and suggested that the Tsar request a visit.

Next up the hoist, a tall, thin intense-looking man, carrying an attaché case, making sure that Kitchener does not have to talk to his boss when he reaches the top. This is John Maynard Keynes, representing the Treasury and there to assist the dynamic Munitions Minister and former Chancellor,

David Lloyd George, who follows behind, irritable and restless, his dapper moustache blowing in the wind.

The rain lashes their faces as they struggle under cover as their teams follow up the hoist. The north easterly wind is now rising into gale force. The smoke from the *Hampshire*'s four tall funnels is blown down, backwards and forwards across the deck. As soon as the dignitaries are aboard, greeted by the Captain and hurried below for lunch, the *Hampshire* makes her way towards the great boom which guards the fleet from enemy submarines. Two small destroyers follow in her wake.

Outside the comfort of the fleet anchorage, the gale hits the *Hampshire* with shocking force. The fleet commander, Sir John Jellicoe, has suggested that they take the westerly route around the Orkneys to avoid the worst of the wind, without realising that – only three days before – the German submarine U75 has laid twenty-two mines by Marwick Head, directly in their path, under the impression it was somewhere else.

Below decks, Kitchener smokes as the ship swings from side to side, while Lloyd George and Keynes are locked in impassioned debate about the Treasury papers. All are nervous of vomiting in front of the others. It is a tough, slow journey and the two escorts are forced to turn back by the heavy seas, so that *Hampshire* is alone at 7.50 p.m., when she is torn apart by a huge explosion. Sirens wail all over the ship. Steam fills the companionways and it is clear by the immediate list that she will not stay afloat. Ten minutes later, she is gone.

Kitchener is last seen pacing the freezing quarterdeck as the ship goes down. Lloyd George is seen remonstrating with the Captain. There are no reports of Keynes. Most of the crew die in the freezing tumultuous sea, within sight of land.

On board his flagship, in the wireless telegraph room of the *Iron Duke*, Jellicoe is given the news, just five days after his return from battle and the loss of 9,000 British sailors. He sits down heavily and buries his face in his hands. The wartime icon and victor of Omdurman, the man who could have been Prime Minister, and the economist who could have changed the world, are all at the bottom of the sea.

~

1 June 2011
To: Professor Charles X. Hackenbacker
Economics Department
Oscar Romero University
New Mexico 87654
USA

Dear Chuck,

I was leafing through the pages of the latest edition of the *Journal of Economic Mysticism* the other day and found the article by your colleague – the one where he claims to have glimpsed some kind of parallel economic universe where an obscure British Treasury official rescued the world.

You know my view on these things. If something has happened, then it *had* to happen. That's the way we economists look at things. So I thought I would send you some ammunition against this kind of nonsense in case it comes up in your department. I am avoiding email; we don't want a repeat of the hacking incident we had last time.

Now, as you know, your colleague suggests that this is all about the career of a Treasury official called John Maynard Keynes, son of the economist John Neville Keynes. Keynes accompanied Lloyd George on his fatal trip in the *Hampshire,* and my colleague suggests that what should have happened was that neither of them actually went in the end. Both men therefore lived to have their impacts on the world.

Let me go through his suggestions one by one.

The first thing he claims is that Lloyd George would have become Prime Minister in December 1916. This is probably quite true, but – as we know – there was no new Prime Minister in 1916, and Asquith soldiered on until the U-boat and convoy crisis the following year, at which point the Conservatives intervened and the place went to the Conservative leader Andrew Bonar Law. Perhaps, as he suggests, Lloyd George could have held the wartime coalition together, split the Liberal Party and allowed the Labour Party to move into their space. Perhaps he would have brought Churchill back in from the cold: 'I would rather have him against us every

3

time', said Bonar Law.[1] Perhaps, but this is just part of his dream world. That isn't what happened, is it?

These things are perhaps more in my remit than yours, since they concern British history. But, as you will recall, Bonar Law managed to moderate matters at Versailles but then instituted a disastrous series of imperial tariffs, Beaverbrook's price for making him getting him the top job. This led to ferocious trade competition with the United States, and truly desperate balance of payments difficulties, leading to more spending cuts, strikes and riots before they were dismantled by the Liberal government of 1924.

Your colleague says that Lloyd George would have built 170,000 homes, controlled the rents and provided unemployment insurance, and doubled old age pensions. Maybe he would have done. He certainly had a more mellifluous way with words. I'm sure he could have come up with a better slogan than Bonar Law's 'houses fit for soldiers in genuine need'!

But then, as your colleague says, even under Lloyd George, the spending cuts of the 1920s reversed most of these achievements. That is why they had to wait for the Liberals to come back into power, an event sadly overshadowed by the business of ousting the ancient Asquith and replacing him with Donald Maclean. The idea that the Liberals had split by then and a majority Labour government was possible is laughable. Please poke fun at your colleague for that on my behalf.

These were difficult years for the Liberals, as you know. They had inherited a disastrous economy, limping along after the post-war spending cuts put through by the fearsome 'Chamberlain Chopper'. And we can only imagine what kind of dynamism and ideas Lloyd George might have brought to problems if he had not been residing at the bottom of the North Sea at the time. Perhaps they would not have had to rely on the handful of Labour Party votes to force through the Irish peace treaty after so long, and to unravel the tariffs and trade barriers.

Perhaps they might have prevented the Conservatives returning to the Gold Standard. They might have prevented the Great Depression. Who knows? Still, your colleague is undoubtedly right – if Lloyd George had lived, things would have been different. There would have been a great deal more peers of the realm, for starters.

Then we get to the interesting part. Your colleague suggests that this Keynes, who – in this parallel universe he speaks of – was dropped from sailing on the *Hampshire* at the very last moment, became the critical figure in economics in the twentieth century. He says he formulated a series of ideas which you and I know as 'Kaleckian', after poor Michael Kalecki, who suggested something similar – that markets cannot produce full employment on their own, because the wealthy save rather than spend in the bad times.

This is the idea, which you may recognise, that governments should run their economies at full capacity, increasing aggregate demand by borrowing to invest. It was a theory not so much for Liberals, though Keynes was a Liberal, but to underpin Social Democrats. As a result, your colleague's parallel universe is full of Social Democrats; ours is not.

We know Keynes as a minor member of the Bloomsbury Group, but primarily as the expert in Indian currencies who persuaded Lloyd George not to suspend gold payments in July 1914, and to issue an emergency currency instead. I believe the notes were called Bradburys, after the man who signed them. What we also know about him (he was only 33 when he drowned) was that he and Lloyd George loathed each other. When Lloyd George asked his opinion in a railway carriage in France, he said: 'With the utmost of respect I must, if asked for my opinion, tell you that I regard your account as rubbish.'[2] So your colleague's idea that Keynes and Lloyd George would have worked together in the 1920s to develop these ideas in practice – and that they led to the New Deal in the US – really doesn't stack up. How could they have produced *We Can Conquer Unemployment* together?

As we know, even without Keynes, there was a tentative New Deal in the USA, but it only lasted until the economic collapse of 1937–38. Perhaps this Keynes would have had such status by then that he would have been able to stiffen the backbone of policy-makers. Perhaps his policies of borrowing to invest could then have become the orthodoxy after the Second World War. I doubt it myself.

We all know what actually happened. The big new Liberal idea, developed by the leading economists of the 1930s – Irving Fisher, Henry Simons and the Chicago School – was quite different. What actually became the orthodoxy after the Second World War was Simons's approach to liberal economics: anti-trust, monopoly-bashing and the 100 per cent money system of banking.[3]

That was the gist of the plans proposed by the Macmillan Committee in 1930. I find your colleague's idea that the Macmillan Committee was designed as vehicle for Keynes a little strange, since he had by then been dead for fourteen years. No, as we know, the future belonged to Simons and Fisher.

'The great enemy of democracy is monopoly in all its forms', said Simons.[4] That was the policy which prevailed among radicals on both sides of the Atlantic after the war, determined to prevent another depression and the rise of more fascistic demagogues – and his other policies too, higher levels of tax on the wealthy, and limitations on the power of advertisers to make people unhappy.

So the big corporations were broken up, as they had been in the days of Teddy Roosevelt. For two generations, the names Shell, BP, General Electric, Ford, Morris, ICI and all the rest of them disappeared. In the UK, the Big Five banks – Barclays, Midland, Westminster, Lloyds and National Provincial – were broken up into their constituent parts and sent back to their local areas to learn about good local productive investment.

'Few of our gigantic corporations can be defended on the ground that their present size is necessary to reasonably full exploitation of production economies', wrote Simons. 'Their existence is to be explained in terms of opportunities for promoter profits, personal ambitions of industrial and financial "Napoleons", and advantages of monopoly power.'[5] That was what we got instead of Keynes.

But the real change, at least in our own universe, was to the way banks work. No more would they take people's deposits and then loan them out again many times over, and risk not having the liquidity they needed in a crisis. They would have to keep 100 per cent of their backing for any deposits they took. There would be no more bank crashes or investment bubbles. Banks would be either investors or warehouses for people's money. The money was created instead by the government, increasing steadily at 3 per cent a year, and bought in by investors for loaning out again to worthwhile productive enterprises.

That was the world without Keynes that we inherited. Your colleague also suggests that the war in Europe ended as early as May 1945, because of the pioneering work that Keynes and his American colleagues did on how to plan to use the whole productive capacity of the nation. That would certainly have helped my parents' generation. We might not have had to rebuild south London from scratch after the V-weapon assault. It would have meant that the Soviet bloc would not have extended all the way to the Rhine.

But even your colleague does not suggest that Keynes persuaded your national policy-makers to drop Harry Dexter White's plan for Bretton Woods – they were not aware at that stage that he was a Soviet agent. Maybe he would have prevented the adoption of flexible exchange rates, maybe not. As we know, what actually happened was that the British negotiators failed to argue effectively for anything else. Or to re-negotiate the humungous British loans in 1946, as your colleague claims Keynes would have done. That is why so many devaluations of the pound took place in the years that followed, and explains its slow decline as a serious currency. That is why Britain was only rescued from economic collapse by Marshall Aid.

I know we had the New Pound for some years, but we were glad to pension if off, quite frankly, along with the lire and drachma, and join the euro – goodness knows what Keynes would have said about that! Well, I know what your colleague says. He thinks Keynes would have said: 'above all, let finance be primarily national'.[6] But really, who knows?

So there we were after the war, with no Keynes to save us, a plummeting currency, no imperial tariffs, little or no empire – because it had been mortgaged to the USA – and when the new Liberal government arrived in 1946 there was no money for the great social experiments some had dreamed of; it was like the 1920s all over again. Huge inflation (no Keynes plan for compulsory savings to keep inflation down during the war), spending cuts, followed by strikes, followed by devaluations. It kept the Liberals out of office for nearly fifteen years afterwards.

What saved us, as you know, was the British plan for a European community and Simons' anti-trust policies. It meant that we had proper banks, hundreds of them, rather than the Big Five that two decades of Montagu Norman at the head of the Bank of England had left us with (did you know Norman was a patient of Jung's, incidentally?). We had local investment and a ferociously productive economy, which is why they called us the English Tiger in the 1970s.

That was the world we knew as we grew up, and it seemed to me that it worked. That was why our Prime Minister Harold Macmillan could say that 'some of our people have never had it so good'. That was why it all felt so prosperous under the Liberal governments of Roy Jenkins in the 1960s, as we rebuilt Britain's manufacturing base in small-scale networks of workshops like those in Emilia-Romagna, or webs of co-operatives like those in Mondragon.

I mention this because it is strange, is it not, that your colleague suggests that both parallel universes culminated in much the same place? The new generation at the Chicago School of Economics, including Simons' favourite pupil Milton Friedman, changed their minds, didn't they?

Friedman and his colleagues came to believe, as you know, that the Great Depression was caused, not because of Wall Street greed or any basic flaw in the economic system, but because the Federal Reserve took so much money out of the economy. He became fixated on the quantity theory of money and came to think that nothing else mattered.

He was such a romantic, Friedman – the perfect balance to your colleague's portrait of this Keynes – and so were the other creators of the new conservatism, like that crazy novelist Ayn Rand. Like Hayek, they started by looking a little like Liberals, but they ended up as libertarians – which means, in the end, that the richest and biggest were encouraged to ride roughshod over everyone else.

Of course, they were helped by the Vietnam War. Your government kept on producing money to keep up with all the bombing and the huge military resources they needed, way beyond Simons's 3 per cent increase a year. Then there was inflation and the whole 100 per cent money idea fell into disrepute. So they stopped and let banks create money again as they used to. 'Politicians are less likely to spend the government's money if they know a large part of it is borrowed', said Friedman.[7] So of course the banks make huge profits from that, and we are heading back to where we started.

And we're back to our present sorry situation, in both parallel universes, with or without Keynes or Lloyd George. Giant corporations which hoover up the money which ought to be going into productive investment somewhere else. Banks which are busily corroding the real economy, and – as a result – the banking crash of 2008, which seems to refute most of what Friedman stood for, though no one seems to realise it.

But the two universes are not quite the same. For one thing, in the world without either Keynes or Lloyd George, we now have a Conservative–Labour coalition in this country. And, ugh, the Labour Party are not what they were in your colleague's parallel world – they are now all union-jack waving, *Daily Mail*-reading intolerance!

For another thing, there is no division that your colleague suggests in the US between old liberalism (tackling monopoly, regulating the money supply) and new liberalism (borrowing and spending). In fact, there is no such thing as a new liberalism. Kaleckian economics is regarded as having been tried and failed – though the extra-parliamentary left are constantly suggesting otherwise.

We also live in a different kind of nation to the picture your colleague painted. The capital of the European Union is in London. The Bank of England is the lead institution for the euro, which provides us with our currency – which suits us very well but is dreadful for countries like Ireland, Greece and Portugal, and certainly not good for Germany now it's extracted itself from behind the Iron Curtain and joined the party. We have a robust and diverse banking system, including thousands of community banks – and our banks survived the 2008 crash unscathed.

Also, there is a different choice between progressives and conservatives on both sides of the Atlantic. Conservatives want corporations to do as they please so that the rich get all the benefits; Liberals want to tackle monopoly wherever they see it so that everyone gets the benefits. That's the dividing line between us, laissez-faire versus free trade. But of course you know all this.

In any case, I can't see that these parallel universe discussions get us anywhere. I don't think it's an economist's job to make predictions about the future, or the past, or anything that can be held as a hostage to fortune. The day we start letting the real world intrude on our theories will be a bad one for economics, let me tell you!

Please don't leave this letter lying around, and I look forward to drinking beer with you on your next five-year sabbatical.

Yours sincerely
Gerald

~

30 June 2011
To: Gerald Banks PhD
Senior Lecturer in Economics
University of Milton Keynes
MK30 6ET
UK

Dear Gerald,

Thank you for your letter, which I have copied and posted back to you for posterity, enclosed in this envelope. You are quite right, of course, and I have mentioned our concerns about the article at the departmental committee. Unfortunately the *Journal of Economic Mysticism* is largely sacrosanct these days, since the Federal Reserve chairman began to use it for communicating his ideas.

My colleague tells me that he is, in fact, planning a sequel! He has decided that he made a mistake about Keynes dying of exhaustion after the loan negotiations in 1946. He says that since both his parents lived until their nineties, it seems likely that Keynes would too.

He says that, had Keynes survived the *Hampshire*, he would therefore in fact have lived until 1973 and – as an old man – became disillusioned with his own theories and became the founder of what we now know as green economics.

Apparently, this is what he might have said on the subject:

The same rule of self-destructive financial calculation governs every walk of life. We destroy the beauty of the countryside because the unappropriated splendours of nature have not economic value. We are capable of shutting off the sun and the stars because they do not pay a dividend. London is one of the richest cities in the history of civilisation, but it cannot 'afford' the highest standards of achievement of which its own living citizens are capable, because they do not 'pay'…

Or again, we have until recently conceived it a moral duty to ruin the tillers of the soil and destroy the age-long human traditions attendant on husbandry if we could get a loaf of bread a tenth of a penny cheaper. There was nothing which it was not our duty to sacrifice to this Moloch and Mammon in one; for we faithfully believed that the worship of these monsters would overcome the evil of poverty and lead the next generation safely and comfortably, on the back of compound interest, into economic peace.[8]

There we are. That was an economic manifesto that I'm glad was never uttered. I don't know where my colleague gets this stuff. I have asked him how he goes about his research, but he just stares knowingly at me in an irritating way and mumbles something about a Subtle Knife.

I gather that Keynes and Schumacher cooperated, just before he died, on a book called *Small is Theoretically Beautiful*.[9] In fact, if Keynes had lived, he believes that he would become increasingly sceptical about money because, as Ruskin put it, 'there is no wealth but life' – a pernicious idea that no serious economist could possibly endorse.

Farewell, old friend. I will be coming over to your country shortly to lecture on genetic probability and the markets.

Yours ever

Chuck

~

In the freezing water off the Orkney coast, in the rusting remains of HMS *Hampshire*, the intermingled bones still remain of David Lloyd George, John Maynard Keynes and Lord Kitchener, a silent testament to a world they might have changed completely – and around them the bones of so many others who, had they lived, might have their own unique shifts in the world we inherited.

Notes

1   Roy Jenkins, *Churchill* (Macmillan, 2001), p. 320.
2   Charles H. Hessian, *John Maynard Keynes* (Macmillan, 1984), p. 124.
3   See, for example, I. Fisher, *100% Money* (Farrar, 1933).
4   Henry C. Simons, 'A positive program for laissez-faire' (Public Policy Pamphlet No 15, University of Chicago Press, 1934), p. 74; in Ross Emmett (ed.), *The Chicago Tradition in Economics 1892–1945* (Routledge, 2002).
5   Simons, 'A positive program for laissez-faire', pp. 90–91.
6   J. M. Keynes, 'National Self-sufficiency', Finlay Lecture, University College, Dublin, 19 April 1933; in D. E. Moggridge (ed.), *Collected Works* Vol. 21 (Macmillan, 1982).
7   Larry Ebenstein, *Milton Friedman: A Biography* (Palgrave Macmillan, 2007), p. 177.
8   Keynes, 'National Self-Sufficiency'.
9   Before he died, Keynes predicted that Schumacher would be the one to inherit his mantle. See Barbara Wood, *Alias Papa: A life of Fritz Schumacher* (Chelsea Green, 2011).

Chapter 2

What if proportional representation had been introduced in 1918?

Robert Waller

Change from the First Past the Post (FPTP) system for electing the UK House of Commons has been intermittently suggested over the past hundred years, most recently in the referendum of 5 May 2011 on the introduction of the Alternative Vote. A typically British variety of more proportional systems has now been adopted for other elections such as those to the Scottish Parliament, the National Assembly for Wales and the Greater London Assembly (all by the additional member system), elections in Northern Ireland and Scottish councils (the single transferable vote), and for the European Parliament (regional list). However every election for MPs at Westminster, where most of the power has always been located, between 1910 and 2010 have essentially retained FPTP, giving rise to debate about both its fairness and its effects.

In this chapter the latter are considered, in the light of the possibility that for general elections from 1918 onwards FPTP might have been replaced by a considerable degree of proportionality in the way that votes are translated into parliamentary seats. This suggestion is not, in its initial premise, mere fantasy. Electoral reform for the Commons was seriously considered by the Speaker's Conference that was called in 1916 and reported in 1917. If the outcome adopted then had been different, many believe that the subsequent history of Britain would have been significantly altered. They may have been disappointed.

Reform of the electoral system, both the alternative vote (AV) and a fully proportional method, the single transferable vote (STV), were both very seriously considered during the second half of the First World War. The work of the First Speaker's Conference began in October 1916, two months before Lloyd George's 'coup' in which he replaced his long-term Liberal colleague Asquith to form a three-party coalition headed by a five-man War Cabinet. David Butler, in his authoritative study of the electoral system in Britain since 1918, declared that 'astonishingly, on proportional representation complete unanimity was achieved'.[1] By 14 December the Speaker reported its first period of its work to the new Prime Minister – and it included a resolution which had been passed recommending the use of proportional representation (STV) for multi-member constituencies,[2] along with AV for all the remainder, single-member seats.[3] The acknowledged expert on electoral reform for this period, Martin Pugh, has argued that Lloyd George missed a golden opportunity fully to back electoral reform at this stage, before he had decided to throw in his lot with the Conservatives as in the December 1918 'coupon election'.[4]

A proposal by Asquith to enact the Speaker's Conference report was passed by the Commons on 28 March 1917 and a consequent Representation of the Bill to that effect on second reading in late May. Even after thorough controversy and debate at the Committee stage, the AV proposal was passed by 151–123 in the Commons on 22 November 1917. However the STV section of the Bill was defeated three times in the Commons, on 11–12 June by seven votes, when heavy Conservative opposition by over two to one outweighed the small but favourable majorities of the other three main parties (all being unwhipped),[5] then again in July and November. However when the Bill went to the Lords the PR-STV idea was not only revived but extended, as members of the Upper House sought to remove AV entirely and replace it with an STV system covering more than 90 per cent of the constituencies in a framework of multi-member seats, in Lord Selborne's proposal of 21 January 1918. By 26 January, five days later, Selborne had prepared a detailed proposal for 25 five-member, 42 four-member, and 50 three-member constituencies in England.[6]

However by a majority of 100 the Commons rejected this measure that might have so transformed the subsequent course of British history, though they did reinsert the alternative vote on 31 January. In a rapid game of parliamentary table-tennis, in early February 1918 the Houses ejected each other's electoral reform proposals, and ended with neither, even though, as David Butler pointed out, 'a parliamentary conference had unanimously recommended another system and although a substantial majority of the members of each House had, at some stage of the discussion of the Bill, voted for one or other of the proposed reforms of the system'.[7]

According to the *Manchester Guardian* Editor C. P. Scott's diary for 28 January 1917, Lloyd George's position was that he would apply proportional representation 'all round or not at all'. It was to be 'not at all' in reality, but let us imagine that the Prime Minister – perhaps already having the intention of cementing his putative personal 'centre' party in coalitions for the foreseeable future – had used his influence in favour of the Lords position on STV, and that, as with votes for women and far more men in 1918, 'all-round' PR had indeed been passed in that seminal Representation of the People Act. Lord Hattersley opined in his recent biography that 'Lloyd George was a coalition man',[8] and PR would have been an ideal way to all but ensure coalition government.

If we assume PR could already have been in place for the December 1918 'coupon election', Lloyd George's coalition would still have won an overall majority, especially as the vast majority of Irish members would still have been Sinn Feiners, who did not take their seats on principle. The Labour Party would have been more rewarded for their advances since the previous election eight years before for, with over 20 per cent of the vote, PR should have given them nearly 150 MPs rather than the 52 actually won under FPTP.

As the reform of electoral systems is highly unlikely to alter the onset, course or aftermath of wars, including their overwhelming economic consequences, there is no reason to believe that the events of the years 1918–22 would not be as happened in reality, with Lloyd George's coalition coming to an end after the legendary expression of backbench Conservative power at the Carlton Club meeting on 19 October 1922. However, we must assume that the election that followed the next month would commence the divergence in history, as the Conservatives were far short of winning a majority of votes, achieving only 38.5 per cent of the UK share – which in FPTP reality was enough for 55.9 per cent of the seats, well ahead of the very divided opposition. As Labour and the two bitterly divided Liberal parties (still led by the feuding Asquith and Lloyd George) would have been highly unlikely to form a coalition between them, especially as two of these three had refused LG's coupon less than four years previously, Baldwin would still have formed the government in November 1922 – except as a minority.

It could be argued that we should no longer assume that Baldwin's government would have taken the same course as it did 'in the real world' in 1923. However, it seems reasonable in this, as other counterfactual exercises, to work on the principle of less difference from reality in the early stages, and it can also be argued that the effects of PR would not be fully understood in its early years. Finally, as A. J. P. Taylor pointed out,[9] there seemed little rational reason why Baldwin should have revived the 'terrible controversy' of protectionism anyway; he must have realised that it would be likely that it would end in his defeat when he called the election of December 1923 to give a mandate to tariff reform. He may have been worried about a revived coalition between Lloyd George and the Conservatives, and wanted to drive a wedge between them, or it may have simply been a matter of principle.

Assuming that proportional representation did not, initially at least, mean an end to all political principle, it is posited that the 1923 election did take place, and produced a similar result in terms of votes. With the Conservatives obtaining 38 per cent of the vote, and Labour and the temporarily reunited Liberals 30 per cent each, this produced a hung parliament in any case (a rare election in which FPTP produced a fairly proportionate outcome), and we assume that the Liberals backed a minority Labour government for the reasons they did in the real timeline – and withdrew that support for the same reasons after just under a year. However, the October 1924 election would have meant that Baldwin again did not gain an overall majority, attaining under 47 per cent under FPTP – and the Liberals may have come up with more than 339 candidates, knowing that votes gained even in their many hopeless seats would still count towards electing MPs.

This would have given Lloyd George another potential opportunity to regain a place in government. Differences with Asquith had again re-emerged, and LG could have mobilised enough of his old supporters to split earlier than he did (in 1931), to provide enough support for Baldwin to achieve his overall majority, especially after a promise not to revive the spectre of tariff reform. We do know that in 1924 LG 'was adamantine in his refusal to provide the Asquithian-dominated Liberal Party organisation with funds,[10] and in *The Goat in the Wilderness* John Campbell accused him of a Machiavellian action to oust Asquith, to smash his own party and to rule the rump:

> He soon became equally impatient of Asquith and of Labour, and resolved to be rid of both. He therefore worked with the Tories to bring down the government and force a general election, for which the Liberal Party, lacking adequate financial help, was unprepared.[11]

Chris Wrigley has summed up Lloyd George's position thus:

> During the 1920s, LG moved this way and that for political advantage, sometimes veering towards Conservatives to explore possibilities of a new political grouping and at the same time making advances towards Labour.[12]

PR would have been ideal for those manoeuvres.

In our counterfactual, industrial relations still came to dominate the mid-1920s, but LG proved an enthusiastic junior coalition supporter in the Conservative strategy to crush the 1926 General Strike, unlike in reality; the attractions of power and office can have potent effects on policy positions. His role as a man of the people on his road to power way back in the 1909 Budget was certainly long behind him.

There are several different types of proportional representation, and it was a well-advised choice in 1918 to opt for the single transferable vote.

Regional lists and the additional member system both transfer power from the voter to the parties, denying the opportunity for voters to vote out an individual MP whose representation is deemed unsatisfactory, due to the party control of the order of the lists. STV, however, uses a preferential system, with one vote with second, third, fourth (and so on) choices being applied until candidates are either eliminated for lack of support or reach the necessary quota to be elected, thus ending such evils as the wasted vote and tactical voting. As applied in multi-member constituencies, for example of three, four or five representatives, it also does not break the link between the MP and his seat; in fact, in theory it improves the link, as voters can even express a preference between candidates of the same party, either on a personal basis (for example if a government minister is thought to be neglecting the constituency), or on political lines, giving a possible choice between more left- and right-wing candidates from the same party, or even choosing politicians with a local base in part of the larger seats – all strategies that have been practised in Irish elections under STV.

Unfortunately, in our counterfactual all the major parties soon realised that these characteristics meant that STV gave voters a dangerous amount of democratic choice and power at their expense – and adopted the policy of only putting up as many candidates as seats they believed they could win, as well as tightly controlling all their nominations; this is essentially what happened when STV was used in Scottish local elections from 2007.[13] This negated one of the democratic advantages of a system that remained very attractive, on paper.

The 1929 election saw a swing against the Baldwin-LG government, with Labour almost becoming the largest party for the first time, and the non-LG Liberals were only too keen to support MacDonald as he formed his second minority administration. The electoral system encouraged the Labour leader to aim for moderation, even more than in reality because of the PR-determined need to occupy the centre ground. However, the method of electing MPs cannot stave off a great depression, whether it originates outside the country or not, so his second government met the same fate as it did in reality.

In 1931, therefore, there was a similar outcome to the actual course of history, with the MacDonald-Baldwin National Government coalition gaining just over two-thirds of the total vote, although of course Labour's 31 per cent share meant they returned nearly 200 MPs, not the paltry 52 they managed in reality. The parliamentary system scarcely allowed even this number to form an effective opposition to the coalition that continued through the 1930s, although after the 1935 election its majority was much more slender, having obtained only 53 per cent of the vote, meaning its overall majority was not nearly 250 but more like 50.

The only impact this could have had was somewhat to strengthen the hand of the anti-appeasers within the Conservative Party as the prospect of war loomed again in the late 1930s – or it would have, if Labour had itself not been divided. The Labour leadership was suspicious of the Communist influence on the republican side in the Spanish Civil War, the Parliamentary Party only voted to abstain rather than vote against increased rearmament expenditure in July 1937, and Labour generally welcomed the Munich agreement in September 1938. There were even doubts about the 'Popular Front' later in 1938 as a revival of 'Lib-Labbery'.[14] Anyway, as he had at the end of the Weimar Republic in Germany itself, Hitler ignored PR and its effects, and the war led to Churchill's all-party coalition in any event, while the 1940 election was cancelled, as parliamentary sovereignty allowed.

1945, however, was a different case. Although in the true course of history this was regarded as a Labour landslide, in fact the party did not achieve an overall majority of votes but only 48 per cent, and in our counterfactual Attlee could form a government only with the help of Common Wealth party radicals and left independents. Even this gave him only a slender majority in the Commons, and with 48.6 per cent of the 1945 vote going to Conservatives and Liberals (who gained over 50 MPs rather than just 12), parties strongly ideologically committed against socialism, only part of the programme of the most radical government Britain has ever had could be passed. This did, however, include the bulk of the welfare state provisions, due to the expectations raised during the war, for example by the Beveridge Report (Beveridge himself was a Liberal). In addition, the coal industry was nationalised, as it had effectively been taken under government control for war production, and the private coal companies' control had already been broken.[15] However the more contentious nationalisation of iron and steel in 1951 did not happen, as Attlee had already been ousted in the election the year before.

One of the characteristic effects of PR is the encouragement of consensus politics and the diminution of drastic changes between successive governments, and this is well illustrated by the case of the steel industry, which in fact was the subject of denationalisation by the Conservatives in 1953 and renationalisation by Labour thirteen years later, before finally being re-privatised under the Thatcher government in 1988. It is a matter of deep political debate whether this consequence of the electoral system represents more stable government and policy, or a bar to radical change.

In 1950, Labour achieved 46.1 per cent of the vote – under FPTP enough to be returned with a narrow overall majority of 15, but under PR this would have been overborne by the 52.5 per cent gained by Conservatives (including the remnants who still called themselves National Liberals) and the Liberal Party itself, which, led by Clement Davies, was far more inclined to support the right rather than the socialists. Indeed, in reality, the anti-Labour pacts that were to sustain some of the handful of Liberal MPs through the decade started in 1950, with Donald Wade elected in Huddersfield West without a Conservative opponent, while the Tories alone fought the east division of the town. This arrangement was extended from 1951, with Bolton entering a similar arrangement to Huddersfield, and Davies himself had no Tory opposition in 1951 and 1955 – by which time most of the six Liberals actually returned did so courtesy of a free run. In 1950 Churchill actually offered one of the Tories' party political broadcasts to the Liberal candidate for Colne Valley, Asquith's daughter Violet Bonham Carter, and in 1951 invited Clement Davies to a government post as minister for education.[16]

Given these facts, we may posit that under PR the Conservatives would have governed with Liberal support throughout the 1950s, even though they never achieved 50 per cent of the vote – and we should remember that the Liberals (and other minor parties) would probably have achieved more votes with the proportional system, as they drastically reduced their candidatures to stand in just 109 seats in the UK in 1951 and 110 in 1955. Under the STV system this would have not have had such a diminishing effect on their share of the vote in the larger multi-member constituencies. Consequently we can assume that the course of history in the 'grey decade' would have been relatively unaltered, with a Conservative-led government adopting Conservative policies, supported by a rather sycophantic Liberal leadership, although it is to be doubted whether Clement Davies would ever have played tennis with Winston Churchill, Anthony Eden or Harold Macmillan. Indeed the Liberal Party itself could be regarded in our scenario as little more than a shadow of the National Liberals, until a younger group of grassroots activists rebelled against the leaders, who they accused of going 'Tory-native' in government.

However, that did not happen until the mid-1960s. Since there was much less reason to vote Liberal as a way of objecting to a Conservative government, there had been no Liberal revival based on by-election victories against Conservative incumbents such as those at Torrington in 1958 or Orpington in 1962. Alec Douglas Home was thus able to form a fourth successive Tory administration in 1964, despite getting fewer votes than Harold Wilson's Labour – due to the continuing support of the 'old guard' Liberal Party leaders. But as his government was seen as ever more tired and out of touch with the 'swinging sixties', and mercilessly panned by the energised new waves of satirists, encouraged by the electoral system the Liberals split, with a new younger group of MPs, led by Jeremy Thorpe, moving over to support Wilson, still spouting his 'white heat' line and as leader of the Opposition engaging in photo-shoots with the Beatles. After a seminal grassroots Liberal conference, eliciting echoes of the heroes of the 1922 Committee, the government changed in 1965, without an election.

This was a new departure for the UK, but by no means unlikely under a PR system, as the practice of the Free Democrats in Germany was to show. Even in 1966, Labour could not achieve more than 50 per cent of their vote on their own – in fact, no party ever had, nor probably ever will, under PR, because it encourages small parties and independent candidates to stand much more than under FPTP, making the chance of an overall majority effectively impossible. Because of their agreement, after the 1970 election the Lab/New Lib coalition survived, even though the Conservatives won more votes than Labour after the economic crises of the late 1960s. Edward Heath declared that the will of the people had been thwarted, but Mr Wilson retorted that he had been returned to power with a clear mandate of over 50 per cent of the electorate, and that Mr Heath might well practise his sulking, as he was likely to need it on later occasions.

However, for the time being, Mr Wilson was wrong. He had either underestimated or overestimated his coalition partners.

Due to the militancy of the unions and associated economic problems, and even more because of the prospect of Heath making a renewed bid for EEC entry (while Wilson, faced with a deeply divided party, sat on the Channel-fence), the Liberals switched again in early 1972. The government again changed without an election. Enoch Powell left the Conservative Party due to his perception of the fraudulence of its European position, but despite calls, did not form a breakaway party – even though it would have had a considerable chance of success under PR, due to his position on race and immigration – because he was against PR on high principle. Instead he went to Ulster.

The Heath-Thorpe government succeeded in its application to join the European Economic Community, but the unions, led by the miners, continued to cause trouble. In February 1974 Deputy PM Thorpe refused to let Heath call a divisive election, insisting that the coalition should complete a full five-year term, that consensus, not confrontation, was the right way to govern, and that the Liberals expected loyalty from their partners in administration. Therefore Heath staggered on, but after the 1975 election Labour obtained the most votes – but of course no majority, as it was under PR – and the Liberals switched yet again to back Labour, stressing that it was their democratic duty to support the party that had received the highest popular acclaim. Mr Heath continued to occupy Downing Street for some days, but although it was rumoured that Jeremy Thorpe himself had been willing to consider his offer of a renewed coalition, particularly with the role of Home Secretary for himself, his Liberal Party colleagues vetoed the idea.

The late 1970s Labour-Liberal government (Callaghan-Steel after two changes of leadership, for different reasons) was so beset by stagflation and union troubles that the new Conservative leader Margaret Thatcher came as close to winning a majority of the popular vote in 1980 as can be imagined under STV. The opposition was very divided partly because minor parties, including the extreme right National Front, did better than under first past the post. The NF managed to get a few MPs elected in 1980 in the West Midlands and North of England, but most were soon disqualified for non-attendance and/or criminal activity. The NF split, partly due to an argument about the sexual preferences of their leading figures, and for the time being the far right sank out of sight.

The redoubtable Mrs Thatcher had no truck with coalitions (apart from with the Ulster Unionists) but she could never command enough support in the House to push through her more radical measures, although most parties did support her over the Falklands. She again nearly won a majority with 45 per cent of the vote in an election called shortly thereafter, in 1982.

However, she could not pass such strong anti-union measures, due to her lack of an overall majority, so there was no full Thatcherite revolution (although the unions still grew much weaker and lost over half their membership because of the inevitable decline of manufacturing industry and coal mining). When she proposed a poll tax to replace local authority rates, opinion poll ratings led the party to remove her in the late 1980s and replace her with a more emollient compromise candidate who might return to a coalition approach – John Major.

As Labour had swung to the left after pressure from grassroots militants, and Trotskyite entryism, even though the main parties were fairly close in the 1987 election, Major formed a government with the Liberal-SDP Alliance as junior partner. The SDP had been created a little earlier than in reality due to the encouragement PR gives to splits and new parties, almost immediately after its leading members, the Gang of Four, had lost their cabinet positions at the 1980 election. For the same reason they had not joined with the Liberals quickly, but the Alliance and then the merger to form the Social & Liberal Democrats was cemented when Dr David Owen gained a promise from the Liberals that they would on no account form a coalition with his loathed former colleagues.

Major's thoroughly centrist government lasted into the 1990s, and through the 1992 election, when it did surprisingly well (not that it would have mattered what the shares or totals of the votes were as long as the coalition held). With the Liberals pushing him not to resist the advance of Euro-federalism, however, the Conservative right became even worse 'bastards', and with the birth and rise of New Labour, in 1997 Tony Blair's remodelled party won the most votes by far. Of course Blair had no majority, but the Liberal Democrats were happy with him, his social democratic (to put it mildly) policies, and his promises of massive constitutional reform, as were the Nationalists with his devolution proposals. Dr Owen, on the other hand, left the political scene with some venom.

Nationalists had consistently returned more MPs due to PR. In 1975, for example, the SNP had taken 30 per cent of the Scottish vote, which gave them 21 seats, and even in 1980, after a relative collapse of their share, they retained 12. The prospect of continuous representation on this scale enhanced the need for devolution to both Scotland and Wales – as it had in the late 1970s, given the increased number of nationalists elected under PR. However, in the earlier decade this justification was not strong enough to overcome the bitter divisions within the Labour Party and the staunch unionism of the Conservatives at the time – and oddly, PR had seemed to limit the threat of a massive SNP breakthrough compared with the magnifying effects of FPTP. Meanwhile, in Northern Ireland there had long been a much better representation of the minority Nationalist/Republican tradition than under FPTP, though this had little effect while the province was largely ruled by a Unionist majority at Stormont.

Even without a majority, with Blair's constitutional reforms – mild though they turned out to be, including incorporating the European Convention on Human Rights into British law, but with no concession of a codified constitution or a bill of rights entrenched in law, and there is a big difference between a human rights act (easily suspended, amended or repealed) and an entrenched bill of rights as in the US codified constitution – and moderate pro-EU stance, and even more the economic climate, the Liberal Democrats remained satisfied with him and with New Labour, so he remained comfortably in office, with another election producing a similar result in 2002. 'The Project' was sailing along nicely until 2003, with Blair completing the privatisations of telecoms, water, gas, railways, coal mines, and almost all other public sector industries (and air traffic control) that Thatcher and Major had struggled to achieve in their minority and coalition administrations.

However, his coalition partners did not let him join the US in their war of revenge on Iraq, and the Prime Minister – denied his mission, however liberal the intervention – resigned in a fit of pique, stating his evangelical determination to bring peace to the Middle East, one way or another. Gordon Brown finally got his chance.

Impossible to work with, after a much more even result in 2005, the Liberals were fed up with Brown shouting at them, especially when Kennedy had quit through ill health and Ming Campbell had been browbeaten; and under yet another leader, Nick Clegg, in 2006 they switched to the smoother Conservative Party leader, David Cameron – without an election, and after lengthy secret discussions. The latest coalition was not really much more electorally successful in the 2007 election than the two parties had been in 2005, but Cameron and Clegg hit it off and again formed a coalition government.

They were immediately beset by a sea of troubles, most of all an economic crunch caused by a banking crisis, and in the run-up to the fixed-term election in 2012 they are a long way behind in the polls. It looks like the Lib Dems are likely to split, or else the Conservatives may do, with the hard-line ideological right wing, ardently supported by the *Daily Telegraph*, considering a bid to incorporate the small but potentially growing band of UKIP MPs, that party being more fairly represented due to the proportional system.

Everyone awaits the 2012 election, but everyone knows the result: a hung parliament, like every one since 1918. It will be over to the politicians yet again, to see what deals can be cobbled together. All parties refuse to say in advance who they might ally with. Interest, and hence turnout, is expected to be low.

Notes

1   David Butler, *The Electoral System in Britain Since 1918* (Clarendon, second edition, 1963), p. 7.
2   Martin Pugh, *Electoral Reform in War and Peace 1906–18* (Routledge & Kegan Paul, 1978), p. 77.
3   Ibid., p. 83.
4   Ibid., pp. 87–91.
5   Ibid., pp. 158–59.
6   Ibid., p. 164.
7   Butler, *The Electoral System in Britain Since 1918*, p. 11.
8   Roy Hattersley, *The Great Outsider, David Lloyd George* (Little, Brown & Co., 2010), p. 477.
9   A. J. P. Taylor, *English History 1914–1945* (OUP, 1965), pp. 206–07.
10 Chris Wrigley, *Lloyd George* (Wiley-Blackwell, 1992), p. 127.
11 John Campbell, *Lloyd George: The Goat in the Wilderness* (Jonathan Cape, 1977), p. 89.
12 Wrigley, *Lloyd George*, p. 126.
13 Colin Rallings and Michael Thrasher, *Local Government Handbook* (*Local Government Chronicle* Elections Centre, 2007).
14 Taylor, *English History 1914–1945*, p. 436.
15 See, for example, Robert Waller, *The Dukeries Transformed* (Clarendon, 1983), p. 217.
16 Martin Pugh, 'Churchill's Strange Brew', *History Today*, May 2011, p. 32.

Chapter 3

What if Lloyd George had done a deal with the Tories in 1931?

Jaime Reynolds

I have sometimes wondered during the past few anxious weeks what would have happened had you been on your feet at the critical moment. Somehow I can scarcely think that, in such circumstances the position would have developed in precisely the way it has … I think your being out of action will be seen as a great part of the tragedy.

Harry Nathan MP to Lloyd George, 13 September 1931[1]

In August 1931 the Liberals and Conservatives came together in the last peacetime coalition government in Britain before 2010. It was formed in a 'hung parliament' amid an international financial crisis in order to restore confidence and defend the pound by cutting public expenditure and reducing the budget deficit. It replaced a Labour government battered and broken by the economic crisis that had begun two years earlier.

But the deal reached in 1931 was very different from that of 2010. There was no real meeting of minds between the two parties either on policy or on strategy. The government was to be temporary, with great uncertainty about what would happen next. No provision was made to protect the electoral future of the Liberals. Although the coalition depended for its parliamentary majority on Conservative and Liberal votes, the Liberals were treated as the third party in the cabinet, over-shadowed by ex-Labour ministers, led by Ramsay MacDonald, who continued as Prime Minister.

In the complex and crisis-driven negotiations of August 1931 that produced the extraordinary and unexpected outcome of a Con-Lib coalition
led by a Labour politician, the Liberals came out badly. This became apparent in October when they were forced into a general election that left the
party fragmented and crushed.

The 1931 crisis was a pivotal moment in twentieth-century British
politics. It was the point at which the three-party system, revived by Lloyd
George in the late 1920s, gave way to the bipolar system that survived intact
for the next half century and, indeed, in many of its essentials, to the present
day. It was the nemesis of the old Liberal Party. Not until the twenty-first
century did British Liberalism recover the ground it lost in those events.

How was it that the Liberals allowed themselves to be drawn into such
a deadly trap? Why did they not strike a harder bargain and insist on a
longer-term agreement, as they did in 2010? And if they had done so, what
might have been the impact on British politics?

At a crucial moment in the crisis, on 27 July 1931, David Lloyd George,
the Liberal leader, a negotiator and political operator of genius,[2] was suddenly taken ill with prostate problems and underwent emergency surgery
two days later. A long convalescence followed, during which he was left
frustrated on the sidelines, unable to participate directly in the dramatic
political upheaval that unfolded in the following weeks.

In time Lloyd George recovered from his illness and remained a formidable political figure for a further decade. If he had not fallen ill in 1931
he would have led for the Liberals in the critical three-party negotiations.
As it was, MacDonald and Neville Chamberlain for the Conservatives
(deputising for Stanley Baldwin who was on holiday) were the two decisive
figures in those talks; Herbert Samuel (deputising for Lloyd George) made
little impact. Lloyd George would have added a third dynamic element that
could have altered the chemistry, and perhaps the result.

A Lib-Lab coalition?

Unlike 2010, a Lib-Lab deal, and not just a Lib-Con coalition, was arith-
metically viable in 1931, as the 1929 election had produced a true hung

parliament with 287 Labour, 260 Conservative and 59 Liberal MPs. Indeed, the most plausible counterfactual outcome if Lloyd George had participated in the 1931 talks would have been a Lib-Lab deal.

Lloyd George had been aiming for this option since late 1929 in a complex and partly concealed series of manoeuvres that culminated in early 1931 in a parliamentary understanding by which Labour ministers consulted the Liberal leaders on legislation, and most Liberal MPs gave the government support in the lobbies. There is evidence – though unfortunately rather thin evidence, as a vital document has been lost[3] – that in early July 1931 this understanding was on the brink of being upgraded into a full-scale Lib-Lab deal, with Lloyd George and other Liberals entering MacDonald's government. This tantalising prospect was put on ice by the financial crisis which blew up in mid-July and then by Lloyd George's illness. But it remained a possibility until the Labour government collapsed and the National Government emerged in late August. There is every reason to believe that if Lloyd George had been on the scene he would as his first choice have continued to follow this avenue.

The Lib-Lab scenario has been explored elsewhere, in John Campbell's biography of Lloyd George between the wars.[4] This chapter focuses on the other key counterfactual possibility: an essentially Con-Lib coalition government not dissimilar to that which was in fact formed, but with the Liberals driving a harder bargain and thereby protecting their own long-term interests more effectively.

The 1931 crisis and Liberal disintegration

The five days it took to form the Cameron-Clegg coalition in May 2010 pale into insignificance compared with the drawn-out crisis of 1931. After a brief honeymoon, the Labour minority government of 1929–31 was faltering almost from the start, sinking beneath the steadily worsening economic conditions following the Wall Street Crash of October 1929 and fruitless efforts to check the rising tide of unemployment and public expenditure, swollen by unemployment benefits. There was already much talk of national crisis by late 1930, but the government's agony really began in mid-July 1931, when a run on the pound began following bank collapses in Germany. It lasted until 23 August, when MacDonald finally gave up his desperate efforts to reconcile the Labour cabinet to a package of expenditure cuts sufficient to win the support of the opposition parties and to pacify the markets.

The emergency National Government formed on 24 August very soon faced a new crisis over the inter-related questions of its own future and the unravelling of its economic strategy. It was understood initially that the government would drive through the expenditure cuts within six weeks or so and then be followed by a general election contested by the parties independently. This was soon replaced by the idea that the National Government should continue in being and submit itself to an election either immediately (as favoured by the Conservatives) or in 1932, when the economic situation stabilised (as favoured by MacDonald and the Liberals). The election uncertainty triggered renewed pressure on the pound and on 21 September Britain came off the gold standard.

The collapse of gold removed much of the original economic case for the National Government, but it had none of the catastrophic effects that were feared in August. As soon as the dust settled the Conservatives resumed their push for an early general election, capitalising on the opportunity to defeat the divided Labour Party, further weaken the Liberals, and in the process undermine the free-trade majority in the Commons.

It was at this point that the trap into which the Liberals had fallen was sprung. After a forlorn rearguard attempt to delay the election, or at least extract guarantees on free trade, Herbert Samuel, to Lloyd George's fury, gave his assent. On 5 October the cabinet agreed to an election with each party fighting on its own programme, under a general statement issued by MacDonald seeking a 'doctor's mandate' to carry through whatever steps were necessary to restore the economy (not excluding protectionist measures). Samuel extracted an empty promise that an inquiry would be held before any proposal could be made to introduce a general system of tariffs.

The election completed the fragmentation of the Liberals. Samuel's group of about 25 MPs stood as supporters of the National Government, but in competition with the Conservatives in many of the 111 constituencies which the party managed to contest. The anti-Lloyd George faction (around 25 MPs) stood as 'Liberal Nationals' under the leadership of Sir John Simon, and in almost all cases their 41 candidates were given a free run by the Conservatives. Lloyd George with his family and a couple of others fought the election independently, in opposition to the National Government.

The election was a massive landslide for the National Government or, more accurately, for the Conservatives (470), flanked by 35 Simonite Liberal Nationals and only 32 Samuelites, facing an opposition comprising 52 Labour MPs and Lloyd George's family group of 4.[5]

The final stage of the crisis for the Liberals came in 1932, with the ending of the free trade system under which the British economy had functioned since the mid-nineteenth century. After a perfunctory inquiry, the Conservatives forced through a general tariff in early 1932 against the impotent opposition of the Samuelites. In September the free-trade Liberals resigned from the government over the Ottawa preferential tariff agreements, though Samuel did not finally lead his party into opposition until November 1933.

The independent Liberals now entered the most wretched period of their decline, returning only 17 MPs at the 1935 general election, with Samuel himself losing his seat.[6] The Liberals had abandoned the field in many parts of the country and had lost about a third of their 1929 vote in the remaining seats that they contested.

What would Lloyd George have aimed for?
As we have seen, the Liberals occupied a pivotal position in the arithmetic of the 1929–31 Parliament, they played a key role in the negotiations that led to the formation of the National Government, and they constituted a crucial element in the coalition's claim to represent the nation and not just the Conservative Party. In the end this counted for very little. The National Government flourished, continuing in office until 1945,[7] but by 1933 the Liberal Party was almost destroyed.

Lloyd George could see this coming. While he was broadly supportive of the formation of the National Government in August 1931, he adamantly opposed the decision in October to hold an election, basically because he believed that it would wreck his achievement, since 1926, of restoring the Liberals as a genuine parliamentary force. An early election would be 'the death-warrant of the Liberal Party as a separate party' and would expose Liberal MPs as 'plucked boobies'. Rather than agree to an election the Liberals should threaten to resign and if that threat failed to force MacDonald and the Conservatives to back down, they should obtain the credit for exposing the Conservatives' partisan manoeuvre and fight alone.[8]

Lloyd George's main objective in any deal would have been to secure the electoral future of the Liberal Party. Almost certainly he would have demanded electoral reform, through the alternative vote (AV). This had been his key condition for cooperation with the Labour government in 1930, and had resulted in MacDonald's agreement to introduce legislation. However Baldwin dismissed Samuel's rather feeble attempt to insert AV into the coalition deal in August 1931.[9] If he had been unable to obtain AV, Lloyd George would doubtless have insisted on a more advantageous electoral pact than the loose and semi-competitive arrangements that were in fact followed at the 1931 election.

Policy objectives would have been of secondary importance. Lloyd George did not dissent publicly, but there is some ambiguity about his attitude to the economy package.[10] While Samuel followed in Neville Chamberlain's wake in pushing for deeper cuts and in making a red line of the 10 per cent unemployment benefit cut, in all probability Lloyd George would have adopted a more flexible and independent stance. This could have given the Liberals more leverage by keeping open the potential of a Lib-Lab deal if the Conservatives did not give ground.

Lloyd George certainly did not give priority to the 'Yellow Book' public works programme that he had promoted in 1928–29. He was flexible even on the issue of free trade, and was ready to accept measures of protection short of food tariffs.[11] Again he would probably have tried to use the trade question as a bargaining counter to extract electoral concessions from the Tories.

What would have stood in the way of a Lloyd George–Conservative deal?

The Liberal meltdown in 1931 is usually seen as yet another stage in the inevitable demise of the party in the face of the internal stresses it faced after 1914 and the rise of Labour. The crisis undoubtedly presented a severe challenge for the Liberals and it would have required considerable leadership, agility and luck to avert the risks it posed. The obstacles in the way of a Lib-Con coalition looked formidable: the Conservative dislike and distrust of Lloyd George, the wide gap in political outlook between the parties, especially over free trade, the fragility of the Liberal Party and its electoral vulnerability. Perhaps these factors would have defeated a political conjurer even of the calibre of Lloyd George?

As in 2010 the chemistry between the three party leaders was important, but in 1931 it did not help the Liberals. Both MacDonald and Baldwin had defined their political careers in the 1920s as opponents of Lloyd George and all he stood for. They had consistently blocked his efforts to return to government.

By 1931 relations with MacDonald, despite his regarding Lloyd George as a rival and an unprincipled adventurer,[12] were less of a problem. As we have seen, he had already been forced to accept a tacit partnership with Lloyd George and may well have been ready to admit him to the cabinet. From August 1931 MacDonald made far more startling adjustments to the extraordinary political circumstances.

The problem was, rather, the Conservatives' enmity towards Lloyd George. Baldwin, who had served in 1921–22 in Lloyd George's Lib-Con Coalition cabinet, had been one of the leaders of the 1922 Conservative rebellion that had led to the fall of that government. He had come to see Lloyd George as 'a real corrupter of public life', a man with 'no moral sense at all'. Nevertheless he was capable of overcoming this dislike and in 1934–35 seriously contemplated an alliance with Lloyd George to strengthen the National Government.[13] Neville Chamberlain, the other key figure in the Tory leadership, who had a grudge against Lloyd George dating from his unsuccessful spell as Director of National Service in 1916–17, was less forgiving but he too did not in practice rule out cooperation.

Tactically the Conservatives were anxious to prevent a Lloyd George-Labour alliance and impatient for an early election and the chance of achieving a protectionist majority; for this, they had even been ready to contemplate conceding AV.[14] Strategically too, coalition with Lloyd George – as long as he maintained a hold on a substantial proportion of the Liberals – followed the logic of Baldwin's long-term objective of drawing Liberalism into the Conservative camp on an anti-socialist platform. In the situation of national crisis in 1931 and given the parliamentary arithmetic, the Tories would have had little choice but to work with Lloyd George, the elected leader of the Liberal Party.[15]

There was also an ideological gap to overcome. The free trade versus protection battle of the early decades of the twentieth century resembled the modern controversy over Europe. It was a key differentiating cleavage between most Liberals and Conservatives. Within the Conservative Party it had led to deep divisions, from the launching of Joseph Chamberlain's tariff reform crusade in 1903 right up to the infighting between Baldwin and the protectionists and die-hards during 1930–31, for many of those years helping to isolate them from power.

However – as with the issue of Europe in more recent times – by the mid-1920s the trade question really only excited a minority of zealots on each side. The attitude of the majority of the political and business elite was increasingly pragmatic. The depressed state of the British economy and the rise of economic nationalism weakened the free-trade cause globally. Equally the old tariff reform platform of imperial preference was basically a political project with limited economic relevance for Britain or the Empire.[16] In practice, both the Conservative and Liberal leaderships were searching for some middle way, adapting to the political and economic realities in which Britain found itself in the 1930s without causing too much offence to their more dogmatic supporters.[17]

The shape of such a *via media* was in fact emerging. The hitherto unbending free-trade Liberal, Walter Runciman, received wide attention for a speech of September 1931 calling for a tariff on luxuries. He was showing the way towards a compromise formula of 'temporary' tariffs during the economic emergency to prevent dumping and raise revenue to help balance the budget. Such protectionism was considered by many free traders as consistent with their principles, especially if it was used to negotiate reductions in foreign tariffs. As President of the Board of Trade from November 1931 to 1937, Runciman pursued this approach robustly, all the time considering himself faithful to free-trade doctrine, while the Conservative leadership also showed a readiness to give and take.[18]

With hindsight it is clear that the Samuelites' fundamentalism on free trade in 1931–32 was anachronistic and self-destructive. As Peter Clarke has put it: everything 'ostensibly turned on the great issue of tariffs, which for thirty years had caused one political crisis after another; yet as soon as tariffs were implemented they appeared less important, either for good or evil'.[19] It was an issue that needed to be defused and managed. With his flexibility and pragmatism Lloyd George might have succeeded in finding a stable face-saving compromise solution where Samuel failed.

But perhaps by 1931 the Liberal Party was simply too enfeebled by internal conflicts and electoral frailty to force any concessions from the Conservatives? Samuel's defensiveness in the August and September negotiations arose from a sense of the party's weakness, and especially the risk of being outflanked by the Liberal rebels coalescing around Sir John Simon, who stood available as an alternative partner for the Tories. This is clearly a big difference compared with May 2010, when the Liberal Democrats were solidly united under the undisputed leadership of Nick Clegg, and riding high electorally.

However, the threat posed to Lloyd George by the Liberal rebels should not be exaggerated. The Simonites only became an organised faction quite late, from mid-September 1931, and even then were a somewhat loose and inchoate formation.[20] Sir John Simon was not an effective leader. His lack of human warmth won him little personal following. He was also tortuously hesitant in deciding which course to take, only resigning the Liberal whip in June 1931 and not declaring decisively against free trade until mid-September. He was not much interested in leading a party.[21] Moreover, the Liberals missed a chance to bury the hatchet with the rebels when the National Government was formed. For about three weeks the party recovered much of its unity, with all sides warmly backing entry into the coalition. A number of the rebels, including key figures like Runciman and Ernest Brown, could have been won back with appointments to the government, but this was prevented by bad luck and Lloyd George's vindictiveness.[22] With Lloyd George on the scene, a more magnanimous response to the waverers, and the possibility of some kind of electoral deal, the Simonites would have found it considerably more difficult to attract sufficient support to mount a credible claim to represent Liberalism.

Working backwards from the 1931 election results, the electoral weakness of the Liberals seems very plain. But that was after everything had gone wrong. The party had splintered, Lloyd George had departed with his election funds, the Liberal Nationals were up and running, and the Conservatives were aggressively challenging the Samuelites in many constituencies.

Viewed from August-September 1931, the election landscape looked very different. Although the Liberals seemed to have lost ground since 1929, and the Conservatives were confident of gains, there were no opinion polls to confirm voting intentions. The Tories were gripped by a real fear that if they took office to carry through expenditure cuts without MacDonald and the Liberals on board, they could be faced by a rejuvenated Labour opposition at the polls, and a second front against Lloyd George. There is absolutely no doubt that with his charisma and money Lloyd George would have put up a much better show as leader of the Liberal campaign than Samuel managed. At the least he would have stood a far better chance of bluffing the Tories into a more advantageous electoral arrangement.

A final obstacle in the way of a satisfactory Con-Lib deal was MacDonald's involvement. The possibility of a National Government emerged in the August inter-party consultations, but without the Labour Party, this could only credibly claim to represent Labour voters if MacDonald took a leading role by remaining Prime Minister. It was Chamberlain who grasped that this solution would serve Conservative interests and drove it through.[23] Such a National coalition would deepen the Labour split and spread responsibility for pushing through the expenditure cuts across the political spectrum.

However, the scenario of MacDonald breaking with Labour looked far-fetched. Leaving the party he had 'founded, nursed, cherished, built up' would be like 'killing his own child',[24] and his instinct was not to go down this road. Baldwin too was sceptical about such a coalition and reluctant to cede the premiership. Even as late as the night of 23 August, after the Labour cabinet had fallen, the Conservative and Liberal leaders came away from a meeting with MacDonald convinced that he was determined not to remain in office, and they began to discuss the more likely possibility of a Con-Lib coalition.

The fact that MacDonald's potential role and hesitations became the focus of the negotiations in August was not to the advantage of the Liberals. It distracted attention from the default option of a Con-Lib coalition and reduced the value of the Liberals to the Conservatives by offering MacDonald an alternative way in which to symbolise the 'national' complexion of the next government. It also made the possibility of a Lab-Lib deal more remote. Basically the Liberals became a junior third party in the negotiations, despite their much larger contribution to the government's parliamentary majority than MacDonald's paltry National Labour following. Similarly, the tussle in September/October over the timing of the election became a battle for MacDonald's support. In the end he threw his weight behind the Conservatives, leaving Samuel high and dry.

It would have only required a signal from the Liberals to deflate the pressure for a MacDonald-led government and thus to have put themselves at the centre of the stage. It seems highly plausible that Lloyd George would have done this – after all, why would he want to share the limelight with MacDonald? Instead Samuel simply seconded Chamberlain in his efforts to woo MacDonald, to such an extent that he is often – inaccurately – considered to be the main promoter of the National Government.

~

David Lloyd George, Deputy Prime Minister of the Con–Lib Coalition

Buckingham Palace, conference of the Conservative and Liberal Party leaders, 10 a.m., Monday 24 August 1931 (the previous evening Ramsay MacDonald's final efforts to hold the Labour government together had collapsed and he had tendered his resignation as Prime Minister).

King George V turns to David Lloyd George, saying that 'he trusted that he and his party would serve under Mr Baldwin and he hoped that he would feel able to lend the new government his support through the present economic difficulties in accordance with the understanding between the parties concluded last night'. At the end of the meeting the King remarks that 'he acknowledged Mr Ramsay MacDonald's decision not to accept office in the new cabinet with great personal regret'.

Shortly afterwards Stanley Baldwin and David Lloyd George stand together at the entrance to 10 Downing Street and wave to the surrounding photographers. After nine years in the political wilderness, Lloyd George has finally regained office in a new Conservative-Liberal coalition.

It is only many years later that historians revealed the truth of the remarkable moves that led to the formation of the coalition; how at one stage in the talks the extraordinary notion of a three-party coalition led by Ramsay MacDonald had been seriously considered until Lloyd George had ruled it out, insisting that he would never ask MacDonald to suffer the painful and humiliating break with his party that this would inevitably entail. At another point of high tension, Lloyd George had declared that he and his party would rather 'die fighting on the left' than agree to a rushed election designed only to serve 'the interests of the bankers and the landlords'. The negotiators even contemplated the constitutional innovation of a referendum on the alternative vote, but it was decided instead to seek a mandate at an election, to be delayed until 1932.

It was clear all along that the most difficult issue to settle would be tariffs, and this was still unresolved right down to the final negotiations on the evening of Sunday 23 August. While Stanley Baldwin offered Lloyd George every assistance to release his party from the 'dead hand' of 'pure free-trade dogma', an unusually emotional Neville Chamberlain declared that he was determined 'to set the seal on the work for tariff reform that his father had begun but had been forced to leave unfinished, even if that vision were to be fulfilled not exactly in my father's way but in some modified form'.[25] For Lloyd George the fundamental issue was: 'what future will my Liberal colleagues have with their electors if we make this sacrifice?' We will never know exactly what assurances Baldwin gave Lloyd George when he took him aside for a whispered conversation. But the result was that a short while later a contented Baldwin and a beaming Lloyd George shook hands after initialling the document held by Chamberlain, as Herbert Samuel stiffly looked on. Apparently the Welshman's silver tongue had worked its magic yet again. Or perhaps it was Baldwin's sixth sense for his party's long-term advantage that had won the day?

The cabinet appointments were completed within twenty-four hours. They included Stanley Baldwin (Prime Minister, Conservative), David Lloyd George (First President of the Council and Deputy Prime Minister, Liberal), Neville Chamberlain (Chancellor of the Exchequer, Conservative), Sir Samuel Hoare (Foreign Secretary, Conservative) and Herbert Samuel (Home Secretary, Liberal). There were surprise appointments of Liberals hitherto among the critics of Lloyd George, including Walter Runciman as President of the Board of Trade and Ernest Brown as Scottish Secretary, while many others received junior appointments.

Despite initial rumours that Sir John Simon would be elevated to the House of Lords and would receive the Woolsack, it seems that the Liberal leader vetoed this possibility, thus finally ending the political prospects of his one-time rival. Some months later Simon announced that he was joining the Conservative Party, but none of his erstwhile Liberal supporters followed in his footsteps.

The new government pressed ahead with the expenditure package that the MacDonald government had failed to agree. The Labour opposition continued to argue that the cuts went too far and were unnecessarily hard on benefits and public-sector salaries. As we now know, this was largely true. The suspension of the gold standard in mid-September and the rapid stabilisation of the pound at a sustainable lower level dispelled much of the pressure from the markets. This forced devaluation, rather than the government's deflationary measures, revived the economy. Unemployment peaked in late 1932, after which prosperity grew outside the depressed areas. The government was able to restore the 1931 cuts by 1934.

The collapse of the gold standard also removed a key argument for protective tariffs as the weaker pound assisted exports and discouraged imports. Nevertheless, as accepted by the Liberals in the coalition agreement, the Conservative Chancellor Chamberlain was free to go ahead with his establishment of a Royal Commission on Tariffs which, in spring 1932, duly reported in favour of a general industrial tariff covering key sectors for the duration of the economic crisis and a renewed drive to negotiate tariff reductions at international level. Tariffs on key foodstuffs and industrial raw materials were specifically ruled out. Although the Chamberlain-Runciman Tariff Bill encountered loud opposition from the imperial preference group, led by Leo Amery and the Beaverbrook press, it rapidly passed into law with the support of all but a handful of coalition MPs. Lloyd George easily saw off an attempted grassroots rebellion by free traders at the 1932 Liberal conference, and only a handful of fundamentalists split away to form a Free Trade Liberal Party, that lingered on until the war.

In May 1932 the coalition went to the polls to seek a mandate for its economic recovery programme and the introduction of the alternative vote. Secret negotiations over Easter 1932 between Lloyd George and Chamberlain (deputising for Baldwin, who was taking a break in the south of France) settled the details of the pact. The two parties contested the election as separate organisations and in quite a number of constituencies even put up candidates against each other – but not where it mattered. In marginal seats contests were avoided and messages of support from the party leaders made plain to the voters which candidate coalition supporters should back. It reminded many of the 1918 'coupon' election. Thanks to Lloyd George's money and his capable organiser, Colonel Tweed, the Liberal election machine was restored to health, and candidates were nominated in over half the constituencies. Tactical voting ensured a landslide for the two coalition parties, with 340 Conservatives (+80) and 110 Liberals (+50) returned. Labour were reduced to 160 (−130).[26]

The Labour Party had put up a stiffer fight than some had expected. Under the moderate leadership of Arthur Henderson, and from 1933 the youthful Herbert Morrison,[27] Labour avoided the lurch to the left that some had predicted. Part of the blame for the economic crisis and the collapse of the MacDonald government had worn off since autumn 1931. Any feeling of betrayal focused on Philip Snowden, who loudly denounced his former comrades. Ramsay MacDonald kept his silence, retiring to Scotland to write his memoirs, *My Life for Labour* (1934), which detailed his contribution to the rise of the Labour Party and said remarkably little about the 1931 crisis. As Earl MacDonald of Lossiemouth he ended his life as an adored elder statesman of the Labour movement.

The coalition remained firm throughout the 1930s. Personal relations between the party leaders were unexpectedly warm. Chamberlain and Runciman got on excellently,[28] while before long Baldwin was saying of Lloyd George that 'I even rather like him'.[29] The introduction of AV for the 1937 general election generally reinforced the alliance between the parties, apart from a few left-wing Liberals who drifted over to Labour. It was only after the war in 1945 that the two parties reasserted their independence, and although both lost seats in the landslide to Labour, AV ensured that the Liberals remained a significant third party, with over 50 MPs throughout the 1950s.

With the compromise on free trade, there was little ideologically separating the Conservative and Liberal leaderships, although traditional tribal loyalties ruled out any fusion of the parties. Besides, their distinctive brands widened the government's appeal. The Labour vote had recovered to its 1929 level: it was the pooling of votes against Labour that kept it at bay.

On the economy the two parties shared a commitment to sound money and industrial rationalisation. But in fact it was cheap money and the boom in housing, cars and consumer durables that fuelled the recovery in the South and the Midlands. Where the Liberals made a difference was in wrapping together the government's industrial policies, public works, and help for the depressed areas in a British 'New Deal', which Lloyd George projected with his characteristic dynamism. After Baldwin handed over the premiership to Neville Chamberlain in 1936 the Liberals were compensated with the Treasury, where Chancellor Runciman carried out the first experiments in applying the doctrines of his chief adviser, the Liberal, Maynard Keynes.[30] It is perhaps for these reasons that the 1930s are widely perceived as an era of economic novelty and achievement rather than of narrow-minded orthodoxy in the face of intractable depression.

The Liberals provided crucial support for Baldwin over Indian self-government, in the face of a sustained rebellion until 1935, led by Winston Churchill, with the support of some eighty diehard Conservative MPs. Churchill attracted more Liberal support for his later campaign for rearmament, but he remained an isolated figure. Quite simply, there was little appetite for a second dynamic force in the government alongside Lloyd George.

It was the looming threat from Hitler that proved to be the most divisive issue in the government. Initially Lloyd George pushed hard to reach an understanding with Germany on the back of the remarkable mutual admiration revealed during his visit to the Führer in Berchtesgaden in 1936. But when this seeming opportunity passed, he demanded a tougher line against Hitler and more energetic efforts to secure an alliance with the USSR. Lloyd George was privately contemptuous of Chamberlain's handling of the Czechoslovak crisis in 1938,[31] but other Liberals, including Samuel and Runciman, backed the Munich agreement.[32] In 1939 the Liberals, working in tacit alliance with Churchill, stiffened the government's realisation that Hitler would have to be opposed by force. This paved the way for the formation of the Churchill wartime coalition in May 1940, with Lloyd George and Sinclair in the war cabinet.[33]

~

1931 and 2010

The contrasts between politics in 1931 and today are obvious, but many features of the political landscape are curiously familiar. It was a time of economic dislocation and coalition experimentation, just as now, and many of the choices facing politicians seem strangely similar. However, instead of following the 2010 option of a negotiated Con-Lib coalition – the 'natural' course in the circumstances – in reality a highly unusual variant was chosen instead.

The real outcome in 1931 was the worst conceivable for the Liberals: 'whereas the Simonites were swallowed whole by the National Government, the Samuelites were ... spat out'.[34] The failure of leadership, the disunity and the abandonment of a large part of their electorate to their rivals very nearly destroyed the party.

But 1931 could easily have turned out differently: 'contingency manifestly played a very large part'.[35] If Lloyd George had been on the scene, if MacDonald had followed his Labour instincts, or if Baldwin had asserted his right to the premiership, the pivotal event of inter-war British politics would have taken a different course and most probably would have led to a Con-Lib coalition which would have given the Liberals a rosier future.

Even if our counterfactual had developed less benignly for them, if Lloyd George had not achieved a deal with the Tories, if he had not secured AV and if he had been forced to lead the bulk of his party into opposition, it is difficult to imagine that the outcome would have been as catastrophic in the long run.

Hung parliaments and coalition politics are perilous for third parties and in 1918, 1924 and 1931 crushed the old Liberal Party. The Cameron-Clegg coalition looks likely to end with a setback for the Lib Dems, but if they can escape the disarray and devastation that overtook the Liberals in 1931 that setback may be only temporary.

Notes

1 J. Campbell, *Lloyd George – The Goat in the Wilderness 1922–31* (Cape, 1977), pp. 304–05. The factual content of this chapter relies especially on Philip Williamson, *National Crisis and National Government: British Politics, the Economy and Empire, 1926–32* (Cambridge University Press, 1992).

2 'He was an unrivalled negotiator: on top of his brief, full of bounce, sure of himself, forceful, engaging, compelling, endlessly patient.' A. Letwin, *Lloyd George and the Lost Peace – From Versailles to Hitler 1919–1940* (Palgrave Macmillan, 2001), p. 5. See Letwin further on Lloyd George's negotiating brilliance (Chapter 1) and on Chamberlain's difficulty in coping with him (Chapter 6).

3 F. Owen, in *Tempestuous Journey, Lloyd George, His Life and Times* (Hutchinson, 1954), published a memo, now lost, dictated by Lloyd George claiming he had been offered a senior cabinet post. See Williamson, *National Crisis*, p. 252n.

4 Campbell, *Lloyd George*, pp. 307–08.

5 13 National Labour and 4 National and 2 National Independent MPs were also returned on the government side. Six of the Labour candidates elected were unendorsed.

6 Four Lloyd Georgeites were returned, and reunited with the Samuelites after the election.

7 It was widened to include Labour and the independent Liberals in 1940.

8 Williamson, *National Crisis*, p. 440.

9 Ibid., p. 342. The AV bill introduced in February had passed third reading in the Lords on 21 July, but expired with the collapse of the Labour government.

10 Ibid., pp. 324, 355.

11 Ibid., pp. 439–40.

12 D. Marquand, *Ramsay MacDonald* (Cape, 1977), p. 528.

13 P. Williamson, *Stanley Baldwin – Conservative Leadership and National Values* (Cambridge University Press, 1999), pp. 228–29.

14 Chamberlain had reacted positively to Lloyd George's (insincere) overtures for such a deal in June 1931; see Williamson, *National Crisis*, p. 250.

15 Williamson dismisses the notion that the National Government was aimed to exclude Lloyd George, noting that 'the possibility that Lloyd George might enter some "national government" was what first made Neville Chamberlain think that Conservatives might be well advised to join too. In reality fear of Lloyd George was a reason for involving, not excluding, him from any broad coalition.' Williamson, *National Crisis*, p. 517.

16 Compared to the late 1920s, by the late 1930s British exports to the Dominions were over 20 per cent lower, while imports from the Dominions had increased. 'Whoever

got the best of the bargain at Ottawa, it was not British industry'; Peter Clarke, *Hope and Glory: Britain 1900–1990* (Penguin, 1996), p. 176.

17 See further in F. Trentmann, *Free Trade Nation – Commerce, Consumption and Civil Society in Modern Britain* (Oxford University Press, 2008).

18 Runciman, though counted as a Liberal National, retained his links with the free-trade Liberals for several years, remaining President of the National Liberal Federation until 1934. See further in D. Winch, '"Very Peculiar Circumstances": Walter Runciman and the National Government, 1931–33', *Twentieth-Century British History*, vol 11, no. 1, 2000, pp. 61–82.

19 Clarke, *Hope and Glory*, p. 177.

20 The Liberal Nationals established a separate organisation only on 5 October 1931.

21 See D. Dutton, *Simon: A Political Biography of Sir John Simon* (Aurum, 1992).

22 Samuel tried to offer Runciman the War Office, but could not contact him in time. Lloyd George vetoed Brown. Williamson, *National Crisis*, pp. 354–55.

23 Ibid., Chapter 9. For a more modest assessment of Chamberlain's role see Graham Stewart, *Burying Caesar – Churchill, Chamberlain and the Battle for the Conservative Party* (Weidenfeld & Nicolson, 1999), chapter 3:III.

24 Williamson *National Crisis,* p. 325, quoting Neville Chamberlain letter.

25 See Chamberlain's speech introducing the Import Duties Bill, 4 February 1932, House of Commons.

26 This assumes that there would have been a large swing against Labour but not as huge as the true 1931 swing, which reduced Labour to 52 seats. It suggests that Labour would have won about the same number as they in fact won in 1935 (154). The Liberals would have won the seats they held in 1929 (59) plus about 20 of the actual 1931 gains by Liberals or Liberal Nationals (excluding a few 'freak' gains from Labour), plus about 30 more gains in seats where the Liberals were strong and might have expected to win under a fairer arrangement with the Conservatives.

27 In reality, both Henderson and Morrison lost their seats in the 1931 election, but the seats were regained in 1935.

28 This was true; see Winch, 'Very Peculiar Circumstances'.

29 Williamson, *Stanley Baldwin*, p. 229.

30 Although Keynes's role was limited after his heart attack in 1937.

31 Following the analysis of Lloyd George's views in Letwin, *Lloyd George and the Lost Peace*, Chapters 5 and 6.

32 In reality they took this position publicly; see Lloyd George's Commons speeches of 3 October and 19 December 1938. Runciman was sent by Chamberlain to negotiate a deal over the Sudetenland. Samuel was the most prominent independent Liberal to support the Munich agreement.

33 In reality, there were no Liberals in the war cabinet, although Sinclair sometimes attended. Churchill offered Lloyd George a seat in the cabinet in 1940, but he declined.
34 Clarke, *Hope and Glory*, p. 176.
35 Williamson, *National Crisis*, p. 518.

Chapter 4

What if Attlee had sent Dalton to the Foreign Office and Bevin to the Exchequer in 1945?

Ted Morris

The years that define our world were those which fell immediately after the Second World War. There was very good reason for the memoirs of Dean Acheson, US Secretary of State in the period, being entitled *Present at the Creation*; for the economic and political structures created in those years settled the agenda for a generation and are only now, and to a limited extent, being superseded.

For Britain, these are the years of the Attlee governments of 1945 and 1950, a political landscape inhabited by giants, a 'big five' of Clement Attlee, Ernest Bevin, Hugh Dalton, Sir Stafford Cripps and Herbert Morrison, with Aneurin Bevan and Hugh Gaitskell maturing fast as politicians of the front rank; and an opposition front bench under Churchill's rather distant leadership while the Conservative Party was being rebuilt by the more active efforts of Anthony Eden, R. A. Butler and Harold Macmillan. It is a time when we can be forgiven for believing that our history was made by great men, and that the country was not simply borne along on a tide of socio-economic trends.

In a world created by these men, however, it is a matter of established history that, at very much the last minute, the destiny of two of these political giants suddenly changed. In 1945 Attlee reversed his initial intention to appoint Dalton to the Foreign Office and Bevin to the Treasury. This was such a significant event that the relevant chapter in Professor Pimlott's biography of Dalton is even entitled 'The Switch'.[1] We know how history actually played out: Bevin spent five tumultuous years at the Foreign Office, the years of Hiroshima and Nagasaki, the start of the Cold War, actual civil war in Greece, Marshall Aid, the Berlin airlift, the formation of NATO, the decisions to quit India and Palestine and to develop a British nuclear deterrent. At the end of those five years, Bevin was dead.

Dalton's time at the Exchequer was briefer but no less eventful. He set the post-war fashion for boom and bust cycles: a misleading but triumphant upswing followed by crisis and retrenchment. Dalton's contribution was that the cycle was seldom shorter or more pronounced. No boom was ever more glorious than Dalton's, no bust ever more crushing. His resignation in 1947 over a trivial budget leak was the departure of a broken man; although he later returned to Cabinet, Dalton's career never again scaled the same heights.

The switch that was

At one level Bevin and Dalton had much in common. They were both figures of the same generation and of the Labour right. They were the two men who, more than any other, had fought in the 1930s to drag Labour away from pacifism as a response to the fascist dictators. Both men were also, on the face of it, well suited to take on either job. But in so many other ways they could not have been more of a contrast.

Ernest Bevin was an illegitimate, uneducated West Country carter, who created Britain's largest trade union and represented, and was the epitome of, the working-class Labour movement in an otherwise noticeably middle-class Labour leadership. Bevin was a believer in power, and knew how to exercise it. He was also the rock on which Attlee's premiership stood; so long as Ernie stood behind Clem, as he unwaveringly did, then Attlee was secure from intrigue.

Hugh Dalton was an early example of another Labour tradition, the upper-class intellectual 'renegade'. Eton- and Cambridge-educated, a professional economist and the son of a long-time canon at Windsor and former tutor to the future King George V, Dalton had rebelled against his father's life as a courtier. In those days, when public-school socialists were rarer animals, Dalton both invited and cheerfully provoked the jeers of his Tory adversaries. His personality combined self-importance with self-doubt. He was an endless intriguer, who always felt a kind of class cringe, with his belief that the likes of Attlee and himself were only stewards for a party that really belonged to the working class. Rightly considered one of the big five of the Labour government, he was still not remotely in the same class as Bevin in terms of self-confidence, force, will or political weight.[2]

In May 1945, Dalton told Attlee of his wish to be Foreign Secretary; he and Attlee appeared to be working to that outcome. On 26 July, Bevin indicated his preference for the Treasury. On the morning of 27 July, Attlee told Dalton that he was 'almost certainly' heading for the Foreign Office, and they discussed the appropriate clothing for Potsdam (no formal wear necessary, as Stalin apparently did not dress for dinner). But later that same afternoon, Attlee sent for Dalton and explained that he had changed his mind; Dalton was to go to the Treasury[3] and it was to be Bevin who accompanied Attlee on the flight to Potsdam the following day.

There are many theories as to why Attlee changed his mind. Dalton dwelt for years on the question of who Attlee had seen at lunch, for he felt that Attlee must have been 'got at' between the two meetings. That may be a red herring – Attlee may have lunched with his most unpolitical wife[4] – and it is more likely that Attlee was weighing up a range of considerations. The most intriguing element was the role of the Palace, which would make this one of the last controversial exercises of the Royal Prerogative. Certainly the King disliked Dalton and would not have enjoyed the regular dealings arising from Dalton's occupancy of the Foreign Office. His Private Secretary records that the King 'begged him [Attlee] to think carefully' about the appointment and pressed for Bevin in his place,[5] seemingly stemming from a personal dislike, going back many years through the long and complex relationship between the Daltons and the Royal Family.

But there were other factors in play. The Foreign Office officials actively disliked Dalton, probably as much as he disliked them,[6] and they (naturally) wanted to have the cabinet heavyweight Bevin in the job; the Permanent Secretary, Cadogan, had access to Attlee and almost certainly lobbied him along these lines. Dalton considered the officials as class-war adversaries; Bevin made the famous comment that people were grateful for these public schoolboys when they were piloting spitfires in the Battle of Britain. Attlee had been warned that Dalton's appointment to the Foreign Office would have been led to senior resignations, while Morrison had added a concern that Dalton's notorious temper was unsuitable for diplomacy (after five years of the notoriously touchy Eden, the Foreign Office staff may have been forgiven for yearning for a quieter life). Conversely, while Dalton felt less confident about the Treasury, he did at least have the technical qualifications that Bevin was felt to lack. And there was the complication of Bevin's long-running feud with Morrison ('Herbert is his own worst enemy'; 'Not while I'm alive, he ain't'[7]); with Bevin at the Treasury, both men would have had more scope to clash over domestic affairs.

What if: the switch that wasn't

We cannot know which of these factors clinched the argument for Attlee as he ruminated on cabinet makeup over lunch on that 27 July 1945. But what if Attlee had decided to stick with his original choice? This would not have been a simple question of switching one personality for another, but about a power relationship and the position of the centre of gravity of the government. It was a decision that would have had a direct bearing on the choices made by the government in subsequent years.

Bevin was regarded as the strongest figure in the Labour leadership, both at the time[8] and subsequently by historians. He was always going to be the dominant figure in the Labour Government, so whichever office to which he was appointed would inevitably exercise the greater influence. If the switch had not taken place, then that dominant office throughout the Attlee government would have been the Treasury rather than the Foreign Office. So what if the switch not taken place?

The Treasury dilemma

The arithmetic faced by the Chancellor, as described in a paper to the cabinet by Lord Keynes, was simple but daunting. Britain was outspending its income by what in those days was a staggering £2.1 billion a year, covered in roughly equal parts by lend-lease from the US and support from elsewhere in the sterling area, notably Canada.[9] A highly optimistic view of export growth could imagine this gap being closed over the course of a Parliament, but inevitably a deficit would accumulate in the next four years. The only option was to obtain continued support from the US of around $5 billion, ideally by a grant, but if necessary by a loan.

In the event, the loan was secured, but for $3.5 billion, and it came with the attached time-bomb of a requirement for full sterling convertibility by 1947. Dalton chose to close his mind to the draining away of the precious dollars while he pursued (famously, and with hubris destined to come back to haunt him, 'with a song in my heart') the implementation of Labour's expensive manifesto commitments.

The counterfactual impact of Bevin at the Treasury

As Bevin strode into the Treasury on that first morning at the end of July 1945, he may have been forgiven for having momentary doubts about his lack of economic experience. Self-doubt was, though, not Bevin's style, and any misgivings would have been banished once he met his senior team, from Permanent Secretary Sir Edward Bridges – a Rolls Royce even among Whitehall mandarins – down to Burke Trend as his PPS, and Lord Keynes as an adviser. This machinery would have had Bevin purring with pleasure. He would do what he did best: paint the strategic picture and allow a first-class team to ensure delivery.

Within a few weeks Bevin was faced with an urgent challenge: with the second atomic bomb on Nagasaki came the end of the war – sudden, very welcome of course, but sooner than expected. The problem was that by this time Britain was utterly dependent on lend-lease, and a week after the end of the war, and to the consternation of the British government and its advisers, lend-lease was abruptly terminated. The rational case may have been there for its continuation, but rationalism and American domestic political considerations mixed no better then than in any other period.

The immediate reaction was a decision to send Keynes to Washington to negotiate a new financial arrangement. Having slept on it, however, Bevin had second thoughts – in his inimical style. Keynes may have had a god-like reputation,[10] but Bevin was in awe of nobody; he had a very different relationship with him than did Dalton, for whom Keynes was his former tutor. And Bevin had spent a lifetime negotiating, often from the weakest of hands. It was what he knew how to do. It was what he was born to do. There was never the slightest chance that Bevin would let an adviser, however distinguished, go off to Washington with plenipotentiary powers on an issue as fundamental as this, leaving Bevin fumbling for news at the far end of a telex machine. Bevin was going to Washington himself.

The negotiations were a success of sorts; Britain did not receive the grant that some had expected, and that Marshall Aid would demonstrate was soon going to be politically possible, but the loan was on better terms than at one stage seemed likely. Bevin and Keynes formed an unlikely but effective duo. Keynes was the epitome of the urbane and witty don, but he was insufficiently business-like for the hard-bitten American negotiators. No one ever made that criticism of Bevin. The US insisted upon dollar convertibility, but Bevin's threat to walk away not just from the talks but, as a result, Britain's global commitments, led to it being postponed from 1947 to 1949, two further years that were to prove crucial.

Keynes died a few weeks after arriving back in the UK, worn out by his exertions. Bevin was aware that he and Keynes had only borrowed time, and he was determined to use it to the full. Early legislation – the Exchange Control Act, the Bank of England Act and the Borrowing (Control and Guarantee) Act – gave the Labour Chancellor control over the key financial levers. But Bevin's style was always to operate on a basis of consent. He soon achieved dominance over the economic agenda in a way that would be unknown by a Labour Chancellor for another half a century.

During the wartime coalition the Lord President of the Council had exercised a wide array of powers on the home front, and Herbert Morrison had theoretically inherited the national economic planning coordination brief in 1945. But the Chancellor, too, sat on the Industrial Sub-Committee of the cabinet, and on that battlefield Morrison was swiftly routed. Bevin's sway over the economic front remained unchallenged until 1950.

One immediate effect is that efforts at economic planning did not lie stillborn in the jealous wasteland between Treasury and Lord President's Department; Lionel Robbins, the brilliant head of the Economic Section, was persuaded by Bevin not to return to the LSE in late 1945 but to continue in his role. For Bevin, the key to the future was going to be planning rather than a strategy of cheap money, as his colleague Dalton had argued during the war. Over the next two years, the President of the Board of Trade, Sir Stafford Cripps, became an increasingly strong ally as the leading apostle of planning, and Bevin was happy to let Cripps make the running in developing what became known as the National Plan. The next few years were not going to be spent just living hand to mouth, but with an eye to the longer term.

Bevin started to acquire a confident swagger. He was getting his own way in cabinet. And not being a professional economist, he was, oddly, enjoying a better press, because he knew his limitations and was prepared to rely on the best advisers in the Treasury and elsewhere.

As the wags put it, even Ernie couldn't prevent the 1947 great freeze, but as the coal shortage became apparent going into that winter, what he could do was insist on executive powers as chairman of the Cabinet's Coal Committee. He immediately saw through the evasions of the Fuel and Power minister, Manny Shinwell, who was swiftly despatched from office and became a bitter but ineffectual enemy on the back benches. The April budget incorporated, over some cabinet hostility, a heavy 15 per cent cut in defence spending. These hard choices placed Bevin in the odd position of being more in sympathy with cabinet left-wingers such as Aneurin Bevan, keen to preserve reconstruction, and aligned against old allies like Foreign Secretary Dalton. Still, as Bevin reflected, since Morrison was vociferously opposed to the proposals, he had to be on the right lines.

As precious manpower switched from the army into industry, coal exports grew and the trade gap narrowed further. The dollar drain was

$315 million in January,[11] but by May the gap had closed to $75 million and still falling. At this rate it was just about sustainable. It had been a close-run thing, and Bevin mused that it would have been well-nigh impossible to land the economy on an even keel if he had accepted the commitment to full sterling convertibility for that year, but the crisis was over before it had effectively begun. And Britain was spared the unprecedented industrial fuel rationing that might otherwise have occurred.

As effective father of the TUC in its current form, Bevin was never going to gainsay proposals to nationalise coal and the railways, nor gas and electricity. But some plans could wait. Others were put off indefinitely at substantial savings; steel nationalisation alone would have cost over £2 billion and brought two million workers into the state sector – a fine socialist goal, but at what price! Bevin knew he controlled the levers that mattered; he did not need to nationalise the industries to be in control of the commanding heights of the economy.

Bevin's hardest cabinet battles were over the implementation of Beveridge's proposals for the welfare state. Nobody spoke more obviously for Labour's heartland than Bevin, and this may have been decisive: if Ernie said that we had to tighten our belts, then it clearly was not a decision he came to lightly. And here, oddly enough, he found himself allied with Morrison, who was opposed to some of the sweeping national aspects of the plans which he saw as undermining his cherished local government. Once the decision had been made to rely on the exiting friendly society framework to administer the new National Insurance plans, thus saving the cost of 2,000 civil servants in Newcastle, the shape of the new Jerusalem had been set. Jim Griffiths, the responsible minister, wasn't happy at Bevin's insistence that the proposals had to be self-funding, but he couldn't argue with the saving, projected as £369 million in 1948 alone.[12]

Next up were Aneurin Bevan's proposals for the National Health Service. There had been no attempt to cost the likely upsurge in demand for free health care. Bevan's airy but entirely uncosted estimate was £150 million of running costs a year;[13] Bevin could see there were some battles he couldn't win, so he did not challenge the estimate. But he took care to ensure that Bevan was taken at his word, and the outgoings were capped at that level for the rest of the Parliament. And, together with Morrison, he successfully argued against the huge national bureaucracy Bevan had originally proposed in favour of greater reliance on existing mechanisms of local delivery. It wasn't that Bevin was instinctively against schemes of Napoleonic scale, he just objected to footing the bill. Where Bevin was able to be more supportive to Bevan was in capital spending, and not just for the hospitals, where the estimated need was for £500 million to replace ageing Victorian buildings, but even more so for housing. In 1945, 40,000 people lived in disused service camps,[14] and an estimated 1,250,000 new houses were needed in all to replace bomb damage as well as the surviving slums. The Bevin/Bevan partnership on housing, initially simply an alliterative gift to lazy journalists, became the stuff of political legend.

With overseas commitments slashed, having declined to be locked into unplanned and open-ended welfare commitments and with a pragmatic appetite for nationalisation, Bevin had achieved an extraordinary degree of balance in the economy. In the first half of 1948, exports started to soar and the balance of payment deficit was wiped out.[15] By the time sterling became fully convertible in 1949, the dollar and gold outflow had been stemmed. The speculators took one look at Bevin and sought a different game to play than sterling.

Bevin at the Treasury: the verdict

Could Bevin have implemented this fundamentally different approach to the nation's finances? David Marquand suggests not:[16] that the whole Labour leadership took for granted Britain's role as a world power, which would have doomed any occupant of the Exchequer to plough essentially the same furrow as that fated for Dalton. What I would argue is that only Bevin would have had the political breadth to realise that the alterative needed to be tried, and the credibility – and sway in the cabinet – to achieve it. With the economy in balance in 1948, the country would have been better able to withstand the global downturn. So no sterling crisis in 1949; Bevin would still have died, worn out, in 1950, but with a dollar exchange rate still at 4.03:1. Instead of a succession of currency crises haunting his successors until the end of fixed currencies in the 1970s, a strong pound would have underpinned a strong record of low inflationary growth. Most tantalising of all, in those circumstances, long-term industrial investment would not have ranked third behind maintaining imports and keeping up the currency reserves[17] when the once-in-a-lifetime opportunity of Marshall Aid started to flow in 1948.

Bevin would have survived in office long enough to take the credit, rather than Cripps, for the 1948–50 recovery, and with Marshall Aid well spent it would have been a more real recovery. Gaitskell as his successor would have had an easier time at the Treasury, with more opportunity to burnish his reputation before going into opposition. There would have been even less for the Conservatives to disagree with on the welfare state, so the continuity of 'Butskellism' would still have been there, but a less costly welfare state would have been less of a drag on the economy, and Britain's performance in the 1950s would have more resembled that of continental Europe than the anaemic reality.

And, little noticed, one of the more far-reaching decisions would have been taken in October 1946 – not to develop an independent British nuclear deterrent. To be precise, the decision was over whether to build a gaseous diffusion plant for the production of uranium. In the real world, Bevin's voice swung the cabinet committee decision;[18] as Chancellor in our counterfactual history, his voice would have been at least constrained and possibly arguing for the counter view entirely. The cost of successive generations of nuclear deterrent of at best doubtful value – fleets of V bombers, the abortive Blue Streak, Polaris, Chevaline, Trident and the rest – would not have been there to bloat and distort the defence budget.

The Foreign Office dilemma

Whoever occupied the Foreign Office would have faced a yawning gulf between Britain's pretentions to a global role and its actual abilities – as very much the poorly trailing third of the three major victorious powers – to live up to them.

The extent of Britain's military commitments, as it sought to live up to its perceived role as a world power, were enormous. Military expenditure overseas in 1945 totalled £700 million, accounting for the whole of that year's financial deficit.[19] In December 1946, Britain's armed forces stood at 1,400,000,[20] well over the ceiling of 1,100,000 which the cabinet had agreed only at the start of the year. And that was at a time when Dalton's view was that the economy was short of manpower by around 650,000.[21]

Britain's view of itself, and its corresponding military ambition, was global. The navy maintained extensive and balanced fleets in each of the Pacific, the Mediterranean and home waters, as well as sizeable detachments in the Indian Ocean, the West Indies and elsewhere. One can perhaps understand why the army maintained some 200,000 troops in Germany, 60,000 in Austria, 50,000 in Italy, the same again in India and not many fewer in Greece,[22] but it is less obvious from today's perspective why there were at one stage 92,000 British troops assisting the Dutch to re-impose control in Indonesia.[23]

The government agonised long and hard over these costs, but they all took as read Britain's continuing global role. Remember that at this time the intentions of the Soviet Union were unknown. We can now judge that the Soviet steamroller was not inexorably heading to the Channel, but at the time, with a steady succession of central European governments being subverted to communist control, this was far from clear. Dalton and his successor Stafford Cripps argued for restraint on defence spending, but were unable to carry the cabinet. How different might it have been with a more powerful hand on the Treasury purse strings?

The counterfactual impact of Dalton at the Foreign Office

Hugh Dalton had aspired to the Foreign Office for many years – an odd ambition given that his brief time as a junior minister from 1929 had not been happy, and nor had he come to terms with how changed were the new realities which he would have to face. Potsdam was to be a difficult baptism of fire. Neither Russian nor American intentions for Europe were at this stage clear, certainly not as clear (to the politicians at least, if not yet the wider public) as the fact that the wartime alliance was a thing of the past. The gap was clearly there between American and British views of the world. For many Americans, the priority was to bring the troops home from Europe and to avoid continued entanglement. It wasn't 1918 all over again, but the parallel was not entirely false. British politicians of all parties realised that it would be impossible to maintain the balance in Europe without American assistance, but attempts to persuade the Americans of this new reality were far from welcomed.

The Russians were already probing Western resolve. The key theatre was the group of countries known at the time as the northern tier: Greece, Turkey, Iraq and Iran. This was the decisive battlefield of the early days of the Cold War, with the prize beyond them of the Middle East, the oilfields and the strategic routes through the Suez Canal.

Dalton appreciated the unwelcome irony that as Foreign Secretary his toughest battles were fought at home, around the cabinet table. Twice at the end of 1945, as part of the policy agreement on the use of the American loan, and again in early 1947 as the harsh winter closed in, the cabinet took an axe to the defence budget in a way that had not been seen since the days of retrenchment following Waterloo. Dalton and the Defence Secretary, A. V. Alexander, protested vigorously about the implications, and there was much sympathy around the table with their arguments. Attlee, especially, found the choices agonising, but Bevin was adamant that if Britain did not cut its cloth and adjust to the new realities now, harder choices would inevitably follow. The choices being made were hard enough: a reduction in armed forces personnel to below a million by June 1946, no new bases in the Middle East and a virtual embargo on commitments east of Suez, and nearly half the fleet in mothballs (the protesting First Sea Lord had struggled to answer Bevin's question as to who might be a foreseeable adversary for the Navy, unless he planned to declare war on America).

It was not long, as is always the way, before the specific implications were seen. The first crisis developed over one of the more far-flung commitments, as Dalton had to find a way out of the diplomatic mess that was Indonesia, where Sukarno had proclaimed independence. Given the choice of fighting him on behalf of the Dutch or acquiescing, Dalton had no choice but to give a guarded welcome to the new regime. Lord Mountbatten had given an estimate that almost 100,000 troops would be needed to secure the country, and that just was not a realistic political option. The Dutch were furious, of course; it was not until some years later that they could look on the French morass in Indochina and conclude that they may have been well served in being forced to disengage early from their colonial role. Ironically, Britain's reputation among the newly emerging nationalist movements across the region rose immediately: cutting and running had proved at least to be a better long-term bet than fighting on. In truth, right through the war the Americans had regarded the Pacific as their own patch where Britain had little or no say,[24] despite the presence of substantial forces, so in practice there was little influence to lose.

Greece, though, was more of a test. The Greeks were in desperate need of support after a savagely damaging war.[25] Stalin may have given his word not to push for Soviet advantage, but if the opportunity presented itself, it was unlikely that he would fail to seize the opportunity. The right-wing and pro-royalist Populist Party won the elections in March 1946, but proved to be inept and irresponsible.[26] Dalton may have wanted to stay and fight, and made dire warnings of the consequences, but the cabinet had only just agreed the defence package and were in any case aware of the post-First World War precedent, when trying to intervene in the Near East had proved a thankless task. Molotov's regular denunciations of the 'crimes' of British troops in Greece may have been something of a formality, but they were not without either purpose or effect. Dalton faced the unwelcome task of flying to Washington to tell James Byrnes, his opposite number as US Secretary of State, that responsibility for Greece and Turkey were being dumped in the US lap. The Truman administration at this point were divided over how to respond to the situation and did not move fast enough to forestall the ensuing communist takeover, aided by the Yugoslavs, who moved immediately to occupy Salonika.[27] Stalin's triumph was completed early in 1949 with the signing of the Greek-Soviet agreement, which saw the granting of naval facilities at Piraeus; the Russian dream of a warm-water port, held since the days of Peter the Great, were at last fulfilled.

The shock to the West was immense but, contrary to the predictions of the doomsayers, the dominos did not fall. Italy was helped by the fact that Dalton had had a strongly pro-Italian prejudice since his service there in the First World War.[28] His diplomatic efforts proved crucial in stiffening American resolve, and the crisis was over when Alcide de Gasperi removed the communists from his cabinet in May 1947. The Christian Democrats swept to a resounding electoral triumph in the general election of the following year. By this time the now-galvanised Americans had also made clear that Soviet encroachment on Turkish sovereignty, especially around the Straits, would not be tolerated. Turkish anti-communism was boosted by the addition of Greece to the Soviet camp and the pressure from Moscow was resisted.

Palestine had long been seen as an insurmountable problem, though Dalton had always been a committed Zionist and his strong feelings made it a priority. More precisely, however, the difficulty lay in how to reconcile Jewish aspirations for an independent state with Britain's continued relations with the Arabs. As Dalton soon realised, however, he was chasing a mirage: closing Palestine to Jewish immigration would never be enough to satisfy Arab nationalism. The removal of the British military presence was a different matter.

As in Indonesia, force of circumstance would drive the issue. Early in 1946, Dalton moved deftly to reconcile Egyptian opinion with a package of early phased withdrawal of British troops from the whole country, not just the Canal Zone – which he presented as the price for Egyptian support for the partition of Palestine. Jerusalem would be run jointly by Jordan and the new Israeli authorities as an open city, which was an immense boost to Jordanian prestige (had British departure been delayed further, Dalton reflected that opinions on all sides could well have hardened against this pragmatic outcome). Without Egyptian or Jordanian support, there was no question of armed intervention by the other Arab states, and so in 1946, to a background of Jewish delight and continuing but low-level unrest among the Arab population, the state of Israel was born. General Sir Alan Cunningham, the last British High Commissioner in Palestine, was a bemused observer of the joyous celebrations but was relieved to be leaving without widespread bloodshed either at the time or – more remarkably – without it being a prospect for the immediate future.

Dalton's greatest challenges came over the future of Germany, where the Soviets opposed Anglo-American proposals for German economic rehabilitation. This was tackled at a succession of seemingly interminable Council of Foreign Ministers meetings beginning in the summer of 1946 in Paris, then moving on to New York and Moscow. Dalton would not be the first to find his Soviet counterpart, Molotov, to be heavy going, and Dalton's own notoriously short temper led to a number of explosive conference sessions. Early in 1947, Truman had appointed General Marshall as Secretary of State; he proved far more effective than his predecessor. But for Dalton, handicapped in his attempts to shore up British influence by the very visible dismantling of the armed forces, the introduction into the conferences of the more assured Marshall proved to be the last straw.

Dalton suffered a nervous collapse in 1947 and was succeeded by Sir Stafford Cripps, the only feasible successor in the Labour ranks now that Morrison's career was in such decline. While a more accomplished diplomat, with previous experience of dealing with Stalin and Molotov from his time as Ambassador to Moscow during the war, Cripps suffered from both poor political judgement and his own ill health. He failed to coordinate a truly effective European response to Marshall's proposals for a general aid package in 1948, which resulted in emboldening the opposition in the more isolationist Congress. The bill to Congress advocated $17 billion in aid, but in the end the agreed amount was only half that.[29] Marshall resigned shortly afterwards and the result was a shaky European recovery through the 1950s and the drift of Germany towards neutrality in the wake of this less-than-wholehearted American support.

The impact on longer term politics

David Marquand paints the intriguing picture that the 1947 crisis revived the credibility of the Conservative opposition, beginning the process which led to Aneurin Bevan's resignation from the cabinet in 1951 and culminating in the defeat in the election that year and the Labour splits of the 1950s.[30] I prefer to look at the very human ingredient. By 1950 the leaders of the government had been in office for a decade of unprecedented and virtually unrelenting crisis. It was enough to take Bevin and Cripps to their premature graves and left their colleagues sick and exhausted. Labour was always likely to have left office in 1951, although thirteen years of opposition was certainly not pre-ordained. The Conservative government would have reaped much of the benefits of Bevin's firm stewardship of the nation's finances, but there would not have been the corrosive memory of a Labour government running out of money which so undermined the 1959 election campaign, when Gaitskell's ill-considered tax and spending commitments were seen as the decisive factor. That election could have seen Labour's return rather than Macmillan's triumph.

What would have been the effect on the internal politics of the Labour Party and the fortunes of the key players? Herbert Morrison's career was already starting to sag badly by 1951,[31] and would certainly have been eclipsed more swiftly if he had been in continuous conflict with Bevin in the period. There would only ever have been one winner to that argument. Hugh Gaitskell's upward trajectory was probably inevitable; as Bevin's health declined, he would increasingly have needed support from a junior, who would have steadily become de facto Deputy Chancellor and his likely successor. In reality Gaitskell fulfilled that role for an ailing Stafford Cripps; he would have done so equally for an ailing Bevin in a counterfactual history.

Harold Wilson may well not have prospered. It is plausible that with sufficiently regular proximity, Bevin would have found Wilson to be irritatingly supercilious, sufficiently so as to see Douglas Jay take the first available economic role in the cabinet in his stead. So no Board of Trade taking Wilson into the cabinet at thirty-one, and no mentoring by Stafford Cripps that was such an influence on the young Wilson. His undoubted abilities would have seen his move steadily up the Labour hierarchy in the 1950s, but it would have been without the foundation of cabinet experience, perhaps putting him at a disadvantage when the next Labour cabinet was formed, which, as I have suggested, might have been in 1959.

What of Nye Bevan? Having been tied to reality at the point when the NHS was introduced, Bevan would not spent the next four years becoming increasingly overwrought on the question of the health service's costs. And close cooperation on housing would have given Bevan a second landmark achievement and a yet more popular record with the party rank and file. He would have been the natural successor for the Foreign Office when it became free after Cripps' enforced retirement in 1950, and then a more plausible alternative to Gaitskell for the leadership when Attlee eventually retired.

Conclusion

Britain bankrupted itself during the war by its long, and for periods lone, stand against Nazi Germany. It dug itself further into the economic mire after the war by aspiring to continue to be a great power and by underpinning that policy through its global military commitments. To some extent, we have never rid ourselves of this mindset, as governments of all hues have continually chased a mirage of influence that was supposed to follow from 'punching above our weight'. The one serious chance we had to take a different path was in 1945 – and perhaps if 'the switch' had not happened we would have done so. Had that path been tried, Britain might be a different place today – but the world would have been different in ways not easily foreseen.

Notes

1 Ben Pimlott, *Hugh Dalton* (Harper Collins, 1985), p. 408.
2 David Marquand, *The Progressive Dilemma* (Phoenix, 1999), p. 85.
3 Pimlott, *Hugh Dalton*, p. 411.
4 According to Roy Jenkins, *The Chancellors* (Macmillan, 1998), p. 447.
5 Pimlott, *Hugh Dalton*, p. 415.
6 Dalton had a notoriously bad relationship with his civil servants. The definitive story has Dalton shouting for one of his senior civil servants who was tracked down by a messenger in the toilets. The messenger slipped a note under the door which was pushed back with the reply, 'kindly tell the Chancellor that I can only deal with one shit at a time'.
7 Quoted equally often as Bevin on Morrison and Bevin on Bevan.

8   For example by the Conservatives: Eden to Cadogan, in D. R. Thorpe, *Eden* (Chatto & Windus, 2003), p. 320.

9   Corelli Barnett, *The Lost Victory, British Dreams, British Realities, 1945–1950* (Macmillan, 1995), p. 3.

10 Pimlott, *Hugh Dalton*, p. 428.

11 The actual monthly average for the first half of 1947; ibid., p. 483.

12 Barnett, *The Lost Victory*, p. 134.

13 In fact the 1949–50 cost was over twice that, at £330 million.

14 David Marquand, *Britain Since 1918* (Weidenfeld & Nicolson, 2008), p. 122.

15 Conceivable, as it actually was achieved in the second half of that year.

16 Marquand, *The Progressive Dilemma* p. 89.

17 Barnett, *The Lost Victory*, p. 374.

18 Memorably demanding that there was a 'bloody Union Jack on top [of the A-bomb]'.

19 Edmund Dell, *The Chancellors* (Harper Collins, 1996), p. 68.

20 Marquand, *Britain since 1918*, p. 128.

21 Edmund Dell, *The Chancellors* (Harper Collins, 1996), p. 69.

22 Barnett, *The Lost Victory*, p. 50.

23 Alan Bullock, *Ernest Bevin, Foreign Secretary* (Oxford University Press, 1985), p. 152.

24 Ibid., p. 31.

25 Eight per cent of the Greek population had died in the war, ten times the UK fatality rate; ibid., p. 48.

26 Ibid., p. 248.

27 Not so far-fetched; the Turkish ambassador in Athens said that Yugoslav occupation of Salonika would take place the day after the British left; ibid., p. 248.

28 Jenkins, *The Chancellors*, p. 437.

29 As opposed to the actual $12.4 billion.

30 Marquand, *The Progressive Dilemma*, p. 87.

31 Ibid., p. 103.

Chapter 5

What if Richard Nixon had become President of the United States in 1961?

Neil Stockley

On 8 November 1960, Senator John F. Kennedy, the Democratic Party nominee, was elected President of the United States. In the closest presidential election since 1916, Senator Kennedy defeated his Republican Party rival, the Vice President, Richard M. Nixon, by a mere 118,550 votes out of 68.3 million cast for the two of them, or 49.9 per cent to 49.6 per cent of the popular vote, with the remaining 0.5 per cent for minor candidates. In the electoral college, Kennedy won comfortably, by 303 votes to 219, with 15 other votes going to Senator Harry F. Byrd, a Democrat from Virginia.

In John F. Kennedy, America had a vibrant young president, the first born in the twentieth century. He had promised to 'get this country moving again' and to explore an exciting 'new frontier'. Kennedy's presidency would prove eventful, from the Bay of Pigs fiasco and the building of the Berlin Wall to the Cuban missile crisis. He also had to contend with the growing US entanglement in Vietnam and, at home, demands from the growing civil rights movement for legislative action. On 22 November 1963, however, the Kennedy era was brutally cut short by an assassin's bullet. The fallen young president left behind a grief-stricken nation, the enduring myth of Camelot – and the tumultuous politics of the 1960s, whose aftershocks have been felt now for over four decades.

Given that the outcome of the 1960 election was so close, we have to ask: what might have happened if Nixon had won? What would he have done differently, in foreign and domestic policy? Would Nixon have been the same sort of president that he eventually became, after he returned from the political wilderness and won the 1968 presidential election?

~

In 1959, Earl Mazo published a biography of Vice President Richard M. Nixon.[1] He predicted that if Nixon became president he would be: 'perhaps the hardest driving chief executive and the most controversial since Theodore Roosevelt. There would be nothing haphazard, nothing bland about his administration, nor any doubt about its political identity.' Mazo also suggested that a Nixon administration would be 'conservative on domestic matters and internationalist in foreign affairs'.

Mazo was correct about Nixon's style of government and his approach to America's role in the world. Yet nobody really foresaw how tough – and how adventurist – Nixon's foreign policy would be, or how radical and innovative some of his domestic policies would turn out.

We should never forget that one of the biggest surprises about the Nixon administration was that it happened at all. His victory in the presidential election of 1960 was as remarkable as it was narrow. The Democratic Party nominee, senator John F. Kennedy of Massachusetts, had a number of advantages. He was younger and richer and projected more vitality than Nixon. Kennedy had the stronger vice presidential running mate in Senator Lyndon B. Johnson of Texas and he won the now-forgotten first television debate. After eight years of conservative Republican rule, under the grandfatherly President Dwight D. Eisenhower, the country could have been ready for the new sense of purpose and dynamism that Kennedy promised.

Yet Nixon was undoubtedly the more experienced of the two candidates. Two experimental election-day surveys in the 'swing' states showed that floating voters concluded, by a narrow margin and at the last minute, that he was more likely to preserve the nation's prosperity and see off the mounting threat from the Soviet Union. In his last, famous debate with Kennedy, Nixon went on the attack, and as before, his aggressive style of campaigning worked.

Nixon ran the better campaign. He shrewdly campaigned in every state, tactfully avoiding the issue of Kennedy's religion, and wisely saved his trump card, President Eisenhower, until almost the end of the campaign. On the defining issues, Nixon finally gained the upper hand, calling for a balanced budget and showing great fortitude over the defence of Quemoy and Matsu. Whereas Kennedy peaked a little too soon, Nixon did so at just the right moment.

The deciding factor may well have been his late decision to spend the weekend before election day on the stump in Illinois. Despite brazen attempts by the mayor of Chicago, Richard Daley, to rig the results in Cook County, Nixon won the state by a margin of less than 1 per cent. The result in Illinois, with his wafer-thin victories in Missouri and New Jersey, was enough to give him 275 votes in the electoral college to Kennedy's 247.[2] He won the popular vote also, by a margin of 49.6 per cent to 49.5 per cent. Richard Milhous Nixon, 35th President of the United States, accordingly took the oath of office on 20 January 1961.

Nixon's inaugural address was an uncompromising but workmanlike call to arms in America's unceasing contest for superiority with the Soviet Union. As expected, his first administration consisted mostly of safe 'establishment types' and moderate Republicans, many of whom had served under President Eisenhower. C. Douglas Dillon became Secretary of State, while the Vice President, Henry Cabot Lodge, acted as a co-ordinator of cold war policy. Allen Dulles remained as CIA director. Fred Scribner was the Secretary to the Treasury and John Mitchell the Attorney-General. Robert B. Anderson went to Defense and Fred Seaton to Agriculture. The new Health, Education and Welfare secretary, Charles H. Percy, had not held office under Eisenhower, but he was a successful businessman and one of the Republicans' rising stars.

The sense of continuity and conservatism did not last long, however. Within months, there was a clear shift away from President Eisenhower's approach, most obvious in foreign affairs. For years, the Republicans' rhetoric had been based on unrestrained hostility to the Soviet Union. They also sought a permanent contest with communism. Nixon was determined that America would be bolder, more active and, if necessary, more aggressive in its efforts to win the cold war. The most important lesson he drew from World War II was that the communists should never be appeased; any negotiation should take place only from a position of dominance.

Soon after they took office, Nixon, Dillon and Anderson concluded that while the Soviet Union had a small operational arsenal of intercontinental missiles, they could also enlarge that arsenal very substantially. Nixon and his colleagues decided to insure against any Soviet military build-up by dramatically increasing the defence budget by 40 per cent in the administration's first two years. By 1965, America's number of inter-continental ballistic missiles (ICBMs) had grown from 200 to 800 and the country had a new fleet of thirty Polaris submarines.

Missile defence was not a new concern of Nixon's. After the launch of Sputnik in 1957, he had privately warned that the Eisenhower administration's reluctance to spend money on defence would enable the Soviet Union to take the lead in weapons technology. As always, political considerations were not far from Nixon's mind; he had tried to warn Eisenhower that the Democrats would play this card. Sure enough, Kennedy claimed throughout the campaign that the Republicans had allowed a 'missile gap' to develop between the United States and the Soviet Union. The new president was determined that he would not be left so exposed on the issue again. He and Secretary Anderson kept returning in their public comments to the promise and attainment of American superiority.

Nixon was determined to stand up to the Soviet Union anywhere and everywhere, and to resist any further communist advances. As Vice President, he had urged Eisenhower to 'go in' and achieve victory, in North Korea, in Vietnam, in the Formosa Straits, in Hungary and in Cuba. Each time, he had watched, frustrated, as Eisenhower pursued a policy of restraint. Now, as President, Nixon had his own opportunities to go for victory and he seized them.

First, Nixon 'went in' to Cuba. Soon after he took office, the CIA revived a plan, developed the previous year, for an American-trained force of Cuban exiles to invade southern Cuba and overthrow the fledgling left-wing government of Fidel Castro. Behind the closed doors of the previous administration, Nixon had supported the invasion plan, even though he took the opposite view in public during the 1960 campaign.

In late March, after much deliberation, Nixon decided that the invasion should go ahead, with American support. Crucially, he acceded to a request from Allen Dulles that the US should provide the exile brigade with full air cover. The exiles landed at Playa Girón (the 'Bay of Pigs') on 17 April and, after nearly a month of intense fighting, during which there were some 2,000 casualties, they took control of Havana. A new, moderate regime took over and Castro fled to Venezuela.

On the evening of 18 May, the President appeared on all three major networks to pledge that his administration would take 'any action necessary' to 'resist aggression by our enemies ... We will commit American prestige to defend freedom and we will be prepared to commit any amount of power to obtain our objective,' he intoned. The administration's intent was made perfectly clear to the whole world.

Second, Nixon 'went in' to Laos and then, fatefully, to Vietnam. The previous administration had committed millions of dollars in aid and teams of military advisers to prevent the takeover of Laos by the leftist Pathet Lao. Shortly before the changeover, President Eisenhower warned his successor that this effort was on the verge of failure and the US military might need to intervene.

His advisers convinced the President that a diplomatic solution based on a neutral government could not prevent a civil war in Laos; worse, a Pathet Lao government would allow parts of the country to be used as a supply route by the Viet Minh in neighbouring North Vietnam. The president was convinced that Cambodia, Thailand, Malaysia, the Philippines, and perhaps even Australia and Japan could fall to the communists if the United States did not save Laos and South Vietnam. He believed that America could now stem the tide of communist advances in South East Asia and the Pacific.

In May 1961, Nixon committed 10,000 American troops and advisers to support the Royal Lao regime in Laos. The Pathet Lao were soon subdued and the situation in Laos stabilised. Crucially, a precedent had been set for United States military engagement in Vietnam.

The previous year, a full-scale revolt had broken out against the regime of Ngo Dinh Diem, president of South Vietnam. Nixon was a long-standing supporter of Diem; soon after he took office, he assured the South Vietnamese that they had the support of the American people in their fight 'to make their young republic strong and safe from communist encroachment'.

In March 1961, Nixon despatched Vice President Lodge to Saigon to meet Diem and his advisers. Lodge reported that Diem could be sustained in office – if the United States backed him up with military advice, combat troops and equipment, especially helicopters. Later that year, another group of advisers maintained that the war could be won if infiltration from the north was stopped.

The following November, Nixon told Republican congressional leaders that the United States had 'an unparalleled new opportunity to roll back the communist tide, not only in South Vietnam, but in South East Asia generally'. His triumph in Cuba had strengthened Nixon's conviction that America could prevail, but only by being strong and determined. At first, he hoped and expected that economic and military assistance would be sufficient to guarantee success. By the end of 1962, there were some 16,000 American military advisers in South Vietnam.

As the conflict dragged on into 1963, Nixon was persuaded that new counter-measures had to be taken against the north. Right from the start of the US intervention, American troops in Laos had been authorised to cut the Ho Chi Minh trail. In September 1963, the administration began to extend the war to North Vietnam. Twenty thousand US combat troops were sent to Vietnam. The South Vietnamese air force was equipped and trained to bomb the enemy's roads, bridges and supply routes into the south. United States forces also helped the South Vietnamese army to run a parallel campaign of guerrilla warfare over the border, to harass the enemy in the north.

Predictably, Nixon's actions over Cuba, Laos, Vietnam and missile defence met with dismay in Moscow. The Soviet premier, Nikita

Khrushchev, was deeply disappointed by Nixon's accession to the presidency. Khrushchev remembered all too well his personal duel of words with Nixon during their famous 'kitchen debate' in 1959. The exchange left him convinced that the advocate of American capitalism was not just tough-minded but also strong-willed. Now his worst fears were realised.

Khrushchev believed that Nixon would be prepared to suppress, by force if necessary, progressive movements in the Third World. He could also use force to preserve the status quo in Berlin. Then, the new president turned down Khrushchev's suggestion that the two men should meet in the summer of 1961 (Secretary Dillon had advised that the issues at hand could be addressed, for the time being, by lower-level diplomats). For his part, Nixon believed that the Soviet premier would continue to 'probe and prod' to find weak spots. He was sure that if met with firm resistance, Khrushchev would back down.

In October 1962, Nixon's theory was put to the ultimate test. After the administration's initial displays of strength, Khrushchev trod carefully. He was, however, coming under intense pressure from hardliners in the Kremlin who argued (with some justification) that the United States was trying to shift the military balance in its favour before asking for a diplomatic settlement of the issues on which the two superpowers were in dispute, including Berlin and the nuclear arms race. The Soviet premier remained angry that the future of Berlin remained unresolved. Khrushchev was also embarrassed by the fact that every year, tens of thousands of people escaped from the eastern sector to West Berlin. Throughout 1961 and the first half of 1962, Khrushchev made a number of demands for a settlement of the status of Berlin, which Nixon brushed aside. The President also increased the military budget and scaled up the presence of US forces in West Berlin. Nixon made an especially bellicose speech at the end of July 1962, arguing that nothing less than the future of the free world was at stake in the argument over the city's future.

Khrushchev acted to end the impasse. On the morning of 13 August 1962, East German troops closed the border between East and West Berlin and started to build a concrete structure to divide the two parts of the city.

Nixon responded boldly, immediately demanding that Khrushchev order the East Germans to tear down the wall. As thousands of additional US troops were airlifted into West Berlin, a military conflict, escalating into a war fought with nuclear weapons, seemed inevitable.

Then, Khrushchev blinked. East German troops demolished the incomplete wall, though the border between the eastern and western zones remained closed and the streets and buildings in the area of East Berlin closest to the border were torn up and made into the so-called 'zone of death', guarded by an array of machine guns and patrol towers. The number of escapees from the east slowed considerably, though in later years, Western Europe still had to contend with an escalating refugee problem. Most importantly, Nixon secured the future of West Berlin, and the communists had not advanced. Given that Khrushchev's critics in the Kremlin had wanted him to invade West Berlin, now he looked especially weak.

Nixon pressed on with the United States' military build-up and toughened up his rhetoric about greater military superiority in nuclear weapons and delivery systems. At the end of 1962, he broke the three-year Russian-American moratorium on nuclear testing, believing – correctly – that Khrushchev was about to do the same. Within a year, the United States had conducted forty atmospheric tests and the Soviet Union just three. A new nuclear and missiles arms race had begun, which the Soviet Union had no realistic prospect of winning; we now know that the American effort was much greater than was really necessary.

In December 1963, Khrushchev was finally forced to resign. A more hard-line leadership took over in Moscow, in which Leonid Brezhnev became the dominant figure. The new regime immediately resumed efforts to seek military parity with the United States, by building more nuclear weapons with ICBMs and updating their fleet. The biggest, most expensive and most dangerous arms race in human history was under way.

With his attention focused so much on foreign affairs, it is hardly surprising that Nixon's record on domestic issues is often overlooked. Many of his policies reflected his moderate brand of conservatism as well as the temper of the times. As expected, the President started by governing carefully and cautiously, always keeping a close eye on the public mood before putting forward substantial new initiatives. He faced political constraints as well. Some were obvious: both houses of Congress were under the control of the Democrats. Other constraints were less apparent but years later, in his memoirs, Nixon blamed 'the Eisenhower types' whom he had kept on for the administration's caution.

Despite this, a great deal was achieved in his first term. As he had promised, President Nixon presented Congress in March 1962 with a bill to provide health care for retired people, by establishing limited federal support for private insurance plans. After some partisan power plays, the bill was passed in May 1963, but with an increased level of federal funding.

In November 1962, Nixon vetoed a Democrat bill to provide direct aid to schools and federal support for teachers' salaries. The following summer, Congress and the administration reached a compromise, to support the schools by using special grants and loans to the states.

Nixon could still surprise and confound Congress, the public and his own party. His second and third budgets contained public housing construction programmes worth $3 billion in total. This was no 'small-government' Republican. In 1964, he put forward world-leading legislation to curb air, water, and pesticide pollution, regulate ocean dumping, and protect coastal zones and marine mammals. Some critics charged that Nixon was simply playing politics on the eve of the election. They forgot that the President came from a staunchly Quaker family.

It was over civil rights that Nixon was most radical. As Eisenhower's Vice President, he had been a public and private champion of civil rights, to the extent that he had risked the ire of white southern voters in the run-up to the 1960 election. Nixon believed that his failure to make a public comment after Martin Luther King was arrested in Atlanta, Georgia, during the campaign had cost him at least a million Negro votes.

At first, President Nixon's instinct was to delay action until the public was more ready to accept new measures on civil rights. He eventually realised that the campaigns of civil disobedience by Negroes in the south, the march on Washington for freedom and jobs at the end of 1962, and pressure from moderate and liberal Republicans in Congress, meant that the issue could be delayed no longer. In early January 1963, he signed an executive order banning racial discrimination in housing. The following month, in one of the most momentous acts of his presidency, Nixon presented Congress with a bill to prohibit racial discrimination in employment, public accommodation, publicly owned facilities and federally funded programmes. The historic legislation was passed in April 1964, despite the fierce objections of southern Democrats and some Republicans.

The President was able to secure passage of the Civil Rights Act for three reasons. The first was a simple matter of numbers. With Nixon triumphant in foreign policy and the economy performing well, the Republicans had made impressive gains in both houses of Congress at the 1962 mid-term elections. Second, the President formed an unlikely alliance on civil rights with the Senate majority leader, Senator Lyndon B. Johnson, Senator Kennedy and other leading pro-civil rights Democrats.

The third explanation stems from a dark moment in Nixon's presidency. On 22 November 1963, Lee Harvey Oswald, a troubled loner and a devoted supporter of the deposed Castro regime, tried to shoot the President as he greeted a crowd in Miami, Florida. FBI officers apprehended Oswald before he could fire on the President, and the would-be assassin was later put on trial and imprisoned for life. Nixon handled the episode with considerable grace and fortitude. Most Americans were shocked and stunned by the assassination attempt and, whatever their opinions of him or his policies, rallied around their President. For a time, it seemed that he could do no wrong. Nixon leveraged what Johnson later called 'the President's new halo' to pressure members of Congress to pass the civil rights legislation.

Despite the political opportunities presented by the events of 22 November 1963, and for all his political gifts and achievements, Nixon never really succeeded in winning the respect or affection of the American people. He rarely inspired them to think differently about themselves or what more they could do for their country or what their country could achieve in the world. He could not speak to a growing feeling, especially among younger Americans, that the United States should do more with its power and prosperity. This mattered when big issues, such as civil rights or Vietnam, were at stake.

(Maybe Senator Kennedy might have provided the sense of hope about the future that some Americans seemed to yearn for in the 1960s? This was argued at the time; but as stories of his womanising and health problems became public, and after a number of embarrassing photos and tape recordings mysteriously appeared in the press, it seemed much less plausible. Ill-health forced Kennedy to retire from the Senate in 1964 and he died six years later, aged just 53.

Or perhaps Nixon could have used something bolder, more visionary, and more romantic – a more ambitious space programme, maybe – to rally his compatriots in the contest for supremacy with the Soviet Union? The President had balked at the potential costs. In any case, one of his first acts upon taking office had to been to approve the launch of Alan Shepard's *Freedom 7* on the planned launch date of 5 March 1961. Shepard became the first man to journey into space, beating a Soviet cosmonaut by a month. The pressure seemed to be off the Americans, and their manned space programme ended quietly in 1964.)

Instead of a sense of hope and idealism, an air of negativity and suspicion often hovered around the Nixon White House. In 1960, another biographer, William Costello, had warned that Nixon 'understands the use of power but not the unwritten constraints on its use'.[3] Recounting how the Vice President had tried to intimidate federal workers accused of leaking, sensitive documents, Costello warned that '[in Nixon's] administration, anyone running afoul of policy, even inadvertently, could expect only the swiftest and most merciless reprisals'.[4] This observation proved remarkably prescient. One of Nixon's foreign policy achievements had unintended consequences and what followed could have brought him down.

During 1962 and 1963, left-leaning parties and movements had come to power in Colombia, Venezuela, Peru, Argentina and Brazil. The Nixon administration had little understanding of the social and economic forces at work in Latin America and had not developed a preventive strategy. They had also failed to foresee that the ousted Castro would provide a source of inspiration for nationalists, leftists, communists and anti-Americans of all stripes. Nixon and his advisers perceived events in Latin America through the simple prism of the Cold War. They reacted with crude force, backing successful military coups against the democratically elected governments and assisting Cuba-style revolts against the others, and supporting the ruling dictatorships elsewhere.

In their drive to keep the region free of leftist leaders, the administration supported some unsavoury allies, using counter-insurgency measures and training police and security forces who were often cruel and brutal. These tactics came under fire from liberal commentators in America, who pointed to the poverty and inequality that remained unaddressed in the region. The United Kingdom and other European allies were also critical. The United States had stood up to communism, but whether it was a force for good, for democracy or for freedom was now open to question.

The administration's Latin America policies were also strenuously criticised by parts of the mainstream media, most notably the *New York Times* and the *Washington Post*. In February 1964, the *Times* featured an extensive set of leaked State Department, Defense Department and CIA documents that revealed the extent of the administration's deception and outright lies over the covert wars in the region. An enraged Nixon, backed by the Attorney General, John Mitchell, ordered retaliation against those responsible. They started by searching out and prosecuting the leakers, who were eventually imprisoned. On Mitchell's instruction, administration operatives threatened and harassed the publishers of the *Times* and the *Post*.

The President was convinced that the leaks and the criticisms were simply the partisan handiwork of his old liberal enemies, out to avenge his past victories against Jerry Voorhis, Alger Hiss, Helen Gahagan Douglas and John F. Kennedy, and deny him the second term and the decisive electoral victory that he craved. All through 1962 and 1963, new questions and allegations bubbled away about the mysterious loan of $205,000 that the business magnate Howard Hughes had made to Donald Nixon, the President's brother.

Nixon left nothing to chance in his efforts to win re-election. He asked Mitchell to head up the Committee to Re-Elect President Nixon, which operated independently of the Republican National Committee. The key aides were H. R. Haldeman, an advertising man, and John Ehrlichman, a lawyer. Both had worked on the 1960 campaign and had impressed Nixon with their toughness and take-no-prisoners approach. Haldeman and Ehrlichman set up a team, partly based in the White House, that organised a variety of dirty tricks, dubious incidents and media leaks to embarrass Democrats and liberal commentators.

It all seems ludicrous now, because there was never any serious doubt that Nixon would be re-elected in 1964. The President had stood up to the Soviet Union in Berlin, forced the communists out of Cuba and was working to do the same in South East Asia. The administration had an impressive record on domestic reform. The American economy was enjoying its longest ever period of continuous economic growth. Nixon had faced an assassination attempt with dignity and courage.

In August 1964, as widely expected, the Democrats nominated Senator Hubert H. Humphrey of Minnesota for President and Senator Christopher Dodd of Connecticut for Vice President. They were a much weaker ticket than the Kennedy-Johnson team of four years earlier. Senator Humphrey was a well-liked and respected senator, best known for his advocacy of such liberal causes as arms control and a nuclear test ban. The Nixon campaign skilfully played on this record, charging that Humphrey would cave in to the Soviet Union and the North Vietnamese, roll back America's missile defence programme and over-spend on social programmes. The Democrat's long-standing record as a strong advocate of federal action on civil rights was received badly in the southern states.

Vietnam appeared to be the most obvious threat to the President's prospects of re-election. By the summer of 1964, it was clear that Nixon's strategy of widening the war was not working. Liberals began to question the morality of America's involvement and some even expressed doubts that the war could be won. But Vietnam was still not a major issue for most voters and Senator Humphrey's vagueness on how he would prosecute the war differently from the administration played into Nixon's hands.

The turning point in the campaign came on 2 August, when a North Vietnamese vessel was alleged to have fired on American warships in the Tonkin Gulf. Nixon seized the initiative, and ordered the US Air Force to launch retaliatory strikes against North Vietnam. For the first time, the United States itself was firing on the north. Humphrey and the Democrats had little choice but to fall in behind.

'The communists are testing the United States during an election campaign, and that means we must take firm action', Nixon told the nation. He asked Congress to pass a resolution giving him authority to use 'all necessary measures' to 'repel any armed attack' against American forces. The President was also authorised to 'take all necessary steps' to 'prevent further aggression' and protect any nation covered by the South East Asia Treaty in 'defence of its freedom'. The resolution was carried overwhelmingly. Nixon now had congressional permission to do whatever he wanted in Vietnam. And the President appeared as tough, determined and in command as ever.

Nixon campaigned energetically, offering 'no apologies' for the retaliatory strikes and promising 'absolutely no let-up' in his efforts to defeat the communists. Victory in Vietnam was at hand, he maintained, if only America stayed the course. The President also promised that in his second term, he would be much more innovative in tackling poverty and deprivation at home. Nixon won 403 electoral college votes to Humphrey's 135 and triumphed in the popular vote by 56.6 per cent to 44.4 per cent. In the Senate, the parties were now tied and in the House, the Democrats' majority was reduced to just 20 seats.

Nixon now had an historic opportunity to change America. There were many new faces in the cabinet in January 1965, as an emboldened President sent the 'Eisenhower types' packing. The most interesting appointment was the new Secretary of State, Nelson A. Rockefeller, former Governor of New York, the hero of the Republican Party's liberal wing who might once have been a serious rival to Nixon.

Nixon's top priority was victory in Vietnam. Negotiation with Hanoi was an option but the President was sure that any diplomatic solution would lead to a communist takeover of the south. Escalating American involvement was the only viable alternative. From January 1965, Nixon committed more ground troops, and by end of the year, 150,000 American servicemen were in Vietnam, and a draft had been brought in at home. He ordered the US air force and navy to commence a bombing campaign against North Vietnam. Two months later, they started bombing suspected Viet Cong bases in south Vietnam and US troops were ordered to search out the enemy and engage in combat.

Over the following four years, the Nixon administration dropped more bombs than had been used in the whole of World War II, in a futile attempt to force the North Vietnamese and the Viet Cong into submission. Yet the enemy did not buckle and the conflict carried on. Meanwhile, across America, campuses were in open revolt, with the country split down the middle over the country's involvement in Vietnam. In New York City, Chicago, San Francisco, and Boston, even middle-class Americans took to the streets in protest.

Racial tensions boiled over and there were riots in Washington DC and Los Angeles, fuelled by the extent of Negro poverty and joblessness. Nixon's personal popularity ratings collapsed, as he was unable to convince his compatriots that the costs and the casualties were worthwhile, that the war could be won.

At the 1966 elections, the Democrats, now galvanised and united against what they called 'Nixon's war', were rampant. They took 95 seats in the House from the Republicans – a post-war record – and 13 in the Senate. More than 600 Republican state legislators were defeated. One of the Democrats' most striking results was in California, where the long-serving Governor, Pat Brown, easily held off a challenge by a former B-grade movie actor called Ronald Reagan. Reagan's widely ridiculed candidacy and extreme views have provided a rich mine of material for satirists ever since.

In February 1967, after further military defeats, and with 30,000 Americans having died in combat, Nixon reluctantly concluded that the war could not be won and that the economic and political costs were proving too great. But he was also firm that America's honour had to be upheld. The President pursued a new strategy: letting the South Vietnamese fight the war for themselves. Nixon announced that the United States would gradually withdraw its troops and instead concentrate on providing its allies with military hardware. This seemed the most likely path to victory, and it went some way to meeting the objections of the growing numbers of Americans who wanted peace in Vietnam. In July 1967, he announced that American troops would start coming home, 20,000 at a time, with the troops' withdrawal proceeding as quickly as the South Vietnamese army was re-equipped and upgraded.

Rockefeller had brought to Washington as his senior counsel, the brilliant Dr Henry A. Kissinger of Harvard University. Kissinger proposed a 'linkage' strategy, similar to that previously used by President Truman, which would provide the Soviet Union with inducements to stop supplying munitions to Hanoi. Nixon and Rockefeller quickly recognised Kissinger's plan as a 'win-win' solution: the north's supply of munitions would be cut off; the Diem government would remain in power; both the US and USSR would be able to lower their enormous spending on nuclear weaponry; and détente could resume.

There was a further advantage to both sides. Communist China, an enemy of the United States and an increasingly vigorous critic and rival of the Soviet Union, would be left isolated. This prospect had enormous appeal to Nixon. Mao Tse-tung had sent nearly half a million troops to Korea and Vietnam and had financed and trained insurgencies in other countries. Nixon believed that the United States could benefit if tensions between Moscow and Peking were ramped up, or if China became worried about a possible rapprochement between the US and the USSR.

In May 1967, Kissinger travelled in secret to Moscow, to begin discussions on a new arms control treaty. Later, Nixon and Rockefeller took over the negotiations. The first outcome of these talks was a partial test ban treaty, which banned nuclear tests in the atmosphere. (Ironically, this was one of the very policies that Nixon's campaign had used to attack

Humphrey.) A nuclear non-proliferation treaty was signed and ratified in 1967. The following year, an arms control agreement, the first of the Cold War, froze the number of ICBMs at 1968 levels, preserving (but only just) American superiority. The Nixon administration went on developing missiles with multiple nuclear warheads, as well as arming their allies in Europe, the Middle East, Latin America and the Pacific. The Soviet Union scaled down its assistance to North Vietnam. The US began selling wheat to the USSR. Détente appeared to be working.

Nixon wound down the number of US troops in Vietnam, to 50,000 by June 1968. He ended the draft and campuses were largely pacified. In October 1967, Rockefeller began peace talks involving both Vietnams and the Soviet Union, but they proceeded very slowly and frequently became bogged down on technical matters. At their heart was a basic disagreement. Le Duc Tho, the North Vietnamese leader, insisted that the Americans must withdraw; then and only then, would he hand over their prisoners of war. For his part, Rockefeller demanded that Le Duc Tho accept a divided Vietnam and renounce the use of force.

Meanwhile, in order to show that he would not be pressured, and to gain bargaining chips to use during the talks, Nixon continued to arm the South Vietnamese army and escalated the bombing on both sides of the border. The horrific campaign reached its zenith with a massive bombing offensive on Hanoi on 30–31 March 1968. Afterwards, the peace talks finally collapsed. When Nixon left office, in January 1969, there was still war in Vietnam. This was to be Nixon's greatest disappointment and his greatest failure.

In domestic policy, Nixon's second term started with another landmark piece of civil legislation. In 1965, the President used the afterglow of his electoral victory, and the new dispensation in Congress, to secure the passage of a Voting Rights Act, to prohibit states from imposing any 'voting qualification or prerequisite to voting, or standard, practice, or procedure ... to deny or abridge the right of any citizen of the United States to vote on account of race or colour.'

The Voting Rights Act had a long-term political impact. As a result of Nixon's boldness on civil rights, neither party has gained a firm electoral hold over the southern states, and the Republicans must still work hard to win the support of the region's white voters.

Otherwise, Nixon could point to few domestic policy achievements in his second term. The administration developed some interesting plans for welfare reform, based on a negative income tax, but these were not tabled in Congress until the middle of 1966 and were eventually killed off, after the election debacle, by an alliance of budget-cutters and social security advocates. An innovative new student loan scheme did not appear until the start of Nixon's last year in office.

Today, we are left with the impression that Nixon had not spent the same amount of time working out what he wanted to do on domestic policy as he did with foreign affairs. The President was, inevitably, distracted by big events on the world stage. The media began to report in detail on the plight of those on low incomes, living in poverty and unable to afford health care. Crime rates soared, especially in the major cities. A growing number of Americans wondered what kind of society they were living in. As a result, the Democrats had a potent set of issues to run with in 1968.

The President had another distraction in his second term. In the summer of 1965, some of the more unsavoury activities of the Campaign to Re-elect President Nixon came to light. Stories emerged that the campaign, possibly with the help of senior administration officials, had placed illegal wiretaps on Democratic Party strategists and *Washington Post* journalists. A leak from someone in the administration suggested that the White House had tried to stop an FBI investigation into the allegation. Then, the trail stopped dead.

Democrats in Congress tried to summon Mitchell (who was still at the Justice Department), Haldeman (now a senior counsel in the White House) and other leading administration officials to testify before congressional committees. They also tried to subpoena FBI and Justice Department documents. But the administration kept on claiming executive immunity. The situation was rich in irony. Twenty years earlier, a young congressman called Richard Nixon had demanded that officials in the Truman administration should testify before Congress. Now, his claims that officials in the Nixon administration should not have to appear on Capitol Hill rang hollow.

The game of cat and mouse carried on until the 1968 elections. What did the President know and when did he know it? We still do not know for sure. A 'smoking gun' implicating the White House was never found. Bitter liberals protested that 'tricky Dick' had got away with it once more time. Such is politics. But the 1964 campaign left a bitter aftertaste which has never really gone away.

Richard Nixon departed the White House on 20 January 1969, after eight momentous years as President. Thanks to him, the United States prevailed in the Cold War. Thanks to Nixon, there was a new détente with the Soviet Union. Thanks to Nixon, America started to include black people as equal citizens. Thanks to Nixon, the Republican Party stayed firmly in the middle ground of American politics, with the Goldwater right kept well to the fringes, where they have remained ever since.

We should never forget, however, the many ways in which Nixon came up short. He let the arms race against the Soviet Union go on too long and his efforts to forge a lasting peace were too late and lacking in ambition. He made sure that China was left out in the cold for least a decade more than was necessary. He failed to win victory or to secure a lasting peace in Vietnam, leaving behind an unstable and dangerous situation in South East Asia and a world economy racked by double-digit inflation. He failed to mount a war on poverty at home to match the vigour of his wars against communism abroad. He ignored the cries of the 'other America'.

And we should never forget that the republic Nixon handed over to Robert Kennedy was more divided and more uncertain of itself than it had been for 100 years. There can be no doubt who is responsible for the sense of regret over opportunities lost and the rancid atmosphere that still pervades American more than four decades later. Nixon's the one.

Sources

Stephen E. Ambrose, *Rise to Globalism: American Foreign Policy Since 1938* (Penguin, ninth (revised) edition, 2010)

Stephen E. Ambrose, Nixon: *The Education of a Politician, 1913–1962* (Simon & Schuster, 1987)

Stephen E. Ambrose, *Nixon: The Triumph of a Politician, 1962–1972* (Simon & Schuster, 1990)

William Costello, *The Facts About Nixon: An Unauthorised Biography* (Viking Press, 1960)

David Greenberg, *Nixon's Shadow: The History of an Image* (W. W. Norton and Company, 2003)

Andrew L. Johns, 'A Voice from the Wilderness: Richard Nixon and the Vietnam War, 1964–1966', *Presidential Studies Quarterly*, 1999

Richard M. Nixon, *RN: The Memoirs of Richard Nixon* (Simon & Schuster, 1990)

Richard Reeves, *President Kennedy: Profile of Power* (Simon & Schuster, 1994)

Notes

1 Earl Mazo, *Richard Nixon: A Political and Personal Portrait* (Harper & Brothers Publishers, 1959), cited in Stephen E. Ambrose, *Nixon: The Education of a Politician, 1913–1962* (Simon & Schuster, 1987), p. 622.

2 There were also fifteen unpledged electors.

3 William Costello, *The Facts About Nixon: an Unauthorised Biography* (Viking Press, 1960) cited in Stephen E. Ambrose, *Nixon: The Education of a Politician, 1913–1962* (Simon & Schuster, 1987), p. 622.

4 Ibid.

Chapter 6

What if Harold Macmillan had not resigned in 1963?

Mark Stuart

The Prime Minister sat up in his hospital bed. He was feeling much better than he had for the last week. He looked down at the draft resignation letter a junior aide had helped him craft prior to going into the operating theatre the day before:

> I regret to inform Your Majesty that I have reached the decision, having been taken gravely ill, that I cannot hope to continue to conduct Your Majesty's business for any extended period. Accordingly, I now tender my resignation with the assurance that I shall ever be
>
> > Your Majesty's faithful and obedient servant,
> >
> > Harold Macmillan[1]

Macmillan stared at the letter for a while, casting his mind back to earlier, happier, times in the summer when his government had signed the Nuclear Test Ban Treaty. In the afterglow of that diplomatic triumph, he had deftly handled a potentially hazardous meeting of the Tory backbench 1922 Committee. He picked up his diary by his hospital bed:

> 27 July 1963: Our MPs are now coming in heavily to support me and other ministers. This confuses the Opposition and is also a healthy sign generally.[2]

He skipped to a later entry:

> 2 August 1963: The *Daily Mail* opinion poll has shown a tremendous swing
> back towards us. Only six per cent or so behind Labour (instead of eight-
> een or twenty per cent) and I have risen equally or more in public favour.[3]

And then there had been that long conversation in October with his son,
Maurice, after which he had written:

> 6 October 1963: I am beginning to move (at the last minute) towards
> staying on – for another two or three years. Maurice says that although it
> would be difficult to win for a fourth time, yet it might be done, by a sort
> of emotional wave of feeling ... After all, we have brought them both
> Prosperity and Peace.[4]

Macmillan gazed back at his resignation letter to the Queen. What a
difference twenty-four hours had made. The previous morning, he had
experienced excruciating pain in both his stomach and his lower back.
During a visit to the gentlemen's room, his urine had turned to blood. He
could remember thinking, 'Blazes, my damned prostate has gone!' Just to
cap it all, his doctor, Sir John Richardson, was on holiday in Windermere.
His wife Dorothy had hastily called Dr King-Lewis, and, after a short
examination, he had diagnosed renal colic. Though in tremendous pain,
the Prime Minister had managed a relieved smile on hearing the news –
no problems with my prostate then, he thought. The doctor suggested
immediate surgery, telephoning Alec Badenoch, the country's most eminent consultant urologist. Badenoch had conducted a quick lithotomy to
remove the offending kidney stone.

While the operation had taken place, the King Edward VII Officers'
Hospital switchboard had received calls from a succession of Conservative
MPs, objecting to the potential leadership of any of Reginald Maudling,
Alec Douglas-Home, Rab Butler or Lord Hailsham.[5]

Macmillan reflected for a while on the merits of these four potential
successors. While Maudling's tax-cutting Budget in the spring of 1963
had proved popular, his star as Chancellor of the Exchequer had waned
somewhat over the summer. The trusted figure of Lord Home held the

best chance of uniting the party, but he had indicated that he wouldn't in any circumstances seek the leadership. Rab Butler could be quickly discounted: he was one of life's cardinals, forever destined never to become Pope.[6] Perhaps his family friend, Lord Hailsham, was Macmillan's spiritual heir? They were fellow puritans, Hailsham having famously declared of the Profumo affair, in a stormy interview with Robert McKenzie, that: 'A great party is not to be brought down because of a scandal by a woman of easy virtue and a proved liar.'[7]

An aide came in to inform Macmillan that Hailsham had precipitously renounced his peerage on the eve of the Conservative Party conference at Blackpool.[8] There were even reports that his campaign team had already been formed, and that ghastly 'Q' buttons were being pressed upon unsuspecting delegates at the Winter Gardens.[9] On hearing the news, Macmillan had been furious at such undignified behaviour. No, he thought, I'm damned if I'm going to be forced out of office, all for the sake of a kidney stone. He reflected on the lack of an obvious successor. The only advice he trusted had been from Alec Home back in September. He flicked through his diary:

> 18 September 1963: He [Home] fears that there will be complete disunity in the Party and that great troubles will follow. I may be forced to stay. I replied 'In that case I shall be "drafted" – not a "limpet"'. I don't want it to be thought that I am just clinging on.[10]

Reading that diary entry clinched it. Macmillan's autumn of uncharacteristic procrastination was over. He crumpled his resignation letter into a ball and cast it into a wastepaper basket. 'Supermac' would outfox his critics one last time.

After a meeting with his aides, the Prime Minister resolved to put paid to the leadership hopes of his potential successors. A visit from Her Majesty to the hospital would be guaranteed to take the edge off Maudling's party conference speech. Photographers could be tipped off beforehand to snap the Queen as she left the hospital. Perhaps a photograph of Her Majesty by his bedside? No, that would be vulgar. A shot of the

Queen leaving the hospital would suffice. In his delicate state, it would be unwise to travel up to Blackpool for the conference for a couple of days, but the Prime Minister resolved, without prior warning, to address the party faithful in the closing speech.

A few days later, on Saturday, 12 October 1963, Macmillan ambled up on to the stage at the Winter Gardens to a thunderous reception from Tory delegates, many of whom were mightily relieved after the febrile atmosphere of the previous week. When the applause finally died away to just a few stray hoots from the crowd, the Prime Minister began:

> Well, my Lords, Ladies and Gentlemen, it appears as if, as Mark Twain once said, 'the reports of my death are greatly exaggerated.' [Sustained applause.] I do most sincerely apologise for being otherwise detained earlier this week. You can imagine it: the excruciating pain, the cries of anguish, the sheer agony [pause] especially after I informed Mr Wilson this morning that I was carrying on [laughter]. But it was remarkable how quickly 'Nye's Little Dog'[11] was brought to heel [more laughter]. You see, I simply had to emerge from my hospital bed to preserve the good life which we have enjoyed for the last decade and more.
>
> In today's Britain, people are basking in a degree of comfort and well-being such as I and my comrades could not have dreamed of when we slogged through the mud of Flanders nearly fifty years ago. This change in our fortunes has been brought about, not by discarding our moral and religious values, as Mr Wilson would have us do, but by having the courage to grasp what is new and fresh, so that a constant process of renewal and reinvigoration takes place in our national life. This change won't come about, as Mr Wilson falsely promised last week, by means of 'white heat' or a Socialist-style 'revolution'. No, this is a silent, Conservative revolution, creating opportunities for living the good life, a life of prosperity and freedom.[12]

It became known as Macmillan's 'Good Life' speech, earning him the longest standing ovation in the history of Conservative conferences. For a few months, the Prime Minister drew level in the polls with Harold Wilson.

Some commentators considered that Supermac's greatest moment came in the aftermath of President John F. Kennedy's assassination in Dallas on 22 November 1963. Macmillan's grief was genuine; it was as though he had lost a close relative. Perhaps fortunately, the Prime Minister had the weekend in which to compose himself, but when the House of Commons returned on the following Monday, he found the right words to speak for the whole nation:

> When that terrible news came on Friday, everyone in this country – and, I think, in every country – felt stunned by the shock of what seemed to us – to each one of us – a personal bereavement, and to the whole of humanity, struggling in this world of darkness, the sudden and cruel extinction of a shining light.[13]

Macmillan recalled the President's visit to Birch Grove, the Prime Minister's country house, that summer:

> From the very first moment that the President's helicopter flew in and landed in the park until his departure there was a feeling of excitement combined with gaiety which has left an indelible memory for all concerned … I can see him now, stepping out from the machine, this splendid, young, gay figure, followed by his team of devoted adherents. Never has a man been so well or loyally served.[14]

Three-quarters of an hour into the Prime Minister's eulogy, a few wicked Conservative MPs from the 1959 intake placed bets with one another on whether or not Macmillan, now in typical rambling mode, would ingratiate himself with Jackie Kennedy.

> Our thoughts at this time are, of course, with Jack's wife, Jackie. She has, as we all know, shown the most wonderful courage to the outer world in these last few tragic days.[15]

Several large five-pound notes surreptitiously changed hands on the Tory backbenches.

~

For all his latent, if outdated, charm, had Macmillan not retired in 1963, the final outcome of the following year's general election would have been largely the same – a narrow win for Harold Wilson and the Labour Party. From the middle of 1962, Macmillan had lost his sureness of political touch, becoming mired in a glutinous mixture of sackings and sleaze.

The Prime Minister's disastrous 'night of the long knives' Cabinet reshuffle of July 1962 was, in the words of D. R. Thorpe, 'one of the most damaging errors of Macmillan's premiership, and he was never to recover the initiative'.[16] Normally possessing the most acute of political antennae, the Prime Minister had erroneously believed there was a conspiracy against him. In particular, his decision to sack Selwyn Lloyd – a loyalist if ever there was one – as Chancellor seemed unnecessarily savage. The event even provoked Anthony Eden to complain that Lloyd had been badly treated, a rare example (back then, at least) of a former Prime Minister intervening to savage the incumbent.[17]

That autumn, the Vassall Case revealed openly for the first time the Prime Minister's inability to deal with matters of a sexual nature – often blamed on his wife Dorothy's long-standing affair with Tory MP Bob Boothby, about which Macmillan did nothing. So when it came to allegations of a homosexual affair between Thomas Galbraith, a former Civil Lord at the Admiralty, and a civil servant, John Vassall, a Soviet spy, the Prime Minister sat back, doing nothing to dissuade Galbraith from resignation, and reinstating him just a few months later. The ensuing debate in the House of Commons in November 1962 was badly mishandled, particularly in the government's failure to agree to a full public inquiry.[18] Moreover, the subsequent imprisonment of two journalists the following March for failing to reveal their sources about Vassall[19] meant that Macmillan lost the support of the press. The fact that the newspapers had turned against the Prime Minister in a big way meant that they were ready to pounce when the Profumo Affair erupted a few weeks later.

During the famous Profumo debate in the House of Commons in July 1963, Macmillan attempted to give what he referred to as 'a full and detailed account of my connection with this unhappy story'. Indeed, at times it seemed as if any crimes during the affair had been personally committed against the person of the Prime Minister. Referring to John Profumo's lies about his affair with Christine Keeler, Macmillan opined:

> For what greater moral crime can there be than to deceive those natu-
> rally inclined to trust one, those who have worked with one, served one,
> and are one's colleagues? ... I find it difficult to tell the House what a
> blow it has been to me, for it seems to have undermined one of the very
> foundations upon which political life has been conducted.[20]

Despite such candour, Macmillan showed himself to be wholly out of touch with changing morals in society with his revealing admission that: 'I do not live among young people much myself'.[21] Donald Johnson, the maverick Conservative MP for Carlisle, one of twenty-six Tories to abstain over the Profumo affair, summed up the mood of many: 'I have encountered nobody but Rip Van Winkle still living in the days of Harold Macmillan.'[22] The press reaction the following day was even more damning: 'Mac: The End' (*Daily Mail*); 'The Stag at Bay' (*Daily Mirror*); 'The Lost Leader' (*Daily Herald*); and most surprisingly 'A Broken Man Close to Tears' (*Daily Telegraph*).[23]

In a very real sense, Macmillan had already played his biggest policy ace and lost, in the shape of General de Gaulle's veto of Britain's application to join the European Economic Community in January 1963. In Volume Two of his official biography of his grandfather, Alistair Horne argues that de Gaulle's veto was 'a devastating blow', claiming that 'the central plank of the government's policy had just broken and Macmillan had nothing to put in its place in order to fight a viable and victorious election campaign'.[24] Although elections are rarely won and lost on matters of foreign policy, in this instance the Prime Minister's foreign and domestic policies were intimately linked. As Macmillan famously recorded in his diary at the time of de Gaulle's veto:

> 28 January 1963: All our policies at home and abroad are in ruins ... our
> popularity as a Government is rapidly declining. We have lost every-
> thing, except our courage and determination.[25]

~

De Gaulle's veto left Macmillan without a clear narrative with which to take his party into the 1964 election, which he contrived to delay until the last possible moment. Instead, he settled back into his rather tired old mantra, that the Conservatives had brought 'prosperity and peace'.

Set against Harold Wilson's message of change after 'thirteen wasted years', Macmillan began to give the air of a politician whose time was up. Privately, leading figures in the Labour Party had been delighted at Macmillan's decision to carry on as Prime Minister. As Richard Crossman had foreseen as early as June 1963, 'As long as he [Wilson] has Macmillan opposite him, old, effete, worn out, a cynical dilettante, the contrast between Harold's character and Macmillan's is an overwhelming advantage to Harold and the Labour Party.'[26] Although a sizable grouping of Tory backbenchers, especially from the 1959 intake – apart from a few mavericks like Humphry Berkeley,[27] MP for Lancaster – shared this view, the bulk of the party realised that there was no clear successor and that the election was too near for a last-minute change at the helm.

Meanwhile, the political satirists, led by *That Was the Week that Was*, mercilessly lampooned Macmillan's hangdog Edwardian persona.[28] Television audiences were treated to fresh sketches from the comedian Peter Cook, the most memorable featuring the Prime Minister on the grouse moor, accidentally shooting a peasant instead of a pheasant. This new brand of political satire was especially powerful because it had the express aim of wounding the ruling elite. As Jonathan Miller, one of the four members of *Beyond the Fringe*, remarked at the opening of the Establishment Club, 'the air resounds with the armourer's hammer. When battle is joined one can only hope that blood will be drawn.'[29]

There was therefore a real sense that whereas 1959 had represented Macmillan at the peak of his powers, from 1962 onwards the Prime Minister had 'seemed left behind by the tide'. As Anthony Sampson later observed, Macmillan 'could not convey any sense of excitement or optimism for the future generation, for he did not feel it.'[30]

As the 1964 election approached, in private the incumbent Prime Minister increasingly complained of tiredness, having served in No. 10 for over eight years. Meanwhile, the British economy was now being over-taken by the country's European rivals, and the balance of payments figures continued to worsen, showing a deficit of £98 million in late September 1964. Wilson, the trained economist, went on the offensive, claiming during an election campaign speech in Norwich that 'Britain is obtaining prosperity on the slate'.[31] For the rest of the election campaign, Wilson mercilessly hammered the Tories' 'broken record' on the economy, a charge that seemed to stick, especially after Reginald Maudling, the Chancellor, had been forced to own up to a £800 million loan from the International Monetary Fund the previous autumn.

As polling day neared, Wilson successfully portrayed Macmillan as an 'old Edwardian politician no longer suited to the jet age'. It was a jibe that stuck. Journalists had a field day when Macmillan was photographed apparently asleep outside a country hotel in Tewkesbury. The Prime Minister's attempts to laugh it off as a 'well-earned catnap' could not disguise the age and energy gap between the two rival candidates. In a speech the following day, Harold Wilson referred to 'the tired old men who govern us from the grouse moors', calling for 'a new, dynamic leadership that can take Britain into a modern era, one that will make *all* the people proud'. The Tory air of defeatism was not helped when Rab Butler referred to a 'strong undercurrent of [sic] Labour', when two opinion polls were published both showing a healthy Labour lead.[32]

Wilson won the general election in 1964 with a slender overall majority of thirteen. Macmillan was badly bruised, and voices in the Conservative Party increasingly blamed their defeat on 'The Old Limpet'.

The new Prime Minister proved a master conjuror, juggling competing personalities in his new government, and playing the world statesman when the Rhodesian Prime Minister Ian Smith made his Unilateral Declaration of Independence in November 1965. Macmillan carried on as a lame-duck Leader of the Opposition before stumbling badly over Rhodesia, making the fateful decision to support Wilson's stance on oil sanctions against the Smith regime. MPs on the Tory right, many of whom still had not forgiven Macmillan for his retreat from Africa, engaged in open revolt in the House of Commons. On 21 December 1965, only a third of the Parliamentary Conservative Party reluctantly supported Wilson's oil sanctions order in the division lobbies, while a damaging 95 Conservatives voted against. Including abstentions (numbering around 80), the bulk of the Tory party was now ranged against Macmillan.[33]

This time round, Macmillan knew his time was up. Rather than go quietly, however, he could not resist conniving to ensure that Rab Butler was once again denied the Tory leadership. It was part of his DNA to interfere in this way. All that his decision not to retire in 1963 had done was to postpone the inevitable attempt to fix his succession.

For Macmillan, the priority became preventing a rout at the hands of Wilson, who, with his paper-thin majority and the Tories in disarray, was liable to call an election at any time. Macmillan quickly weighed up the merits of his potential successors. All along, he had considered Butler 'a dreary figure who would lead the Party to inevitable defeat or to a worse defeat than was necessary'.[34] His time had come and gone. Although Reginald Maudling was still a serious contender, Macmillan thought him too laid back: what was required was a natural campaigner, capable of rousing the party faithful.

Macmillan's first choice was therefore Quintin Hogg, the darling of the Tory associations from his time as Party Chairman in the late 1950s. Although Hogg's campaigning style was considered 'too American' by some of the old guard in the party, it was felt that something had to be done to counter Wilson's slick political style. Although Macmillan feared deep down that Hogg might have wobbled had he ever held the premiership, leading the party in opposition played to his strengths as a combative politician.[35] The old Tory 'magic circle' was therefore pressed into action, soundings were taken, and Hogg duly 'emerged' as leader.

The fact that the Conservative MPs had failed to elect their new leader led to howls of protest from Iain Macleod, who penned an angry letter in the *Spectator* in January 1966, attacking the 'customary processes of consultation'. Newer MPs muttered their disgust that the young technocrat Edward Heath had been overlooked for the leadership. The Tories' penchant for picking toffs had been preserved for a little longer.

Sensing Tory disarray, Wilson called an early election in the spring of 1966, winning a landslide majority of 102. His application to join the EEC, however, was rebuffed by de Gaulle in November 1967. Hogg chose not to stay on as Conservative leader. Although he was not directly to blame for the Tory defeat, he recognised the problems that his appointment to the post caused in the modern age. Before standing down, he hurriedly reformed his party's leadership election system so that Conservative MPs could now vote in a secret ballot.

The Conservative leadership election was held just before Christmas 1967. In the first round of voting, Reginald Maudling narrowly defeated Edward Heath by 126 votes to 120, with Enoch Powell winning a creditable 46 votes on the back of a strong anti-immigration and anti-EEC platform. Heath's support had dwindled now that Britain's European entry was seen as a non-starter. Meanwhile, Maudling's star had risen again, following an unexpected leak in *The Times* from Richard Crossman's unpublished diaries, in which Harold Wilson had apparently commented in June 1963: 'The one thing I am really frightened of is Maudling.'[36]

In the second round, tactical voting held sway, with almost all of Powell's supporters switching to Maudling in order to stymie Heath's chances. The final result was Maudling 170 against Heath on 122. A despondent Ted Heath told awaiting reporters that, 'While I accept the result, and wish my new leader well, I fear that Britain's best hope of joining the Common Market has just been snuffed out'. Heath then announced his retirement from frontbench politics, aiming to pursue a career in sailing instead. The grammar-school generation of Tory MPs had suffered a rebuff from which they would never recover.

Conclusion

The outcome of the 1964 election remains of interest to political scientists and historians alike as it was decided by the slenderest of political margins.[37] In the real world, Harold Wilson only scraped home with an overall majority of three. Labour's total number of votes actually fell for the third election running, and Wilson amassed the lowest popular share of the vote

(44.1 per cent) of any majority government since 1922.[38] Given the closeness of the result, it has therefore proved fascinating to speculate if Macmillan would have won that election had he not been forced to retire through ill health in October 1963. There will be plenty of people who will disagree with the crystal-ball gazing outlined here, most prominently Richard Lamb, biographer of Macmillan, who is adamant that:

> Nearly all political observers agree that if Macmillan had remained leader, which his health in fact permitted, or had Rab Butler been Prime Minister, their mastery of politics and debate and their political skills and experience would have given them a marked superiority over the astute but less consistent Harold Wilson, and brought the Tories to power for better or worse for a fourth term of office.[39]

Such a view overestimates Butler's leadership skills and understates Macmillan's waning power, while denigrating Wilson's undoubted political skills. If anything, Wilson's decision to play the class card against Sir Alec Douglas-Home, the 'Fourteenth Earl', would have worked even better against Macmillan, because at least under the former's leadership the Tories were able to draw a line under their past failings in government. If nothing else, Home had an untainted and honourable sense of duty about him, qualities which mattered more to voters brought up to be deferential than they do today.

Perhaps the most intriguing 'what if' connected with Macmillan staying on a little longer after his likely election defeat is that the antiquated system for selecting the Conservative leadership would have not been reformed in 1965, but two years later. My view is that Macmillan was a serial manoeuverer who, no matter when he stepped down, would have tried to interfere in his own succession. In that sense, Iain Macleod's outcry against the 'customary processes of consultation' in January 1964 would merely have been delayed for a couple more years.

What is much harder to predict is which Conservative leader would have been elected in the wholly different political circumstances of 1967, as opposed to 1965. That Edward Heath might have not have been elected to lead the Conservative Party raises all sorts of fascinating questions over the resolutely grammar-school type of leader that followed in his wake – not least, Margaret Thatcher. Just as profoundly, had Heath not been elected in 1965, would Britain ever have joined the European Economic Community? Surely that would make another interesting political 'what if'.

Notes

1   Adapted from Harold Macmillan's actual resignation letter, dated 18 October 1963. See D. R. Thorpe, *Supermac. The Life of Harold Macmillan* (Chatto & Windus, 2010) p. 621.

2   Harold Macmillan, *At the End of the Day, 1961–1963* (Macmillan, 1973), p. 487.

3   Ibid., p. 487.

4   Ibid., p. 497.

5   In real life, it was the Buckingham Palace switchboard which started receiving calls from senior Tories when it emerged that Macmillan was in hospital; Thorpe, *Supermac*, p. 561.

6   Butler had used the Papal analogy about himself as early as July 1963; Anthony Howard, *RAB. The Life of R.A. Butler* (Jonathan Cape, 1985) p. 304.

7   Thorpe, *Supermac*, p. 541.

8   The Peerages Act, passed in the summer of 1963, allowed existing and new hereditary peers to renounce their peerages. A Tory 'revolt' in the Lords ensured that the Act came into effect immediately, thus allowing Lord Hailsham the possibility of challenging for the Tory leadership before a general election.

9   Geoffrey Lewis, *Lord Hailsham. A Life* (Jonathan Cape, 1997), p. 224.

10 Macmillan, *At the End of the Day*, p. 494.

11 Hugh Dalton's contemptuous tag for Harold Wilson, following his resignation from the government alongside his mentor, Aneurin ('Nye') Bevan, over the introduction of prescription charges in April 1951.

12 Adapted from Macmillan's farewell message to conference delegates, reproduced in Macmillan, *At the End of the Day*, pp. 505–07.

13 HC Debs, 25 November 1963, Vol. 685, col. 42.

14 Macmillan, *At the End of the Day*, p. 472.

15 Adapted from a Macmillan letter to Jacqueline Kennedy, dated 18 February 1964; Thorpe, *Supermac*, p. 586.

16 Ibid., p. 522.

17 Ibid., p. 525.

18 Macmillan instead established the Radcliffe Tribunal, comprised of three civil servants.

19 The two jailed journalists were Reginald Foster of the *Daily Sketch* and Brendan Mulholland of the *Daily Mail*.

20 HC Debs, 17 June 1963, Vol. 679, cols. 55–56.

21 The full extent of Macmillan's detachment from reality is always missed in this truncated quote. The Prime Minister was responding to being laughed at, having tried to explain to an incredulous House that Profumo's letter to Christine Keeler, beginning with 'Darling', was 'a term of no great significance'. HC Debs, 17 June 1963, Vol. 679, col. 65.

22 Quoted in John Ramsden, *An Appetite for Power: A History of the Conservative Party since 1830* (Harper Collins, 1998), p. 192.

23 Howard, *Butler*, pp. 303–04.

24 Macmillan had briefly explored the possibility of holding an election in the spring of 1963; Alistair Horne, *Macmillan, 1957–1986, Volume II of the Official Biography* (Macmillan, 1989), pp. 447, 449.

25 Macmillan, *At the End of the Day*, p. 367.

26 Quoted in Thorpe, *Supermac*, p. 548.

27 In the spring of 1963, Berkeley made a speech calling for the Conservative leadership rules to be reformed. In July 1970, he applied to join the Labour Party, having been defeated as a Tory MP at the 1966 election. Humphry Berkeley, *Crossing the Floor* (George Allen & Unwin Ltd, 1972).

28 Anthony Sampson, *Macmillan. A Study in Ambiguity* (Pelican Books, 1968), p. 233.

29 Horne, *Macmillan, 1957–1986*, p. 454.

30 Sampson, *Macmillan*, p. 234.

31 David Butler and Anthony King, *The British General Election of 1964* (Macmillan, 1965), p. 134.

32 Ibid., p. 118.

33 In real life, the Conservative three-way split on the issue of Rhodesian oil sanctions inflicted considerable political damage on the fledgling leadership of Edward Heath. Mark Stuart, 'A Party in Three Pieces: The Conservative Split over Rhodesian Oil Sanctions, 1965', *Contemporary British History*, Vol. 16, No. 1 (Spring 2002), pp. 51–88.

34 Thorpe, *Supermac*, p. 624.

35 On 4 October 1963, Macmillan's son-in-law, Julian Amery, had asked Macmillan if Hailsham would make a good Prime Minister. Macmillan had supposedly replied, 'Dear boy, that is secondary. The thing is, can he win an election?' Quoted in Lewis, *Hailsham*, p. 217.

36 Quoted in Thorpe, *Supermac*, p. 548.

37 For a revisionist view, see Steven Fielding, 'Rethinking Labour's 1964 Campaign', *Contemporary British History*, Vol. 21, No. 3 (September 2007), pp. 309–24.

38 Butler and King, *The British General Election of 1964*, p. 297.

39 Richard Lamb, *The Macmillan Years, 1957–1963: The Emerging Truth* (John Murray, 1995), p. 501.

Chapter 7

What if the UK had never joined the EEC?

Richard Briand

'Never Glad Confident Morning Again?'
A History of Britain Since 1970, by Harris Roberts

One of the most intriguing counterfactuals in British political history is what if Sir Edward Heath had not been too stubborn to listen to his Chief Whip Francis Pym's advice that the crucial vote on 28 October 1971, in which the House of Commons would be asked to agree to the principle of UK entry into the EEC, be made a free one?

In that case, the number of Labour MPs willing to risk the wrath of their party might have outweighed the number of Conservative MPs willing to vote against their own government. Heath was too stubborn, however, and the vote was lost. 'Each man kills the thing he loves', wrote Oscar Wilde, and the Prime Minister's obduracy had ruined his dream of integrating Britain into Europe – just about the one success that would have redeemed a government that seemed to bear out the famous adage of his old foe Enoch Powell that 'all political careers end in failure'. The third failed British attempt to enter the EEC reinforced the impression, already left by de Gaulle's two vetoes, that Europe was to British post-war governments what the quest for Irish home rule was to governments of the late nineteenth and early twentieth centuries. It was the political equivalent of a tar baby, or the upas tree. Going back to it would be, to use Enoch Powell's mordant phrase about writing political memoirs, like a dog going back to its own vomit.

Certainly opposition leader Harold Wilson needed little encouragement to avoid European entanglements. The Bennite left in his own party, which saw the EEC as a capitalist club in which its ambitions of nationalising large swathes of private enterprise would be constrained, led him to issue the formula that a future Labour government would not apply to join the EEC 'for the foreseeable future'. This latest concession would provoke the resignation of his deputy leader, Roy Jenkins, followed by others in sympathy. Jenkins, whose grand manner and polished vowel sounds had been the subject of one of Bevan's more playful quips ('Lazy? How can a boy from Abersychan who sounds like that be called lazy?'), was already regarded with suspicion by the more left-wing 1970 intake of Labour MPs, but his resignation ended any hopes he had of winning the Labour leadership. It also assisted the election of the next Labour government when it gave Enoch Powell, already at odds with Heath on immigration and economic policy, a casus belli behind his call for the election of a Labour government in the February 1974 general election. The above-average swings to Labour in the West Midlands marginals certainly helped to produce the defeat for Heath that had Powell singing the 'Te Deum' after he saw the headline: 'Mr Heath's election gamble fails', on the front page of *The Times* the morning after the general election.

It is, of course, possible that had Heath listened to Francis Pym, and Britain had joined the EEC, the wily Wilson might just have managed to keep Britain in via a referendum. The British, at that time more deferential to the political establishment, in a way hard to imagine in the wake of the people of Hartlepool electing a football mascot as mayor in 2002, may well have done the bidding of centrist politicians such as Jenkins and Jeremy Thorpe, not least against a no campaign represented by such polarising figures as Tony Benn. They may also have taken the view that the country was in no state to leave even a Christmas club, given its high inflation and troubled industrial relations at the time. A successful referendum campaign may have led to even more clashes with the left over such issues as whether Britain's MEPs should be directly elected. It would probably have led to even more instances of ministers notionally bound by collective cabinet responsibility voting against the government's policies in the NEC. It may also have given the Prime Minister, James Callaghan, another means of ridding himself of the turbulent priest of the Labour right, Roy Jenkins, by appointing him as President of the European Commission. As it was, Callaghan rid himself of Jenkins the same way in which Winston Churchill rid himself of Lord Halifax, by appointing him ambassador to Washington. The idea, recently mooted in the Biteback collection of counterfactuals, *Prime Minister Cameron ... and other things that never happened*, that the upright Callaghan might have risked accusations of nepotism by making his son-in-law, Peter Jay, ambassador to Washington seems rather fanciful.

As for the Conservatives, the spectre of the Bennite left, and fears of what Lord Hailsham called 'an elected dictatorship', led to, alongside renewed musings of the desirability of a bill of rights and proportional representation, a feeling that EEC membership might be desirable after all, not least for the very reasons that led the Bennites to oppose it, such as constraining nationalisation. With the Conservative victory of 1979, such talk faded. The new Conservative Prime Minister was as nowhere near instinctively pro-European as her predecessor, and saw the prospect of applying for membership (and the risk of a veto) as a tiresome distraction from slaying other dragons, such as excessive trade union power. Besides, she reasoned, her policy of abolishing exchange controls would be just as effective (if not more so) in keeping Britain safe from socialism as EEC membership. The very prospect of a future Labour government had also been lessened by the internal civil war that followed Labour's defeat, and the creation of the SDP.

Roy Jenkins gave his Dimbleby Lecture after returning from Washington. In a parallel universe where Britain had joined the EEC, it might be suggested that arguments over whether a Labour government should stay in were important – even instrumental – in the formation of the new party. As it was, David Owen and Shirley Williams found plenty of other reasons for alienation from Labour. These included the passing of mandatory reselection of MPs, the raucous 1981 Wembley special conference, at which Owen was shouted down for defending the deployment of cruise missiles in Britain, infiltration of the Labour Party by the Trotskyite Militant Tendency, the National Executive Committee's refusal to publish the Underhill Report about said infiltration, and the creation of an electoral college for the party leader in which the trade unions would have the largest percentage of votes. And if the defectors were disappointed by Denis Healey's concession of an electoral college, they were more disappointed still by his failure to run a more robust campaign in the 1980 leadership contest.

The United States, operating on Henry Kissinger's aim of having a single number for Europe to ring in a crisis, had urged successive British governments to join the EEC, but President Reagan was keen to avoid undue pressure on a Prime Minister who had showed less hesitation than other NATO allies in supporting the installation of cruise missiles. The public apathy, or even hostility, to the EEC had also been reinforced by the wave of patriotism that followed the successful effort to retake the Falkland Islands from Argentina. What was seen as the equivocal attitude of EEC members such as France and Eire did not exactly aid public enthusiasm for any further efforts by Britain to join the EEC. Having felt the full force of Mrs Thatcher's handbag at NATO summits, Francois Mitterrand and Helmut Schmidt felt little enthusiasm for renewed British efforts to join. Indeed, such reservations were later reinforced by the Prime Minister's hostility to German reunification following the end of the Cold War. While such reservations were shared by President Mitterrand, Mrs Thatcher's opposition was felt to have been expressed in an unduly shrill fashion, and seemed to show what existing EEC members regarded as Britain's unhealthy obsession with the Second World War.

Not that European leaders had to worry about what they regarded as Mrs Thatcher's undue shrillness for much longer. Thatcher resigned as Prime Minister on the tenth anniversary of her accession to power, having been persuaded by her husband Dennis, and by Willie Whitelaw sitting as an unpaid minister without portfolio. Indeed, historians will see Whitelaw's role in Mrs Thatcher's orderly exit, avoiding either election defeat or a tearful defenestration by her own party, as a service to his party to rank alongside the way in which he persuaded her to abandon an electorally ruinous poll tax in favour of Nigel Lawson's plan for a radical reform of the rates. The foresight of the Whips' Office in delaying the Vale of Glamorgan by-election until after her tenth anniversary also helped, as the Iron Lady would not have wanted to resign after a Labour victory.

Nigel Lawson had once been seen as a likely successor, but his star had faded following the inflation caused by a combination of the 1988 budget and the lowering of interest rates in response to fears of a global economic depression following Black Monday in 1987. As so often in Conservative leadership elections, the candidate with the fewest enemies won, and Mrs Thatcher's successor was Sir Geoffrey Howe, despite relations between the two having grown increasingly strained. The new Prime Minister later admitted that the moves towards a European single market had made him consider a renewed British effort to join the EEC, but the hostility of Thatcherites towards the qualified majority voting (QMV) that had accompanied the single market put him off. The hostility of the Thatcherites, and the Murdoch press, would be increased still further by talk of a 'social Europe' and a social charter.

As someone who had served as Solicitor-General in the Heath government, Sir Geoffrey was also wary of the damage that yet another unsuccessful bid might do to his own premiership. After all the cruel jibes about Mogadon Man, he was determined to turn his lack of flashiness into a strength, and recast his lack of charisma as Baldwinesque imperturbability. Ironically, this proved an asset during a general election which took place against the backdrop of a recession caused by the need to raise interest rates to correct the inflation which resulted from Lawson's mistakes. Lawson had paid for these errors with his job in Sir Geoffrey's first cabinet reshuffle, with a stir being caused by the promotion of his deputy, Treasury Chief Secretary John Major. 'Dull and duller', mocked the *Daily Mirror*. Yet with Labour still behind the government in the economic competence ratings, some in the opposition ranks wished their own party had two reassuringly solid figures, not just Shadow Chancellor John Smith. If the government could not argue that 'Britain's booming. Don't let Labour ruin it', it successfully maintained, nonetheless, that things would be even worse with Labour, and was re-elected with a greatly reduced majority.

If, however, Sir Geoffrey was wary of another failed bid for EEC membership, he was also mindful of how Britain had lost out from not being a member. True, Britain's fishermen were flourishing in a way in which they would not had they, under EEC membership, had to share their waters with foreign vessels, particularly those which registered themselves as British. British consumers could still enjoy cheap butter from New Zealand, whereas one survey found that British membership of the EEC's Common Agricultural Policy (CAP) might cost the average British family of four around twenty pounds a week. Yet these benefits were, according to business leaders, cancelled out by having to trade with an EEC protected by tariff walls. Inward investment was also hampered; Nissan and Honda, for example, had declined to open car factories in the North East. As it happened, a third way was offered with the creation of the European Economic Area (EEA) in 1994, an agreement struck between the European Free Trade Area, EFTA (of which Britain was still a member) and the EEC in which EFTA members would be offered access to the EEC's single market without having to join the EEC. *The Sun*'s succinct take on this was: 'Never mind the bollocks, we've got the free trade!'

It was, however, the last high point for the government, and the last policy initiative that resonated with public opinion. As with other long-serving administrations, such as the Conservative government of 1951–64, it seemed exhausted and careworn, an impression reinforced by a series of scandals. In addition, the new Prime Minister, John Major, incurred the wrath of the Thatcherite right when it turned out that he was not one of their own, but rather a member of the party's centre right. And apart from sheer boredom, the public's mood had changed. It was less enthused by tax cuts, and more concerned with public services. Rail privatisation also proved unpopular, particularly in commuter constituencies. As in 1964, economic recovery did not prevent a government defeat. The economic recovery of the mid and late 1990s made a Labour government, particularly one led by Tony Blair, seem a reasonable gamble. So in 1997, for the first time in eighteen years, Britain had a Labour government, with a majority of forty.

For the new Prime Minister, Tony Blair, the UK's failure to take part in the Messina Conference was one of the great missed opportunities, along-side the rupture of the progressive alliance by the split between Labour and the Liberals in the earlier part of the century. If his plan to repair that break was stymied by the opposition of Gordon Brown and John Prescott, he was determined to heal the rupture between Britain and the Continent. EU membership for the UK fit neatly into his vision of globalisation and global interdependence. EU membership would, he believed, enhance the UK's bargaining power in GATT rounds and negotiations with the new World Trade Organisation. As it said on the Labour membership card after the new Clause Four was passed, 'Together we achieve more than we achieve alone'. A good example was the way in which the second Bush adminis-tration's proposed tariff on steel imports had been shelved after the EU reacted by proposing retaliation against US exports to the EU, particularly those from electorally critical swing states (i.e. orange juice from Florida). Besides which, EEA membership was, Blair thought, an unsatisfactory half-way house, in which the UK had to abide by single market regulations (often 'gold plated' with overzealous assiduity by British civil servants), but had no say in making them. Its lack of representation in the European Commission and European Parliament had led to jokes about a 'fax democ-racy', in which the UK had instructions from the European Commission faxed to it. Facing the same situation, Britain's erstwhile EFTA stablemates, Austria, Sweden and Finland, had joined the EU in 1994.

Yet, under pressure again from Gordon Brown, and careful not to offend the Murdoch press, Blair would leave EU membership until a second term had been secured. While there was frustration at the slow progress made in improving public services, the electorate felt that Labour needed more time to put right the under-investment which had taken place during the Tory years, and deserved another chance. In the meantime, Blair's determination to enter the EU was strengthened still further by its increasing role in humanitarian intervention. If Blair was exasperated by the opposition of German Chancellor Gerhard Schröder to the commitment of ground troops in Kosovo, he was more impressed by the role the EU peacekeeping mission played, alongside the efforts of President Boris Trajovksy, in helping to prevent a civil war in (the Former Yugoslav Republic of) Macedonia. While wary of those on the liberal left who wanted a united Europe to be a counterweight to the US, Blair thought that a more influential European Union, with Britain as a member, could offer a makeweight for liberal intervention should an isolationist US president be elected in the future. He had, after all, had enough difficulty persuading the liberal interventionist Clinton to consider the use of US ground troops in Kosovo.

As irony would have it, however, the last of what Blair considered his humanitarian interventions, the Iraq War, would derail his bid for EU membership. President Chirac had already upbraided him for his 'rudeness' over Britain's desire for CAP reform. Britain's backing for the Iraq War, however, would enable Chirac to repeat de Gaulle's argument in 1963 that Britain was too different from the rest of Europe, too close to the US, for it to be an EU member. As with Macmillan and Wilson, a veto would further confirm a loss of authority inflicted by other defeats.

Of course, had Heath listened to Pym in 1971, and thereby realised his dream of taking Britain into the EEC, Conservative divisions over Europe may have led to an Atlanticist in favour of the Iraq War having become Tory leader instead of Kenneth Clarke. In this case, Tony Blair might have escaped the electoral repercussions of the war's increasing unpopularity after Iraq descended into post-war chaos. Clarke's opposition to the war caused considerable consternation within his party. When, however, he offered a non-aggression pact in which he agreed to renege on his earlier support for a renewed effort to join the EU, only Shadow Defence Secretary Liam Fox resigned. The initial surge in support for the war, and an onslaught by the Murdoch press, made Clarke's position look shaky. Once, however, Iraq sank into chaos, it was Blair's position, not Clarke's, that looked insecure. With the Conservatives ahead in the polls from 2003 onwards, Murdoch's customary support for opposition parties likely to win power would overcome his backing for the Iraq War, and his desire to punish those who opposed it. As it was, future historians will note that the difference between the Suez and Iraq conflicts, both of which bitterly divided public opinion and which were opposed by the main opposition party, was that the Conservative Party escaped electoral defeat through the resignation of Sir Anthony Eden, whereas the Labour Party suffered a set-back when it was led by the conflict's architect.

The Conservatives' return to office after a decade out of power was, however, to be a far from happy affair. The new Prime Minister, while not quite reneging on his own part of the non-aggression pact, nonetheless annoyed the Eurosceptic centre of gravity in his own party by musing publicly on the EU's achievements, and how much better off the UK would have been had it joined, either in 1957 or in the early 1970s. His scepticism over building more prisons also alienated the law-and-order right of the party. Chancellor John Redwood's response to the financial crisis, refusing to renationalise Northern Rock and following Ireland's example of swift and extensive cuts to public expenditure, led to extreme unpopularity for the government. It was, therefore, no surprise when the 2010 general election led to a resounding victory for Gordon Brown's Labour Party. In the mean time, following the troubles that afflicted the Eurozone, British public opinion was as unreconciled to EU membership as ever.

~

In reality, Heath did listen to Chief Whip Francis Pym's advice that the vote be made a free one for the government benches. The vote was not lost, and Britain did enter the EEC (as it was then known) in 1973.

It may be argued that, even had the vote been lost, Heath could have done what John Major did over two critical European votes, and make it a vote of confidence. Yet this would have been a hazardous move. The second reading of the bill on 17 February 1972, for example, was a vote of confidence, but no less than fifteen Conservative MPs voted against their government. The Heath government won by twelve votes (unlike the eight who rebelled against the Major government in 1994, the whip was not withdrawn). It only did so, however, thanks to the votes of the Liberal MPs and 'a small Labour abstention ... made up of almost equal proportions of old men who had decided their political fate no longer mattered and young men with the gallantry of 1916 subalterns',[1] something which saved the Heath government in many other divisions as well. Had, however, that vote been lost, and the subsequent general election won by Labour, taking Britain into the EEC may well have been beyond even Harold Wilson's ability to manoeuvre.

Are there any other plausible scenarios in which Britain might not have entered the EEC? A situation in which Edward Heath was a victim of a third veto, or one in which Heath waited for de Gaulle to leave office, only to be overcome by the oil crisis, the second miners' strike, and the upsurge in violence in Northern Ireland, might be slightly implausible. Many regard de Gaulle's resignation over a lost referendum in 1968 as a convenient pretext to go when in reality his authority had already been undermined. Indeed, some even suggest that de Gaulle held the referendum knowing that he would lose. In any case, he died in November 1970.

Less far-fetched would be the election of a Prime Minister less enthusiastic than Heath about trying again for EEC entry – had, for example, Reginald Maudling won the 1965 Conservative leadership election (as outlined in a previous chapter), or if Hugh Gaitskell had not died in 1963, but had instead lived to fight and win the 1964 election. Certainly anybody less committed than Heath to European integration might have been deterred by opinion polls that suggested de Gaulle's second veto:

> ... had sapped whatever enthusiasm there might once have been for a fresh initiative. Two thirds of the population were said to be opposed to the principle of British entry. Two thirds of Conservative voters were certainly no more enthusiastic than Labour, and a substantial section of the Parliamentary Party believed that British entry could only be achieved at the cost of betraying the Commonwealth.[2]

The other credible scenario in which Britain may not have entered the EEC is presented by Philip Ziegler, the official biographer of both Harold Wilson and Edward Heath. It has been widely noted that Wilson had plans for another attempt at EEC entry. Ziegler, however, is sceptical that

Wilson's second attempt would have proved any more successful than the first, when:

> He did not have Heath's unyielding determination to succeed. Nor was he well viewed by the French. Pompidou's visit to London in 1966 had been a disaster. Wilson had caused grave offence by failing to turn up at a dinner at the French Embassy on the plea that his backbenchers had demanded an emergency debate on Vietnam: the French Prime Minister had interpreted this as being a deliberate slight which showed that Britain did not genuinely regard France as a future ally. Even though he might have hesitated to overrule his European partners with the brutality shown by de Gaulle he could have made the progress of the negotiations incomparably more difficult.[3]

An even more realistic scenario, though, is if Harold Wilson had resigned as Labour leader after the 1970 general election defeat, to be replaced by James Callaghan. Callaghan, 'the keeper of the cloth cap', had shown his ability to detect the Labour Party's centre of gravity when he opposed *In Place of Strife*, and he knew that the party's instincts were tipping against EEC entry. A Labour special conference in July 1971 opposed EEC entry by five to one, over a hundred Labour MPs signed an Early Day Motion opposing entry on terms 'so far envisaged' in January 1971, and Andrew Marr estimates that the PLP opposed EEC entry by two to one.[4] Callaghan had also shown a personal scepticism about EEC entry in his 'language of Chaucer' speech in April 1971 – though this Euroscepticism would later dissipate through his experience of the 'renegotiation' as Foreign Secretary. As his biographer, Kenneth O. Morgan, has noted, Callaghan would become more Euro-enthusiastic with age.[5]

Had, however, Callaghan succeeded Wilson as Labour leader after the 1970 defeat, he may well have committed a future Labour government to withdraw from the EEC, a commitment which Callaghan would almost have certainly have kept had he, and not Wilson, defeated Heath in the February 1974 general election. An earlier Callaghan government merits, of course, a counterfactual chapter in itself ...

Notes

1 Roy Jenkins, *A Life At the Centre* (Pan Books, 1992), p. 338.

2 Philip Ziegler, *Edward Heath* (Harper Press, 2010), p. 272.

3 Ibid., p. 271.

4 Andrew Marr, *A History of Modern Britain* (Pan, 2009), p. 328.

5 Kenneth O. Morgan, *Ages of Reform* (I. B. Tauris, 2011), p. 194.

Chapter 8

What if Rupert Murdoch had not bought *The Times* in 1981?

Simon Buckby and Sam Cannicott

He won the prize primarily because he was the only one who promised not to close the daily paper. Tycoons like Robert Maxwell and Tiny Rowland, separate consortiums led by former editors Harold Evans and William Rees-Mogg, and rival newspaper owners Associated (*Daily Mail*) and Atlantic Richfield (*Observer*) had all sniffed around. But in 1981, after almost a year of industrial action during which neither title had even been produced, the Canadian proprietor Lord Thomson of Fleet chose to sell *The Times* and *The Sunday Times* to the Australian.

'The most exciting challenge of my life', he called it. 'And the rocket boost for my career', he might have added.

~

Keith Rupert Murdoch was born in Melbourne in 1931, the only son of a regional newspaper owner. Bullied at school, his dad arranged a placement for him at the *Birmingham Gazette*; after a third at Oxford and a stint on the *Daily Express*, he assumed control of the family business, aged twenty-two, on his father's death. In 1950s' Australia he easily stood out as a dynamic operator, collecting several suburban and provincial papers through a policy of aggressive acquisition with debt. By the early 1960s he had founded Australia's first national daily newspaper and seized a controlling interest in New Zealand's daily, *The Dominion*.

His first foray further afield came in Britain in 1968, when he bought the already sensationalist Sunday tabloid, the *News of the World*, founded in 1843. The following year he paid only £800,000 for *The Sun*, an ailing mid-market daily that he immediately re-launched as a red-top tabloid, a year later adding topless models on page three. These two were run as stablemates, with relatively few staff and shared printing presses that made them extremely profitable as sales soared. *The Sun* overtook the *Mirror* for the first time in 1978.

Not only was the new owner happy to see his papers become more sexual, but their populism also fitted with Murdoch's idea of himself as an outsider. 'I'm rather sick of snobs who tell us they're bad papers, snobs who only read papers that no one else wants', he said. 'I don't believe people who read *The Times* are better than those who read *The Sun*, they're just different'.

This self-propagated mythology of Murdoch as anti-establishment is very strong. Right from the beginning he used his two tabloids to tout his favourite causes. As early as 1970 *The Sun* called for the abolition of the honours system. And in 1973 the *News of the World* promoted the memoirs of Christine Keeler, who had brought down the War Minister, John Profumo; the backlash of powerful interests against this serialisation hardened Murdoch's hostility to the hypocrisy and decadence of the British upper class, as he moved his home to New York and bought his first newspaper in the United States.

This explains why Murdoch so assiduously cultivated Lord Thomson at the end of the 1970s. Founded in 1785 as the *Daily Universal Register*, the London *Times* was the British elite's newspaper of record; the 'top people's paper' as the tabloids put it. As it suffered from falling circulation, chronic labour relations and disaffected ownership, Murdoch saw his chance. Through News International, the company he controlled, the crude Australian claimed the news-sheet of the British toffs. The barbarian was now inside the gates, owner of the castle. And from this bastion, he could and did maximise his power and influence on the country that had at first rejected him.

~

By the time of his eightieth birthday, in March 2011, *Forbes* magazine listed Murdoch as the very lucky thirteenth most powerful man on Earth. Having just launched the world's first tablet newspaper, the *Daily*, and on the brink of his biggest ever deal – the £8 billion buy-out of the BSkyB satellite broadcasting company – while his offspring jockeyed for their share of the inheritance, Murdoch could reflect on a life that had taken him a long way from the *Adelaide News*.

Yet within a few months, his awesome dominance of the British media, cultural and political landscape was exposed and shattered with a speed, and through a popular uprising, akin to those which had brought down Eastern European dictators in 1989. Industrial-scale illegal phone hacking, along with widespread bribery of Metropolitan Police officers, had been going on for years at the *News of the World*. When the never-believable defence that it was all the work of a 'rogue reporter' was proved to be a corporate cover-up, Murdoch's life-work slid away from him. The *News of the World* itself was ruthlessly shut down after 168 years, journalists and senior executives resigned and faced criminal proceedings, and the BSkyB deal was withdrawn in the face of universal opposition in the House of Commons. Murdoch was forced into humiliating public apologies and stripped of his dignity before a Parliamentary Select Committee, where he cut a sad figure, admitting it was the most humble day of his life. Judicial enquiries were set up in Britain and called for in the United States, destroying Murdoch's reputation, along with his family's grip on the News Corporation empire that he had founded.

Without the platform created by owning *The Times*, however, it is highly unlikely that Murdoch's reach would have extended so far in Britain, or his fall been so dramatic. He would probably have focused even more on the United States, which delivered 75 per cent of his annual income, and perhaps done better in China. So let us assume that in fact Murdoch was outbid in 1981, say by Tiny Rowland, who did actually acquire *The Observer* just two years later. What would have happened over the past thirty years to our newspaper industry, our television industry, our public discourse and our politics without the enormous impact of Rupert Murdoch?

~

Newspaper industry

Back in 1981, journalists still used typewriters, sub-editors revised the text by pen on slips of copy paper, and these were handed to runners who took them to print supervisors who allotted them to a typesetter or tapper. The metal type produced by him (it was always a man) was read and fact-checked on a galley proof by one of an army of trained readers; corrected copy was reset and the metal slugs put into an iron page on the stone, finally ready for printing. This may have been only three decades ago, but it feels as if it could have been three centuries. And we mostly have Rupert Murdoch to thank for that.

Lord Thomson had accused the typesetters of killing *The Times* through over-staffing, restrictive practices and resisting the introduction of computerised technology. He had taken on the print unions by halting production altogether, but they had called his bluff by striking for almost a year while happily earning their income from other sources. Murdoch learned much from this lesson.

At the time, following deep public spending cuts and the bitter miners' strike, it felt brutal. But, in retrospect, it was probably the only way to break the stranglehold that the print unions were using to choke the newspaper industry to death. The new production plant was under secret construction in Wapping as early as 1982; brand-new off-the-shelf computer technology was installed; experts from the US taught sub-editors how to typeset on screen; and a new distribution system was set up through 800 brand new trucks and vans, not unionised trains. On 25 January 1986, News International published four million newspapers without the unions.

After Wapping, Murdoch continued to be a creative innovator in the technology of the newspaper industry, his first and truest love. In 1990, he was the first to invest in colour printers, changing the look of papers forever. A generation later, he was the first to charge customers for their news from the internet, by imposing a paywall around *The Times* website rather than trying to cover costs solely from advertising, and the first to launch a replica newspaper designed specifically for a modern outlet, the online tablet.

~

If Murdoch had not bought *The Times* in 1981, it would have all been so different. He would almost certainly have treated Britain like Australia, a country of his early development left behind in the search for greater riches elsewhere. And he would probably have switched earlier and heavier to online opportunities. Instead of failing with Myspace, he would have had the time and clout to create a genuine rival to Facebook.

The Times itself would have gone under. Tiny Rowland, like all the other bidders, had refused to guarantee he would keep it open, and when he inevitably failed to solve the industrial relations problems that had brought it to its knees, it would have closed within five years.

Without *The Times*, Murdoch would have been a bog-standard owner of down-at-heel tabloids that felt as modern and relevant as a saucy seaside postcard. *The Sun* would have been more of a smutty comic than a powerful instrument to shift public opinion. The *News of the World* would have been little different in content and impact to the *Sunday Mirror*.

Murdoch would have had far less motive to force the move to Wapping, so it would have fallen to others to provide the financial investment and political will necessary to impose technological change on an antiquated industry that was essential for its very survival. We know that none of his immediate contemporaries did it. The most likely candidate would have been Conrad Black, the self-regarding Canadian who took over the *Telegraph* group in 1985. But, as he later proved, Black was too greedy, too pompous and too bullying, not smart or strategic enough to beat the unions.

Without the great leap forward in technology, all newspapers would have declined much faster than they did. They would have fallen back on even more ridiculous gimmicks to bolster sales: more bingo and TV tie-ins in the tabloids, more DVDs of old films in the Sunday press, and more dinosaur wall-charts in *The Guardian*. There would have been even more features and lifestyle sections, even more comment infiltrating news, and even more dependence on celebrities and sensationalism to attract readers.

With no *Times* to act as the powerful pivot between left- and right-wing media, British newspapers would have become even more aggressively divided along political lines, as they are in other European countries.

There would be a much more assertive liberal press. *The Independent* would not have fallen victim to price wars, would not therefore have gone tabloid or launched the spin-off *i*, and would instead have remained a journal of conscience. It would have had more success in reforming the Downing Street lobby system through its boycott of Bernard Ingham's off-the-record briefings in the late 1980s. Meanwhile, although *The Guardian* would have been denied a purpose in defining itself as anti-Murdoch, it would have taken a more influential stand against the ever-tightening restrictions on civil liberties. Perhaps, over many years it would have published each Friday on its front-page skyline (no doubt alongside adverts for that day's celebrity-designed wrapping paper) a running count of the number of CCTV cameras in Britain.

The *Mirror* would have battled a still brash *Sun*, but one which lacked the powerful political overtones and aura of self-importance it was able to cultivate when Murdoch also owned *The Times*. So the *Mirror* would have had the space to maintain its historic tradition of campaigning and investigative journalism in the school of Paul Foot. It might have been the *Mirror* that broke the scandal of MPs fiddling their expenses, or bankers gambling away our economy. And we would never have heard of Piers Morgan, once Murdoch's golden boy, who developed his intrusive editorial style at the *News of the World* before dragging the *Mirror* and later CNN down-market.

Meanwhile, the *Telegraph* would have been even more Tory and even more anti-European under Black, as he would not have to fret about any bleed of readers to the middle-ground *Times*. Conversely, without the competition of a *Times* that later went tabloid and devoted many of its front-page splashes to social policy stories, the *Daily Mail* might not have been quite so rabidly right-wing in its editorials. In fact, it would have expressed outrage at the public scandal of taxpayers funding prisons to teach minor offenders how to become career criminals.

In any case, they would certainly all have had lower circulations and weaker holds on our policy debates and public opinion. They would also not be in the vanguard of the rush to new formats on the internet. That role would probably have been played by the television news-gathering organisations, allowing more room for ersatz players like the *Huffington Post* in the United States to flourish in Britain. There would undoubtedly be no pay-walls, and no tablet newspapers, leaving the old business models to gently decline. Perhaps, if Murdoch had not bought *The Times*, children in schools today might even be taught in their history lessons what newspapers were and the influential role they played until the end of the twentieth century.

~

Television industry

You could choose between BBC1, BBC2 and your regional ITV outlet. That was it in 1981, a very long way from the literally hundreds of channels that these days are beamed into our set-top boxes, some in HD and even 3D, with red buttons, live pauses and record facilities all built in. And Rupert Murdoch can take much of the credit for that revolution.

Straight after buying *The Times*, Murdoch told the BBC that he thought the public would be better served if there were as many television channels as there were newspapers.

When cash-strapped Sky Television went to auction in 1983, Murdoch snapped it up for just £1 plus outstanding debts of around only £10 million. At first, he made the same mistakes as others, wasting money on cable and wrongly assuming that the driver for consumer take-up would be movies, which is why he bought Twentieth Century Fox.

It was only once he moved from cable to a satellite system out of Luxembourg, beyond the jurisdiction of British laws on media ownership but facilitating access to British viewers via reception dishes, that he finally saw the way ahead: using the profits from his newspapers to cross-subsidise

the purchase of the rights to broadcast football, the real magnet for consumer demand, along with the give-away of satellite dishes.

None of Murdoch's competitors had his ability to weather the essential
heavy losses in the early phase of investment to enable them to lead the
drive to satellite broadcasting. And once Sky was in the lead, Murdoch
used his power to beat back his rivals. He merged Sky with the rival British
Satellite Broadcasting on his terms in 1990. He easily saw off ITV Digital
through the aggressive marketing of his premium sporting rights. And
he blocked BT, Virgin and every other attempt to set up a pay-TV cable
service to rival his monopoly of the satellite platform.

The BBC has long been intimidated by Murdoch's commercial clout,
his freedom from quality standards, the power of his cross-media outlets
to impact on public and decision-maker opinion, and his ability to cross-
subsidise. It has lagged in the race to digital, but since the resignation of
the Chairman and the Director-General following the Hutton Inquiry in
2004, the BBC has been paralysed with fear.

Seizing a further advantage, James Murdoch, Chairman of BSkyB, used
a notorious MacTaggart Lecture at the Edinburgh Television Festival in
2009 to demand greater constraints on the public service broadcaster. At
the height of hubris, the Murdochs pressed on with a bid to buy out the
rest of BSkyB and entrench their own power in the television industry.
With blinkered eyes and grovelling for a political quid pro quo, David
Cameron's government later gave the green light, only to be forced into a
re-think amid the scandal spreading from the *News of the World*.

~

If Murdoch had not succeeded in getting *The Times* in 1981, he would have
been much less interested in Britain in general, and he would not have had
the base, the confidence or the funding to pump-prime Sky in particular.
There is no reason to believe that he would have become such a significant
player in our television industry.

Had Murdoch bothered buying Sky at all, he would probably have cut
his losses once he failed to beat British Satellite Broadcasting to the first

three satellite channels when they were offered for auction by the government in 1986. Having already bought Twentieth Century Fox, he would have turned faster to the United States and the establishment there of Fox TV. And that would have meant Britain's technological drive would have been far slower.

Even if BSB had ever finally spotted that football was the content that could trigger the demand for satellite, it was in no position to cross-subsidise the purchase of the necessary broadcasting rights. Football would have stayed on the terrestrial channels; ITV would have won the rights in the 1992 auction. The demand for satellite dishes would have remained sluggish. Without the boost of freely or cheaply distributed squarials, home take-up would have stagnated among the early adopters who alone can never push technological consumerism to a tipping point.

There might have been a longer life for cable services. There might also have been better free-to-air viewing and ITV Digital may have lasted longer. But the date for our national digital switch-over would surely have slipped back from 2012 to at least 2020, and it would probably be around then before we saw anything like Sky Plus, High Definition, 3D or movies-on-demand.

Of course, sports coverage, especially the much-hyped Sky Sports Super Sunday football coverage, would not have been revolutionised. Plodding highlights would have continued to be wrested between ITV and BBC for years. Sky News, an award-winning service with few but extremely influential viewers, would not exist. Rejecting rolling news as too sensationalist, the BBC too would not have a 24/7 service, choosing instead to invest in high-quality, in-depth news and current affairs analysis while boosting its local coverage in the regions. We would not have the absurd rush to speculate about 'breaking news' as it happens, so although we might get our reports slightly later we could be more confident that they were accurate. Perhaps the ITV News Channel is the best that we could get.

BSB lacked Murdoch's reach into the United States, from where he pillaged content for Sky in Britain. Instead, BSB sustained a more traditional model of television, where power was held not by the broadcaster but by the producers of programmes. This would mean that we would be in thrall far less to content imported from the United States. *The West Wing, The Sopranos* and *The Wire* would still have made it across the pond. But Sky Atlantic, pumping over-promoted but sub-standard comedy and drama into our living rooms, adding to the impression that American culture is in some way superior, would not have been born. And HBO seasons would have been rivalled in quality and cultural impact by BBC and Channel 4 series. The British television production industry would be one of the most creative and resourceful in the world, as it was in the 1960s and 1970s.

This in turn would have had a beneficial impact on arts as well as current affairs, with a premium on stimulating analysis and investigative journalism, rather than the race to be first with breaking sensationalised stories. Melvyn Bragg would still have a home on terrestrial channels. *Question Time* would not feel the need to have gormless celebrities on its panel each week, and *Panorama* would still be a flagship programme with properly resourced journalists. We would not be drowning in a dirty tide of game shows, cooking programmes, so-called reality output, house-buying porn and cringe-making celebrity-based challenges.

Quality, not ratings, would be the watchword with our public service broadcasters. Viewed through this prism, and without the colossus of Murdoch's empire standing on its shoulders, the BBC giant would not have been brought so low. Instead of getting caught out rigging the phone-in vote to name *Blue Peter* pets (so *Match of the Day* might still be offering prizes for its famous Goal of the Month competition) and exaggerating its accusations against Tony Blair's claims for going to war in Iraq (we would never have heard of Andrew Gilligan), the BBC would still be guided by Reithian values.

~

Public discourse

'I call my cancer Rupert,' the playwright Dennis Potter controversially said just days before his death in 1994, 'because that man Murdoch is the one who, if I had the time … I would shoot the bugger … there is no one person more responsible for the pollution of what was already a fairly polluted press.'

Since the *News of the World* illegal phone hacking scandal broke, this encapsulates what is probably a consensus shared by the nation: that Murdoch's media have been in the forefront of trashing journalistic ethics, invading personal privacy, mixing news with entertainment to create the bastard child of infotainment, and generally degrading the quality of public discourse in Britain.

For years, Murdoch's papers have been accused of bursts of homophobia, sexism and racism to sell papers. He has been more than willing to allow his media to initiate populist campaigns, often aimed at the very lowest common denominator, which have distorted complex public policy issues, sometimes leading to perverse public attitudes and poor policy-making. This has been true on broad fronts like pushing an aggressive authoritarianism on crime and migration (with a reckless disregard for the facts), and on narrow issues such as how to resettle convicted paedophiles once they have served their sentence (the *News of the World* campaign for a so-called 'Sarah's Law' led to attacks on innocent paediatricians on the south coast).

Murdoch's media has long been charged with fomenting the celebrity culture that now debases our public life, as well as increasing our collective prurience – creating a nation of Peeping Toms – and undermining the rights to privacy of the rich and famous. And this is all in the bogus name of confected public interest. In large part a response to this obsession with real or invented scandal, there has been a huge rise in libel actions. At one extreme, Elton John received a record £1 million in damages from *The Sun* in 1987 after it alleged he had had sex with under-age rent boys. At the other, even the Queen successfully sued *The Sun* – for breach of copyright when it published the text of her annual Christmas message two days before broadcast. The invasions of privacy that Murdoch's red-tops pioneered – starting with reporters rifling through rubbish bins – has in turn led to the widespread use of super-injunctions, through which wealthy and powerful people aim to protect themselves, even from legitimate journalistic enquiry.

Few have been the victim of Murdoch media intrusion more consistently than the Royals. As early as 1952, soon after Elizabeth II's coronation, Murdoch wrote: 'I personally entirely deprecate this thoroughly new theory that the Monarchy is above criticism'. In 1992 alone, there was Squidgygate (when *The Sun* set up a special phone line which enabled callers to eavesdrop on a 30 minute tape-recording of a private conversation involving Princess Diana) and the Fergie toe-sucking scandal (when *The Sun* splashed with zoom-lens paparazzi photos of a topless Duchess of York). Many assume that Charles Spencer had the Murdoch red-tops in mind when he effectively blamed the intrusive media for the death of his sister.

This pattern of behaviour – the total disregard for morality or laws – metastasised into the systemic hacking of mobile phones, pinging (using mobile signals to track people's whereabouts), blagging (journalists pretending to be someone they're not in order to access private information) and bribing of Metropolitan Police officers. With up to 4,000 cases, the victims were not restricted to celebrities, but included murdered teenager Milly Dowler and relatives of those killed by terrorist atrocities or on active service in Afghanistan and Iraq; frankly, it could have been anyone. The outrage was revolutionary and this disgrace will undoubtedly dominate Murdoch's obituaries.

Yet it is not that Murdoch was uniquely to blame for all of this. It is that his papers were usually the worst offenders, and in setting the standards lower and lower he had the clout to drag the others down too. The whole system has been corrupted, and he must bear much of the blame, along with the failure of public agencies, which were too cowed by his commercial power and hold on public opinion to do anything about any of it.

~

If Murdoch had not taken control of *The Times* in 1981, he would have had far less influence on public discourse. Standards would undoubtedly not have slipped so far so fast, at least in mainstream coverage, as they have not in other European countries. It is noteworthy that national radio, a medium in which Murdoch has no interest, has not suffered the same slump. Trivia and sensationalism, law-breaking and lying may well have continued to find a home in the margins, but the most influential media would have felt the commercial freedom to uphold higher ethics.

Crucially, there would have been more balanced coverage of complex policy issues, which in turn would have led to better public policy-making. Of course, there would be a place for populist campaigning. *The Sun* might still have encouraged vigilantes after the Tony Martin case, for instance, while the *Mirror* would have highlighted the lessons of Terry Matthews, a hapless minor offender who, when put in prison, was indoctrinated into organised crime and later murdered a police officer. But there would also be limits. *The Sun* might even still be widely read on Merseyside, as it would not have told lies about the behaviour of Liverpool football supporters after ninety-six of them tragically died at Hillsborough in 1989. Most importantly, the context for public policy debates would have been less dominated by one voice, less hysterically skewed, more keenly contested, and therefore with a healthier chance of better policy outcomes.

There would have been faster moves to change public attitudes about, and outlaw, sexism, racism and homophobia. In 1986, Clare Short would still have failed in her bid to ban Page 3, which might still exist but would surely be seen as a cheap and dirty anachronism. Throughout the 1980s, the government's AIDS awareness campaigns would have been more successful, possibly saving more lives.

If war was politics by other means for Clausewitz, then sport has long been war by other means for much of the populist British media. Without the cloak of respectability conferred by sharing a stable with *The Times*, *The Sun*'s xenophobia would have been ignored like that of a deranged aunt. The hoary old stereotypes and insults would still have screamed out – 'Let's Blitz Fritz' at Euro 96, for instance – but the widespread reaction would have been embarrassment, as the other tabloids failed to respond in kind.

Football itself would not play such a central role in our national culture. The Premier League may have been created anyway, thanks to a breakaway of the leading clubs, but without the vast sums of Murdoch's money that inflated players' wages and egos as well as ticket prices. There would be no 'Skyjacking': more matches would kick off at 3 o'clock on Saturday afternoons, and football would not dominate the TV as well as the back and front pages of the papers. Ironically, this lower profile would have bred a different kind of success. English clubs would not have attracted so many foreign superstars or got to so many Champions' League finals, though there might have been a wider variety of domestic league and cup winners. There would have been more home-grown players, creating a better England team, led by a manager whose vocabulary stretched to more than 100 words, capable of lifting the World Cup in 2010.

In the wake of the illegal phone hacking scandal, it should not be forgotten that the *News of the World* scooped many major and legitimate investigations. Even without *The Times* under Murdoch's control, Mazher Mahmood would have continued to pose as a 'fake sheikh' for the *News of the World* or perhaps the *Sunday Mirror*, rightly winning awards for undercover stings that have brought more than a hundred criminals to justice. John Higgins would have been revealed for his apparent willingness to throw snooker frames for cash, several Pakistan cricketers would have been caught out as bribe-taking match-fixers, and Wayne Rooney would have been exposed for earning huge sums from the notion that he had a model marriage while simultaneously paying prostitutes. Pictures of the idiotic Prince Harry fancy-dressed as a Nazi would still have been published. In fact, good journalism would thrive – in the newspapers that survive, in broadcast and increasingly online.

Without the power that Murdoch derived from owning *The Times*, however, there would have been a more strictly drawn line of public interest. Either the newspapers would have behaved more responsibly, kept in check by a code of conduct properly enforced by an effective system of self-regulation, and the Press Complaints Commission would not have been held down by the very strongest interest that it is meant to be monitoring (how can it be that Neil Wallis, Deputy Editor of the *News of the World* at the time the phone hacking was at its height not only went on to work as PR adviser for the Metropolitan Police force but back then also served on the PCC Code of Practice Committee?); or there would have been proper external regulation.

Most likely, the PCC would have been scrapped and external regulatory authority would have been vested by Parliament in Ofcom, with genuine powers of policing and sanction. The first whiff of criminal phone hacking or police bribery would have prompted a thorough investigation and tough action, preventing the secondary scandal of a corporate cover-up.

Either way, the rapid decline in journalistic standards would have been arrested and public discourse better respected. There would have been, at the least, less widespread phone hacking, nor such institutionalised corruption of the police to get at private information, and we would never have heard of Andy Coulson or Glenn Mulcaire. It would also be much less likely that judges would have felt empowered to issue super-injunctions, building privacy laws for the rich and powerful by back-door case law. The distinction between legitimate enquiry and moral-free invasions of privacy would not have been so blurred, and elected politicians would not have been so afraid to challenge unelected media barons when they appeared to over-step the mark.

~

Politics

Murdoch's recently acquired *Times* published a famous letter in 1981 signed by 364 senior economists, arguing that the government's monetarist policies had no basis in economic theory, would deepen the recession and should be abandoned. Yet *The Times'* new proprietor decided that his anti-establishment and free-market approach chimed with that of Margaret Thatcher, who he championed in 1983 and 1987.

By 1992, after the poll tax had removed Thatcher, and dithering over Europe had already started to weaken John Major, the race was so close that BBC exit polls initially called it for Neil Kinnock. At the start of the election campaign, Labour announced plans to introduce new cross-media ownership rules, forcing Murdoch to break up his empire by either selling his papers or abandoning Sky. No wonder that by polling day *The Sun*'s front page pleaded: 'If Kinnock wins today will the last person to leave Britain please turn out the lights'. After Major in fact won a wafer-thin majority of just 21, the myth of Murdoch's power over politics took deep root. 'It's The Sun Wot Won It' was both the boast of the red-top tabloid and the lament of Labour's red-topped leader.

All calculations were transformed by Black Wednesday, 18 September 1992, as Britain was humiliatingly ejected from the European Exchange Rate Mechanism. That night, Kelvin MacKenzie, the editor of *The Sun*, spoke to the prime minister and arrogantly told him: 'Well John, let me put it this way. I've got a large bucket of shit lying on my desk and tomorrow morning I'm going to pour it all over your head.'

This was the context in which New Labour decided to prioritise courting the media, especially News International. In 1995, Tony Blair famously flew halfway round the world to fawn over Murdoch at a News Corporation conference in Australia. Although this has subsequently been widely ridiculed, it was completely understandable at the time. With almost no media accountability, proprietors like Murdoch as well as successful editors like Paul Dacre at the *Daily Mail* were a significant barrier to politicians, especially from the left, being taken seriously by the public. But in going so far to seek this anointment, Blair – like Gordon Brown and David Cameron after him – deepened the capture of the political system by Murdoch and the media class.

The obeisance worked. *The Sun* switched its support, and Blair won three successive general elections without having to worry about criticism from Murdoch. Cameron learned these lessons, paid the necessary homage, and won the crucial support of Murdoch in 2010. No wonder Murdoch was invited through the back-door of 10 Downing Street to be thanked for his support.

The Australian-born US citizen's hidden hand was revealed at the last general election in other ways too. It was Sky that forced Gordon Brown to accept the leaders' debates. And after Nick Clegg starred in the first of them, David Yelland, a former editor of *The Sun*, explained: 'Make no mistake, if the Liberal Democrats actually won the election – or held the balance of power – it would be the first time in decades that Murdoch was locked out of British politics. While it would be wrong to say the Lib Dems were banned from Murdoch's papers ... I would say from personal experience that they are often banned – except where the news is critical.'

The anti-establishment tycoon appeared to own not just huge swathes of our media, and sections of the Metropolitan Police force, but large parts of our politics too. This is not so far from a mafia.

~

Even without the authority of *The Times* behind him, Murdoch would no doubt still have deployed *The Sun* for Thatcher. But, in 1983, Michael Foot, Tony Benn and the longest suicide note in history would still have done for Labour's chances. And, in 1987, Thatcher was in her pomp and Labour had yet to begin the long road to reform, so the Tories would still have won again. As Alastair Campbell would later have written in Volume 14 of the Reliable Witness Edition of his *Diaries*: 'Of course the feral beasts help shape the context of political battle. That's why we need to deal with them actively. But voters are not stupid. It is usually their views of the real political situation, not a false perception fostered by Rupert Murdoch, which determines elections.'

Yet in 1992, uniquely, the main two parties were so closely matched that a dominant media intervention could have effectively determined the outcome. Without *The Times* to back *The Sun*, and with other media evenly split, no external force was powerful enough to push John Major over the line. Neil Kinnock might still have screwed it up himself, with even more displays of over-confidence than just at the Sheffield rally. But it is likely that he would have gone on at least to prevent Major reaching his majority, and quite probably to form a government of his own.

As Kinnock then floundered with the ERM crisis, however, most media and crucial swing voters would quickly have turned against him. As he would have confessed much later in his memoirs: 'At that time, we just weren't ready for the realities of power'. It is possible that he would have gone on to lose the following election to an unreconstructed Tory party under, say, Michael Portillo, and recent political history would have been utterly different. But it is more likely that, as Gordon Brown (at the time, Chief Secretary to the Treasury, blocked by John Smith as Chancellor) dithered over what to do, Blair (Home Secretary) would have been impatient enough to mount a coup in time to win the following election as New Labour, leading us back to a familiar story.

Though emboldened by the urgency of his dramatic assumption of power, Blair would still have failed to redress the slide to anti-Europeanism in Britain that had begun when pro-Europeans complacently believed the argument to have been done and dusted after the 1975 referendum. It was not just fear of Murdoch that stopped him; it was fear of the voters. Britain would still be outside the euro, and the furore over the signing of the so-called European Constitution would have been no less vicious and politically divisive.

Without a new and relevant appreciation of the country's changed role in the world since the loss of Empire, repeatedly harking back to 1945 and 1966 for its memories of glory, Blair would certainly still have felt obliged to cuddle up to the United States. We would still have been sucked into Iraq and Afghanistan after 9/11.

And at the Treasury, Brown would still have harboured his self-defeating grudge at missing out on the top job. So although there were many major achievements, New Labour's domestic reform agenda would still have been checked. When Blair was finally forced out, Brown as his inevitable successor would still have appeared to be victim, not commander of events, despite his deft touch in international forums in preventing the collapse of the global financial system.

These were the decisive political issues of New Labour's years in office, and although the influence of Murdoch was apparently visible in the repeated acts of deference paid to him by successive prime ministers, in fact events would all have panned out much the same even if his role in Britain had been much smaller. Even with *The Times*, he just was not as directly powerful over our politics as he, and many others, believed.

By 2010, Labour was burned out, having failed to fulfil its massive potential. David Cameron and the Tories would still have won most seats. There may have been no televised leaders' debates, yet the Liberal Democrats might still have held the balance of power. For without the active apathy towards them of the powerful Murdoch media, neutered by the lack of the establishment *Times* in his portfolio, the third party would have gradually been making solid progress for the past twenty years.

~

As the thirteenth most powerful man on the planet, Rupert Murdoch has consistently been one of the two or three most powerful people in Britain in the thirty years since he bought *The Times*. As such, he must take the responsibility – both the credit and the blame – for at least shaping much that has happened here over that time. Without the authority that flowed from his ownership of the Establishment's paper, his awesome media empire and his influence would have been much diminished.

While the course of elections would have unfolded more or less as history teaches us it did, all of these governments would have fared better without the spectre of a super-charged Murdoch hanging over them. Britain would have had a less powerful but better quality media: higher standards of public discourse; far fewer incidents of illegality and corruption; more balanced public attitudes and more considered public policy.

All this would have come at a cost, however. We would have had a less technologically advanced television industry, albeit with a stronger local production sector, and there would have been an even faster decline in our newspaper industry. A price worth paying?

Bibliography

William Shawcross, *Murdoch: The Making of a Media Empire* (Touchstone, 1997)
Michael Wolff, *The Man Who Owns the News* (Vintage, 2010)

Chapter 9

What if Mrs Thatcher had settled with the miners in 1984?

Adrian Moss

'The miner's strike of 2001–02 and the assassination of the Labour Party'

It was an outrageous plan – but it worked. At the end of August 1984, increasingly irate at the futility of the miners' strike and recently convinced that the dash for gas was a strategic calamity in waiting, Mrs Thatcher invited her two closest confidants, Norman Tebbit and Lord Whitelaw, to an informal meeting at Chequers. It was a warm and balmy day and they took tea in the garden under the shade of a mighty cedar. When at last they had finished some introductory chat about holidays and children, Mrs Thatcher, in a few simple sentences, delivered her bombshell. Tebbit and Whitelaw, astonished, sat in their chairs with mouths open and eyes wide and unblinking. While she filled in a few more details the two men sat in stunned silence, as the birds in the garden sang to the dull droning of a combine harvester in a far-away field.

It was the most perfect of perfect plans. Neither the government nor the miners would lose face, allowing both to emerge with what would be considered victories by their own sides. In every detail the audacity of the plan was quite simply astonishing. The strike could be ended almost amicably and the long-term future of the mining communities could be secured. As a distant rumble of thunder presaged a coming storm on that warm August afternoon surely not one of those present could have foreseen that the deal would cause a cataclysm of quite biblical proportions to a government whose formation was still thirteen years away.

Two days later the planned secret meeting took place in a country house (loaned by a loyal party donor), just a few miles from the A1 at Stamford. Special Branch officers surreptitiously ensured that the fields and woodlands were clear of any snoopers, the entire property was swept for bugs by MI5, and cars with blacked out screens were hired to pick up the attendees from quiet rendezvous locations in the surrounding countryside. The entire operation was conducted with the sort of secrecy only ever read about in spy novels.

The meeting began at 0930 and by 1130 there was a unanimous show of hands passing the one motion under discussion. The plan was thus accepted and the miners' strike of 1984 was settled bar the shouting (though, as we know, there was to be a lot of shouting). Delegates from South Wales, Yorkshire, Lancashire, Durham, the Midlands and Derbyshire joined the facilitators for beer and a buffet lunch in the elegant dining room. After a considerable amount of congratulation, back-slapping and laughter, they left to begin the implementation phase. There were no delegates invited from the Scottish or Kent fields.

The details of the plan are of course now widely known. In a nutshell the deal saw a continued government subsidy for the vast majority of mines as part of a twenty-five-year strategic energy plan, in return for a binding non-strike agreement. All of the outstanding 6,782 court cases against law-breaking miners, except for those seriously violent crimes which could not be ignored, were to be dropped. In similar fashion, any outstanding complaints about police brutality were to be made to disappear. The Chairman of the Coal Board, Ian MacGregor, was to be sacrificed in return for the head of Arthur Scargill, and this latter act of treachery was carried out in simple fashion. To the horror of the minority of militants still left on the committee, the NUM Executive called an EGM and simply made the post of President of the NUM redundant. This assassination would echo round the courts for many years and nearly went close to bankrupting the NUM but by 1987 Scargill had been legally disenfranchised and dethroned.

He emigrated to Florida in 1990 and little has been heard of him since, although he has appeared on Libyan TV from time to time, most recently in the rather confusing Libyan version of *Celebrity Big Brother*.

The miners, barring those in Kent and Scotland, went back to work by mid-September and productivity rose swiftly. Those mines made unstable by lack of maintenance work were subject to a tremendous display of British engineering genius, overseen by a specially commissioned task force, and all were made safe and ready to begin production by March of the following year.

The strike continued to its calamitous and inevitable end in the Kent and Scottish coalfields and while Mrs T always maintained that this was because their militancy had prevented them from being included in the deal, more than one analyst has suggested that the ensuing closures and economic devastation was *pour encourager les autres*. The fact that the Tories were so enduringly unpopular in Scotland, and the mining constituencies in Kent were so few, probably cannot be ignored in retrospect.

And so, throughout the Tory 1980s and '90s, while every other publicly held bastion fell to the privateers in a frenzy of asset-selling, coal production bumbled on under the rather undynamic management of the National Coal Board. However, by the end of 1996 two things had become obvious. First, the country had decided that it could, all things considered, get along quite nicely without the Conservatives for the foreseeable future and, second, environmental politics was becoming a force that could no longer be ignored.

The first of these manifested itself in 1997 when a grinning Tony Blair swept in to Downing Street on a perfect May morning. A discredited, scandal-ridden and woefully tired Conservative Party had been given an absolute whipping; constituencies which were Tory to the core had fallen to the shiny, new, breath-of-fresh-air Labour Party. A new dawn had broken for Britain.

We don't tend to have revolutions in Britain but this was about as near as we are ever likely to get. After nearly eighteen years of Tory rule the incoming Labour government had a manifesto which, in essence, was all about being nice to people. We were going to be a nice country doing nice things for each other and doing nice things for other countries around the world. The economy was set to boom (after a token period of restraint), so there was going to be pots and pots of money to splash about doing nice things. There would never be another recession because we had a Chancellor so clever and so cunning that his mighty intellect would prohibit them from ever happening again. We were to have an ethical foreign policy, so there would be no more wars or support for dodgy leaders, and, best of all, the massive majority in the House of Commons meant that the incoming government could totally, root and branch, reform everything that needed reforming. And there were an *awful* lot of things that needed reforming.

The citizens of Britain bathed in their good judgement. They were set for good times; they were going to be prosperous for a thousand years; they would be nice to everyone; they would banish the nasty party to justified exile. It was evident that they couldn't have been more delighted about the prospect. Even the bitterest and most jaded of political commentators looked at the joyous, flag-waving crowds in Downing Street that morning and asked themselves: what on earth could possibly go wrong?

In 1998 the Kyoto Protocol was 'opened for signature', although it was not to be until 2002 that the EU and its member countries signed in full. Climate change, or global warming, as we called it back then, was an issue which had barely flickered in the minds of most of the UK population. In 1999 data released by the US National Oceanic and Atmospheric Administration, the UK Meteorological Office and the World Meteorological Organisation confirmed that the global climate was changing rapidly. The only cause, they concluded, was human economic activity, and if we were to avert a global disaster governments had to act swiftly to counteract the effects. The green movement had of course been banging this drum for many years but for others it had appeared a fair way down the list of political priorities. With this report governments and major global institutions like the UN began to realise that the problem of anthropogenic global warming was the most important issue of the day.

As with every issue that has the word 'disaster' somewhere about its lexicon, the media went into overdrive. We were all going to die. Africa would be uninhabitable in twenty years; the ice caps would melt within thirty; only the Munros, the Cumbrian mountains and Snowdonia would poke out of the North-East Atlantic; there would be food riots by 2010 and mass destruction of species by 2011. How could we be so foolish as to have ever let poorer countries in on the secret of electricity and the internal combustion engine? We had to act now before we *destroyed the Earth*. (Such splendid and delightful arrogance caused more than a few chuckles in various geology departments.)

The general public shrugged their shoulders a bit and the reporting got ever more wild and inaccurate; the most outrageous liberties were taken with the truth. Transatlantic flying was the same as child abuse, screamed George Monbiot in *The Guardian*; the BBC listed earthquakes as the sort of natural disaster which could be caused by people driving to work; mainstream newspapers informed us that the greenhouse effect was destroying life on Earth (the very opposite of which is true), and then gave us the image of a sad polar bear as the ubiquitous illustration for any story with the word 'climate' in it.

While the media went off the scale, scientists worked on finding proof (with a fair-weather eye on the ever-burgeoning research funds being committed to the issue). Charities, seeing which way the wind was blowing, diverted funds, redrew their organisational charts and spent fortunes on staging and attending fancy conferences. As it became increasingly apparent that too many economists and not enough paleoclimatologists were getting involved, politicians at last grasped the issue of climate change, took a deep breath and decided that *something must be done*.

In the UK the challenge was taken up by all the major political parties, who began a not insignificant, yet never-ending, game of 'I'm greener than you'. A cynic may well say that it is always those with no chance of power who have the best (and often simultaneously ludicrous), policies but both the Lib Dems and the Greens had made the issue a central plank of their thinking and in doing so they ensured that both the Labour

Party and the Conservatives had to address it with ever-increasing commitment.

When Tony Blair received his copy of the Richardson Report in the summer of 2000, things began to happen. His normal habit was to get someone else to read such reports and then supply him with detailed executive summaries, but with the sense of vision he was to become famous for, he took it on holiday with him to Bermuda. In between games of tennis and dips in the infinity pool, he read the whole thing from cover to cover. And then read it again. When he returned, tanned and refreshed (relieved to know that the country hadn't gone to rack and ruin in his absence), he sat with Alastair Campbell and Peter Mandelson on the sofa overlooking the Downing Street lawns and drew up a list of immediate actions. The main thrust was that £100 million would be set aside for green policies (on reflection, a paltry sum), and a call would be issued to all businesses and environmental groups to work together. The more obvious long-term action was to live, eat and breathe commitment to green issues, mention them at every opportunity and thus assume the role of Tony Blair – Earth-protector (to fit snugly alongside Our Tone – regular guy, and Prime Minister Blair – Champion of the Free World). The other major, and as it turned out, game-changing, decision was to play a proactive, energetic and enthusiastic role in any international agreement which addressed climate change. Among all the other myriad issues of the day this particular issue had strayed across Tony's radar and he was locked on.

At the time the Secretary of State for Energy and Industry was a fairly over-worked Stephen Byers, but in a reshuffle held just before Parliament reconvened that autumn Blair decided that the coming years would require a minister with real teeth. He invited Patricia Hewitt to take on the role and she accepted.

The first time the new cabinet met Blair informed them that the coming years would be difficult ones, that there were massive changes coming to the world, to the country. And. To. The. Party. While this news was hardly different to that given out at the start of any parliamentary term, what Blair presented next blew their collectively responsible minds.

France, he informed them, had stolen a march on all its European neighbours by reducing their CO_2 emissions over the previous twenty-five years. The French had done so by reducing their need for coal and investing heavily in nuclear power, so that 80 per cent of their electricity generation was carbon-free. If they could do it, then so should the UK. Blair's vision was that there should be huge investment in nuclear and renewable energy production, and a significant expansion of gas-fired power production to take up the slack while the other two came on stream. Among those present in the room there was an audible intake of breath. Roughly half the gasps were from those who saw the splendid audacity of the move; the other half were gasps of incredulity at the implications.

John Prescott was the last to get it but the first to burst. How in hell's name were they going to close the coalmines? How could a Labour Prime Minister present such a plan to a Labour cabinet? What legacy would it be for a Labour government to betray the very constituency that formed the party, selected its members, elected them time after time and looked to them as their protectors?

Blair thanked Prescott for his opinions and then went round the table asking for other comments from the cabinet. All those present gave their opinions and they broadly fell into three separate camps: those who supported pit closures as part of a massive reduction of the UK's CO_2 output (predominately those who were urban, middle class and New Labour); those who were fiercely protective of their working-class industrial constituencies (traditionalists like Prescott); and finally those ditherers who were caught like rabbits in the headlights (the Chancellor of the Exchequer). Interestingly, apart from the Prime Minister himself, not one of the newly appointed cabinet came from a significant coal-mining constituency.

Blair took each opinion and noted which of his cabinet were going to be supportive and those who were going to be a problem. He swore them to secrecy and, as a way of buying time, announced the commissioning of an energy review which would report back to the cabinet in the autumn of 2001.

At the turn of the millennium UK electricity production was handled by the privatised energy companies; coal made up roughly 40 per cent of their fuel needs. The Coal Board was required to ensure that coal prices were kept as low as possible to maintain its competitiveness with abundant – and cheap – gas supplies. This required a huge subsidy from government, an unsustainable situation which was a serious bête-noire for the right – not that many people were listening to *them* at the time.

While the Labour Party prepared itself for the oncoming election in 2001, on the basis that no political party could match its spending commitments, Blair and his inner circle knew that unless the coal subsidy was withdrawn then neither could a new Labour government.

When the country eventually went to the polls in May 2001 and Blair won an overwhelming majority on a distinctly unimpressive and apathetic 59 per cent turn-out, the energy review was reaching its final stages of analysis. The steam train that Blair had put in motion the year before was roaring back down the tracks towards the buffers, at full power and completely out of control.

The new cabinet announced soon after the election was, with the odd new face here and there, almost a carbon copy of that which had preceded it. 'Business as usual', was the phrase with which Alastair Campbell chose to describe it to the press lobby but, in reality, it was not business as usual – far from it.

The remainder of that year put paid to any concept of a government quietly managing the country. The events of 9/11 and the wars that followed were horrific enough, but the incipient calamity of the energy review would exceed even them in terms of the impact it had on the political landscape of the UK.

The report put before cabinet in October made many recommendations but, as expected, the major one was that in order to meet international emission requirements and to end the £8 billion per year subsidy, the use of coal in power stations was to be halted without further delay. The government spin doctors could now go and put the boot in. The age of glorious coal-fired enterprise was over; the era of 'dirty coal' had begun.

As expected there was uproar. Prescott resigned on the spot and immediately went to the press despite frantic appeals from No. 10. His statement made the next day's front pages but, on the following Sunday, detailed revelations about his mistresses, his alleged drinking habits and his bulimia took the headlines. In those days, as many could testify, defying the No. 10 Press Office was a very foolish thing to do.

While sections of the review were leaked to the press the government rearranged the parliamentary timetable to squeeze in the Energy Bill, and the battle lines were drawn. When Blair presented the findings and the planned way forward to the members of the PLP the Serjeant at Arms had to ask the police to intervene. In scenes more reminiscent of the South Korean parliament or Saturday night in a major British town centre, fisticuffs and brawls broke out and four members were suspended from the Palace of Westminster estate for a month.

In the coal-mining communities which had 'fought off' Thatcher, the planned closures were seen as a betrayal bordering on treason. Those deeply felt suspicions about New Labour which had been hitherto suppressed by two mighty electoral successes now reappeared. The treachery of these jumped-up middle-class lawyers, teachers and lecturers was compounded by the perception that none of them had ever done a true working man's day of work in their lives. The blind, unquestioning support given by the working classes to the Labour Party over the years had been abused, smashed and kicked into the dirt. The resultant rage in the mining constituencies was ferocious.

The non-strike agreement put in place in 1985 was symbolically burned outside the NUM headquarters and every pit in the country prepared itself for industrial action. When the Energy Bill was published and the planned closures became a formal government aspiration, every miner and mineworker in the country stopped work.

As with Thatcher, Hewitt had prepared for such an eventuality by ensuring a stockpile of fuel which could last well into the spring of 2002. By that time work would have started on twelve new gas-fired stations, the planning of four new nuclear stations would be well under way and decommissioning of eight of the UK's biggest coal-fired power stations would have begun.

The notion of taking eight power stations offline without immediate replacement was scoffed at by analysts, the Conservative Party and the media; the maths of it simply didn't add up and the country, so predicted the BBC, would be facing power cuts by Easter. None of them cottoned on to the fact that the 2GW inter-connector under the Channel was going to be importing the difference between current and future output and that a handsome deal had been struck by the government with the French suppliers. Any temporary shortfall, however long, would be made up by French-generated electricity.

The Energy Bill set out the future and detailed the closure of all but a handful of profitable mines. In a bid to sweeten the pill the government went for broke: in return for incomprehensibly high levels of personal compensation, investment in communities and infrastructural improvement to their immediate areas, the government asked for voluntary redundancies in the coalfields. The next step would be enforced redundancy and closures. The Bill was passed in late November by a majority of just nine. Given that the Labour Party had a nominal majority of 167, the result was alarming. The 79 Labour MPs who voted against the Bill represented the largest Parliamentary rebellion ever recorded and the government only squeaked in with the votes of a handful of right-wing Tories with long memories, who ignored their own party's directive to oppose. That the government had to rely on such support was, to put it mildly, a bit of an embarrassment.

The protests in the mining areas reached fever pitch by Christmas. Despite the ban on secondary picketing thousands of miners tuned up at Keadby Power Station near Scunthorpe, broke through police lines and forced entry into the control room. For twenty-three hours the station produced no electricity whatsoever, and the 2GW inter-connecter briefly buzzed into life to make up the shortfall until other UK plants picked up their production and increased output. Now equipped with mobile phones and having learned lessons from the past, the miners did not hire coaches but travelled in separate cars; they did not widely broadcast their intentions beforehand. Similar but not quite so successful invasions occurred at the gas-fired stations at Immingham, Killingholme, Salt End and Great Yarmouth.

During the spring of 2002 there was a new twist to events. Wherever the miners gathered to protest about the pit closures so the rag-tag rainbow coalition of various green groups and anarchists would turn up too, leading to understandable friction. Those environmental protestors that did try to occupy mines and power stations to demonstrate against 'dirty coal' were shocked to find the levels of violence that their actions triggered. Up and down the country Tarquin with his public-school idealism and greasy hair extensions fought Fred with his fight-or-die pragmatism and steel-capped boots, and on such occasions Fred generally gave Tarquin a terrific beating and then nicked his camcorder.

It was a long, hot summer, the memorable scenes of which are now branded in the public memory – the Battle of Drax, the burned-out rainbow convoy on the M18 near Doncaster and the horrific Tredegar ambush.

With the Labour heartlands of South Wales, the North East and urban Yorkshire in complete turmoil the 79 MPs who had voted against the government controversially gathered in Newton Ayliffe in the Prime Minister's constituency to decide their next moves. Their mass resignation of the Labour whip on the Town Hall steps later that day rocked the political establishment to its foundations.

Blair's majority, now just nine, had been irrevocably slashed. That the 79 rebels wouldn't resign and re-fight their seats was seen by those still sheltering under the New Labour flag as completely scandalous. When Dennis Skinner, inevitably one of those 79, decided to call their bluff he stood as an 'Old Labour' candidate in the ensuing Bolsover by-election and was returned with a massively increased majority of 34,000. All the other candidates, including the official ('New') Labour Party candidate, lost their deposits. Thereafter no new calls were made for the remaining 78 to re-contest their seats and the remaining New Labour 'loyalists' made their penne al pesto, drank their organic Chinon and drew the curtains against the world in their lovely North London town houses.

By January 2003, Old Labour had become legally incorporated and established as a party in its own right; it fought the 2005 election as such. Despite the Tory party still being a totally unrealistic alternative, the splitting of the Labour vote saw Blair fail to reach a majority by some 22 seats. Having become exhausted with the fight and now wanting to spend some quality time with his money, Blair handed the reins over to Gordon Brown with an inner glee and the satisfied smile of someone who had long dreamed of an opportunity to extend such largesse.

As Dr Edward Miliband, Senior Lecturer in Politics at Sunderland University, notes in his book *Dirty Coal and the Assassination of the Labour Party*:

> As the financial disaster of the deal became clear, and the incompetence of Hewitt's forward planning unravelled, so the lights began to go out. The result was that the wheels simply fell off the Labour Party. It became a static wreck, semi-abandoned on the side of a road to nowhere.

Ultimately hounded from office, the election of 2006 saw final witness to the death of the New Labour dream. It also put an end to two-party politics in a manner surely no one could have foreseen.

The acceptance that the original plan which saw an end to the 1984 miners' strike was Mrs Thatcher's strategic masterpiece has rarely been challenged, but the long-term outcome was a seismic shift in the political balance of the UK which changed the landscape for ever. The splitting of the opposition to the Conservatives into three almost equal parts has ensured Tory electoral success for many decades to come, and although it is to the detriment of broad-based political accountability this one-party dominance will continue until at least two of the opposition parties come to some formal coalition agreement. At the moment and for the foreseeable future this seems perfectly unlikely. Members of the Old Labour Party and the Labour Party still do not even talk to each other outside Parliament, and there is still deep distrust of the Lib Dems by both.

Mrs Thatcher's original desire was to end a futile and damaging strike and secure a self-sufficient national energy source, yet in doing so she smashed the Labour Party beyond recognition. There are those who somewhat outlandishly subscribe to the view that this was her intention all along. Her scientific knowledge was strong; by the mid-1980s she knew full well about global warming and understood that the issue would be a major global driver in the coming years. She must have known that, inevitably, one day the Conservative Party would be replaced in government by the Labour Party, and that the whole concept of 'dirty coal' would be a time-bomb that would eventually explode in the heart of their key constituencies.

Could it be that the deal that ended the miners' strike in 1984 was but the first action of a long-term assassination plan, drawn up with chilling efficiency and executed with devastating consequences? Among scholars and analysts this debate is likely to continue for years, but the episode proves without doubt that the very best type of problem in politics is that which ultimately becomes someone else's.

Chapter 10

What if Margaret Thatcher had won the 1990 Conservative leadership contest?

Graham Kirby

When the Prime Minister invited Margaret Thatcher to No. 10 in the summer of 2010, it was a significant political event. The sun shone in a clear and light sky as the limousine left her home in Chester Square and moved towards Britain's narrow seat of power, through the traffic of Belgravia, past Buckingham Palace and up the Mall, then down Whitehall to the Cenotaph before swinging past the great iron gates the erection of which she herself had authorised. The policemen there, sombre-faced, stood to informal attention as she passed them by – not peering tearfully out of the car window this time – and the fortress barriers crashed shut. Slowly, so slowly, getting out of her silver car, 'the Lady', resplendent in a light blue (any political significance there?) dress and coat, once more milked the attention of the assembled journalists and photographers. Visibly frail, at times she felt it necessary to hold on to one of the railings in front of the gleaming black door. The tall frame of her successor towered over her, yet somehow her presence and the very fact of her visit told a different story beyond mere physicality. Every subsequent occupant of the most famous address in the country had paid a form of homage – some secretly – to the most dominant political figure of the late twentieth century and the longest-serving modern prime minister.

First-time voters at the recent general election were not old enough – some had not even born – to witness her last, dramatic, defiant sweeping exit from Downing Street, past the straggling band of protesters chanting

'Maggie! Maggie! Maggie! Out! Out! Out!' for the last time (except when they later recounted stories of political derring-do – exaggerated, of course – to their bemused grandchildren). She may have been out but she would not let herself be forgotten. Few characters in history have had that magnetic ability to attract mythology, and that capacity for self-dramatisation – Elizabeth I and Winston Churchill are two others – but Thatcher was certainly one of them. Of course, she attracted in near-equal measure the contempt and undying hatred of those who blamed her policies and her for the divisions of wealth, the destruction of old communities in the march of harsh free-market economics and the breaking of the post-war consensus. Yet few would deny that she had forged, like Vulcan in the white heat of political fire, the country in her image.

'Is it good to be back in Downing Street, Lady Thatcher?' cried impertinent reporters, but their calls were received only with an enthusiastic wave and silent smile before the young premier with a gentle hand guided his predecessor inside the Georgian house. The scene, pictures of which would make every newspaper and evening broadcast, was over in less than a matter of minutes, and the great door closed behind her, the victor of the Falkland Islands, the Iron Lady, Denis Healy's Great She-Elephant, That Bloody Woman and winner of – how many general elections was it, again?

~

The roots of the politics of the 1990s stretch back to the crucial events of the winter of 1990 and Michael Heseltine's leadership challenge. Of course he did not win – there was never any serious prospect of that – but the result was closer than many expected. Events which at the time seemed inevitable could all have played differently. Some even say that Thatcher came perilously close to being toppled and replaced by a greyer figure, probably Douglas Hurd. It does not seem likely but the fractious nature of politics over the following ten years or so were a result of the Prime Minister's dark victory of December 1990.

The mood among the Tory troops was restless, the polls were not good, most of the MPs were dealing with complaints about the Community

Charge on the doorsteps and at their surgeries, the Eastbourne by-election had produced a massive swing to the Liberal Democrats – derided as a dead party only weeks before by 'the Lady' in her conference speech. Finally, there was the prospect of war in the Middle East following Saddam Hussein's invasion of Kuwait in August. The year before, Sir Antony Meyer had challenged for the leadership; his insurgency had been crushed but the number of ballots against the Prime Minister and of abstentions were not inconsiderable; suddenly, unhappy backwoodsmen, the dispossessed and the never-possessed, seriously began contemplating a life after Thatcher. Westminster in such moods is infectious and claustrophobic, feeding upon itself like some ravenous beast that wants of reason. And then came Sir Geoffrey Howe's resignation on 1 November.

Suddenly what had been before just whispers became open contention until his famous 'conflicts of loyalty' speech nearly two weeks later; quiet, gentle and understated, as ever, the dead sheep eviscerated Mrs Thatcher's leadership style. 'It is rather like sending your opening batsmen to the crease, only for them to find, as the first balls are being bowled, that their bats have been broken before the game by the team captain.' The former Chancellor and Foreign Secretary cruelly turned the Prime Minister's words against her (something that had been happening too often of late) before he produced his *coup de theatre* to a stunned and silent House of Commons, calling on his colleagues to 'consider their own response to the tragic conflict of loyalties with which I have myself wrestled for perhaps too long'. Thatcher's face was near-inscrutable as her expression barely moved, but perhaps beneath the make-up and behind those blue eyes one could just detect a hint of the hurt Howe had inflicted.

Conflict became full-on and bloody war in the Tory party. A challenge was 'inevitable'. On his doorstep the day after Howe's speech Heseltine declared his candidacy, claiming that *he* now had a better chance of leading the party to victory at the next general election. Wisely Mrs Thatcher ignored entreaties to bring forward the closing date for the contest to 15 November (with the first round taking place on Tuesday 20 November); instead, the ballot was to be held on 10 December. The next week, as

Thatcher went to Paris for the OSCE conference, the febrile atmosphere reached a frenzied state. As Tarzan toured the tea-rooms, charming and flattering MPs for their votes, the contrast with the remote and distant leader, who seemed more interested in far-off countries of which most MPs knew nothing, was stark.

It was Norman Tebbit who turned the tide upon her return, forcing a reluctant Thatcher to pitch herself in and grub around for votes 'before that bastard Heseltine screws us all' (as he later told the BBC). But perhaps more important was the censure debate. With memories of the Westland debate obviously in her mind, Thatcher was later to write: 'He [the leader of the opposition, Neil Kinnock] never let me down: he gave a speech as if I had just lost rather than was still fighting the leadership election'. As her campaign manager, Tristan Garel-Jones, predicted, the clamour died down; the long nature of the campaign meant that Heseltine, who had roared out of the stables at the start, peaked too early. When the Chairman of the 1922 Committee, Cranley Onslow, announced the results, they were:

Thatcher	212
Heseltine	146
Abstentions	5
Void/Spoilt	16

In *The Downing Street Years*, the Prime Minister described the reaction as one of relief rather than jubilation. The phone started ringing with supporters offering their congratulations; Trade Secretary Peter Lilley was first on the airwaves congratulating the Prime Minister on a 'substantial and decisive victory', while John Major, recovered from a recent operation on an infected wisdom tooth, read a supportive statement in front of the gates of his constituency house, The Finings.

No second ballot was needed, but the Prime Minister's position was still uncertain; a large minority within the Parliamentary Party had voted against her and, although she had won the support of 56 per cent of the electorate, her margin of victory, just satisfying the 15 per cent rule, was slim. The narrative of a convincing win held for most of the next day until it was noticed that Malcolm Rifkind and Kenneth Clarke, Secretaries of State for Scotland and Education respectively, had offered only brief and perfunctory statements of support while a testy meeting of the Blue Chips, the dining club of the 1979 intake of Tory MPs, was reported by Alan Clark; Michael Mates toured the television studio claiming a moral victory for Heseltine and hinting at a seat at the table.

The next evening, Wednesday 11 December, Mrs Thatcher gathered her cabinet as a collective in her rooms behind the Speaker's chair to face down any potential threats. Rifkind stirred uneasily in his chair, they say, as the prime ministerial attention turned on him, and Clarke was forced to declare that it would be 'absurd' for her to stand down now. When he went on to say that he was personally happy to support her for another five or ten years, a rare prime ministerial joke lightened the atmosphere: 'We wouldn't ask you to do that, Kenneth'. Once she had quelled the dissenters, she went on make a number of small policy concessions on the poll tax and Europe. The next day's photo-opportunity in Downing Street with Thatcher and Heseltine – he could hardly refuse – stunned Westminster: the rebels had been outmanoeuvred. The wound had been cauterised, but it was a victory gained through gritted teeth.

Victory in the Gulf War on 28 February 1991 finally moved the previously obstinate opinion poll ratings in the Conservative Party's favour, further enhanced by Mrs Thatcher's opportunistic visit to liberated Kuwait before President Bush. This time, however, there was no rejoicing. Instead, if anything, Thatcher seemed dissatisfied with the military achievements, and pushed for Saddam Hussein's removal from power.

From one victory to forms of another. John Major's 'budget for growth' in March raised VAT by 2.5 per cent to knock £140 off poll tax bills, and raised child benefit. While hawkish Tories privately noted the party's reputation for lower taxes might be compromised, the headlines praised the Chancellor, with *The Observer's* William Keegan judging the budget to have been delivered with 'considerable political flair'. Inconceivable only a few months before, it was now Kinnock who was on the back foot and whose leadership was being questioned. Tony Benn was reported as saying that Kinnock couldn't knock the skin off a rice pudding, and a profile piece on John Smith in *The Sunday Times* raised the prospect of a swift Labour coup. Fed by Central Office, headlines began to speculate on a snap general election, with June (long considered a lucky month for the Conservative Party) most favoured. When the results of the local council elections in May were much better than expected, with the Conservatives nudging 40 per cent, it was no surprise when Thatcher emerged from Downing Street to say that Her Majesty the Queen had granted a dissolution of Parliament for a general election on 6 June.

What *was* surprising, however, was the imagery. Advised by Gordon Reece, Thatcher was flanked by her ascendant Chancellor and the holders of the two other great offices of state as well as her Party Chairman, Ken Baker, and senior cabinet members. That evening Heseltine was seen rallying the troops and calling for a fourth election victory; Tory unity was once again the message of the day.

It couldn't last; the peace of December 1990 was too fragile to hold, and when the Labour campaign got off to a slick start, aided by Benn's and Skinner's votes against the manifesto at the NEC, it coincided with the media beginning to notice that whenever Thatcher appeared she was accompanied by a more popular party colleague. Soon the decision to call the election one year earlier than necessary, with grim economic figures fronting the business pages and rising unemployment, was questioned by off-the-record sources. People noted that Thatcher in 1991 was not the same political animal as she had been in 1983 or 1987. When the polls showed Labour creeping into the lead for the first time in two months, the debate once more focused on the question of whether the Prime Minister had outlasted her political life and outlived her political judgement. For all her sheer force of will, those faceless voices wondered whether a fresher figure could pull off the possibility of one more victory.

As the election debate stayed focused on public services, the country began facing the serious possibility of the first Labour victory for seventeen years, with Neil Kinnock as Prime Minister and everything that would mean. John Smith's shadow budget on 19 May was an attempt to demonstrate Labour's intent, promising to raise the top rate of income tax from 40 per cent to 50 per cent and phase in the removal of the ceiling on national insurance contributions to pay for pension and benefits increases. The immediate response was, on the whole, positive and the next batch of polls showed an average Labour lead of 4 per cent. 'Dogs bark, cats miaow and the Labour Party puts up taxes,' replied the Chancellor at the next morning press conference. The response was part of was a concerted attack, devised by Saatchi & Saatchi, that became known as the 1991 'tax bombshell' campaign. Standing next to a giant poster of an engraved bomb that claimed every family would pay more than £1,000 per year in extra taxes, the Prime Minister said: 'The last thing we need now is more taxes from an unreconstructed Labour Party'.

Except for a two percentage drop in Labour's lead, however, the polls did not move significantly in the Conservatives' favour. Former Downing Street press secretary Bernard Ingham appeared on *Newsnight* to declare that the party's campaign was being hampered by the Conservatives' unwillingness to unleash the Prime Minister to full effect, but each party was successfully using the other's leader to mobilise their core supporters. The only question was which raised a greater fear: Kinnock let loose on Downing Street, or Thatcher redux?

~

General election night 1991 remains one of the most exciting in recent years. For the last week of the campaign the two parties had slogged it out fiercely and ferociously. As Kinnock cosied up to Paddy Ashdown, Thatcher attacked the Labour leader's patriotism and derided him as *Commissioner* Kinnock. While the Prime Minister asked if Britain could afford a Labour government, Kinnock asked the country if they could face another four years of 'That Bloody Woman'. When Thatcher defended the union in Edinburgh, Kinnock held the famous 'Manchester Rally' where he presented his colleagues as a cabinet in waiting. The 11,000 strong American-style convention was lauded by the press as representing 'the new consensus'. While the *Mail*, *Telegraph*, and *Times* all gloomily supported the Conservative cause but predicted a Labour victory, to various degrees *The Guardian*, *Independent* and *Financial Times* promoted the virtues of Labour. The two red tops split as expected, one for each party. Supercilious commentators lamented the harsh attacks on the two leaders while reporting them rapaciously, and most yearned for each party to be led by almost anyone but the actual person who did lead them.

As ten o'clock approached, the BBC started to roll with its usual grandiose music and images of the three main party leaders. No one watching knew what to expect. A grey-haired and visibly flushed David Dimbleby welcomed viewers to what he promised would be the most dramatic and exciting general election night since the war. John Cole, Anthony King and Peter Kellner all looked sombre; the only prediction they offered was that it was close and it was exciting. On the first strike of Big Ben, the polls closed, and Dimbleby, his notes waving about in his hands, declared: 'Our view is that this election is too close to call – we're saying it could be anything from a slim Labour majority to a hung parliament with Labour short by ten seats. The likeliest outcome is Neil Kinnock becoming Prime Minister and having to put together – having to make some arrangement with the other parties, and rely on other parties to vote him in, to get the three hundred and twenty six he needs.' As each commentator spoke, the only thing that was clear was that nothing was clear.

The television displayed an anxious Kinnock sitting with Glenys, while the closed black door of No. 10 represented the Prime Minister, who was said to be 'quietly confident'. Paddy Ashdown was at home in Vane Cottage, in his words, 'with a beating heart', which must have been a relief to all those who voted for the former Royal Marine and Special Boat Serviceman.

Manfully the commentators struggled with the tangible tension, and party hacks ruthlessly continued to take pieces out of each other, unaware that for everyone else the battle was over – old habits die hard. The strong Belfast tones of John Cole were heard tripping over themselves to make it plain that he had no idea what would happen, except that both

Mrs Thatcher and the Liberal Democrat leader had ruled out a deal while the only possibility – *if the exit poll was correct*, he said carefully – of Mrs Thatcher remaining as Downing Street was with a pact with the Ulster Unionists. The increased turn-out in the marginals proved to each side that they had got their vote out, but the worry was that the other side had achieved the same.

Just before eleven o'clock, Dimbleby edged the BBC prediction slightly towards the Conservatives. At seven minutes past, Sunderland South returned Chris Mullin with a 15,000 majority and a 4 per cent swing, while a couple of minutes later in Torbay, the spy-thriller writer Rupert Allason held on to his seat with a reduced majority after a large swing to the Lib Dems. It was not until Basildon was declared as a Labour gain on a 4.5 per cent swing that the predictions began to take shape: perversely, that this was not going to be the triumph for which Labour had hoped. All through the night the results – flying in the face of the opinion polls – shifted in the Conservative Party's direction in a very uneven and unpredictable fashion. A grim-faced Kinnock easily won his Islwyn seat and a stony-faced Thatcher was returned in Finchley. Chris Patten lost Bath to the Liberal Democrats' Don Foster and Malcolm Rifkind lost his seat as the Conservatives slumped in Scotland. By the middle of the night the pundits were confident that Margaret Thatcher's party would remain the largest party, but in a hung parliament.

At nearly three o'clock, the prime ministerial Jaguar rolled into Smith Square to a crowd of cheering but confused supporters and a rabble of reporters. Emerging from the back seat she declared, almost tripping over an errant John Sergeant: 'Naturally we are very pleased that we got the greatest number of votes and disappointed that it is not *quite* enough to win an outright majority. So it is our intention to form another administration.'

The political world was stunned; so stunned that no one knew quite how to respond. The next morning, as the final results came in, Labour spokesmen declared that the Prime Minister had lost the moral right to govern the country, but the door of No.10 remained firmly shut and the Prime Minister unseen. At about eleven o'clock the final results were in, and the BBC declared that, on a turn-out of nearly 80 per cent, the new state of the parties was:

Conservatives	311	(15 short of a majority)
Labour	290	(36 short of a majority)
Liberal Democrats	26	
Ulster Unionists	9	
Others	15	

Margaret Thatcher's Conservative Party had won nearly 13.5 million voters, only 200,000 less than in 1987 and nearly a million more than Labour. With no official news coming from No. 10, the media turned to experts for their opinions. Vernon Bogdanor was chivvied willingly out from his lair in Brasenose College to declare that it was well within Mrs Thatcher's constitutional right to remain as Prime Minister and dare Parliament to vote down her Queen's Speech. Charles Kennedy, the Liberal Democrat spokesman on Europe, told ITN that it would be a 'very chilly day in hell' before his party would support Mrs Thatcher. The Cabinet Secretary, who had prepared papers for Mr Kinnock's cabinet meeting the next Thursday, washed his hands of the affair, stating that it would be constitutionally improper for the civil service to intervene in political matters. After a brief statement before supporters in Cowley Street, Paddy Ashdown was seen being driven away to an undisclosed location.

Saturday brought news that Thatcher was in talks with the Ulster Unionists. Nobody could say with any certainty what their demands were and no one could find anyone to talk to. A perfunctory statement at 3pm from Walworth Road read that the Labour Party was in talks with the Liberal Democrats to seek a 'new programme' upon which to govern the country. Then at just gone 5pm Mrs Thatcher emerged from her Downing Street bunker to declare: 'We are delighted to remain the largest party in Parliament but, of course, disappointed not to win enough seats with which to form a majority government. The Conservative Party cannot form a majority government but neither can the two main opposition parties. The question now for all parties is how best a parliamentary majority can be established that reflects the desire of the country. I believe that the Conservative Party, as the winner of the highest number of votes and the largest number of seats, is best placed to form a government that can take forward the country until fresh elections are called.'

By Sunday all of the minor parties, bar the Ulster Unionists, had declared they would vote against any new Thatcher programme. Alan Beith confirmed that the Liberal Democrats would begin detailed discussions to form a coalition government with Labour, with the support of the nationalist parties. Kenneth Baker declared that the situation was far from certain but that since the Conservatives remained the largest bloc in Parliament it was their intention to put forward legislation for the Queen's Speech on 25 June, when Parliament returned.

With the markets haemorrhaging by mid-week and a press cry for some news from the negotiating parties, Neil Kinnock and Paddy Ashdown appeared together at a joint press conference to declare that they had come to a broad agreement in principle and were willing to form a rainbow coalition with the smaller parties. Due to the knife-edge parliamentary arithmetic, however, they were unable to guarantee a majority for their programme. A growing crowd of Labour supporters flocked to the iron gates of Downing Street calling on Thatcher to go, while Sir Geoffrey Howe twisted the knife he had carefully left in the Prime Minister's front only six months before, calling her on her to resign. The next weekend the Sunday papers were declaring a 'constitutional crisis' – the only wonder was that it had taken them that long. Little noticed was a report by Andrew Pierce in *The Times* on Monday morning that Robin Butler was sending over a group of civil servants to the inter-party negotiations, with one anonymous minister saying that he was 'in office but not in power'.

As she later wrote in her memoirs, the Prime Minister believed that she had won the election and had a right to put her programme before Parliament, even though the Labour Party and Liberal Democrats just outnumbered her party in number of seats. With the small trickle of Conservative MPs saying that the Prime Minister's position was untenable in danger of becoming a torrent, one by one, senior ministers trooped into the Cabinet Room to tell the Prime Minister that the game was up. It was not that they did not personally support her, it was that any proposed programme of legislation would get voted down in Parliament even with the support of the truculent Unionists, and Kinnock and Ashdown would be in Downing Street anyhow. Nobody, it seemed, wanted to see her *humiliated*. It did not occur to them that she would not find this in the least humiliating. 'Treachery, with a smile on its face', she later sneered. 'They're a weak lot. *Weak.*'

The next morning, after cabinet – and two weeks after the general election – Margaret Thatcher emerged for the last time as Prime Minister, clearly upset and her eyes red, to say that she was leaving Downing Street for the last time as Prime Minister after twelve 'wonderful years'. She was pleased that she was leaving the country in much better shape than twelve years before. 'It's been a tremendous privilege', she ended, 'to serve this country as Prime Minister, wonderfully happy years, and I'm immensely grateful to the staff who have supported as well as those supporters who voted for me. But now it is time for a new chapter to open and I wish the new prime minister all the luck in the world – whoever he may be. Thank you very much. Goodbye.' With Denis by her side as ever, she crouched in the black Jaguar, the cameras flashing at her tearful face through the bulletproof glass as the car pulled out and away from Downing Street and past the protesters.

At last, she was gone.

~

The immediate reaction to the new government was one of relief; it was as if the nation collectively exhaled a huge release of tension built up over twelve years of heroic battles and roller-coaster confrontations. Prime Minister Neil Kinnock found himself more popular than he had ever done as leader of the opposition. The public also seemed to like the new team: Ashdown as Foreign Secretary, Hattersley at the Home Office, Kaufman as Environment Secretary. It was much fresher than its predecessor, too, with bright young faces like Tony Blair (Education), Gordon Brown (Trade and Industry), Mo Mowlam (Chief Secretary to the Treasury) and Charles Kennedy (Europe Minister). As the Tories descended into recriminations, the new government boasted of a 'new consensus', and commentators speculated as to a new era of political consonance. The coalition government produced a programme of constitutional reform from devolution in Scotland and Wales, a royal commission under Lord Jenkins to report on voting reform and an elected Lords. Public services, such as Education and the NHS, were to receive unprecedented new levels of funding. John Smith's emergency budget, delivered in his usual reassuring style, was a relief compared to the ardent radicalism of Lawson and Howe. Whereas 'The Lady' had stood at the despatch box and declared 'No! No! No!' to Jacques Delors, Ashdown and Kinnock spoke of being at 'the very heart of Europe'.

The opposition, as they now were, were too concerned over their own future to respond effectively to the new government, but David Cameron, then a bright young thing at Conservative Central Office, dubbed them 'the coalition of the losers', a portent of feelings to come.

The first battle was to come over Europe, after Kinnock emerged from the negotiating table at Maastricht to declare a settlement which included a single currency, a social chapter and enhanced powers for the European Parliament, political union and foreign and security policy. 'Game, set and match to Europe', quipped the Shadow Foreign Secretary. The MP for Finchley, never one to gather a coalition around her, started her campaign for a referendum on the new socialist treaty. However, it was more the reaction of the Labour left that was to prove decisive. Unnoticed by the press, dazzled by the gloss of Labour's spin machine and an embrace of all matters continental, there remained a significant section of the Labour Party which still favoured withdrawal from Europe. They were the same group of tribalists and former trade unionists who were highly critical of Kinnock's failure to win a majority; they were later to be dubbed by him as the never possessed and the demonically-possessed.

Kinnock's decision to postpone parliamentary scrutiny of the new treaty to the 1992–93 session proved crucial. With a busy parliamentary programme, his decision was understandable and at the time he was in a turf war with Smith over the European exchange rate mechanism. Kinnock favoured a devaluation of the pound within the ERM to stave off the currency traders, but he faced political opposition from his Chancellor and the Trade and Industry Secretary. In June 1992 the decisive Danish referendum vote against Maastricht, and the French decision to put the treaty to a popular vote made the position of those countries, trading at the bottom end of the ERM, increasingly impossible to hold. On 16 September, with the pound coming under relentless pressure, Kinnock, Ashdown and Smith gathered in Admiralty House. With Smith threatening resignation, Kinnock was persuaded by Ashdown to support keeping sterling in the ERM, with an increase in the base rate to 15 per cent. However, the Prime Minister's sceptical position was well-known, traders were unconvinced and sterling collapsed. Despite another announcement by Smith that rates would rise immediately to 20 per cent, he was forced to announce that evening, at a dark press conference in front of the Treasury building, that Britain would leave the European Exchange Rate Mechanism.

The government faced the worst press since its election the year before; both Kinnock and Smith faced calls for their resignation, while Ashdown incurred the loathing of the Europhobic press for his own role in the affair. Cabinet members such as Bryan Gould were openly rebellious. After a stormy party conference, which should have been Kinnock's opportunity to herald the achievements of his government's first session, the government's approval rating went into negative. It did not matter that entry had been negotiated by the last government; the lesson the Conservative press took was that you couldn't trust Labour on the economy. Reports circulated that the Prime Minister had been climbing up the wall on 'Black Wednesday' and was close to a nervous breakdown. Labour's Maastricht rebels inflicted defeat on the government by supporting a Conservative amendment on an opt-out on justice and home affairs. When Robin Cook and Bryan Gould later resigned rather that force through the treaty in a confidence motion, Kinnock was caught on camera calling the pair 'wankers'.

Eventually, a government reshuffle in June 1993 saw Smith demoted and Gordon Brown, who had been mysteriously absent from the debacle of Black Wednesday, become the new Chancellor.

When Croatia and Serbia seceded from the Republic of Yugoslavia, few predicted the bloody conflict that was to arise from the 1992 referendum on independence by Bosnia and Herzegovina. Europe and America seemed paralysed, unable to prevent the massacre and ethnic cleansing of the Bosniak population. While Ashdown and a hawkish Home Secretary, Tony Blair, urged intervention, the Prime Minister was all too aware that he did not have a parliamentary majority for action, and nor was President Clinton, who reportedly found the Welshman a verbose 'lightweight', to be persuaded. Britain's inability to influence her major partner, as well as his perceived weakness, became another stick with which to beat the hapless Prime Minister.

In 1994, Thatcher's replacement as Conservative leader, the pro-European Douglas Hurd, became the first Tory leader since Austen Chamberlain not to be elected prime minister after a no-confidence vote by his increasingly sceptical party. Under the Hurd-Macgregor rules, two contestants went forward to a ballot of party members. The more Eurosceptic of the pair, John Major, won out over Michael Heseltine. Major seemed to offer a competence that the present government did not. His temperate and well-mannered style – although perhaps a tad Pooterish – was a welcome contrast to the unpredictable and foul-mouthed Kinnock. 'Majmania', as new Shadow Culture minister Edwina Currie dubbed it, swept the country. The press seemed to have forgotten Major's role in ERM entry and, when, in January 1995, he pledged a referendum on the European single currency, he played a tactical hand that once again opened up divisions within and between the governing parties.

~

It is easy now to dismiss the 1991–95 government as a chaotic failure. History, however, will judge it more fairly, as Anthony Seldon has said in *Kinnock: Prime Minister*, placing it in the middle of the second tier of post-war governments. After all, it enacted a whole raft of constitutional reforms, including freedom of information, the Human Rights Act and a partially elected House of Lords, although the 1994 'AV Plus' referendum was lost on the back of the government's unpopularity. Robin Cook was elected First Minister of Scotland in 1994 and a young Peter Hain became leader of a coalition between Labour, Plaid Cymru and the Liberal Democrats in Cardiff. Overcoming right-wing opposition, the age of consent was lowered to 16 for gay men and Section 28 was reversed, although gay marriage was defeated in 1994. Free entry to museums was introduced and Roy Hattersley's abolition of charitable status for private schools provided funding for an expansion of the schools building programme. Crime fell for the first time in two decades, and the economy sluggishly recovered from growth after the longest recession since the 1930s. Inflation and interest rates remained relatively high by European standards, but unemployment fell to under 1.5 million by the time of the 1995 election.

The strain of the constant negotiations needed between the parties to get legislation passed had its toll on the government. By the time the government fell in March 1995, over the Welsh Parliament (Amendment) Bill, Neil Kinnock had aged dramatically, and fought a lacklustre and incoherent campaign in the subsequent election. Despite a small revival in the coalition's fortunes during the campaign the combined forces of the two parties could not hold back the Tory tide.

It is impossible to say whether his successor, John Major, might have made a decent stab as prime minister in the absence of the continuing infighting within the Tory party. Elected on a manifesto promising a renegotiation of the Maastricht treaty, the realities of a small parliamentary majority forced a rethink. When Major failed to secure withdrawal from the social chapter, the spectre of his predecessor but one loomed large, and Norman Lamont and John Redwood resigned. It is perhaps not fair to talk of Major's 'unpopularity', since he remained far more popular than his party. It was more a sense of quiet disappointment over his failure to deliver anything more than a deficit reduction plan and lower inflation. His public service reforms promoting diversity in the public sector ran into early opposition, and while he proclaimed Britain 'open for business', unemployment crept stubbornly above 1.5 million.

It was with bitter irony that the unimpeachably honest Prime Minister watched the Freedom of Information Act used to disclose his MPs' expenses; published in *The Times*, they discredited politicians from all parties, but mostly his. It was little consolation to a party mired in sleaze that Labour's former Transport Secretary had used taxpayers' money to buy a set of croquet mallets. Such was the popular disillusion that even after the bomb attack on Chequers he gained no popular credit for his Downing Street Accord with Bertie Ahern, the Irish Taoiseach, in 1998.

After Tony Blair defeated the former Chancellor in the 1997 Labour leadership election, his energetic rebranding of his party made victory at the next election seem all but certain. No one, however, not even Shadow Foreign Secretary Peter Mandelson, predicted that Labour would win by the biggest margin since 1966.

It is perhaps too soon to tell the tale of that premiership, as the uncertain nineties became the buccaneering noughties, but as Britain experiences its second coalition government in two decades, there are already mumblings of dissent from the senior party that they have given too much away, made too many concessions. While the polls are mixed, each day seems to hold new headlines of splits or potential splits between the parties; Nick Clegg, the Deputy Prime Minister, has gone from hero to zero in a matter of months thanks to his support for the hike in tuition fees.

Political fortunes rise and fall – they rarely rise again. After ten years of Tony Blair, perhaps the lesson of Margaret Thatcher's premiership, as Lord Brown of Kirkcaldy has said, is that two terms is usually enough in modern politics. Although Thatcher successfully redefined the modern premiership, her inflexibility nearly led to a crashing defeat at the hands of her own MPs and the drama of her last days in office – now impossible after the Elections and Constitutional Reform Act.

It is, perhaps, a cautionary tale which the new Prime Minister, David Miliband, is already pondering.

Chapter 11

What if the coup against Gorbachev in 1991 had succeeded?

Christian Walker

A People's History of the USSR:
The Authorised History of the Soviet Union
Published by CPSU Publishing, Inc.
(International Edition: Authorised for sale only outside the USSR)

Chapter Five: Reform and Counter-Reform

On 11 March 1985, Mikhail Gorbachev was elected General Secretary of the Communist Party of the Soviet Union. With the acclamation of the People's Representatives, many hoped that the unassuming and genial Gorbachev would lead the Soviet Union into a new golden age of prosperity, strength and dignity.

The Gorbachev regime's first major policy initiative of note was *perestroika*, which Gorbachev announced at the XXVIIth Party Congress in 1986, and which would permit greater pluralism in Soviet politics, and greater economic reform towards the free-market. Gorbachev assured the People (and those unconvinced within his own government) that this policy would maintain the Communist system, while delivering more effective governance for the proletariat.

The policy of *glasnost* was equally controversial. Ministers generally accepted the idea that greater freedom of speech would free the proletariat from the perceived restraints of doctrine and ideology, enabling them to bring much-needed innovation to the Soviet economy (something which was now possible thanks to the sixty-year Soviet commitment to progressive education). But many loyal comrades argued against these reforms, claiming they were systemically incompatible with established Marxist principles, that political pluralism and unmonitored media outlets would lead to social chaos, and that the free-market would merely create slaves to the dollar. But as good Citizens who themselves sought nothing from their tenure in government but the metaphysical advancement of the Workers, and the final eradication of all poverty,[1] they trusted Gorbachev's wisdom as General Secretary, and his word as a Communist, and ultimately supported his reforms.

Those more cautious members of the Politburo, however, observed with growing horror how accurate their initial assessments were, with the 'reforms' precipitating the most taxing period in the Soviet Union's august history, benefiting only the anarchists and democrats who seek to destroy socialism itself. The Republics – our bulwark against capitalism and a continual representation of the blood Soviet soldiers paid for banishing Nazism from Europe – became weak. This weakness was caused by General Secretary Gorbachev, who openly flouted the established egalitarian principles and legal obligations concerning the provision of mutual assistance between the Soviet Republics – the concept upon which the entire Union and, indeed, Marxism itself, was founded.

While strong both morally and ethically, and institutionally superior when compared to the uncertain and ineffectual governments of the capitalist West (whose only loyalty lies not to the People but to the American Dollar), the concerted and continual attacks simply became too much for Republics which relied upon Moscow's assistance to fend off outside aggression. American-backed religious leaders, who made a mockery of their own religious texts through selfishly seeking to push back the unavoidable, ever-present march of Socialism, attacked Union policies in the most farcical ways imaginable. European and American political leaders, united by their love of greed (and fear of superior Marxist principles enlightening the populations over which they claimed dominion) also used this moment of internal reflection within the Union to attack. The General Secretary, now aligned with the forces of chaos, prevented those loyal to the dignity of the Soviet Union from acting in defence of their brothers and sisters in the Western Republics. As a result, the Soviet Republics of Poland, Czechoslovakia, Hungary, Albania, Bulgaria, Romania and even East Germany – for which so many in the Red Army had died liberating during the Great Patriotic War – fell to the forces of organised capital. It was clear to what true loyalists remained in the Gorbachev regime that decisive action must be taken. As painful as it was to admit, it was now clear that General Secretary Mikhail Gorbachev, appointed to defend the light of socialism in its most trying hour, was now himself an enemy of our enlightened philosophy.

The coup
The Soviet loyalists constituted a disparate group of patriots. The civilian wing of the group was led by Vice-President Gennady Yanayev. The highest-ranking member of the government after Gorbachev, his grudging acceptance of the need for change enabled a constitutionally and morally legal change of General Secretary. The military wing was led by Defence Minister Sergei Sokolov. Marshal of the Soviet Union and Hero of the Soviet Union, Sokolov was the officer commanding the Union's glorious liberation of Afghanistan in 1979, and in 1988, as Defence Minister, he had physically wept as he oversaw the USSR's humiliating withdrawal from that doctrinal backwater. He was ably assisted by Marshal Sergei Akhromeyev, Chief of the General Staff, who had not only commanded forces in Afghanistan, but also East Germany and the Baltic Republics, garnering both military experience and the respect of the Socialist governments found there. Both developed an intense dislike for Gorbachev when he tried to remove them in the wake of the Matthias Rust affair.[2] Gorbachev's attempt to use the affair to neuter the influence of the armed forces through dismissing their most respected leaders only further alienated him from his own military – and created two powerful enemies in the form of Sokolov and Akhromeyev.

Gorbachev's removal occurred on Sunday 19 August 1991, the day before his 'New Union Treaty'[3] was due to be signed by the President of the Russian SFSR,[4] Boris Yeltsin. With the Union in a precipitous state of collapse, Gorbachev had decided to take a break at his dacha in the Crimea. Vice-President Yanayev led a delegation comprised of the Chairman of the KGB, the newly created Prime Minister of the USSR, and key military officials and representatives of the Ukrainian SSR.[5] Even now, the loyalty of these comrades to the office of the General Secretary (if not to the man himself) clouded their thinking; they begged Gorbachev to declare a state of emergency, and allow the proud Soviet officials to do what was necessary to preserve the Union. Gorbachev obstinately refused. Seeing no other alternative, the General Secretary was, with the greatest of reluctance on the part of the loyalists, placed under house arrest by officers of the KGB. The war to take back the USSR had begun.

Marshals Sokolov and Akhromeyev were still in Moscow. The two Soviet Army soldiers, unfamiliar with the dark arts of politics but well-acquainted with the noble profession of war, made a fearsomely effective team: Sokolov a strategist and a thinker and Akhromeyev an instinctively proactive leader of men. Sokolov remained in his office at the Defence Ministry at Arbatskaya Square, calling various Warsaw Pact leaders and ranking Party officials to secure their support – which was unanimously received. Meanwhile, Akhromeyev retired to the subterranean command complex beneath Army Headquarters. Designed to run the country in the event of nuclear war, the complex gave effective command and control over the entire Union. The Marshal quickly made contact with the officers leading the four operational strategic commands, as well as various key force commanders throughout the Union. He instructed General Nikolai Kalinin, commander of the Moscow Military District, to bring the Tamanskaya Motorised Infantry Division and Kantemirovskaya Tank Division into Moscow, with other officers tasked with despatching forces to other key cities throughout the Union, in anticipation of public disorder – particularly Leningrad; a known den of democrats.

The seat of the Russian Congress, the White House, was surrounded by troops and sealed, for the protection of the delegates within. Some argued that the delegates did not deserve such protection, with the once supreme Russian Congress having degenerated into a rabble of anarcho-reactionaries; but military leaders were not willing to allow angry civilians, now gathering outside the White House, eager to strike at those threatening to destroy their beloved Union, to storm the Parliament. The most problematic delegates were arrested, and detained at a KGB site outside Moscow, to ensure their absolute safety. Unregulated media outlets, prone to using moments of institutional weakness to propagate myths and half-truths and generate further disorder, were seized and taken off the air; a 'Declaration of the Soviet Leadership', outlining the transfer of authority, played on loop on all remaining channels, outlining how Vice-President Yanayev's assumption of power was legal and constitutional.

The untimely death of Russian President Boris Yeltsin on that first day of the New Regime was a major loss to the Party. In Kazakhstan to promote the New Union Treaty foisted upon him by his notional superior, Mikhail Gorbachev, Yeltsin was flying back to Moscow. The loyalists' most secret, most prized asset, he was to go directly to the White House and explain to the People why Gorbachev's ill-considered 'treaty' would only result in the untimely demise of the Union – a demise which should be prevented at all costs, given that the USSR is the only institution capable of resisting the continual attacks of the capitalist imperialists. When his plane encountered mechanical difficulties and crashed somewhere over the wide expanse of the Ural mountains, the inability to locate the aircraft in the intervening years combined with the 'timing' resulted in some blaming the New Regime itself for his death! But this is nonsensical: why would the loyalists, who were striving for the reintroduction of law and order within the Union, cravenly kill a man in contravention of that law which they clearly, based on their actions, held so dear? The fact that this has since become the considered view of many in the United States Congress and British Parliament unfortunately illustrates the vast gulf that still exists between our nations.

But while the death of Yeltsin was a great loss to the new Soviet government, it was an even greater loss to the 'democrats', who held out hope that Yeltsin would, for some unknown reason, serve as shepherd to the herd of cats which their group constituted. Without a popular figure to rally around, their cause – already rife with factionalism[6] – splintered and degraded in the face of a united military and civil authority. On 22 August 1991, Defence Minister Sokolov was joined by KGB Chairman Viktor Chebrikov, now returned from the Crimea. Seeking to end the stalemate in the capital, they ordered Alfa Group (the elite special forces element of the KGB) to begin planning to retake the White House from the Post-Reaganite Neo-Reductionists who were making efforts to fortify it from the inside, and begin the painful process of sweeping away the enemies of social stability.

The New Government of the New Union

The first week of the New Regime was a testing time. All loyal Communists were on their guard against reactionaries both within the Union and without – reactionary elements, always present in Soviet society but tolerated by the good graces of state and citizenry alike, acted in our moment of weakness to seek the return of the dangerously incompetent Gorbachev to the highest political office in the Union. The loss of life on both sides caused by this struggle was unavoidable, and reclaiming the White House on behalf of the People marked the high point of the disorder in Moscow. Martial law became necessary to maintain order, after suspiciously co-ordinated 'spontaneous' protests had broken out.[7] Over the course of the following weeks, the KGB began judiciously detaining key agitators and unrepentant sympathisers, giving a degree of necessary stability to the new leadership, which announced plans to establish a more effective New Union Treaty, enshrining the continued centrality of the Union in Soviet political life (something which some 74 per cent of those remaining in the USSR supported) and introduce greater political freedoms. Quickly followed up with Gorbachev's televised resignation as both General Secretary and a member of the Communist Party, citizens, most of whom had agitated out of fear for the future rather than a desire to break the back of the Union, returned home, and the Union began the slow process of social recovery and political consolidation.

The revised New Union Treaty outlined the relationship between the Union and its composite Republics, as well as the make-up of the new government. It took a year to draft, during which time General Secretary Yanayev maintained the state of emergency in all military districts. The military advised, and the civilian leadership agreed, that military force and KGB alertness was a necessary evil in order to maintain the very coherence of the Soviet Union against the disparate alliance of capitalists, anarchists, liberals and nationalists still seeking to undermine it. The New Union Treaty published in the summer of 1992 surprised many in the West, who presumed that the new leadership was comprised exclusively of hard-line Communists, and that the Treaty would be similarly configured. In fact, the treaty was a victory for the pragmatic loyalists, led by Marshal Akhromeyev and Prime Minister Pavlov, and a defeat for the hardliners, led by the respected General Secretary Yanayev.

The old Union, as institutionally elegant as it was, was dead; the new leadership accepted that the people would no longer accept the Communist Party's total monopoly on political power. Vladimir Zhirinovsky, leader of the Liberal Democratic Party and a critical supporter of the loyalists from the outset, played a central role in bringing around others to this view. The People could now elect whoever they should so choose (provided candidates did not breach electoral law[8]) to serve in the Congress of People's Deputies, in a proportionately representative system. Support for this revolutionary measure was contingent upon the General Secretary – or President, as he would be known in the new, multi-party Union – being elected by the Congress, and not by the People directly. The still powerful Communist bloc in government believed that it would be impossible for the people to accurately judge the Marxist-Leninist philosophies of competing Presidential candidates – which *could*, in theory, result in the people accidently electing a capitalist. Liberals accepted this, provided the President would hold limited powers, in comparison with those held by the General Secretaries of old. Republic Law once again became subservient to Union Law, so as to preserve the fundamental integrity of the Union. As such, the New Treaty represented a perfect marriage of the traditional and the progressive, the old and the new, the stable and the radical.

Consequently, the proclamation of the treaty met with near-enough universal approval from all sections of society, with the exception of the die-hard anarchist democrats who believed that only an entirely democratic system – and the destruction of the Union which such a system would represent – was acceptable. Their cause would eventually be co-opted by the plethora of nationalistic political parties that were formed in the wake of the New Union Treaty's ratification, and the treaty marked another milestone in the return to social stability. The first Union-wide election to the People's Congress, held in December 1993, was organised with a visible military presence on the streets to dissuade terrorist attacks. Because of this, no such terrorist assault occurred, and the election was a success, with a 22 per cent share of the vote for the Liberal Democratic Party, 18 per cent for the Communist Party of the Soviet Union, and 14 per cent for the Agrarian Party, with the rest being shared between some sixty-five independent nationalist and democratic organisations.

The three largest parties voted together in support of Liberal Democratic leader Vladimir Zhirinovsky's appointment as the first President of the Soviet Union. As a friend of the loyalists who had removed Gorbachev, he worked well with the Communist bureaucracy in the Kremlin, and respected the Communist power base in the KGB by retaining Chairman Chebrikov – something he later regretted, as the Chairman was more than experienced enough to ensure Zhirinovsky's efforts to subtly dismantle the KGB became bogged down in bureaucratic wrangling. His term as President was noted for normalising relations with the West, together with beginning to transform the Union's economy from entirely planned toward a mixed state-capitalist system, where firms funded directly by the state competed both with one another and with wholly private (usually foreign) firms in a capitalist system. This allowed individual Russian citizens to create businesses, own land and accrue wealth, while protecting the proletariat from the destructive avarice of unregulated capitalism.

The legal and practical acceptance of political pluralism led to a transformation of the powerful Kremlin bureaucracy, transforming it from the guardians of Communism to the advocates of the state – regardless of where that advocacy led.[9] Western firms, forging clandestine links with Soviet 'companies' (bureaucrats who sat on corporate boards), provided the technology and the capital necessary to begin exploiting the Union's vast untapped natural resources out beyond the Urals – in exchange for a slice of the profits. This somewhat replenished the state finances, which were in a pitiable state, but many Communist Deputies suggested that the policy was rash, and served to merely 'export Soviet wealth overseas'. At the time, however, the strategy was hailed as a master stroke.

The constant need to ensure the Union would not be overrun by NATO tanks meant cutting budgets for social services provision across the board, and a degradation in their quality. Whereas a Communist government would have attempted to mitigate these effects through direct socio-economic action, the Liberal government of Zhirinovsky could only tell citizens to cope with the downturn as best they could, and use the increased wealth to keep the military – a pragmatic base of support, at best – on side. His policy of open access to information revealed that sexually transmitted diseases, poverty and wealth inequality were all steadily on the rise. The severe economic dislocation caused by this transformation, while prophesised by many Communist academics, was unexpected by the majority of the population. This led to a decline in support for the Liberal Democrats in each successive legislative election, with the Communist vote holding steady and growing support for the nationalist parties. In 1999, with the Liberals declining to just 9 per cent of the vote, the Liberal, Communist and Agrarian (KLA) coalition was broken apart when the Communists, now the largest party in the People's Council, and the nationalistic Fatherland Party, supported Zhirinovsky's replacement by the first Communist head of state since the death of Konstantin Chernenko in 1985.

Gennady Zyuganov had honed his political skills in the propaganda department of the Communist Party, where he became a noted and vocal critic of the Gorbachev regime. With his approval as President being contingent upon the appointment of a strong Prime Minister to serve as 'a friend of the Kremlin' and counter his more Marxist-Leninist policies, a raft of reforms to further cement the economic restructuring of Zhirinovsky were implemented; he also attempted to centralise authority within the Office of the President – something his backers in the Communist Party, Fatherland Party, and the few remaining, but still powerful old-guard 'New Regime' members all supported. While the role of the increasingly powerful Prime Minister, and the centrality of the KGB, seemed beyond reach, Zyuganov succeeded in passing new anti-terrorism legislation which relocated local powers previously assigned to the Oblasts back to Moscow. He took advantage of a thawing in relations between East and West to aggressively exploit oil and gas reserves in the Union, primarily through Gazprom.[10] His policy of maintaining Soviet dominance in Eastern Europe and pushing for the Union once again to become a world power was well received by nationalists, despondent at the perceived decline in Soviet power during the Zhirinovsky years, despite high levels of military spending.

The Republics
The Republics' response to the advent of the New Regime was mixed. While the sight of our erstwhile Republics in the far west abandoning the Union was highly distressing, it did have its positive side: at the same time as they abandoned their fellow Comrades who had sacrificed so much to liberate them from Fascism, they also took with them significant portions of the neo-imperialist malcontents who, up until that point, had resided within the Union, doing everything possible to destroy it. With no more East Germans seeking to tear down the Berlin Wall, Poles seeking ever-greater representation or Romanians demanding hand-outs from Moscow, a semblance of stability had returned to the remaining Republics of the Union – in short, the troublemakers had joined a different gang, and both gangs were better off for it. Gorbachev, widely viewed in the Communist Republics as a Russian splinterist who sought the demise of the peripheral Soviet Republics in order to make Russia stronger, was not missed. His

downfall was welcomed by all governments of the Union, with the exception of elements within the Russian Congress. While levels of disorder in the first week of the new administration were high, all could be contained by native military forces, without necessitating Soviet military intervention. Belarus, the Central Asian Republics and Ukraine were largely calm, and the New Union Treaty further strengthened intra-Union solidarity.

Under the new treaty, Republics continued to have their own governments, with a degree of political pluralism in line with that put forward for the Union as a whole – provided a majority supported them. In Belarus and Kazakhstan, a majority did not. Authorities in Moscow accepted this, not wanting to force the issue – and recognising that the old system, while unacceptable in Russia and hence no longer viable for the Union itself, was not necessarily discredited throughout the wider USSR. Suggestions that secret police forces in Belarus or Kazakhstan forced the population into voting a particular way are massively exaggerated; as successive Communist leaders have pointed out, the simple fact is that for many parts of the Union, the old system worked, and produced stability.

This, however, was not the case for the Baltic Republics or the Caucasian Republics. The Baltic states had, since before the Gorbachev regime, served as a nest of anti-Union splittists. They used the confusion that existed in the wake of Gorbachev's removal to take advantage of our momentary weakness and declare outright independence, in what proved to be a horrible miscalculation. With Estonian independence formally declared on 20 August, Latvia on 21 August, and various imperialist foreign states officially recognising Lithuania's previous declaration of independence from 11 March 1990, their assertion of sovereignty was proof, if any were needed, that the Union needed strong leadership if it was to survive such cowardly acts of betrayal as those advocated by the anti-progressives in the Baltic Republics.

Marshal Akhromeyev knew that such ideologically backward rebels could not be negotiated with – indeed, he had witnessed with growing fury the Gorbachev regime fruitlessly humiliate itself before the world as it alternated between peacefully engaging with terrorists and then authorising military engagement but at a level insufficient to break the backs of the enemy. He advised then-President Yanayev to reinforce the Baltic Military District with significant force from the Leningrad Military District, Belarusian and Northern Group of Forces, and begin offensive operations to isolate and destroy the continuing subversive elements within the Baltics. Chairman Chebrikov similarly despatched considerable KGB resources, including Alfa Group, to the region. The resistance movement was well organised, well financed, and difficult to break, with CIA support in direct contravention of international law. The numerical strength of the insurgents was difficult to ascertain, with a high leadership turnover making it difficult to establish links with rebel commanders, but the KGB believes that the principal contact between the resistance and their American backers – and the name most frequently mentioned by captured resistance members – is Latvian terrorist Anastasija Misulovina, aka 'the White Widow'. Her background is unknown, but she is well educated (at the expense of the Union), and believed to be fluent in English, having made frequent trips to the capitalist West in her youth.

The question of how best to deal with Baltic terrorism continues to dominate Soviet political discourse, being the central issue in both legislative and Republic elections. The Liberals are alone in advocating a steady transition to independence for the entire region, with other parties supporting varying degrees of authority. After several terrorist attacks in Moscow, and many more in Leningrad, together with the continued inability of the Baltic SSRs to govern themselves, the population as a whole has hardened in support of 'retribution' enabled through a policy of military occupation, with the Liberal aim of independence being perceived as a dream harboured by a small Moscow metropolitan elite, much like the idea of an elected President.

Marshal Akhromeyev and Defence Minister Sokolov similarly felt that the moves of Georgia towards *de facto* statehood also necessitated a military response, but at this President Yanayev and his faction, natives of western Russia who looked with dismissive disdain upon the rugged people and mountainous terrain of the Caucasus, demurred, believing the cost of subduing Georgia would be too high and the reward too small. They believed that the Baltic Republics represented a geo-strategic threat in a way which the Caucasian region did not. Nevertheless, realising that the military and the bureaucracy would not tolerate full long-term intervention in the Baltics while Georgia, romanticised by many as a cultural 'heartland' of the USSR, moved towards full independence, they authorised a small, and ultimately ineffectual, intervention. The result was similar to that in the Baltics, albeit of a lower intensity, with less global attention and with fewer casualties, owing to the smaller troop numbers involved. During the Zhirinovsky presidency, the mission began to drift, and owing to a reluctance to expand it further,[11] independence for Georgia became the accepted policy in the Kremlin and became a reality in 1998. This independence was predicated on a guarantee that the new nation, like Poland, Czechoslovakia, Hungary and Romania before it, would never join NATO; the USSR would maintain its precious and much-valued 'sphere of influence' – a notional, if not entirely practical, recognition of Soviet authority by the international community.

As Lieutenant-General Stefan Fernandez, former Spanish Special Forces, now assisting the Soviet ground forces' policing action in the Baltics, recently remarked, 'in Estonia, Lithuania and Latvia, the Soviets are forced to fight a dirty war against individuals willing to die for their cause. To "win" in the Caucasus would have required a far more expanded, long-term operation, which could have cost the USSR its very existence if fought alongside the high-intensity operations in the Baltics. I think that even the Soviet General Staff would now accept that it is perhaps for the best that President Zhirinovsky allowed the Georgians to go their own way.'

Foreign relations

The foreign relations of the Union have undergone something of a transformation over the past twenty years.[12] While the original anti-Gorbachevites supported the preservation of the Union and the maintenance of high military readiness, even they recognised that the 'old' Cold War, based around massive military spending on both conventional and nuclear forces, was bankrupting the state. So once the New Regime was secured, considerable effort was made to re-engage with the West, specifically the United States, in an effort to maintain much-needed grain shipments and aid. This began with the New Regime's immediate and vocal recommitment to START I, a treaty heavily associated with Gorbachev and which had been nearly a decade in the making. Equally associated with the treaty was US President George Bush. Many within his Republican administration, led by Secretary of Defense Dick Cheney, publicly voiced fears that the New Regime would abrogate the treaty in order to humiliate the United States – much to the chagrin of Secretary of State Baker, who felt differently, but kept his opinions to himself. When the New Regime declared its intention to respect the treaty, not only did it personally enamour the New Regime to the US President (in a practical if not a moral sense), it also critically undermined the most vociferously anti-Soviet elements within the US Administration. With the grudging gratitude of the United States and the diminishing reputation of those wishing to continue the Cold War, grain supplies to the East continued unabated.

But the recommitment to START I did create problems; it led to an assumption on the part of the United States that the New Regime would continue to destroy the very Union upon which Soviet greatness was founded, allowing the various Republics to quietly go their own way, and come to worship profit in the same way Americans do.[13] The robust policy advocated by the Kremlin toward the Baltic Republics was obvious in its necessity; yet the United States, principal *agents provocateur* in those sovereign Soviet Republics, expected the Union to meekly accept the creation of US client states within striking distance of Leningrad, and allow the will of the people of Latvia, Lithuania and Estonia to become twisted by the Western-induced madness of a minority. Marshal Igor Sergeyev, former Defence Minister, voiced the views of many when he remarked that, 'were it not for CIA operations in the Baltics, the resistance would have been wiped out long ago'. The United States has always denied assisting the insurgents, but its leaders, most notably President Powell, have expressed affinity for their cause, and the US's strategic interest in creating a client state on Soviet territory is obvious. But as President Zyuganov said during his 2001 state visit to the People's Republic of China, 'a higher percentage of the Baltic population voted in 1999 than Americans voted in the Presidential elections in 2000. I will not abandon the people of those SSRs who tacitly accept the Union's fundamental right to govern.'

The breakdown in relations during 1992–96 was primarily caused by the inexperience of President Bill Clinton in foreign affairs, and the minor role foreign policy had played in the presidential election of 1992. When Clinton won the presidency he was compelled, in the words of National Security Adviser Tony Lake, 'to deal with the vision thing'. Unable to develop anything more coherent (or original), Clinton fell back on the traditional hypocritical approach of American policy – exporting 'democracy'. The progress, or lack thereof, of the USSR in improving a US-defined 'human rights' record became the foreign media's focus for every public high-level meeting between the US and USSR. But, with burgeoning economic relations promising to benefit both powers, the cooling off in relations was effectively managed. While both men disagreed on a great many things, they knew that their real enemies resided within their respective legislatures. Clinton did everything possible to prevent the US Congress passing legislation which demanded trade relations be linked to 'human rights', while Zhirinovsky empowered the pragmatic bureaucracy to stop the Communist-dominated Chamber of Deputies from nationalising all foreign firms. British market analyst Jennifer O'Neill, of Morgan Stanley Global Wealth Management Group, summed up the relationship when she remarked that, 'penetration of Soviet markets and acquisition of western oil technology makes up for any hurt feelings in the White House or the Kremlin'.

President Powell, a Republican, was stuck between two competing forces when he assumed the presidency in 2000: while he wanted to 'punish' perceived Soviet transgressions in the Baltic Republics, as an advocate of free trade, and financially supported by oil firms reliant on exploring Soviet oil and gas fields, there was little he could realistically do to oppose Soviet policy. His inability to act was best exemplified when the United States, far from downgrading trade with the USSR, sponsored Soviet entry to the WTO in 2005. Rather than the revolution many predicted during the election campaign, Powell's presidency marked an evolution in relations: by organising regular yearly summits between the two leaders, he institutionalised much of the Soviet-American relationship, such as the independent neutrality of the 'BEE' countries ('Breakaway Eastern Europe' – the states which left the Union in the 1980s, but are still considered within the Soviet sphere of influence[14]) and the steady reduction in nuclear weapon stockpiles – the former being unpopular in the United States, the latter in the Soviet Union. But, as one official close to the Soviet Prime Minister remarked at the time, 'the United States has a massive numerical and technological advantage in nuclear weapons, possessing counter-force capabilities that could potentially neutralise the entire Soviet arsenal in a first strike. In which case, it is in the interests of the USSR to make meagre reductions in low-quality, low-grade weapons, if it means a reduction in the US's high-quality, high-grade weapons. As for Polish independence … neither the US nor the USSR seriously supports those weapons I just mentioned being used in the defence of Poland. We've moved on from that kind of thinking, and the new settlement recognises that.'

While the powers continue to disagree over the issue of Yugoslavia, with the United States claiming that the KGB is clandestinely funding Yugoslav Communists, and the USSR publicly deriding American efforts to break up Yugoslavia into its constituent elements, the relationship is fundamentally robust, thanks to its pragmatic, economic foundations.

The twenty-first century
With the dawning of a new century come new problems. Around the world, the rebirth of Progressive Socialism has resulted in the reestablishment of many old organisations – and old feuds. With the proto-capitalist 'European Project' floundering amid yet another apparent malaise in direction and necessity, the French and Italian Communists have reconstituted themselves and, with the assistance of the CPSU (operating independently of the USSR) have garnered far greater support than at any point during the

Cold War. In Britain, former politics student Simon Cowley formed the Democratic Workers Party, but has seen his support sapped by former classmate Simon Matthews, who has formed the Workers Democratic Party. Said Cowley, 'the differences between us might seem minor to the bourgeoisie, but to the proletariat, they're big, important distinctions that will determine how this country will be run once the revolution comes'.

One of the key factors inducing greater support for Marxist-Leninism among the global proletariat is the issue of globalisation. With the breaking down of barriers to trade between the various power blocs, global trade has sky-rocketed. It is now easier than ever before for global firms to produce components in locations where it is cheap to do so, and sell finished goods for a premium in the developed world. Some, such as the developed United States, have benefited disproportionately from this; others, such as the Soviet Union, benefit less so, and some, such as many nations in Africa or Asia, do not benefit at all.

Rather than fruitlessly trying to oppose the tidal surge of globalisation, the Union has sought to manage it for its own ends, allowing Western companies to operate in the USSR. We have also tried to provide a voice for those whose rights are ignored by the continuing march of American capitalism: our friends in Angola, Cuba, Ethiopia, Vietnam, and Mozambique receive what financial and military assistance we ourselves are able to provide, as well as a voice on the UN Security Council through the Soviet delegation. The People's Republic of China has also decided, after decades of inaction, to join us in helping the poor and dispossessed peoples of the world to help themselves, and protect them from the proponents of universalised capitalism, and for this the entire world is grateful; the Soviet Union needs all the help it can get in repelling militant capitalism.

Another ever-present factor of the twenty-first century is the threat posed by international terrorists, particularly those financed by the United States, who seek to undermine the Soviet position in the Baltic Republics. Such terrorists are naturally clustered in the Baltic region itself, but there have also been isolated strikes both throughout the wider Union and at representations of Soviet power globally, the most recent of these being the attack on the Soviet carrier *Leonid Brezhnev* while in port at Kaliningrad. The infrequency of such attacks is seen as a validation of the Soviet mission in the Baltic Republics, with military operations there disrupting the enemy and 'taking the fight to the insurgency'.

The 'terrorism' endured by the United States at the hands of the *Mujahideen* is fairly inconsequential in comparison, but it has led to unprecedented cooperation between the American and Soviet security services, owing to the large low-level Muslim insurgency plaguing Southern Russia, as well as the USSR's previous experience with the CIA-backed *Mujahideen* in Afghanistan.[15] As British secret service official Hadlee Bennett, once dubbed the 'international man of mystery' back in his field days, remarked, 'this cooperation is still extremely limited, being borne out of the need, rather than the desire, to work together'.

Economic development has both benefited from and advanced the cause of technological development, and this advancement is perhaps best embodied in 'the internet'. What we now call the internet was developed as a method of transferring rudimentary statistical information. The ability to display images over this system developed in the 1990s, with British computer scientist Tim Berners-Lee developing the hyper-text transfer protocol, which standardises the way in which electronic information is transferred, allowing people all over the world to upload content accessible by all other users. However, as KGB Chairman Putin constantly reminds us, this system poses very real security threats, particularly in the context of the terrorist menace. It is for this reason that the Soviet Union maintains a tightly regulated internet system, with monitoring of Soviet users' activity being standard practice. Together with the People's Republic of China, the USSR has reached agreement with Google over how best to prohibit Citizens accessing information harmful to the Soviet state, such as instructions on how to construct a bomb, or propaganda websites purporting to be legitimate news sources.

In conclusion, there were many on 19 August 1991 who, upon witnessing the transference of power to the New Regime, looked with concern towards the future, fearing for their family and way of life. Such concern was misplaced. Domestically, the Union is stable; while it fights a war against an embattled insurgency in one part of the country, the leadership remains committed to societal stability. President Zyuganov has been elected President after each successive round of elections, with the People's Congress now dominated by his supporters, with his loyal Prime Minister, and the Kremlin bureaucracy, ensuring that his will is done. The security services maintain a judiciously watchful eye over the various anarcho-democratic movements still operating within the Union, but they pose no real threat; by their very nature, they remain splintered, divided and ineffective as a form of opposition, criticising each other as much as they do the supreme source of authority in Moscow.

With the wealth of the resources beyond the Urals finally being tapped, the state treasury is once again being replenished, with many political scientists claiming that the twenty-first century will be noted for the rise of the 'BUIC' (pronounced 'Buick') states of Brazil, the USSR, India and China. The USSR is in no position to militarily rearrange the current international order, but many expect it to play a part in the realignment which will be necessary once the power of the aforementioned states supersedes that of the US; the recent announcement by the PRC concerning its refurbishment of the former French aircraft carrier *Foch* represents a significant step forward in this aim. In short, anyone who expected the Soviet Union to simply wither and die in the wake of the Gorbachev regime may be considered, in the light of the past twenty years, somewhat naive.

As Jean-Baptiste Alphonse Karr once said, 'the more things change, the more they stay the same'.

~

Author's postscript
To write this fiction, I referred to *Armageddon Averted* by Stephen Kotkin, and *The Cambridge History of Russia: Volume III*, edited by Ronald Suny.

To write an alternate history positing a successful coup against Gorbachev is at once both surprisingly simple and surprisingly challenging. When one looks at the names and positions of those involved in the real, failed, 1991 coup, you could be forgiven for double-checking your history books to confirm it did actually fail – from the Vice President to the Interior Minister to the Prime Minister, to the Chairmen and Deputy Chairmen of the KGB and armed forces, it is frankly difficult to see how it could collapse, when seemingly every high-ranking official except for Gorbachev was involved in it. But collapse it did, and this owed first and foremost to the ineffectual leadership of those at the head of the coup, with middle-ranking bureaucrats being unsure of what exactly they were supposed to do. A good example of this is how Yeltsin, a known enemy of the coup, was allowed to fly back to Moscow on the day of the coup, travel to his dacha – which was being guarded by anti-Gorbachev KGB guards – and then travel through Moscow, arriving at the Russian Parliament where he promptly stood on a tank, in defiance of authority, and began rounding up a cadre of officials to countermand the instructions of the putschists.

So the first thing to do in order to render the possibility of a successful coup credible was to replace that leadership: the principal civilian players are all still present, but they are overshadowed by a stronger military element. Historically, Gorbachev utilised the German aviator Matthias Rust's landing in Red Square in 1987 to remove Marshals Sokholov and Akhromeyev. Members of the traditionally-minded Soviet military aristocracy, the two were already considered powerful enemies to Gorbachev – who was unique among Soviet General Secretaries for not only not having fought in the Great Patriotic War, but also in never having served in the military in any capacity. Sokholov and Akhromeyev's replacements were selected for their docility to Gorbachev rather than their competence, and consequently the military did not bother Gorbachev again; although it did side with the coup, its assistance was minimal, ill-led, and ineffective.

The key here is not necessarily the 'competence' of Sokholov and Akhromeyev, but their support from within the wider Soviet and individual Republic militaries, combined with their commitment to ousting Gorbachev. This immediately transforms the coup, with the military now at its centre, rather than at the side-lines – so in my version, Yeltsin is quickly killed, in the traditional Soviet manner – a quiet and unfortunate 'accident', the kind involving a couple of MiGs and an air-to-air missile. Historically, while divisions were indeed despatched to Moscow, rather than compelling protesters to return home, commanders on the ground and individual soldiers instead elected to merely keep the peace, and liaise with Yeltsin and his supporters. And Alfa Group, while on alert, received various contradictory orders before ultimately being recalled from duty.

The greatest divergence between reality and my alternate history is naturally found in the fortunes of the states involved with or proximate to the Soviet bloc. Perhaps the first thing to note is that, with the collapse of regimes in Poland, Romania, East Germany et al, many of the 'troublemakers' were no longer part of the Soviet system, protesting against it: by the time the coup occurred, with a couple of (very notable) exceptions, the only Republics left were those which genuinely supported the idea of the USSR, both state and people. But whereas historically the bloc evolved (or devolved, depending on your view) into the Commonwealth of Independent States, in my history the new government does not tolerate continued declarations of independence. The evidence to support this presumed policy is based on what the plotters did while in power. While they were unable to make many decisions during their regime's short existence, one of the first was to institute an immediate naval blockade of the Baltic Republics – giving a strong indication that there would be no tolerance for those states to merely follow the Eastern European countries in going their own way should the coup succeed. As a result, the independence of the Baltic States and Georgia is contested by Soviet force.

The plotters did, however, recognise that the old Union was over: the idea of sending the tanks back into East Germany was never seriously considered, either historically or in my fiction above. Instead, an 'arrangement' is made with the United States – an arrangement akin to that made historically (where the US pledged that no East European state would enter NATO), but in my fiction, this pledge is observed, owing to continued Soviet military power necessitating continued American respect for and recognition of the 'Soviet sphere of influence'. The destruction of the USSR represented the destruction of that sphere, in American eyes; so the continuation of the USSR, quite logically, can be seen to represent the continuation of that sphere of authority. Additionally, there seemed to be a general recognition among the plotters that the Communist Party could no longer hold a monopoly of all political power, and it would be a mistake to believe that the coup was launched to preserve Marxist-Leninism; the motives of the coup leaders were to preserve the Soviet state, and to preserve their own commanding roles within that state.

The character and tone of my alternate Soviet Union is largely based on current Russian political dynamics: a president whose power is defined largely by 'who they know' in the bureaucratic web of Moscow, but with a general trend toward centralising authority; a legislature which generally does what it's told, a people with a healthy pride in their nation, strong respect for authority, and fairly high levels of distain for democrats. A state with very little in the way of social provision – historically, this is because the Russian economy imploded, here, it is because the small trickle of wealth which does exist is shunted into military spending. The prosecution of the war in the Baltics is roughly analogous to that in Chechnya, except on a far larger scale. While the war defines 'elections' at every level, it does so within a tight band of opinion – the nationalistic nature of the USSR results in overwhelming support for the war itself, with differences only really existing on the issue of how it is prosecuted, not whether it should be prosecuted in the first place.

How to deal with the alternate Soviet economy was quite easy – when the USSR really did collapse, there was a view that democracy and wealth-creating free markets were co-dependents of one another, but China has taught us that it is quite possible to not only have the one without the other, but that the United States will do everything possible to assist in that endeavour. And, while the dawn of the 'information age' was seen as a final nail in the coffin of authoritarianism, it has proven anything but: now, secret police forces are more efficient than ever, keeping the details of the populace that previously would have required a warehouse of filing cabinets on a single, searchable computer drive. Firms such as Google are more than happy to assist regimes with money (such as China) in gating off whichever sections of the internet the regime does not want the people to see.

In terms of wider foreign relations, I have argued that outcomes in my alternate history would not be as different as one might expect. This is because, while the ideology and individuals involved would clearly change in my reworked history, the systemic pressures and variables, particularly at the international level, would be fairly constant. George H. W. Bush would still prefer to work with, rather than against, the USSR – he had, after all, been working with General Secretary Gorbachev for quite some time, and with some success. Bill Clinton would still win the 1992 election (there's no reason to believe George Bush would not again tell everyone to 'read his lips', after all), and he would still come into office largely unfamiliar with foreign affairs, on the back of a presidential election predominantly focused on domestic affairs, owing to the poor state of the US economy.

Perhaps the biggest difference between my reality and genuine reality is that in mine, Francis Fukuyama's *The End of History* seems a lot more ridiculous a lot more quickly, and so while Clinton still builds a vision based around the age-old American canard of exporting democracy, in a roundabout 'provided-we-ignore-the-Saudis' sort of way, it is more tempered by reality – the failure of people-power to totally destroy the USSR would cast a long, conceptual shadow over the 1990s. Colin Powell gets a promotion from Secretary of State to President; this is based on my belief that if a Communist returns to lead the USSR in 1999, then the GOP will elect a candidate strong on national security in the primaries, and the American people will agree with them in the 2000 presidential election.

The USSR's place in contemporary society would similarly be defined by the international system as a whole, which is largely as it is now: a United States undisputed in global power, but with others – such as China and India – catching up. So if the USSR adopts an economic policy similar to that of China, and accesses a portion of the vast mineral wealth beneath its frosted soil, there is no reason to believe that it would not also be ranked among the pantheon of states growing faster than the US – and with a crucial role to play in the coming power transition from North America to Asia.

What if …

Notes

1 Poverty which constitutes the principal legacy of the Tsarist monied capitalist elite and aristocratic landed gentry, protected internationally by the Post-Reaganite Neo-Clintonistas.

2 See Appendix Four: 'The Truth of Matthias Rust', which details both the CIA funding used to purchase his aircraft, his stated desire to humiliate the Soviet Union and bring glory to the West German regime, and his unfortunate crash in Pskov Oblast, as well as pathetic attempts by western media outlets to suggest that Rust was some sort of 'apolitical' pacifist.

3 A Treaty to be ratified by all Republics, which would serve to further the reforms of Gorbachev, and effectively destroy the USSR.

4 Soviet Federative Socialist Republic.

5 Soviet Socialist Republic.

6 Some focused on seeking greater acceptance of capitalism, some wanted only more political pluralism; some sought to disband the Union, some advocated retaining the Union.

7 This led Marshal Sokolov to later claim in his book, *The Revolutionary Reformers*, that much of the disorder in that first week was not the product of organic discord on the part of the Citizenry, as is often argued, but rather the result of CIA strike teams seeking to destabilise the Union.

8 See the article by Dr. Gunter Walzenbach, 'Soviet Electoral Law: Stifling Democratic Debate, or Protecting Social Stability?', *Global Governance*, July 1995, for one of the more even-handed debates on the need for Soviet electoral law to safeguard the Union from the forces of splittism.

9 See Pavlov's book, *How the Kremlin Destroyed Soviet Communism* (CPSU Publishing, 2007).

10 The private company in which the Soviet state owns a controlling share – with it now being the largest extractor of oil and natural gas in the world.

11 For more details, see Maldrinov's article in *International Security*, October 1999: 'The Resurgence of the Soviet Pragmatists: The Presumed Social Costs of Baltic and Caucasian Escalation'.

12 Westerner Adam Quinn argues in his article, 'Through the Looking Glass: A Neoclassical Understanding of Soviet Policy', that this can best be explained through analysing the enigmatic bureaucracy of the Kremlin, who as previously mentioned, only perceive ideology in terms of 'furthering the aims and preserving the dignity of the Union', and infuse successive governments with a similarly pragmatic outlook.

13 This was best represented in Francis Fukuyama's much pilloried 1989 article 'The End of History?' which put forward the notion that it was Capitalism (and not, as

Marx accurately claimed, Communism) which represented the zenith of humanity's socioeconomic evolution, and that all nations of the world would in the future adhere to Capitalist tenets. The book that followed did not sell well in the Union.

14 The so called 'Baker-Pavlov Line', named after Secretary of State Baker and Prime Minister Pavlov who, at their first summit, agreed upon a line drawn in red pencil on a map of Europe defining the Soviet and NATO spheres. It is not recorded who drew the line.

15 See Rabinsky's most recent book published by CPSU Publishing, Inc., *The CIA: A Secret History*, detailing how all major terrorist groups currently plaguing the world have been linked to the CIA at one time or another.

Chapter 12

What if Gordon Brown had stood for the Labour leadership in 1994?

Peter Riddell

For Gordon Brown, it was both an historic and a moving occasion. As a historian, he knew the symbolism of addressing the elite of the international financial world in the ballroom of the Mount Washington Hotel in Bretton Woods in New Hampshire – where, in July 1944, Keynes had helped to create the post-war structure of the International Monetary Fund and the World Bank. Brown had asked to stay in Keynes' room, marked with a plaque outside. It was moving, particularly because the acclamation that Brown received for his speech in April 2011 at last provided vindication for the painful decision he had taken so many years earlier – it seemed far more than seventeen years ago – in May 1994.

~

The death of John Smith hit Brown deeply. They were very different people, in their approaches to politics and to Labour. Smith was instinctive, even cynical, and naturally easy with people, while Brown was cerebral, one of life's policy wonks, and, by hard experience, suspicious of others. Yet they had been through at lot together over the previous two decades, both at Westminster and in Scotland. And Scotland was the key. They both viewed politics through a Scottish prism. They both mistrusted the English. Neither were metropolitan figures. They were never more comfortable than on their way back to Edinburgh. These instincts were crucial for the manoeuvrings that May.

The long-standing assumption had been that only one of Tony Blair or him should stand when there was a leadership vacancy – and that, of course, would be Brown. After all, he had been the senior in their eleven-year relationship, with Blair learning from him. As Shadow Home Secretary, Blair had successfully taken up his, Brown's, slogan about being 'tough on crime, tough on the causes of crime'. Admittedly, they were not as close as they once were; ever since the 1992 leadership election, Brown had sensed a distancing by Blair, who seemed to be nurturing his own ambitions – or that is what Peter Mandelson reported to him. The three of them had been the great triumvirate of modernisers from the mid-1980s onwards, though Mandelson had been out of favour with Smith. Brown was uncomfortably aware of Blair's ability to strike a chord with the public.

However, as Mandelson put it in his memoirs, *The Third Man*, about the period 1992–94: 'To the extent that any of us thought about what might come after, Gordon and I certainly still assumed that he would succeed John as leader. At that stage, I think Tony did as well, and other MPs seemed to share this view.'[1] Brown was certainly unaware of a conversation in early 1993 which Blair had had with Mandelson. Blair had mentioned that Derry Irvine, his mentor as a barrister, had said that Brown lacked something: 'Tony said he had been struck by the comment, and that, thinking it over, he was "just not sure that Gordon has got quite what it takes to be leader".'[2]

Brown was disconcerted by the widespread media predictions in the twenty-four hours after Smith's death that Blair was the front runner. Brown dismissed this as the usual London media gossip, out of touch with the real Labour Party of Scotland, of his supporters in northern England and Wales, and of the trade unions, which he knew and Blair didn't. Brown was assured by his close allies like Nick Brown (no relation) and advisers Ed Balls and Charlie Whelan that his support was deeper than the early surveys of Labour MPs suggested. And the instant polls putting Blair well ahead were seen by them as merely a response to the media coverage, which would not sway trade union and Labour Party members who held the key to the election. His advisers were suspicious of Mandelson: what game was he playing, and what was he saying privately to the political correspondents whom he had cultivated over the years? To the Brown camp's surprise, a friendly journalist reported back that Mandelson had been trying to stop the Blair bandwagon and talking up Brown's chances.

Brown was therefore determined to press ahead despite all the media predictions and warnings, even from friends, that the odds against him were lengthening. Even though some of the modernisers were saying that only one of Blair or Brown should stand, others thought that both should enter the contest, that the opinion of the electoral college should be tested. The danger of splitting the moderniser vote did not matter under the alternative vote system being used in the leadership ballot – unlike the first-past-the-post system, where another candidate like John Prescott could come through the middle and win. Under AV, if either Blair or Brown was in the top three, the votes of the third-placed runner would largely transfer to the other, who would win. And if Blair and Brown were the top two, it was a straightforward choice of modernisers. Brown also felt that his authentic Labour approach, very much in the Scottish tradition, should be heard in the contest against what his allies saw as the more ephemeral appeal offered by the Blair camp.

Blair and Brown held rather stilted discussions on what should happen. Brown was unwilling to back down and Blair didn't seek to encourage him. Of course, what Blair knew – and Brown and his close allies could not bring themselves to recognise – was that he was already well ahead in the leadership race. Blair was persuaded – and it showed his ruthless side – that it would be better to run against Brown and beat him. So whatever the short-term damage from the contest, a victory over Brown would establish Blair's authority once and for all. The point was well put by Mandelson in his memoirs, in discussing the evidence that Brown would lose to Blair, 'in all probability heavily. For a while, that would have been difficult for him, and possibly bruising for our relations. But an open contest with a clear result ... removed the temptation for him to agonise about what might have been, and brood over the sense that he had somehow been unfairly pushed aside'.[3] The founding troika, as Mandelson put it, could come together again and work closely in government.

Mandelson was right, but, first, it was essential that the contest did not descend into bitter infighting. An agreement about how the campaign would be fought was sealed at the famous Granita supper between Blair and Brown. No promises were made, but it was clearly indicated that the loser would become Shadow Chancellor. Moreover, both candidates agreed to rein in their attack dogs – and that largely worked. Crucially, Brown successfully persuaded Margaret Beckett, elected deputy leader in 1992 and now acting leader after Smith's death, to stay on rather than also stand both for leader and deputy. In that way, she would retain a position of great influence whoever won. In the other part of the bargain, Blair agreed to persuade Robin Cook not to run. Cook, a rival and critic of Brown from their days in the Scottish devolution battles of the 1970s, was convinced that by not entering the contest himself, there was a greater chance that Brown would be defeated. And there was the hint that a big post might be available, perhaps Foreign Secretary, first in opposition and then in government. That left Prescott as the only traditional left candidate.

The campaign turned out to be pretty restrained, despite some sniping from the fringes. It helped that Mandelson had withdrawn to a position of benevolent neutrality, trying to keep the tone of the contest right. The hustings emphasised each of Blair's and Brown's strengths: the ability to communicate a simple message to a mass audience versus the deep grasp of the big policy issues, with Prescott as a cumbersome, but quite effective, contrast, offering traditional values in a modern setting. Blair didn't win an overall majority on the first round of voting, thanks to an unexpectedly strong performance by Prescott, who came just ahead of Brown. While some of Brown's Scottish and trade union votes went to Prescott, Blair still won comfortably with nearly 60 per cent of the electoral college votes.

The outcome was a huge blow for Brown, especially in being narrowly pipped by Prescott in the first round. His long-cherished hopes had been dashed. He was not the leader. The recriminations in the Brown camp were bitter for a time, blaming opportunistic Labour MPs, and, above all, an unstoppable London media bandwagon. But Brown was also a realist. He had been beaten, not by a whisker, but by a big margin. He still believed in the modernisation programme and thought he could still play a major role in helping secure a Labour victory and afterward in government.

Blair handled Brown shrewdly and sensitively. He retained Brown as Shadow Chancellor and gave him a wide remit over domestic economic and industrial policy. But there was no doubt about who was in charge, and Blair insisted that all major economic decisions should be agreed jointly between them. Mandelson was given an important role in the campaign and, despite some tensions, the troika worked well together. But the roles were very different. Brown accepted – and occasionally was reminded – that Blair was the leader and the person who had the final say. But Brown was always acknowledged by Blair as the central figure in the shadow team. After the initial pain, Brown became less driven, more detached and reflective and more at ease with himself, especially after his relationship with his future wife Sarah developed in the second half of the 1990s, leading to marriage in August 2000.

After Labour's landslide victory in the May 1997 election, Brown duly became Chancellor, subject to certain conditions which he was forced to accept. He could not bring Charlie Whelan into the Treasury; he went back to work for the trade unions. And he could not have Geoffrey Robinson, his close ally and backer, as a Treasury minister. Brown grumbled but could do nothing about it. Anyway, he was immediately given his head by Blair to go ahead with making the Bank of England independent on monetary policy.

Stripped of some of his close allies, Brown was forced to depend more on the official Treasury. And despite initial suspicions, Brown found that Treasury civil servants were keen to work with him and he could trust them. Brown was even heard saying that the legacy left by Kenneth Clarke was not too bad.

Relations with 10 Downing Street were eased by the absence of Whelan, while Ed Balls was fully absorbed by preparing a paper on putting neo-endogenous growth theory into practice. Blair's insistence that all key economic decisions be made jointly between him and Brown worked reasonably well – though Blair had to put Brown in his place in October 1997 by insisting that he, as Prime Minister, should make the statement on

British policy towards the euro, the famous 'two tests' statement. Blair later, privately, conceded that Brown was correct to be cautious over the euro.

The first term went pretty smoothly, largely thanks to the strength of the economy. Brown grumbled and moaned from time to time, but he had to recognise Blair's authority, and also his remarkable popularity. Brown was allowed pretty wide latitude most of the time, but was reined in occasionally, notably in scaling back his plans for tax credits. As the 2001 election approached, Brown also accepted that public services such as health and education not only needed more money, after the restraint of the 1990s, but also structural reform to allow greater competition among providers and choice for their users.

Brown became increasingly involved in international financial issues, in part because of his interest in the problems of developing countries, notably those in Africa. He had already increased the budget of the Department for International Development, and began working with Bob Geldof and others on writing off the debt of developing countries. He disliked meetings of European finance ministers, partly because he felt excluded after Britain's decision not to join the euro, and partly because he never felt at home in Brussels with what he regarded as insular EU finance ministers. But he was much happier working with their counterparts from elsewhere in the world, notably with Robert Rubin and Larry Summers in the Clinton administration up to January 2001, but also with his Indian, Brazilian and Chinese opposite numbers. Brown felt liberated when working with them – no longer in the shadow of Blair, but treated as an equal and regarded as a creative and original leader in their frequent global summits.

By contrast, at home, Brown's big defeat in 1994 meant that he could no longer assume that he would succeed Blair – and the subject was never mentioned by either man since. Moreover, Brown recognised that Blair would carry on being Prime Minister for quite a few years, at least well into a second term if Labour won in 2001, and probably into a third term if his popularity held up and the Conservatives continued to fail to change their image as New Labour had done in the 1990s. By then, many new faces would have come along in the Labour Party, and younger, fresher candidates generally won party leadership elections. Brown could not face the thought of a second, humiliating defeat.

He was also aware that, however successful he had been so far as Chancellor, the economy seldom continued on a smooth and benign path for ever. Remaining as Chancellor for too long had tarnished Nigel Lawson's otherwise successful period at the Treasury. For Brown, the creation of the Bank of England Monetary Policy Committee had been a great success and had contributed to a low-inflation, low-interest-rate economy of steady growth. He resisted the temptation to be use hubristic language and was cross when an adviser suggested that he include references to 'no more boom and bust', and the 'longest sustained period of growth for two centuries', in one of his Budget speeches. He thought that was asking for trouble – especially as he had become increasingly worried about imbalances in the global economy and the excesses of some of the banks. It might be better to get out when the going was good, being able to point not only to Bank of England independence and sound public finances, but also to a steady and sustainable expansion of public services (particularly through the building and rebuilding of new schools and hospitals), and more help for the poor at home and abroad. He would be remembered as one of the most successful Labour Chancellors.

So when he met Blair shortly before the June 2001 election to discuss his future, Brown said that he did not want to remain Chancellor for more than a year or two. He then wanted to take up an international job, for which he would need Blair's support. Nothing was said publicly, but the exchange was duly noted by the ubiquitous Jeremy Heywood, the essential link between 10 Downing Street and the Treasury.

Brown had one last task which he wished to complete: to secure the long-term funding of the NHS. While Labour would go into the election sticking to its existing pledge not to raise the basic and higher rates of income tax, nor to widen the VAT base, the party manifesto would fudge the language on other tax changes. Brown and Blair agreed that further improvements to public services – tied to reforms in their structures – would require a one-off increase in taxes. Brown favoured a one percentage point rise in the national insurance contributions of both employers and employees, which would raise much more than a one point increase in income tax. However, any announcement would have to be carefully prepared. Before the election, Brown announced the setting up of a review into health funding under a former senior bank executive, Derek Wanless, which would make its initial report in autumn 2001 and a final report in spring 2002, at the time of the Budget, when he would announce the rise in NICs specifically to finance the NHS.

As we all now know, it did not work out quite like this. The 9/11 attack that September diverted Blair's attention and he asked Brown to stay on for a few months longer after his triumphant spring 2002 Budget. Brown, however, was increasingly unhappy with Blair's unqualified public support for the Bush administration's 'war on terror'. He sympathised with the American predicament but did not believe an attack on Iraq was justified. But he kept his doubts largely to himself, though they were known in other EU capitals and helped his candidacy when a vacancy appeared for managing director of the International Monetary Fund.

Brown took over at the IMF in spring 2003, just as the Iraq war was breaking out. He was relieved to have left the Blair cabinet, and relished the new challenges. His interest in global financial issues quickly made their impact. He pushed reform of the role of the IMF, both in overseeing global financial imbalances and in assisting developing countries. He enjoyed only partial success, because of the doubts of the Bush administration, but his earlier contacts with other finance ministers paid off in securing changes to the IMF's role and capacity. Alan Milburn, his successor as Chancellor, was particularly helpful in securing European support for his initiatives. Brown's warnings about the inherent instability of some of the new financial derivates – particularly those based on sub-prime US mortgages – went largely unheeded, except by those few smart enough to sell them short. Few people – at the top of investment banks and even in central banks – really understood what was going on. However, Brown's early changes at the IMF ensured that the Fund was rapidly able to respond when the global banking and financial crises erupted in 2008.

So when Brown retired from the IMF at the beginning of 2011, he was widely praised – even by the *Wall Street Journal* as well as the *Financial Times* – as one of the few international leaders to have emerged with credit from the financial crisis. That is why the acclaim he received at Bretton Woods in April 2011 so touched him. And back in Britain he had the status of an international statesman, above the party political fray. David Miliband, Blair's successor as Labour leader, wanted to bring him into the Labour/ Liberal Democrat coalition government. But Brown preferred to devote himself to international development and conflict resolution issues in a new non-profit consultancy he had founded with Tony Blair and Peter Mandelson, called – what else? – the Troika.

Notes

1   Peter Mandelson, *The Third Man – Life at the Heart of New Labour* (HarperPress, 2010), pp. 156–57.
2   Ibid., p. 157.
3   Ibid., p. 173.

Chapter 13

What if the United Kingdom had not gone to war in Iraq in 2003?

Tony McNulty

As a successful G20 meeting drew to a close in London on 2 April 2009, Gordon Brown reflected on his last six years as Prime Minister. He would stay as PM for a further year to ensure that the economic recovery took hold, and would then take up the international financial role that beckoned.

He had enjoyed the roller-coaster ride of the last six years, but he was ready for a change. His mind drifted back to the events concerning Iraq and Saddam Hussein that had brought him to the job of Prime Minister.

~

'When Blair assessed the balance of opinion within the Cabinet, he reckoned that without a second resolution he could only "just about get to a majority".[1] It was to Blair's great credit that a first United Nations resolution on Iraq had been secured in December 2002. Even Syria supported UN Security Council Resolution 1441, and it felt like a real triumph. The international community knew that the US did not feel governed by the UN and would attack Iraq without blinking if it felt it was within its interests. It was the work of the UK that led to the first resolution and it was Blair himself who had seen the importance of international consensus. However, this looked and felt like a mighty triumph for all of five minutes.[2]

Part of the problem was that 1441 seemed to mean all things to all people. Even worse, Blair's overwhelming problem was that whatever view people had of the resolution, the very success of achieving it defined the problem as international and put the UN at the centre of any solution. In other words, securing the first resolution meant that a second resolution became essential, not optional.

Despite the constant rewriting of history since, most MPs were clear in 2002 that there might have to be military action against Iraq. The dominant tone of the debate was over the legitimacy of such action under the auspices of the UN and the need for a second resolution. It was about the balance between the need for action and the need to give the inspectors more time for Saddam to comply. The purist anti-war position was articulated by very few MPs. Even the Liberal Democrat front bench was clear that its concerns were around the authority for military action, not the principle of action itself. There was a considerable degree of support for Blair's approach from Labour MPs, and he could be assured of their backing as long as the second resolution route was in play. Blair's concerns about support within the cabinet without a second resolution, however, were very real and even more apparent in the ranks of the Parliamentary Labour Party.

As the year turned to 2003, it was unclear exactly what was going on. For many, the search for a second resolution was in full swing and the whole issue of any military action would only be taken forward within the context of the UN. For them the debate over the role of the UN had been won – no second resolution, no war. For others, the UN was seen as totally irrelevant, a second resolution mere window-dressing, and the momentum behind military action unstoppable.

In February 2003, President Chirac of France made clear to Blair at a meeting in Le Touqet that war in Iraq was not something that the French were likely to support. Although the public face of Le Touqet was unity and deep discussion, the private meetings did not augur well for Blair in his search for a second resolution. Chirac seemed keen to lead an anti-American bloc internationally and Blair left France with growing anxiety, deeply frustrated with the French attitude.

The quest for a second resolution seemed to be increasingly fruitless, and pressure was mounting on Blair to explain where his government would go if there was no such. Blair had hoped that the momentum created by the first resolution would grow behind the second – but all the signs pointed the other way, and it became increasingly clear that Blair possessed no safety blanket. The US had made clear that it did not see the need for a second resolution, though Colin Powell had failed to shift the sentiments of the Security Council to the US view in early February. Many MPs appreciated that the UN route was still open only because of Blair's efforts. But just as the second resolution became all the more unlikely, it became all the more important in political terms. Blair needed it to gain the support of his party for action.

Disquiet on the government back benches continued to build. Without a second resolution, there was likely to be a majority of backbenchers against any military action. The key question for Blair was where the payroll vote would lie. How many of his colleagues in cabinet, and in the wider government, needed the second resolution to support action? Robin Cook had made noises in this direction. Publicly there was little disquiet or discussion, but within government, Cook was vociferous about the need for a second resolution even as Blair and Straw were clear that they had to stick with the Americans. There had been some discussion about a Straw-inspired alternative that would have meant that the UK did not go to war but effectively led the international effort for reconstruction and development under the auspices of the UN. This plan got short shrift from Blair, who was more and more certain that he now had to go all the way with Bush to war, regardless of the fate of a second resolution. As a loyal Foreign Secretary, Straw began to see that he had to go with Blair regardless of the outcome.

Throughout the early days of February, the march to war seemed inevitable; the only real issue was who in Blair's cabinet would support him and the US. Brown had made clear that he fully endorsed the path the government had taken to date.[3] He had seen the intelligence and understood the threat that Saddam posed – but he was also clear that the second resolution was crucial and that it was difficult to see how the government could support the Americans without it. He was appalled by what was now emerging as the public hand-wringing of Cook, Short and Denham, viewing it as indulgent and deeply disloyal. Everyone had serious doubts, but most resisted the luxury of such self-indulgence. Like others, Brown supported the notion that the House of Commons should have a vote if the UK were to participate in any military action, and he wanted to ensure that the government was well-placed to assist in any post-war reconstruction, regardless of whether or not the UK was actually involved in the war.

On 5 March 2003 Germany and France joined Russia in making clear that they would not support any second resolution that endorsed the use of force. The following Security Council meeting on 7 March was deadlocked. The US and UK were not going to table a second resolution unless they could secure the necessary votes for it to pass – which seemed unlikely. The only certainty was that they were now in the end game; the ongoing fudge of supporting the Americans and also the need for a second resolution could no longer be sustained.

The debate within government was intense, but most cabinet members were clear that it should remain internal, in line with collective responsibility. Not even Brown flinched when Clare Short was summarily dismissed for going on Radio 4's *Westminster Hour* and calling Blair's behaviour 'reckless'. Whatever views cabinet members had on the impending military action, all knew that Short's behaviour warranted dismissal. Brown was very clear that a second resolution was essential, but he was not going to rush to support Short and felt that her actions undermined the serious debate that was raging across government.

Blair knew that time was running out on a second resolution. The moment was fast approaching when his twin-track strategy would reach its natural end and the government would have to go one way or the other – alone with the Americans, or together with those who opposed military action without a second resolution. The Americans began to understand the importance of the second resolution for Blair, but were clear that if he felt the UK and his government would be damaged by supporting action, then they would go it alone. Blair thought right to the end that he would get the second resolution; unlike others, however, he was always clear that he would support the Americans regardless, and he knew the dangers. Others weren't so sure. Jonathan Powell, Blair's Chief of Staff, has said: 'When we couldn't get the second resolution, Tony thought, we all thought: "Oh fuck, what are we going to do now?"'[4] But Blair knew what he was going to do.

Things now moved apace. Within twenty-four hours of Short's sacking, Chirac finally shut off the option of a second resolution when he announced that 'France will vote "non" because we believe, tonight, that there are no grounds to wage war.'[5] The only path remaining was to go back to resolution 1441, an argument that many felt had already been lost. Brown made it very clear that this was the end of the road and that the UK could not support unilateral action by the US. Despite his strong ties to America and his avowed Atlanticism, this was a step too far. He told Blair that the government could not support the Americans and that the issue now was how they would jointly decouple the UK from the US on military action and focus instead on how they could help Iraq in a post-conflict situation. Brown assured Blair that he would defend him against any flak over the decision not to support the Americans.

But Blair himself was clear that he could not live with a course of action that walked away from the Americans. He still wanted to support them and he believed personally that resolution 1441 contained all the relevant justifications for action. He wanted to discuss how Brown and the others could help to persuade the party, the backbenchers and the country that we should still support the US. But Brown bluntly told Blair that over half of the cabinet would not support such a course of action. He told him also that the backbenchers knew that disquiet in the cabinet had grown and rebel numbers had risen as a consequence; at the end of February, 122 Labour MPs had voted for an amendment that 'the case for war had not yet been made', and estimates in early March suggested the numbers could be well over 200, after it became clear that no second resolution was forthcoming.

Brown had thought that Blair would accept the reality of the situation and tell the Americans that British support was off – after all, Bush would understand the difficulties. But Blair was adamant; if he could not get the government, Parliament and the country to support the American action against Iraq, then he could not, with any integrity, continue as Prime Minister. When he had told his staff that he was serious about supporting the Americans and that this could be the end for him, he meant it. Brown made clear, however, that if the proposal to support American military action was put to the House as had been promised, then the government itself could be at risk, as half the cabinet and over 200 backbenchers would not support any motion that endorsed the use of force. It was as stark as that. 'If I can't raise support for a cause I believe to be so right, then I have no choice but to go', said Blair. 'It's that simple.'

As the American march to military action continued unabated, the Prime Minister became more and more isolated. The view of the UK government had changed from broad support to the Americans to backing for those who demanded more time for the arms inspectors and no support for military action. Gambling that an all-out personal appeal would shift his cabinet, Blair called a meeting for Sunday 16 March.

He argued passionately for his position. First, he told the cabinet that military action was imminent and that there was no chance at all of any second resolution or support for such action from the UN. Second, he made clear that he would continue to support the Americans, and if this position did not command the support of the majority around the cabinet table he would resign as Prime Minister as a matter of principle. It became clear, however, that he had miscalculated; his threat was not enough to shift his colleagues' views, which now mirrored those of the PLP.

Blair had to go. His resignation was immediately followed by that of John Prescott, declaring that as he was elected Deputy Leader alongside Tony Blair, loyalty told him they came as a pair, and if Blair was going, then so was he. The cabinet unanimously endorsed a proposal that Brown become PM pro tem until the party could elect a new leader. With that, the dramatic cabinet meeting ended, only to be resumed the next day. Blair agreed that he would make a statement only after the government had made its new position clear.

When the cabinet reconvened the next day, Straw and Hoon, key proponents of the previous strategy, had gone too. Brown would deal with the reshuffle in time; the key business now was to determine how to go forward. In the normal course of events, Cook, as Leader of the House, would need to make a statement changing the business of the House to drop the debate on military action in Iraq. It was very clear that Brown would have to make a broader statement first, explaining the change in Prime Minister, why the government was no longer supporting the Americans and what the government would now seek to do instead.

Brown was clear that he did not want the decision to be seen as anti-American. The government did not share the visceral – and, Brown thought, juvenile – anti-Americanism of some on the left and some of their European counterparts. The government was not anti-war or anti-military action – this was about the legitimacy of action now, and the role of the UN. The government could not wash its hands of the consequences of American action and would need to decide what international role it would seek to play in the area.

Brown told the Commons that the Labour Party would select a new leader in due course, that he would act as Prime Minister in the interim, as elected by the cabinet, and that the first item of business would be dealing with the international fallout of any military action against Iraq by the US. He emphasised that the UK remained the US's strongest ally and that his government would work closely with the UN to deal with the consequences of any military action. Brown made clear to the Commons that walking off the international stage was not an option and that he would seek to ensure that the UK led the internationally sanctioned reconstruction of Iraq, continuing to work with the US and others to ensure the development and reinvigoration of the Middle East peace process.

The world watched as, throughout the next evening, US bombers flew sorties over Iraq, delivering the 'shock and awe' that Bush had promised. Some six weeks later, Bush declared 'mission accomplished' as Saddam's regime crumbled and the initial phase of the action was over.

The UK led the international efforts through the UN to ensure the reconstruction of Iraq. As the US still regarded the UK as a key ally, Britain acted as a conduit for them at the UN. Some in Washington, particularly Rice and Powell, were hugely disappointed that the US had found itself alone when war broke out. They knew that Bush had gone too soon, and also that this could still prove to be a disaster, notwithstanding the early military success. Ironically, it seemed that the UK was now in a more powerful position to influence the Americans because it had not supported the initial action.

Crucially, Rice and Powell were successful in ensuring that a fully resourced team in the US Office for Reconstruction and Humanitarian Aid (ORHA) was established and worked with international experts in the UN and the UK. They also ensured that good early decisions were made about reconstruction; they resisted neo-conservative notions of a complete so-called 'de-Ba'athification' of Iraq. Such a policy would have instantly dismissed most of the key middle-ranking administrators, police and army, where membership of the Ba'ath Party was more or less compulsory.

By the end of May, the UK proved successful in securing a unanimous vote on resolution 1483, effectively giving the UN an increasing role in post-war Iraq. This mattered because, with the key middle strata of the army, police and civil service still in place due to the efforts of Rice and Powell, the UN had the people to work with to counter any growing anti-US insurgency that might spring up. Had the neo-cons had their way, some 250,000 army, police and civil servants would be on the streets of Iraq, ripe for recruitment to an insurgency. Rice and Powell would freely admit later that they were only able to get their way on reconstruction in the face of the strength of the neo-cons because the UK had not supported the military action.

There was, accordingly, no fully blown insurgency in Iraq, though the violence did continue for some time. The UN took over more and more responsibility for the reconstruction, and Iraq proved to be far from the disaster that many had predicted. In the US, although not as bad, violent or costly in terms of lives as many had expected, the war soon became very unpopular, and the exposure of what was seen as an increasingly bizarre neo-con view of the world strengthened the hand of Powell and Rice.

Their success in working with the UK and the UN over the reconstruction of Iraq also increased their popularity and political currency in the US and abroad.

The UK came out of the conflict in a strong position. Brown attempted to use his leverage to get the Middle East peace process back on track. There had been discussions before the war over a new roadmap for peace, but many felt that this was just Bush trying to build alliances, and he was not really serious about the peace process itself. The UK would play a leading role in developing a new way forward for peace in the Middle East, as well as in the reconstruction of Iraq.

As the international community started to get a grip on the rebuilding of Iraq, both the US and UK turned their attention to internal matters. Domestic American politics saw intense criticism of Bush, fuelled by the view that if he could not even maintain the support of the UK, then he had failed in a spectacular fashion. Powell and Rice were very keen to make sure that the American public knew about the options put forward by Bush's neo-conservative colleagues, and just how disastrous they would have been for the military and the American body count. It would be interesting to see how Bush fared when he ran for re-election in 2004.

In the UK a timetable was drawn up for the Labour leadership election, culminating with the result of the contest being announced at the Labour conference in Bournemouth in September. When nominations closed in mid-June, it was clear that Brown was the overwhelming favourite, facing a two-pronged attack from Alan Milburn as the 'Blairite' candidate and Clare Short as the weakly endorsed ultra-left candidate. The party agreed to scrap the largely irrelevant position of deputy leader, so there was no contest to replace Prescott.

Brown won the election handsomely, with Milburn in a strong second place and Short a very poor third. The result was announced on the Sunday of the conference, and Brown made a unifying speech in the regular Tuesday afternoon slot that followed. The whole week, though, was distracted by speculation over a general election. Although the government had only been in power for two years, many felt that the new leader should seek his own mandate from the electorate, and the entire coverage of the conference from the time that Brown sat down after his speech was all about its likely date. Labour was still riding high in the polls, sustaining a 7–10 per cent lead over the Tories since Blair's resignation, and more like 10 per cent plus in the first polls after Brown's conference speech.

On the Thursday lunchtime, as the conference was winding down, Brown made an impromptu speech, short and sharp. He said that he had been persuaded by those who had argued that any new leader who was also Prime Minister should seek their own mandate at the earliest opportunity. The country needed direction and he needed the certainty of his own endorsement. There would be an election at the earliest opportunity; he would be going to the Palace as soon as he returned to London.

Neither Charles Kennedy nor Iain Duncan Smith, the leaders of the Liberal Democrats and the Tories respectively, could object to the announcement, as both had complained about Brown's apparent lack of a mandate. In truth, however, the Tories had not got over the 2001 defeat – virtually a repeat of the 1997 landslide – and the Liberal Democrats needed more time to consolidate their 2001 position. It was not to be.

In a largely uneventful election, it soon became clear that people were happy to confirm the change in Labour leadership, were fairly indifferent about the rather lacklustre efforts of the Liberal Democrats and gave some, though little, reward to Duncan Smith's Tories. Labour lost twenty seats – all to the Tories, who also gained two seats from the Liberal Democrats. So Labour emerged with 393, the Tories 188, the Liberal Democrats 50 and others 28 – with the Speaker, who was Labour, this gave an overall Labour majority of 126.

The new cabinet was a prudent mix of those who could be described as Blairite and Brownite. Brown confirmed most of his changes earlier in May when he had restored Cook as Foreign Secretary, Darling had become Chancellor, Blunkett stayed at the Home Office and Prescott at the ODPM, now renamed as the Communities and Local Government Department. There were no comebacks for Straw or Hoon, and many changes in the lower ministerial ranks. Brown's hand was strengthened as two of his key lieutenants, Ed Balls and Ed Miliband, were elected as MPs; it was felt that neither would have to wait long before securing preferment.

Within the Conservative Party there had been rumblings against Iain Duncan Smith even before the election, and many felt that he would have done well to survive the conference season. Although the Tories had gained twenty-two seats the election was still seen as a major disappointment. The Labour Party had effectively won a third landslide, the Tory vote had remained more or less static and the party had still won fewer than 200 seats. Duncan Smith accordingly resigned. Michael Howard was persuaded to step into the breach and was elected unopposed, declaring that the party needed stability and that he would seek to lead the party up to the next election and beyond.

Charles Kennedy's leadership of the Liberal Democrats was also called into question as his party had performed indifferently in the election – but he held on as there was no pressing contender and most of the party membership still supported him. There were some noises off from pushy, disgruntled MEPs led by an unknown named Nick Clegg, but most understood that Kennedy's personal appeal had prevented a worse result than had actually transpired.

So, as the country headed into 2004, the settled view was that the government had done well on foreign affairs, especially in the two areas of the reconstruction of Iraq under the auspices of the UN and the increasing possibility of progress in the Middle East peace process. The UK had decided to bid for the 2012 Olympics and, given the UK's high regard internationally, had some confidence of success.

Domestically, the cabinet was united around a public services reform agenda. Investment in all the key services remained high, but it had come on the back of deals done between Brown and Darling over reform. There was agreement on the need for transformation in all areas; Brown endorsed foundation hospitals and trusts in the NHS, greater local involvement in the health service and a reinforcement of the rewards and targets system. He was keen to work with John Reid to ensure that the government gained a good return from the huge sums that were being invested in the NHS.

Education was also a key issue, one that played to all that New Labour stood for on social mobility, aspiration and advance. Brown knew and understood the power of education. He could never understand why the English state system had fallen so far behind its Scottish counterpart, and worked closely with Education Secretary, Charles Clarke, to improve performance in return for investment. One key area of reform was in higher education, where they worked closely together to see the introduction of a mixed system of fees, of no more than £3,000, and a graduate tax, both payable by those earning over £22,000. This hybrid system meant that the future of funding for universities was secured and top-up fees were outlawed, as had been pledged in the Labour manifesto.

Policing and security had been a key issue for the government since the events of 9/11. Brown knew that the threat from al-Qaeda had been very real before 2001, and it remained so despite the advances in Iraq and the Middle East. On 11 March 2004 a series of bombs on the Cercanias commuter train system in Madrid killed 191 and injured over 1,800.[6] In the same month a number of arrests were made throughout the south of England; an al-Qaeda-inspired group of extremists was planning to plant bombs in the Ministry of Sound nightclub in London, Bluewater Shopping Centre and London synagogues.[7] In August Dhiren Barot and others were arrested as part of a 'dirty bomb' plot.[8]

The government was keenly aware of the balance between security and civil liberties and the way in which the terrorists played on this balance, hoping governments would exaggerate their response. It was also clear that unscrupulous politicians, particularly the Liberal Democrats, would seek to exploit any problems for the government. Recognising the need to strike the right balance, Brown was nevertheless clear that security was paramount. This approach survived the resignation of David Blunkett in December 2004;[9] Blunkett was replaced by Charles Clarke, despite Clarke's rather fractious (at best) relationship with Brown.

In the US, during 2004, John Kerry emerged as the strongest rival to Al Gore during the primaries for the Democratic nomination for the presidency. Gore had not intended to run for a second time against Bush, but felt that the way in which the President had abused his tenuous mandate over Iraq left him no choice. If it hadn't been for the UK, the US would be totally isolated and in dangerous territory. Gore felt that he owed it to the nation to try to repeat the contest of 2000. He duly won the nomination, selected Kerry as his vice-presidential running mate, and won the general election in November, crucially taking Ohio and, unlike 2000, his home state of Tennessee.

At home, the fate of the Tories went from bad to worse. Michael Howard faced difficulties in trying to modernise the party while at the same bringing its traditional base with him. In the June 2004 European elections, the Tories came third, behind the UK Independence Party. Howard was keen to keep his initial promise to stay as leader for the entire Parliament, but was constantly forced to reflect on his position. It seemed as though events conspired against him, as the Tories continued to flatline or worse in the polls. After another bad set of results in the local elections in 2005, he subsequently announced that he would resign – and the search for a new leader by the party conference in October began. The main contenders soon emerged as Ken Clarke, David Davis, Michael Portillo and Liam Fox – with a potential bid from either George Osborne or David Cameron.

In an extraordinarily eventful month, London was announced as the venue for the 2012 Olympics on 6 July, and the London bombs rocked the country on the 7th. Brown was up at the G8 meeting in Gleneagles when the news came through and insisted on flying back to London to take control. In all, 52 people were murdered on London's tube and bus network, with over 700 injured. Despite the positive endeavours of the UK government in Iraq and the wider Middle East, the violent extremists continued their activities – including, of course, the murder of many Muslims.

Brown was clear once more that while there had to be a balance between the struggle against terrorism and civil liberties, a government's first duty was to the safety of the public. His speech in Dunfermline that weekend – subsequently known as the Dunfermline declaration – made clear that he would not side with those who thought the attacks meant that the 'rules of the game had changed', but neither would he join with those who put the human rights and civil liberties of those who would kill above public safety. He demanded that Parliament work with him to secure the security of the nation and told the opposition parties that the country would not forgive them if they played party politics in the wake of the threat.

As Foreign Secretary, Robin Cook had worked with relish on both the development of the Middle East peace process and the reconstruction of Iraq. The bombings of 7/7, however, posed a further huge challenge, as the government prepared for the recall of Parliament in September to discuss its response. Cook took the opportunity for a brief holiday in the Highlands, and died suddenly while out walking near the summit of Ben Stack on 6 August. Brown was quick to make David Miliband the new Foreign Secretary in a bid to finally heal any remaining scars between the competing Labour tribes. Miliband made clear that he would take forward Cook's attempts to develop the UK's foreign policy in an ethical way, while resisting empty gestures.

After witnessing a successful Labour conference in Brighton, with a strong and united Labour Party, the Tories headed to Blackpool with a modicum of trepidation – five declared candidates would present their case for being leader. Although it would be the job of the MPs to whittle the field of five down to two before the party membership voted, everybody agreed that the candidates' presentations at the conference would be crucial for their prospects in the MPs' ballots. Going into the conference, David Davis and Ken Clarke were the frontrunners. It was felt that it was too late for Portillo, Fox was a darling of the right wing but with limited public appeal, and that the youthful and inexperienced Cameron was simply putting down a marker for the future. The speeches broadly endorsed these views. While Davis' speech had been weak, he was still viewed as the only serious right-wing candidate. Portillo and Clarke both played to the modernising agenda, but Portillo seemed tired while Clarke was rejuvenated by the contest, emerging as the front runner after the conference. On a minor note, rather than put a marker down, Cameron was seen as having made a serious error with his speech. He wandered the stage with no notes, in a style that was judged both rambling and arrogant. There was muted applause when he finished and many old hands considered it a rude and juvenile performance that showed his misunderstanding of the party faithful.

In the end, Clarke and Davis went through to the run-off and Clarke emerged as leader by a whisker – by 102,671 to 96,173. He won, it was felt, because more party members were against Davis than were against Clarke. Both Hague and Duncan Smith had fought elections on the sort of right-wing agenda that Davis supported, and it had been decisively rejected by the country as recently as 2003.

Clarke's first action was to make clear that he was not going to be a prisoner of the right simply because the election was so close. He asked Davis to be Shadow Foreign or Shadow Defence minister. but he was not going to give him a deputy role, Shadow Home Secretary or Shadow Chancellor.

Observers suggested that the election of Ken Clarke as the Tory leader saved Charles Kennedy's leadership of the Liberal Democrats. There were strong rumours circulating about Liberal Democrat MPs' concern over Kennedy's apparent problems with drink. They had planned to use the election of 'new blood' as Tory leader as the excuse to strike, but Clarke's success meant that Kennedy's leadership was safe for now. He was claiming to clear up his problem, and was given the benefit of the doubt.

Ken Clarke's election did not mark an immediate turn of fortune for his party, but did herald a different form of politics – much to the annoyance of his right wing and some of the younger Tory MPs. When the Home Office discovered that the prison service and the immigration service had failed to deport a number of foreign prisoners on completion of their sentences, the tabloid press had a field day. The issue broke in the run-up to local elections in 2006; the perfect storm of elections, crime and foreigners proved irresistible to the 'red tops'. It looked for a while as though the government, particularly Home Secretary Charles Clarke, was in trouble, but just as the issue was really heating up, Ken Clarke went on television to defuse the row. Making clear that he regarded the issue as very serious, he nevertheless argued that it was 'not a matter of government policy but a matter of one part of the administration not talking to another part', and that the government should simply get on and fix the problem. When pushed, he said that: 'I have not come into politics to play silly games. The Home Secretary needs to get a grip, but, God knows, I've had my own experience of admin failure – get over it.'

Not only did this intervention save Charles Clarke's job as Home Secretary, it also increased Ken Clarke's national standing. He seemed to tap into a growing yearning from the public to have politicians who spoke normally and were not always looking for a chance to oppose for the sake of opposition. His natural inclination to 'tell it as it is' was reinforced by his confidence that the Tories could not afford to drop yet another leader. This approach meant that Brown could keep Charles Clarke in place to get on with solving the problem. Charles Kennedy could only agree with this approach; to do otherwise would seem to be partisan and churlish.

Charles Clarke accordingly got on with clearing up the mess, stayed on as Home Secretary and dealt with the 'airline plot' in the summer of 2006, when a group of terrorists sought to use 'liquid bombs' to down between three and seven transatlantic airliners.[10] Cooperation between the UK, the US and Pakistan meant that the project was foiled, but it was another reminder of the existence of a very real threat. Charles Clarke had already worked well with the opposition and easily secured agreement to a pre-charge detention limit of up to 28 days in the Prevention of Terrorism Act 2006. These powers were used for the first time in the 'airline plot' and the police did not need more time than this. Ken Clarke and Charles Kennedy both said that, within reason, they would do all that they could to maintain a political consensus on the response to terrorism.

Much of the government's focus from 2007 onwards was on the growing difficulties in the economy. There were rumblings at the turn of the year about the next election. For most of the recent past, most governments had lasted for four years, only staying on for the full five-year term if there were problems, as with John Major in 1997. There was talk that Brown was going to go in 2007 rather than wait until 2008. Labour remained buoyant in the polls, although there were signs of a 'Ken Clarke bounce'. Very unusually, however, Brown announced in March 2007 that as there was no compelling need to go to the country early, the Parliament would run its full five-year term, with the election scheduled for October 2008. Some had tried to depict Brown as a ditherer; the label did not stick after this announcement.

The remaining period before the election of 2008 was dominated by the economy and the emerging global recession. The collapse of Northern Rock was just the first manifestation of economic difficulties in the UK. In September 2007, the building society sought a liquidity support facility from the Bank of England following problems in the international credit markets due to the US sub-prime mortgage crisis. Eventually, Northern Rock was nationalised in February 2008, the first step in a series of decisive actions taken by Gordon Brown to insulate the economy from a run on the banks. Brown took the initiative both at home and abroad and won plaudits around the world for his actions and his international leadership.

Given that Ken Clarke had said only the previous year that the Tories would match government spending; and, furthermore, that he accepted that government spending was part of any recovery from recession, the Tories were fairly mute in response to the crisis. The Liberal Democrat claim that they had foreseen the impending economic crisis was met with derision and the party's Shadow Chancellor, Vince Cable, was derided as a mix between Mystic Meg and Mr Bean.

The Tories were all over the place in response to the economic crisis. Ken Clarke's difficulty, as an ex-Chancellor, was that he did not trust anyone else on his front bench to lead on the economy. This attitude was hardened when a junior member of the shadow Treasury team, George Osborne, thought it would be a good idea to announce a Conservative pledge for a huge rise in the threshold for inheritance tax as a wheeze to scare Brown off any notion of an election in October 2007. This allowed Brown to announce that of course there would not be an election as his government was far too busy working in the national interest to turn the economy around. He was able to capitalise on Osborne's policy by suggesting that the Tories were only interested in the very rich. Ken Clarke was absolutely furious and, unusually, made it known that, in his own words, he 'gave this little boy a right bollocking'.

The world economy settled down, but even the strongest national economies were still shrinking. Brown felt it imperative for an international stimulus package to be developed, saving some of the smaller developed economies from potential collapse, though of course it was Germany and France that would have to sort out any problems in the Euro-zone. Commentators couldn't help but notice that it was Brown as Chancellor who had kept the UK out of the Euro – and a 'bloody good job too!' announced *The Sun*.

With an agreed plan for economic recovery in place and with accolades from the international community for his efforts during the world downturn, Brown headed for the 2008 election with a degree of optimism. It looked as though the country recognised that there was no alternative to Labour, that the Tories were still in disarray and the Liberal Democrats were out of their depth on most issues. The issue for Brown was how long he wanted to go on as Prime Minister. He had relished leading the response to the international crisis and steering the recovery. He had spent his entire career talking about the need for a new Bretton Woods, a new international financial architecture. There was real pressure from international colleagues for him to step up to the plate and give the world the systems it needed to resist or prevent further economic crises.

As he was driven to the Palace to submit his resignation to the Queen and seek the dissolution of Parliament and an election, his thoughts turned again to an international role. 'London holds the G20 in April 2009 – I'll decide by then. By that time there will be plenty of contenders to replace me – Clarke, Johnson, Balls, Ed or David Miliband, Burnham or Yvette – who knows?'

Notes

1   A. Rawnsley, *The End of the Party* (Penguin, 2010), p. 144.
2   Ibid., p. 140.
3   S. Richards, *Whatever It Takes* (Fourth Estate, 2010), p. 181.
4   Rawnsley, *The End of the Party*, p. 153.
5   Ibid., p. 160.

6   In October 2007, 21 people were found guilty on a range of charges from forgery
    to murder. No direct link to core al-Qaeda was ever established, but the attack was
    certainly al-Qaeda-inspired.

7   Operation Crevice, as it was called, successfully disrupted an attempt to cause mass
    murder through bombs planted in public places. Clear links were established back to
    al-Qaeda in Pakistan. In 2007 five of the defendants were found guilty.

8   Operation Rhyme, as it was called, countered a plan to develop and use a dirty radiation
    device or dirty bomb. Again clear links were established with core al-Qaeda and all the
    principal defendants were found guilty in 2007.

9   David Blunkett resigned over personal matters in December 2004 following an inquiry
    into allegations that he had improperly used his position – for which there was no
    subsequent evidence.

10 Six men were found guilty on a range of charges in 2009 and 2010 relating to this plot.
    Again, there were clear links with core al-Qaeda in Pakistan.

Chapter 14

What if David Davis had been elected leader of the Conservative Party in 2005?

Iain Dale

'I wish I'd known he could do that before', whispered one aide to another. 'Wouldn't it be great if he could do it for his conference speech?'[1]

They were listening to Conservative leadership contender David Davis MP make a speech to 250 Scottish Conservatives in Edinburgh in early September 2005. The day hadn't got off to a good start, with Davis junking the text prepared by his speechwriting team. 'Guess I'll have to fly solo', he complained. The two aides shuddered, having the previous day experienced a different sort of 'flying solo' when, following a visit to the Wirrall, the three of them had taken a helicopter ride back to London. Needless to say, it wasn't long before 'action man' Davis was flying the damn thing. 'I'm sure there must be a law against this', pleaded one of the aides, but in vain.

Back to Edinburgh. The two aides looked on in wonderment as Davis wowed his audience, delivering a polished, passionate, insightful and inspirational speech – and all without notes.

The second aide responded: 'Do you think he could still do it? Isn't it a bit late? Is there time enough to plan it properly?' A few of the elderly ladies looked round and tutted disapprovingly. The two aides moved out of the room and started an animated discussion. Would Davis go for it? He loves a bit of a risk, doesn't he? But he's never been confident about his speaking. He surely wouldn't risk his whole leadership campaign on that one speech, would he? Maybe not, but the others may do – Cameron, for example, what's he got to lose? He's got to plan something dramatic at the conference. And Fox. It would be typical of him to upstage everyone, wouldn't it?

The two nodded knowingly, plans already hatching in their minds.

And so it came to pass. All five leadership contenders set out their wares at the party conference. But by the end of the week there was only one speech the conference representatives were talking about – and that was Davis's. How had he pulled it off, was the most common reaction? Where on earth had it come from?

In truth, it had all been very simple. Davis had studied the video of Ann Widdecombe's 1998 conference speech, when she had been the first to break the tradition of speaking from an autocue or from a typescript; it had been an almost evangelical performance. He had also studied Bill Clinton's lectern-less speeches.

Having initially dismissed the idea of delivering such a speech as 'barking mad', he increasingly warmed to it – and, to cut a long story short, pulled it off. In spades. 'The most memorable conference speech from a Tory since the Lady wasn't for turning', said ITN's Tom Bradby on the lunchtime news. It was a remark which provoked the Cameron team's Greg Barker to launch a bitter tirade at Bradby outside his Imperial Hotel bedroom door several hours later.[2] The BBC's Nick Robinson was equally effusive: 'It was the speech which secured Davis not only the leadership, but the affection of his party.' Leading Tory policy wonk Nick Boles, someone everyone had assumed would support Cameron, told Sky News: 'That was what I had been waiting for. It was the speech of a party leader on his way to No. 10. Davis knows what modernising entails and he's got my full support.'[3]

The next day, with only a handful of MPs publicly backing him, David Cameron withdrew from the campaign, having delivered a lacklustre conference performance. 'We got it so wrong', said Cameron's emotional campaign manager, George Osborne, but the writing had been on the wall for some time. A week before the conference, Cameron supporter Ed Vaizey had signalled in an unguarded aside to one of the Davis campaign team that the end was nigh, and that he would soon be transferring his allegiances. Nudge nudge, wink wink.

'Ah, the boy Vaizey', sniggered Derek Conway, 'he can see which way the wind is blowing'. Conway was the Davis campaign's numbers man – the keeper of the records. 'If he comes over, he'll bring a few with him.'

Much to the campaign's surprise, when Cameron pulled out, it was without signalling anything formal to Davis himself, and he made no demands before publicly declaring his support for Davis. 'What on earth is he playing at?' mused Davis's campaign manager, Andrew Mitchell. 'He could have at least asked for Shadow Home Sec.'

A week later MPs trooped down the Committee Room corridor to vote. With Cameron and Rifkind gone, only Fox and Ken Clarke remained on the ballot paper to challenge Davis. At 6.30pm that night MPs crammed into Committee Room 14 to hear the chairman of the 1922 committee, Sir Michael Spicer, read out the result. He rose slowly to his feet, revelling in the moment. 'The results of the Conservative Parliamentary Party leadership ballot first round ...' 'Get on with it', shouted a male voice from the back of the room. Sir Michael started again, as if he was punishing the heckler. 'The results of the Conservative Parliamentary Party leadership ballot first round are as follows: Liam Fox 32, Kenneth Clarke 66, David Davis 100. I therefore declare that Kenneth Clarke and David Davis will contest the party members' ballot.'

Few had expected Davis to win a clear, albeit narrow, majority of MPs. Speculation mounted over whether Ken Clarke would pull out, thereby saving the party the cost of an all-members' ballot. Party activist John Strafford, a doughty campaigner for internal Conservative Party democracy, immediately took to the airwaves to put the case for the vote taking place. Clarke's team were split. His canny campaign manager Richard Chalk relished the battle ahead, but he knew that the numbers didn't stack up and that, barring a miracle, Davis would win by a landslide. He recognised that although party members rather liked Clarke's bluff style, they would never trust his views on Europe. At midday on the Wednesday, he walked into Clarke's office and advised his candidate to pull out. 'I've drafted a concession statement, Ken', he said. 'You may want to consider it.'

On Tuesday I encouraged the Parliamentary Party to send a clear signal to the membership in the country – to tell them who commanded the greatest level of support in Parliament to lead us into the next general election. I hoped that would be me.

Earlier this morning I telephoned David Davis to congratulate him on his vote. In a very short time David has come a long way. I, too, have travelled a journey. But it is one which stops here. I made another call this morning, to the Chairman of the 1922 Committee, Michael Spicer, to tell him I would not be allowing my name to go forward to a ballot of the party members in the country and that I am pledging my support to David Davis as Britain's next Conservative Prime Minister.

I do not pretend this has been an easy decision. There will be many in the party who believe I should allow the membership to have its say. But to carry on when I am clear in my own mind that there is no prospect of winning would be a self-indulgence.

Three years ago, David stood aside in favour of Michael Howard in order to allow the party a chance of uniting before the election. That was the right decision. My decision today, while painful for some, and which I know will be criticised by others, is essential if we are to take the fight to Tony Blair and Gordon Brown as soon as possible.

By standing aside now I want to give David Davis the best possible chance of hitting New Labour where it hurts through the autumn – and I intend to do all I can to help him.

When Michael Howard set the timetable for this leadership election he took a risk. But it was a risk worth taking. For the first time in some years people are actually listening to what we are saying; they are receptive to our ideas; they are willing us to win. Our challenge now is to unite behind our new leader, support him in both good times and bad and carry the fight to Labour.[4]

But five minutes later events took a different course. Chalk took a call from the BBC's Nick Robinson, who informed him that CCHQ were briefing that a Davis coronation was likely to happen by the end of the week. Indeed, this was coming from the party chairman Francis Maude himself, Chalk soon ascertained. 'Get me that fucking Francis Maude on the phone', barked Chalk to a campaign aide. It wasn't a pretty conversation. Chalk accused Maude of scuppering any chance of a concession and wondered what on earth he was playing at.[5] He suddenly became aware of a hulking presence by his side. 'Give me the phone', demanded Clarke. He put it to his ear. 'Francis, you can take your off-the-record briefings and shove them where the sun don't shine. My campaign continues.' And with that he slammed the phone down. 'Onwards!' he declared.

Over the next six weeks the two candidates traipsed up and down the country debating at regional hustings and taking part in TV debates. Neither made a great gaffe and neither wiped the floor with the other. In the result of the final ballot, announced on 6 December, David Davis won with the expected two-thirds share of the vote.

His victory speech was magnanimous. He set out three priorities for his leadership: to unify and modernise the party, to have a root-and-branch review of all party policies and institutions, and to look like an alternative government.

Later that day he started building his shadow cabinet. Although Davis was seen to come from the right of the party, he was also a political realist; he knew that he had to build some bridges with the centre-left. His first call was to his defeated rival. 'Ken, I need you on board', he said. 'Will you serve?' He knew full well what the answer would be, but it suited him to go through the motions.

His next call was to William Hague. This time Davis hoped that the answer would be more positive, as he been at great pains to court Hague throughout the leadership election. Hague had been out of frontline politics for four years, and many questioned his hunger for office. Furthermore, Davis and Hague had never been close, despite both representing Yorkshire seats; Hague had found it difficult to forgive Davis for refusing to serve on his front bench during his own leadership. Whatever his reservations about returning, however, Hague knew his duty.

So, Hague was on board – but not, as all the pundits had speculated, as shadow chancellor or foreign secretary. No, he was to be party chairman, with a remit to shake up the party structures, revitalise the troops, radically change the candidate selection processes and go round the country stirring up enthusiasm. Importantly, it would also leave him time to write his books. Job done, thought Davis. Who could possibly think that would be a bad appointment? Apart, possibly, from Hague's wife Ffion …

But then the difficulties started. George Osborne has only been in the shadow chancellor's job for six months. Osborne and Davis had always got on well, but Davis wanted his own man in the post; he was a keen reader of political history and knew that he and his shadow chancellor needed to work hand in glove. It was Damian Green who got the call. His first reaction was to quote Margaret Beckett when asked by Tony Blair to be Foreign Secretary. 'Fuck me!' he exclaimed. Although on the dripping wet socially liberal wing of the party, Green was as dry as dust economically and had played a pivotal role in advising Davis during the leadership election. Osborne was made shadow chief secretary.

What to do with David Cameron? Cameron and Davis had known each other for a long time. For a brief period they had met each Tuesday and Thursday to work out John Major's best lines for Prime Ministers' Questions, but they had never been close. Davis regarded Cameron with suspicion. He had never warmed to Etonians – but he also recognised Cameron's political skills and his ability to communicate on TV. Davis had received many plaudits for his performance as shadow home secretary and he had shifted party policy towards a much more libertarian stance, in the face of bitter opposition from Michael Howard. He wanted to appoint Cameron to succeed him but needed his reassurance that he would not seek to revert to the old authoritarian ways. It was an assurance Cameron was happy to give. 'Don't worry, David', Cameron joked. 'I'll make sure I have Shami Chakrabarti on speed dial 1!'

In other appointments, Andrew Mitchell became shadow foreign secretary, succeeding Liam Fox, who decided that any other job would be a demotion and flounced off to the back benches. Francis Maude, an ally of Davis in the 1990s, was sacked, and no place was found for Oliver Letwin. Derek Conway became Chief Whip.

Long-time Davis ally Nick Herbert was put in charge of a full-scale policy review, with a remit to report by the summer of 2007. 'Look at everything, Nick', ordered Davis. 'Nothing is sacrosanct. Nothing.' It was a remark Davis was to live to regret. Herbert set about his task with vigour. He was a member of the shadow cabinet but with no specific portfolio. But it wasn't long before he grew frustrated by the inability of his colleagues to think radically and innovatively. Many of them, he felt, were still stuck in the politics of the 1990s. His solution was to ignore them completely while he patiently constructed a policy platform under the old Davis campaign slogan of 'Modern Conservatism'.

~

The next few years proved tough. It took Davis some time to adjust to the rigours of leadership. He resented the fact that he couldn't just ring up a journalist for a gossip, as had been his wont. He hated the glad-handing of senior party bigwigs and hated even more the inevitable schmoozing of party donors. Even worse was the interest the press took in his family. He and the Murdoch empire were already at daggers drawn over his stance on civil liberties, so it came as little surprise when his press spokesman, Guto Harri, took a call from the editor of the *News of the World*, Andy Coulson, alerting him to the fact that the next day his paper would be carrying an interview with the wife of a man who had run a company Davis had shut down while working for Tate & Lyle. The man had committed suicide a few months later.

'That's it,' spluttered Davis, when he was told the news. 'These people are out of control. I never want to hear Coulson's name again.' It proved to be a vain wish.

Herbert's policy review continued apace, but in mid 2006 a serious leak occurred, when the *Daily Telegraph* published a story that Herbert was actively considering a radical proposal to cut the armed forces. He considered the MoD budget to be unsustainable and argued that Britain needed to take a less active role in policing the world. 'DAVIS TO CUT ARMY BY A FIFTH', raged the *Telegraph* front page. Liam Fox, the former shadow foreign secretary, took to the air waves to denounce the proposal. In an interview with Sky News he said: 'No one who calls themselves a Conservative could possibly consider cutting Britain's armed forces by a fifth.' He continued: 'Whoever wrote this paper should be ashamed of themselves. I hope our leader will take action against them.' Meanwhile, shadow defence secretary Patrick Mercer issued a statement which amounted to saying 'over my dead body'. It was a sign of things to come.

William Hague, however, had the party in the palm of his hands. For him, being chairman was the perfect job: no policy work, appearing on the *Today* programme every other day, attending a few strategy meetings at Conservative Central Office (as it had been renamed), and glad-handing party bigwigs. It left all the time in the world to continue writing his history books.

One of Hague's first acts was to reform the candidate selection process. When he had been chairman, Davis had started the process of attracting more female candidates, which had been carried on by Theresa May and Liam Fox. But it had been to little effect. When May argued in shadow cabinet for positive discrimination and the formation of a priority list of female candidates, David Cameron put the counter case. 'We need positive discrimination like a hole in the head', he said. 'Surely we should be going out there and looking for better female candidates and encouraging them to come forward?' Davis concurred. 'Stop putting so many useless men on the list, and increase the proportion of women', he suggested.

Gradually the Conservatives started to rise in the polls. An increasingly unpopular Tony Blair was in constant unarmed combat with his Chancellor Gordon Brown. It looked like a government which was falling apart at the seams. Blair's dominance in the House of Commons was fading as every day passed. Davis proved an unexpected hit at Prime Minister's Questions, regularly besting Blair at the despatch box. 'You were the future once', was one of his best lines, fed to him by David Cameron at their regular Wednesday morning planning session.

In late 2006 Davis and his constitutional affairs spokeswoman, Theresa May, published plans for the creation of an English Parliament. For several years Davis had been concerned at the constitutional imbalance left by Labour's devolution plans. He scented a growing unrest among the English, who saw their hard-earned tax monies disappearing north of Hadrian's Wall and west of Offa's Dyke. And still the Welsh and Scots whinged.

Several years earlier Davis had supported a campaign, run by the maverick Tory MP Teresa Gorman, proposing the establishment of a full-scale English Parliament which would have full control of domestic policy. Davis had formed a secret policy group to consider the future of the Barnett Formula – it didn't have one – and the powers and make-up of a proper English Parliament. His plans were denounced by *The Guardian* as 'endangering the Union' and by *The Independent* as 'stark staring con-stitutional vandalism on an industrial scale'. The public, however, saw it differently – even in Scotland.

Davis was famed for his reputation for wargaming every possible scenario. He knew that his biggest test would come when Blair eventually handed over to his rival. Unlike many of his advisers, Davis knew that he shouldn't underestimate Gordon Brown. He regarded him as a formidable machine operator; what he lacked in empathetic skills, he more than made up for in sheer ruthlessness – which was why Davis always expected Brown to call a general election as soon as he could politically get away with it. He told his closest aides that the most likely date was the autumn of 2007. He told Nick Herbert to ensure that a draft manifesto was ready to go, and to ensure that no one saw the text until he had personally signed it off. He knew it would be incendiary.

What Davis hadn't counted on was the astonishingly impressive per-formance of Brown during his first two months as Prime Minister. He displayed a calm sure-footedness and an ability to react to a crisis which few would have credited him with. Slowly but surely the Conservative lead in the polls evaporated. By the beginning of September it was clear that if Brown went to the country he might possibly pull off an historic fourth Labour win. The Labour Party conference at the end of September took on the air of a pre-election rally. Rumours were rife that Brown would call the election on the day of the Conservative leader's conference speech the week after. It was then that Davis launched what became known inside CCO as Operation Sidewinder.

And it was in those few days that Brown's hubris proved to be his undoing. A visit to Iraq was meant to show a Prime Minister on the world stage, in contrast to pictures of the Conservative leader quaffing champagne at his conference. Instead, Davis's press spokesman successfully persuaded the media that it was a political stunt, using Our Boys to aid his re-election efforts. But the real missile was to come on the Tuesday of the Tory conference. On the Monday the shadow chancellor, spurred on by shadow chief secretary, George Osborne, announced the abolition of inheritance tax for anyone with assets of less than £2 million. The papers loved it. But it was a day later that the Brown stuff hit the fan in No. 10. Up got shadow foreign secretary Andrew Mitchell to announce that a future Conservative government would hold a national referendum on Britain's membership of the European Union. 'We'll give the British people the chance to decide the nation's destiny', he declared. 'We can't put this off any longer, and the Conservative Party will abide by whatever decision the nation makes.' The roar which emanated from the conference hall was louder than anyone remembered – even from the days of the Leaderene herself.

'Master stroke' was the headline on the *Daily Mail* website. 'Davis takes huge gamble', said *The Guardian*. 'Everybody Out' trilled the *Daily Telegraph*. The fact that it was already a Liberal Democrat policy announced by Ming Campbell only two and a half weeks earlier had passed most people by.

Within hours, UKIP leader Nigel Farage announced the disbanding of his party. 'We've achieved our aim', he declared. 'I urge all our members and supporters to hold their noses and vote Conservative, and then vote No in the referendum.'

When the Tory leader heard the news he punched the air. 'Gotcha', he exclaimed to no one in particular. Did he mean Farage or Brown? No one really knew, and frankly, no one cared.

By the time David Davis stood up to make his leader's speech two opinion polls had been published, one showing a three-point swing to the Conservatives and another with a marginal Tory lead.

It became known as the Election That Never Was when Gordon Brown announced the following Saturday that he'd never planned to call an election anyway. The million leaflets being pulped in a south London incinerator told a different story, as Simon Walters reported in the next day's *Mail on Sunday*. 'FRIT & FRAZZLED' declared the front-page headline above a Photoshopped picture of the beleaguered Prime Minister being fed into the incinerator alongside his election leaflets.

~

It was not all plain sailing. One-time leadership contender David Cameron resigned from the shadow cabinet in June 2008 following the loss of a Commons vote over a government bill designed to permit the holding of terror suspects for 42 days without charge. He also resigned his seat, causing an unwelcome by-election in Witney. Davis was furious: Cameron had given him very little notice of his intention. He was so shocked by the young pretender's action that initially he found himself unable to speak. That soon passed, and a stream of vitriol was aimed at Cameron, in conversations with his advisers. 'If he wins his fucking by-election, I'm not having him back', ranted Davis. 'If he does it once, he could do it again.' He came under pressure to replace Cameron with his former rival Liam Fox, but that was never going to happen. Fox would have turned the party's home affairs policies back in an authoritarian direction. And in any case, Fox and Davis had never really got on since they had both served as junior Foreign Office ministers in the mid 1990s. Instead, Davis turned to his long-time ally Dominic Grieve. 'I should have appointed him to start with', he remarked to colleagues.

The next two years were punctuated by leadership election rumours – and for once, they had nothing to do with the Conservative Party. Even so, there were those in the Tory hierarchy who couldn't get used to the Davis leadership. 'I thought that Major chappie as a bit of a pleb but he had nothing on this Davis oik', one Tory peer was overheard saying at a party conference soiree. Davis laughed when he saw it in the Black Dog column of the *Mail on Sunday*. It was something he'd heard many times before during his rise through the Tory ranks, and it troubled him not a jot. Any chips on his shoulders had been despatched many moons ago.

Davis had one or two more surprises up his sleeve. One of his first acts as party leader had been to announce the end of the traditional party conference; the 2007 conference proved to be the last of its kind. In future two three-day events would be held – one a policy forum, where party members would have proper policy debates, and the other an unashamed American-style rally. The overwhelming feeling was one of relief that no longer would the party have to trek to Blackpool and experience rubber-sheeted beds.

Secondly, the candidate selection system was changed so that 50 per cent of candidates on the approved list were women.[6] Associations were still free to choose who they wanted, but the format of selection meetings was also radically changed. Gone were the set-piece speeches, in were filmed TV and radio-style interviews. And the final three candidates were forced to debate with each other, on the platform at the same time.

One thing the Tory leader had despised, both during his time as party chairman in 2001–02 and afterwards, was having to grease up to party donors. He knew he had little alternative, but the thought of listening to another lecture by Stuart Wheeler made him physically queasy. So he set up a secret group to consider the future funding of political parties, led by former party chairman Lord Parkinson. For once it didn't leak.

It had long been in Davis's mind that he should announce a formal commitment to reform party financing right at the start of the election campaign. He knew there would be flak from the trade unions and the Labour Party, but the electoral gains would be huge, especially after the cash-for-honours scandal and the sacking of Labour Party General Secretary Peter Watt over the loans affair. Indeed, Watt agreed to appear alongside Davis at the press conference in April 2010, at the beginning of the election campaign, at which he announced that, under a Tory government, from 2013 no individual company or donor would be allowed to donate more than £50,000 in any twelve-month period. There would be a five-year transitional period in which all parties with any national or European representation would gain an element of state funding, but that would disappear after 2018. There was a minor storm about the BNP being eligible for state funding, but that soon blew over. 'If we can't raise the money to survive, we don't deserve to survive', was the message Davis wanted to transmit. 'We've got to prove to people that we're worth supporting.' He said that a future Conservative administration would make donations of any sort to political parties tax-deductible. In effect, he was suggesting the transformation of political parties into charities.

And so the election campaign continued. It was dominated by the three TV debates between the party leaders. Although they all received high ratings, none of the three scored a knockout blow. Nick Clegg did surprisingly well in the first debate, but Davis was thought to have equalled him by concentrating on the TV audience rather than the audience in the hall. Both stared, gimlet-eyed, into the camera.

The only near-knockout blow to any of the leaders came in the last week, when Gordon Brown was caught on a microphone in Rochdale criticising a woman voter for her views on immigration. Rather like the 'Prescott punch' in 2001 it had the opposite effect to that which political commentators had imagined. Brown became a different politician during the last week of the campaign and gave the speeches of his life. Davis, meanwhile, concentrated on not dropping a bullock. Internal party polling looked good, but the result was on a knife edge. Campaign Director Lynton Crosby said it was the first election in many years that he couldn't call.

Davis spent polling day in his constituency. At 9 a.m. he and his wife Doreen were filmed casting their votes. He spent the rest of the morning in one of his outbuildings, climbing up the wall on his mountaineering equipment.

Reports started to come in of a much higher than expected turnout. What did it mean? Were people turning out to vote to eject Gordon Brown, or was it Labour voters who were turning out in unexpectedly large numbers to save him? Within hours the country would find out.

~

Author's note

I was David Davis's chief of staff from May to December 2005, so I have written this story from that perspective. Some of the events described above really did happen. Some I have adapted and others I have completely made up. If Davis had won, there were several initiatives which would have been implemented which I describe above (albeit perhaps in an exaggerated form) but much of what I write is clearly meant to be fictional.

Or is it?

Notes

1 This conversation took place between Iain Dale and Davis press officer David Hart.
2 In reality the confrontation was between Iain Dale and Tom Bradby.
3 Nick Boles played a leading part in spinning the Davis speech for Cameron.
4 This is a rewritten version of a concession speech Iain Dale had prepared for David Davis that day.
5 This conversation actually took place between Iain Dale and Francis Maude.
6 This had in fact been a Davis promise in the leadership campaign.

Chapter 15

What if Tony Blair had remained as Prime Minister?

Jane Griffiths

'They begged Tony to stay'

The three of them sat disconsolate in the empty room. It had been a long night. A chilly night, after a cool day – not like the blazing sunshine of 1997. Or that election in between that everyone almost forgot – 2001; foot and mouth, wasn't it, or fuel protests? Or something.

This was going to be a terrible election, they all said. Especially party members. The Labour Party was happier in opposition. The three of them knew it, most MPs and all party members outside the madder elements in the General Committees knew it. Opposition was where they were cheerfully headed. Tony had won it for them twice, but – Iraq! *The Guardian* diary! 'Blair stares into the abyss!' Tony had been pictured looking greyer, and older, and more sunken. Every *Guardian* headline pushed Tony's personal poll rating down with the middle classes – which meant the party members: teachers, local authority outreach workers, social workers. Even in the industrial towns of the North – Leeds, Halifax, Bradford – well, those places had universities too, and they certainly had councils, and that was where the party members worked. And they hated Tony. Hated him as much as they had ever hated Thatcher. Hated him more than Yasmin Alibhai-Brown did, which was going some. Was Yasmin a Labour Party member? They thought not.

Tonight, election night 2005, as the dawn broke, the result was clear. Labour had won again. The polls had always said the party would form another government, but their own intelligence said they would not, could not. Not after Iraq, not after George W and his 'Yo, Blair!' (didn't matter whether he had really said it or not, *The Guardian* had said he had, so it must be true. Was as good as true for party members and for most other people too.) As the media got newer, and there was more than email – there were starting to be blogs, and MPs had websites, even some constituency parties had them these days – people had got more trusting, not less. The General Secretary could remember his grandfather, a railwayman who had been an NUR steward and who had voted Labour when you still had to keep quiet about it in front of the vicar, and *he* had never believed anything he read in his paper (the *Mirror* and before that the *Daily Sketch*) as a matter of principle. But people now, they believed it all. People came up to you in the street and said things like: 'Tony's in trouble again!', because they had read it in *The Guardian*, or in the 'Londoner's Diary' in the *Standard*, or even, some of them, in the words of somebody like Kevin Maguire in the *Mirror*, having a cheap go at some defenceless back-bencher who'd got drunk on the Terrace or been rude to someone who wasn't a constituent and was wasting their time. The people never questioned anything these days. So that was it. Tony was going. Except – where was everybody?

The three of them, the General Secretary, his devoted hench-creature with the big calves and flat shoes, and Loyal John, were on their own. People were waiting for Tony to come down to London, for the helicopters to fill the sky above Downing Street again. But they were hearing some worrying stories: media shutdown; nothing to see here; move along now. And yet they had won. True, some seats had gone, though not many, even in the soft south; Reading East, after they deselected that woman with the red hair, but the Reading party were a bunch of thugs, everyone knew that. But in Harlow, in Crawley, in the working towns of the South, Labour had held on to its MPs, and so to the government.

But Tony had to go. The party and the people would never stand for him staying any longer, not after Iraq. The General Secretary remembered that when he went to see his aunties in Southsea just before the invasion of Iraq, they had had their dining table littered with newspapers. 'We like to get the full picture, dear', Auntie Jean had said. Screaming headlines, millions marching waving Saddam Hussein's colours (what was all that about? Made no sense. Marching, yes, Labour's internationalism had pretty much gone out with Michael Foot – but Saddam Hussein? There was no accounting, really there wasn't ...) 'I think Tony will be all right, don't you dear?', said Auntie Sandra. And perhaps it was his aunties he should have believed, not *The Guardian* readers. Because his aunties read the papers, they even believed a lot of what they read, but they still knew what people said and what they thought, and they thought Tony would be all right. And so he was.

But Tony had told the General Secretary privately that he had had enough. There was more he wanted to do, he had said, a lot more. So much of the first term had been wasted, with the wrong ministers, the wrong people talking in his ear, and now there was so much to do with the economy. We had given people money; tax allowances; real money for working people. And were they grateful? They were not. And we had thrown money at the NHS. But that was what people expected Labour governments to do, so they weren't grateful for that either. And anyway, the hospitals were dirty.

It was dealing with the legacy of Thatcher's destruction of the mining and most of the old industrial communities, which had left millions on benefits, sometimes for three generations, with all that that did to communities – teenage pregnancies, drugs – that was the big task for a new term in government, Tony had said, but he shook his head, too, and said he couldn't stand any more of the constant undermining and briefing. Was it just Gordon, the General Secretary wondered privately after this conversation? Gordon had his people around him, they all did, but they melted away when the going got tough. Where were all Alan Milburn's chums now? Loyal John had asked the General Secretary after that meeting if Tony really knew what the PLP thought of him and his leadership. Neither man knew the answer. Tony wasn't that much of a parliamentarian, but he did talk to people. Sometimes he even talked to some of the babes, usually the mousier ones who never made the headlines; he avoided the brassier Patsy and Edina types, who did.

Stories would be out, before the sun was up. They didn't have Sky in here, this was an old building and HQ still operated in an old-fashioned way, but there was breaking news. 'Gordon Brown Fails to Appear at Own Election Count. Were Medics Called to Brown's Constituency Home?' The General Secretary didn't know what had happened. The media-grid people would know, though, and they would be getting ready to brief their chosen journos. What did Tony know? What had he been told? What would he do? Tony was expected to make an announcement about his own future on Monday morning, this had been briefed in advance, and the media were quite frankly more interested in that than in who was going to be Minister of Defence Procurement in the new government.

Gordon was, variously, reported as under sedation at home suffering from severe stress, not appearing in public because of a bad cold, and in hospital suffering from exhaustion – if you got hospitalised for exhaustion the hospitals would be full of us after every election, thought political activists up and down the land that weekend – and it later emerged that an ambulance had been called by Gordon's wife Sarah, who was worried about the stress Gordon was under and about his behaviour.

On Friday night Tony called his trusted people together. Peter, of course, was there already when the little group arrived, but said nothing, standing aloof by the mantelpiece and occasionally jotting something down in a little notebook. Tony told them nothing new. He had had enough, he said. He had plans; he was moving on; the Middle East; a faith foundation (a harrumph at this from Alastair). At last, Tony said with a broad smile, we do do God. He would cheerfully announce an approximate departure date at the PLP meeting on Monday.

But – where was Gordon? Denis MacShane, recovering in Rotherham from a tough campaign despite his safe seat – those Lib Dems could be nasty customers – had an idea. Yes, he found out from an old comrade who knew people that Gordon was a patient in a remote, very private establishment.

He had, possibly, been sectioned. Not at all shocked by this, Denis knew straight away what he must do. He called Tony. A bemused Prime Minister, who had already been to see the Queen, came on the line. 'Come late to the PLP, Tony', said Denis. Some of us need to talk without you first.

'You always do that anyway, don't you?', said Tony with a characteristic smile.

'They're saying Gordon has had a health crisis – but whatever he has had he's not here', said Denis. 'He won't be in London. You will. Come late, though. Please, Tony.'

At the PLP that Monday evening, with the massed ranks of the lobby's finest peopling the committee corridor outside the room, Denis MacShane made what was probably the speech of his life. And in English, too! (Most of his speeches in recent years seemed to have been made in one of the several European languages he spoke, and to impress nobody.) 'We were wrong', he says. 'Our General Committees were wrong.'

'They always are', came several voices from around the room.

'Tony is a winner', said Denis. 'He won it for us. Thirty or forty of us here in this room thought we wouldn't be here tonight, but we are, because of Tony. You know it, I know it, some of us didn't want to admit it even to ourselves, but it's Tony they want. Iraq, neither here nor there on the doorstep. Poodle of the Americans, did you hear *that* on the doorstep? Nor me.'

Up spoke the Blairites in support – but then up spoke Jeremy Corbyn, and up spoke John McDonnell. We on the left, they said, must listen to the people. The people have spoken. If the people had thought what party members said they thought, most of us wouldn't be here today. We are, and we live to campaign another day. Comrades, we have spent too much of our history in opposition – to campaign for what we know we must do, we have to be in government. Tony has said he wants to leave us. No. He must not be allowed to leave us.

Then a pause. All eyes turn to the grizzled Beast of Bolsover, Dennis Skinner, in his usual position near the door, leaning on the wooden barrier. Dennis growls, 'Get him to stay.'

And they do. They beg. They cajole. They plead. They do all but threaten to kidnap Tony or his children. Tony is reluctant – he even blushes. But the certain knowledge that he will not have Gordon breathing down his neck – not now, not soon, probably not ever – puts a quiet gleam in his eye. Caroline Flint in the Treasury team, he catches himself thinking, let's get a good-looking team in every sense of the word, and what are we supposed to do? Gordon has been telling me for ages about the economic cycle, and that booms don't go on for ever, and there could even be a financial crisis coming, and he might be right, what would I know – but he wouldn't let me pull in spending, and when I tried to he briefed against me. And now he's gone. We hope. I can put the Middle East on hold for now, Israel-Palestine is not exactly going to go away in the next few years, is it? It's not like there are going to be uprisings in Syria or anywhere of *that* sort any time soon, is it? And God – well, forgive me, Lord, of course I can't put You on hold, it doesn't work like that, and I can't go into Your proper church, the one in Rome, if I'm going to be Prime Minister for a while longer, but I can go along with Cherie sometimes, and the children are being brought up in it, and – oh well, Lord, I knew You'd understand that I am doing Your work all the time anyway; You do understand that, don't You? Knew You would. OK, glad that's sorted out.

Tony came to himself suddenly. People were still speaking. Back-benchers he didn't recognise. That woman with the frizzy hair at the back, had she just been elected? No, he thought he remembered some rather tedious intervention from her at some point, and having to say something nice about her constituency in PMQs a few weeks before the election was called. Better pay attention, he told himself. This meeting is going to be so briefed, so I had better know what really got said before the newspapers start deciding what they said and what I said.

Oh well, thought Tony, still musing despite himself, I was going to tell them at party conference I was leaving, but I don't think I can do that now – too much work to be getting on with, it'll take a bit longer. But I won't stay until the next election, I'm not getting any younger, and I'm missing Leo's growing up. But the things I've got in mind, that Gordon would never let me do, I can get most of them done in a year, two at the most. Yes. Oh yes.

Cherie was aghast. 'All our plans!', she wailed. 'Now we have to carry on living in that poxy hole in Downing Street!' She wouldn't miss Gordon, though, she less than anyone. She loathed him with a passion that Tony sometimes found a little terrifying, She had never understood their partnership and how they had worked over the years, those Tory years, for a Labour government. Something about Gordon didn't smell right, she had said. And yet, Tony thought, women liked Gordon. He had had some top girlfriends before Sarah came along, better lookers than he, Tony, could … Stop it. Stop it now. And women said, even Anji had once said, Tony remembered, that what they found attractive about Gordon was his smell. He didn't use a special cologne or anything, he just smelled good. Well, apparently he was somewhere pumped full of sedatives now and probably didn't smell so good any more; nothing attractive about smelling of hospitals. Tony had thought at times that Cherie would actually have killed Gordon if she had thought she could get away with it. She had said once that all Gordon's crap over the years had made her understand how people could do murder – just to make that person not be there any more. For ever. Tony was, just a little bit, frightened of Cherie himself.

So, the PLP wanted Tony to stay. In fact they had begged him to. He had never exactly even said he was going, and certainly not when, in any public way, but people had expected it. And it seemed that begging Tony to stay was all Denis MacShane's idea. Finger on the pulse for the first and probably the only time in his political life, Tony thought, spitefully.

Tony's departure somehow went off the boil as a story. The media just stopped asking about it. He had never *really* said he was actually going, or that he had changed his mind. No, Gordon's health was the story. Cue endless think-pieces about what politics did to the brain and the emotions and the mental health. But neither Tony's people nor Gordon's had much of an interest in briefing about Gordon either. It wouldn't help any of their agendas; and certainly wouldn't help the government. Gordon's people in Parliament had their own careers to think about – and there weren't that many of them anyway. And there was all the business of government to be thinking about. Of course the 'Stop the War' crowd still hated Tony; but they always had and always would, and, Tony thought, they weren't interested in stopping any wars at all. In fact they were totally in favour of wars, especially in Iraq, they just wanted the other side to win. They were the warmongers, against Bush'n'Blair.

Better stop wool-gathering, thought Tony, and get out there and face them. Well, there was nothing to face, really.

That night Tony and Cherie talked, side by side in the dark bedroom that was never really dark, because Downing Street never went dark, about the future. Not the immediate future – a third term won, and Tony didn't even have to decide now whether he would serve the whole of it or go earlier – but Tony's own future. Bestriding the world; England was too small for him now. By morning Tony was renewed. He understood it all now. Since the late 1970s he had been trying to impose himself on the world. When he decided he wanted to become an MP there was no clear path for him – no Labour tradition in the family, no relatives who were MPs, no one really properly in politics at all. No, he had had to push, and wheedle, and persuade, and talk to people he didn't like at all, and eventually he had got in, but none of it had been easy. Nothing had ever been easy for Tony, because, it had always seemed to him, he was trying to follow a path which was not the one his background, and his parents, and his early life, had set him on. But he had done it. He had pushed in, and he had got to be Prime Minister.

The Labour Party didn't like him much. They liked John Prescott, and they liked Gordon too, and they *loved* Dennis Skinner. Dennis, and the dwindling band of northern ex-miners in Parliament, and the overweight, drinking, brawling Scots who had a 'wee lassie that works the computer' in their constituency offices, were an exotic breed to the average party member. Most Labour members were more at home with people just like themselves – just like people were everywhere, really – and that meant people a lot more like Tony, with his nice background and his nice soft voice, and yet it was those same party members up and down the land who hissed the word Blair (oh yes, Tony knew they did, whatever the people around him tried to hide from him) with the most profound loathing. When Tony had been to constituency parties in the 1990s after he had become leader, the look on their faces, especially the women's faces, reminded him of his mother's look when he was a child and had watched her emptying the vacuum cleaner bag.

But now Tony understood it, or so it seemed to him on that rather clammy grey day early in the summer of 2005. Something had happened when Gordon went crazy: the scales had fallen from the eyes of the PLP. And now it seemed, because he had been begged, pleaded with, to stay, by Labour MP after Labour MP – he almost expected one of the more sycophantic ones to say: 'Only you can save us, Tony, lead us out of this wilderness and into the promised land' – there was nothing to push for any more. He had come home. He belonged. All his life so far he had had to make powerful friends (Derry) and influential ones (Peter) because none of the places he wanted to be had really wanted to let him in. He knew, like David Owen before him, that he would have been better accepted, and better liked, if he had been a Tory. But somehow he was not a Tory, although his family and background had set Tony on that path. He had followed a different path, and now they wanted him, the country accepted him. The back-benchers' pleadings, orchestrated at first by Denis MacShane – who then didn't need to any more as they were enthusiastically doing it for themselves – had made him something he had never thought himself to be before: powerful.

'How ridiculous', Cherie had said to him in bed that night. 'Of course you're powerful. You are one of the most powerful men in the world. Politics is about power. However people dress it up, that is what it is about. So you of all people should understand where power is. And it is in *you*.' But Tony had never understood that, never really felt it before. Even though he had got a safe seat in Parliament, when better connected men than he had tried to get a seat for twenty years and given up disgruntled; even though he had not been long on the back benches; even though he had not toiled in a succession of junior front-bench and ministerial jobs that no one was interested in, surrounded by civil servants who despised him, until the inevitable dismissal by the Prime Minister or Leader of the Opposition of the day, as he had seen others do, ending their careers in bitterness and drink. No, he, Tony Blair, had held only one office, that of Prime Minister. He had had the ear of the President of the United States – and at any given time, how many could say that? Because he had been *asked* to stay on – after ten years of Gordon, especially, but not only Gordon, trying to push him into the outer darkness – suddenly he could see his way clear, and his life entire. He had a mission, a road to travel, a world to save. In the mean time he had a country to run, and a Europe to influence, and a US President to hobnob with in the interest of democracy, human rights and the rule of law. Oh, and a constituency to represent. But he had been doing that for years already.

Not many people remembered Tony's speech in Chicago in 1999 on humanitarian interventionism; in the UK hardly anyone had noticed it. But that speech, in which he had set out the case for intervention wherever in the world populations were being oppressed, tormented and killed by leaders who denied them the basic freedoms taken for granted in North America and much of Europe, though not in many other places, had been hugely influential, producing a generation of what were called in America liberal hawks (some called them neocons, but that wasn't quite the same thing) – or at least the speech had contributed to that generation's gesta-tion. Cherie had been furious with him for making it – but then she didn't agree with any of it, anyway. Old-fashioned, Cherie was, probably still a unilateralist who didn't understand that Ronald Reagan had been a great reforming, anti-nuclear president who had kept most of the world at peace for a decade or more. Cherie was more worried about what *The Guardian* would say. Well, what price *The Guardian*, now, thought Tony in fierce triumph. Anyway, he never asked Cherie what she thought about any of those things. He was afraid of what she might say.

So, out into the world. The economic cycle; yes, Gordon had warned him about that. But Gordon is no more, and the Tories cannot convince and cannot form a government – they will probably need two more elections to get anywhere near it, and only then if they reform, he thought. But in the mean time, Tony might nationalise a bank or two, not to keep the lefties happy but to keep the British people's mortgages safe, and as an example to the others. Then he had a brilliant idea: the French socialist Dominique Strauss-Kahn must go to the IMF. That would suit everyone. Chirac couldn't stand the bloke, but he and Tony got on terrifically well, in French of course (Tony was proud of his fluency in that language, which very few British politicians, and still fewer Prime Ministers, had ever had). Brilliant. Someone at the heart of the world's money who was One of Us and who might be President of France one day. Yes, Dom was the man. What next?

The economic cycle dipped all right. They always do, like earthquakes and tsunamis, just a bit more predictable. But then it started to get uglier. There were rumours that sent the markets wobbling, talk of bankruptcy protection at the very top of America; it could be the start of a full-blown crisis. Some of the more swivel-eyed market commentators started to talk about runs on banks. The thing with crises is to get at them before they've picked up speed, before the tipping point is reached and firms start laying off workers and people start not being able to pay their mortgages – Tony had learned all that from Gordon. Gordon had wanted full employment. He had said that was the only guarantee against recession. Tony supposed he was right, so that was what his government wanted too – and everyone was in favour of full employment, even the bosses, who don't usually like having to up wages when there are plenty of jobs. Even *The Guardian*. It didn't work quite so much like that any more, now that the workforce was more mobile than it had been in the post-war years; so, a dip but not a crash. Everyone happy – well, nearly. In world terms most of the victims were American blue-collar workers, and nobody had ever cared much about them, not since FDR, anyway.

It couldn't last. The clear direction, the sense of belonging, the sunny confidence about his place in the world, those Tony would keep. When they begged him to stay he had found all those at last, and he would not be letting go of them. But inevitably people, meaning the media, began to wonder What Tony Would Do Next. And of course there were those who had themselves in mind for a future leadership role. Alan Milburn, anyone? No, perhaps not. All leaders stay too long – well, nearly all, Tony said to Alastair one day. Harold Wilson didn't; and Harold won us four elections, which I haven't done yet. Alastair looked uncomfortable. The next day Peter asked for a conversation – about the Middle East. So Tony began to take an interest in it. He hadn't, much, before. He had thought of himself at first as the Prime Minister for Africa. But that hadn't really worked, despite the Sierra Leone success. No, the Middle East it must be. Tony began going there, more than he had ever done before. He read the Koran. He started learning Arabic.

A third-term Labour Prime Minister. The country hadn't had one of those before, not continuously anyway. The manner of Harold Wilson's passing gnawed at Tony. He knew better than to mention Harold's name to any of his own advisers, but Harold had quit while he was ahead, even though it was possible that he had known his mind was going – it didn't really matter, he hadn't stayed around to let people see he was not the Prime Minister, or the man, he had been. And Tony was still young, still good-looking – the grey hairs Iraq had given him were not a disfigure-ment, no one thought so, after all – and not in the same place Harold had been in at all. So, a mission – but first, fend off the doubters. They were mostly in the media, but there were plenty in the constituency parties too, and some of the back-benchers in the more marginal seats were starting to listen to those voices at their General Committees. Deselection was always a risk – once parties started on that they got a kind of taste for it, like sharks scenting blood. The wiser heads could understand that when you start with that, you've got opposition as your future – though of course, opposition is where most of the Labour Party feels most comfortable. That was why the party had never been Tony's spiritual home; he needed government, he needed power, he needed influence, he needed a place on the world stage. And if Tony needed those things, so did Britain, and so did the Labour Party. Obvious, really.

Tony would go. He didn't think they would beg him to stay again, but they didn't need to. They had done it once, and they had been doing the

Lord's work without knowing it. But before he made his announcement he had something to do. Something which would assure him of the place in history he already knew he had, but perhaps not all the world realised it. I'll go, he told those closest to him, on my terms: not pushed out like Thatcher was, not booted out by the electorate – well, let's not think about that one. No, I'll go and I'll tell them when. But first there is Something I Must Do. For the Good of Humanity. Tyranny must be opposed wherever it is to be found.

'What are you going to do, Tony?' asked Denis MacShane, awed.

'Well, y'know, people', said Tony quietly, 'I am the man for the Middle East; and democracy, human rights and the rule of law for those suffering under tyranny will be my goal when I leave this place. But there are some things you have to be in government to do. And toppling tyranny can be one of them. The places I'm thinking aren't even necessarily geographically in the Middle East, but you know what I mean. I'm talking to the chiefs of staff straight after this. Then a war cabinet at Chequers at the weekend. Then, when it's done, I'll be off.'

A hubbub of voices.

'Oh, didn't I say?' said Tony over his shoulder as he strode towards the door. '9/11, 7/7, they're all getting ideas, and their own people don't like it. Libya – Gaddafi was only pretending; Iran, yes; Pakistan even if we need to. We're going in.'

On a dry hillside a shepherd looks up as a sudden wind causes his skinny sheep to bunch together and sand to eddy over the parched grass.

Jets scream overhead.

Chapter 16

What if Gordon Brown had called an election in 2007?

Philip Cowley

Gordon Brown stood on the doorstep of No. 10 and smiled. It was a curious, some said disturbing, smile – rather like a stroke victim attempting to chew gum – and it was seen only rarely. But today he had good reason to grin broadly. Labour's victory in the 2007 general election, which he had called less than six months after becoming Prime Minister, had seen him comfortably back into No. 10. The government's new majority was not huge, but it was manageable, and easily sufficient to last a full four- or five-year term.

For his party, it was a remarkable achievement. Prior to 1997, the Labour Party had never even managed two full consecutive terms of office. It had now won four elections on the trot, and by the next election it would have been in power for at least fourteen years without a break. But the smile was also evidence of the personal achievement that the election victory represented. Brown had become Labour leader in 2007 despite widespread doubts about his electoral appeal. His many critics had also claimed that he was too indecisive to risk everything on an immediate snap election – having waited so long to achieve the position, why would he risk being the shortest-lived Prime Minister since George Canning? – but instead he had seen his chance, gambled, and emerged triumphant.

For two other individuals, though, the 2007 election represented the end of the road. Defeat left the Conservatives, once the natural party of government in Britain, in disarray. Their third consecutive defeat in

2005 had prompted them to take a gamble on the young, and inexperienced, David Cameron. Elected leader in a blaze of optimism, he had attempted an ambitious rebranding exercise in an attempt to detoxify the Conservative 'brand', to make voting Conservative widely acceptable again. At first it had seemed to work and the dog days of the Blair administration had seen the Cameron-led Conservatives move ahead in the polls, but Blair's departure from No. 10 had shifted the ground, producing a visible 'Brown bounce' in the polls, from which the Conservatives never recovered. Cameron had believed he needed a full term in opposition to make the Conservative party electable again, and over the weeks following the 2007 defeat he would attempt to argue that failure merely proved his point – but the argument didn't wash. The lack of any significant electoral progress meant that he joined William Hague, Iain Duncan Smith, and Michael Howard on the list of Conservative would-be Prime Ministers who had tried to displace New Labour only to fail, and the Conservative Party soon descended into vicious infighting over its future direction.

The Liberal Democrats were felt by many to have fought a good campaign, and despite a fall in their share of the popular vote, the popularity of their MPs in their constituencies meant that they held most of their seats. Their leader, Sir Menzies ('Ming') Campbell, had fought a competent if uninspiring campaign, but he had been subject to relentless mockery as a result of his age since he had become leader in 2006. In historic terms, there was nothing unusual about Ming Campbell's age but the cult of youth in modern British party politics is strong, and although the mockery had diminished somewhat during the campaign, it had not gone away. Campbell now reasoned that he would be over seventy by the time of the next election, and questions about his advancing years would continue to dog him and his party. He asked himself whether there was anything he could do about it, came to the conclusion there wasn't, and stepped down from the leadership of the party a few days after the election.

But the morning after the election, on a cold crisp November day, that was still to come. Smiling for the cameras once again, Gordon Brown gave a brief speech – in which he used the word 'mandate' on ten occasions – before entering No. 10.

~

Even before he became Prime Minister in June 2007, those around Gordon Brown – the so-called 'Brownites' – had been considering the possibility of an early general election. But by 'early' they had meant sometime in mid-2008, giving the new Prime Minister a year or so in office and enough time for him to establish himself with the electorate.

Yet once in No. 10, events moved quicker than they had anticipated. The Prime Minister found himself lavishly praised over the handling of three relatively low-level crises in quick succession: acts of terrorism which marked his first days in Downing Street (in which the only person to die had been one of the perpetrators), widespread flooding which hit England and Wales in late July, and an outbreak of foot and mouth disease in August. The Prime Minister and his team appeared to handle these events well, for which they received (exaggerated) praise from across the political spectrum. 'Brown could be a great Prime Minister', claimed Peter Oborne in the *Daily Mail*.

The opinion polls saw Labour move steadily into the lead, and talk of an early election began in earnest, encouraged by some of Brown's aides on the grounds that it might destabilise the Conservatives, or would be an opportunity to close the Blair era, giving Brown his own mandate and emphasising him as 'the change' voters were said to want. In July, the Ealing Southall by-election saw the Conservative candidate come a poor third. Conservative MPs sceptical about the Cameron project, but who had been willing to keep quiet while it produced electoral dividends, began to use the ironic acronym: PODWAS: Poor Old Dave, What A Shame.

At a meeting at Chequers in late July, ministers heard an upbeat polling presentation. Labour, they were told, had an 8 per cent lead over the Conservatives, with Brown outscoring Cameron on most of the leadership attribute questions. A few ministers expressed support for an early election; Jacqui Smith, the new Home Secretary (who held a marginal seat and feared the impact of the money the Conservatives were putting into targeting seats like hers) was the most vocal. But there was no concerted push by ministers for an early poll, and nothing was decided.

Opinion was divided within the party about whether or not to go to the country in the autumn – there were plenty of Labour MPs with doubts about the wisdom of canvassing on cold dark nights in late October or November – and Brown himself remained unsure. Those critics who thought the Prime Minister too indecisive to call a snap election had not entirely misjudged the man. Brown remained doubtful about the idea, aware that to dissolve Parliament and then lose would almost certainly be fatal to his premiership. He was sitting on a majority of over 60, with up to three years left in the Parliament; why risk throwing that away? But those around him continued to apply pressure. Three individuals in particular worked away at the Prime Minister, trying to persuade him that his best chance of winning an election – indeed, probably his only chance of winning convincingly – was a short, sharp, snap campaign.

Spencer Livermore, the Prime Minister's strategy adviser, thought the idea of an early election had been ruled out too hurriedly at the Chequers meeting, and so on his return from holiday in late August he wrote a four-page memo to the Prime Minister, making the case for an early general election. Livermore pointed to the upturn in the polls (which he argued might not last), as well as the prospects for a worsening economy; he suggested that autumn 2007 looked like the best opportunity. Brown, who was still thinking of mid-2008, was taken aback by the memo, but rather than think through its consequences, he put it aside, unattended for almost three weeks while he dealt with other matters.

The party's General Secretary, Peter Watt, was also in favour. In late August 2007 he visited the Prime Minister at No. 10 in and spoke frankly about the party's weak financial position compared with the Conservatives, one that would worsen month by month if an autumn election was not held. An early election was therefore the cheaper option, because it would avoid tying up people and funds for several years and minimise the opportunity for the Conservatives to make use of their funding for key seats.

And third, there was Douglas Alexander, Labour's campaign coordinator as well as Secretary of State for International Development. He had already conducted an audit of the party machine at Victoria Street. He also noted the poor state of the party's finances, but on the positive side the party's voter database was working well. He was convinced that the party's superiority over the Conservatives in this respect meant that they could use their contact data scheme to send direct mail to over three million target households at least four times in a short, blitzkrieg-like, three-week election. The Labour campaign would be funded almost entirely at a national level, with nationally generated direct mail and very little ground war, meaning that the lack of party activists and the poor state of organisation in many constituency parties would be less of a problem. Alexander went on holiday in August to New York, where he arranged a shortlist of advertising agencies for the party to interview on his return.

One of the things that the events of late 2007 proved is that there is no such thing any more as a 'snap', unexpected, election. Preparations are too extensive, and too obvious, to conceal. Despite no decision having been taken, the Labour Party apparatus began to prepare itself for a 2007 contest just in case. Labour set up a media centre in Victoria Street, booked poster sites and prepared personalised letters to key voters in marginal constituencies. Promises of finance were agreed. Ed Miliband and members of the Policy Unit began to draft a manifesto, drawing largely on Brown's leadership acceptance speech. Preparations were made for a leader's tour, and a 'war book' was drafted.

Yet still there was no decision. In his note to the Prime Minister in August, Spencer Livermore had explicitly warned that, whatever was decided, it was important that a decision was taken before Labour went to its party conference. But with no decision taken, the debate entered the pressure cooker of the conference season.

~

Labour Party delegates were in buoyant mood as they gathered in Bournemouth for their annual party conference in late September. Despite a spat over the text of Gordon Brown's speech on 25 September – after *The Times* discovered that it contained many stock phrases from the repertoire of Brown's adviser Bob Shrum, a discovery that caused a blazing row between Shrum and the Prime Minister – the polls after Brown's speech still appeared very positive. A YouGov poll on 26 September showed an 11 per cent Labour lead; an Ipsos-MORI poll four days later revealed an even larger 13 per cent lead.

Behind the scenes, Labour's private polling was not quite so positive. The veteran pollster Stan Greenberg gave a presentation to the Prime Minister the day after his speech in which, contrary to the 100-plus seat majority some public opinion polls indicated, Greenberg cautiously indicated a majority of between 35 and 45. Brown was visibly disappointed. Defending a 60+ majority, he had been looking to improve on it. He called on Greenberg to do further work, as if this extra effort would somehow produce a more favourable result. Yet while these discussions were going on in private, in public almost all the talk continued to be of a forthcoming election, not least as a result of heavy briefing behind the scenes by some of Brown's closest aides and ministers throughout the conference. In the bars, delegates and journalists talked of almost nothing else, and most left the conference convinced the election was coming.

One of the aims of talking up an early election had been to destabilise the Conservatives. With their poll lead gone, Brown's team hoped that the Conservative conference would be full of panicky Tories, scared that the party faced its fourth consecutive defeat. It had precisely the opposite reaction, rallying the party behind the leader, and producing a far more cohesive Conservative conference than would otherwise have occurred. The Conservative Shadow Chancellor and election coordinator, George Osborne, was one of those who thought the Prime Minister was an over-cautious politician, and believed until almost the very end that Brown would not call an election. But in July, as the rumours had increased, the Conservative leadership had moved their offices from the Commons to Conservative Campaign Headquarters at Millbank. Oliver Letwin oversaw the hasty development of a number of policies, adding to the early Cameron stress on personal responsibility and policies addressing traditional Tory themes of opportunity and security.

On 2 October, the first day of the Conservative conference in Blackpool, Gordon Brown paid his first visit as Prime Minister to Iraq, where he promised that British forces would be cut by 1,000 by the end of 2007. He had been warned by aides that the trip would look opportunistic – and his aides were right. Many commentators accused Brown of playing cynical pre-election politics, a charge reinforced when it emerged that the 1,000 figure included 500 troops whose withdrawal had already been announced in July.

And in Blackpool Cameron appeared to call the Prime Minister's bluff, claiming that the Conservatives were ready, willing and able to fight an early election. The conference mood was also lifted by George Osborne's pledge that a Conservative government would increase to £1 million the threshold above which households would be liable to inheritance tax, and the abolition of stamp duty for first-time buyers of homes up to £250,000, all to be financed by a levy on 'non-doms'. The former proposal effectively ended inheritance tax for most middle-class families. Although Labour criticised the concession as a tax break for the rich, it had been exhaustively tested in focus groups for the Conservatives (as it had for Labour) and proved to be very popular, even among the less well-off. It gained positive media coverage and set the agenda for the rest of the week. On Wednesday 3 October, David Cameron gave a polished, notes-free speech, at the end of which he laid down the gauntlet to the Prime Minister: 'So, Mr Brown, what's it going to be?' That evening, many Conservative election staff left the conference early, to return to party headquarters, convinced that Brown had left it too late to call off an election.

Labour campaign strategists and special advisers were called to what turned out to be the decisive meeting at Downing Street on the morning of Friday 5 October. Before them were the results of Stan Greenberg's second marginal seats poll. The meeting was already tense because of the positive reactions to Osborne's speech and rumours that early returns from public opinion polls were showing a Conservative recovery. Greenberg's latest poll showed a 1 per cent Labour lead and a likely Labour majority of twenty seats. But it could, he stressed, be lower still.

Everyone was nervous as Brown entered the room. When the Prime Minister was presented with the numbers he gave no visible reaction, but stood, silently thinking through his options. Everyone else in the room stared at him; one of them described it as 'like watching one of those chess computers going through the million possible moves'. Yet Brown was later to say that he very quickly realised how few options were now left to him. Calling the election was risky, and far more risky than he would have liked, but the effect of not calling the election would be disastrous. He realised how much damage it would do not only to Labour's standing, but also to his own reputation. He tried to think of how best to justify not having an election, how he could avoid looking indecisive and cowardly, how he could avoid appearing to be the worst sort of calculating machine politician, but the best he could come up with were lame explanations that, he quickly concluded, would make him a laughing stock. He had, he realised, backed himself in a corner. There was only one choice left.

'Let's do it', he said, before turning and walking out of the room.

~

Most of that happened, more or less.[1] The first five paragraphs are entirely made up (of course), but almost everything else took place just like that – until the very end. In reality, having allowed speculation about the election to get out of hand, Gordon Brown then baulked at the final hurdle. Presented with the results of Greenberg's second marginal seat poll, he 'dissolved into himself completely' (as one of those present put it). Instead of saying 'Let's do it' before he turned and walked out of the room, his words were something like 'We can't do it' (although accounts differ on the exact phrasing).

No election in post-war history has come so close to being called, only then not to happen. The events of 2007 are sometimes compared to James Callaghan's decision not to call an election in 1978, another of the great what ifs of modern British politics. But the debacle of 2007 was much worse, for two reasons. First, because preparations in 2010 were significantly more advanced than they were in 1978. Brown allowed the extended preparations and the intense scrutiny of public and private polls, printing of election material and preparation of a war book and a manifesto. Labour spent over £1 million preparing for the election-that-wasn't, money the party simply did not have to spare. They had even scheduled their 'Clause V meeting', to sign off the manifesto, as well as a manifesto launch. His advisers, with his connivance, had ramped up expectations of an election to such a degree that the decision to call it off was always going to be seen as a humiliating climbdown.

And second, because although he had fluffed the timing of the election in 1978, Callaghan had at least fought and won a proper leadership contest to become Prime Minister. Brown appeared uniquely weak among modern Prime Ministers because he had neither a mandate from his party, following his 'coronation' in June 2007, nor from the country. When he took over as PM in June 2007 relatively few had commented on the lack of a leadership contest, but after the non-election his unelected status became a running sore for him in focus groups.

Certain political events are sometimes seen as turning points, decisively shaping a party's prospects for the coming general election; examples include the winter of discontent in 1978 and its impact on Labour's fortunes in the 1979 general election, and Britain's withdrawal from the Exchange Rate Mechanism in September 1992 and its effect on Conservative standing for the rest of the Parliament. For most observers, Gordon Brown's 'cancelling' of the planned 2007 election comfortably falls into that category.

It was certainly a crucial moment in the 2005 Parliament, and one which revealed much about the new Prime Minister and his political operation. All modern-day Prime Ministers face constant media speculation about the timing of a so-called 'snap' election. But Brown could have killed it off, or at least dampened it down at any time. Not doing so was deeply damaging, both to him and to his party. Brown's standing was fatally damaged. Labour was never again able to sell him as a 'father of the nation' figure. Instead it faced growing accusations that he was a calculating yet indecisive politician. As one of Brown's closest aides put it shortly afterwards: 'We've handed strength and competence away. We've not just lost it, we've given it away.' Few politicians have trashed their own brand in such a comprehensive way. Asked why things had gone so wrong, one Brown aide later answered bluntly: 'Irresponsibility, inexperience, over-exuberance, immaturity.' He added: 'Not every person who is responsible is guilty of all four.'

Having funked it in 2007, Gordon Brown was then forced also to publicly rule out 2008 as well. A Parliament he had planned would only last three years went on to run the full five. Labour would almost never again lead in an opinion poll, and things would never look as electorally promising for the Labour Party as they did on that Friday morning. Given what eventually happened at the 2010 election – with Labour slumping to their second-worst defeat since 1918 – even the 20-seat majority predicted by Stan Greenberg's opinion polling looks like a wasted opportunity. A conventional wisdom has already grown up around the idea that not calling the election in 2007 was one of Gordon Brown's biggest mistakes, and that had he done so, he would – as in the scenario that began this chapter – have stood on the door of No. 10 victorious, grinning that dreadful smile of his.

Yet no Labour victory, even with a small majority, can be assumed in 2007. For one thing, while Labour's own internal polling was pointing to a small Labour majority, the Conservative private polling was pointing to a hung parliament. Indeed, one private Conservative poll of 120 target seats, distributed only to a very small group at the highest levels of the party leadership just before the election was abandoned, was predicting the Conservatives to gain almost 90 seats (around 70 from Labour, 20 from the Liberal Democrats). This was not sufficient for a Conservative victory but it would have made the Conservatives the largest single party, and produced a result very similar to that which would eventually result in Labour losing office in 2010. If that poll was accurate, then Brown's decision not to call the election may not be as misguided as conventional wisdom holds. The only saving grace for Brown would have been that in any coalition negotiations he would have been dealing with his long-standing friend Ming Campbell, who would have been more amenable to any deal with Labour than Nick Clegg was to turn out to be in 2010; but it would still have been very difficult for a Prime Minister who had thrown away a majority of more than 60 on an entirely needless election to remain in power, whoever he was negotiating with.

Even if we assume that the Conservatives' polling was wrong, and that Labour's polls were the more accurate, given the speed at which the polls were changing, and the volatility in the electorate, who knew what change a three-week campaign could produce? A YouGov poll, conducted on 5–6 October for *The Sunday Times* showed a Tory lead of 3 per cent; the same polling organisation had a week earlier revealed an 11 per cent lead at the end of the Labour conference. A swing of 7 per cent in a week suggested an extremely volatile electorate, and one which could have swung any way in an election campaign. The campaign of 2007 would have been very different from that of 2010 – no TV debates, for one thing – but the Gordon Brown of 2010 was hardly an effective election campaigner; he would have been better in 2007, but may still have struggled. The truth is that no one knows what would have happened in an election that never took place.

More importantly, as the narrative above shows, there are at least two other counterfactuals worth thinking about. The alternative scenario presented earlier is one in which Brown's indecision backs him into a corner, from which he then gambles. But what if he hadn't been quite so indecisive in the first place? What if he had not left Spencer Livermore's memo languishing unread and unattended on his desk, but had instead given it the attention it deserved. And having read it, what if he had decided – early and firmly – to call the election? Having so decided, Labour would probably not have waited until after the Conservative conference before calling an election. Gordon Brown would have stood up at Labour's conference and announced he was going to the Palace on his return to London. The Conservative conference the following week would have been a write-off, swamped in the opening of the election campaign. George Osborne would still have made an announcement about inheritance tax, but like all announcements made in the heat of an election campaign it would have had less effect. Labour would have begun the campaign with a double-digit lead in the polls; we still have to be unsure about the outcome, but an assertive decision to call a contest in 2007 would have been better than a backed-into-a-corner act of desperation.

The converse hypothetical is what would have happened if Gordon Brown had not allowed expectation to run out of control, and stuck with his original plan for a poll in 2008? As soon as stories about an early election began to circulate in the media, he could have realised the potential damage were they to get out of control, and put a stop to them; he would have needed to say nothing publicly, merely tell his advisers to let it be known that there would be no election in 2007. With none of the hype surrounding a forthcoming election, and behind in the polls, David Cameron may have had a difficult 2007 Conservative conference. Labour could then have used the planned combined Comprehensive Spending Review and Pre-Budget Report to build on their lead in the polls. Perhaps Brown's poll lead would have remained high entering 2008, providing the launch pad for a Labour victory in early 2008. An election in an alternative 2008, in which Brown did not make such a hash of 2007, might well have proved better for the party than a rushed election in 2007.

The key decision, therefore, was not whether to have held the election or not, but to have allowed expectations to build up in such a way that not holding it was to prove so damaging.

Notes

1   Indeed, it is based heavily on the account of the 2007 election-that-wasn't in D. Kavanagh and P. Cowley, *The British General Election of 2010* (Palgrave, 2010), Ch.1. There are also good accounts in Peter Watt, *Inside Out* (Biteback, 2010); Andrew Rawnsley, *The End of the Party* (Penguin, 2010); Deborah Mattinson, *Talking to a Brick Wall* (Biteback, 2010); and Steve Richards, *Whatever It Takes* (Fourth Estate, 2010).

Chapter 17

What if Hillary Clinton had secured the Democratic nomination in 2008?

David Bean

On 4 November 2008, Senator Barack Obama was elected as the 44th President of the United States of America. Before his name was entered on the ballot, however, he had to fight a gruelling primary campaign with the former First Lady, Senator Hillary Clinton, as his chief rival. History records that Obama won and Clinton lost.

But what if the result had been different? Could Clinton have found a way to claw her way to the Democratic nomination? Having claimed the prize, how might the electorate have responded to the two quite different presidential tickets that would have emerged? And how might those altered campaigns have responded to the extraordinary global challenges that confronted them throughout the course of the election?

In the following scenario, every event in human history up until our point of counterfactual divergence occurred exactly as in reality, as did all subsequent events the author believes could not have been affected by the change. Only an added dose of deviousness on the part of the Clinton family brings us to the course here related, and – despite the reassertion of certain patterns of events that will be familiar to readers who lived attentively through the period – to a contemporary politics quite distinct from the one our timeline has bequeathed.

~

The video package of welcome, crisply displayed over three massive screens above the stage at Denver's Pepsi Center, was gracious and slick. Yet the ovation that greeted the man who had come within inches of making so immense a piece of American history was distinctly subdued. As the camera panned across the audience – alighting briefly on a gallery of famous faces, among them the Rev. Jesse Jackson's, his eyes glistening with tears – the smiles seemed fixed, the applause laboured. The assembly's demeanour was matched by that of black America's nearly-man, Barack Obama, as he trod in stoic resignation toward the podium. Moments later, he offered the ritual sacrifice of an endorsement speech for the 2008 Democratic Party presidential nominee, his victorious opponent, Senator Hillary Rodham Clinton.

The address – on paper a rousing, and in its delivery at times a poignant, appeal for unity – was rendered forgettable by its half-hearted reception, from a party nigh-on torn asunder by the controversy of its primary battle. Her nomination once thought inevitable, Clinton had been badly shaken by her third-place showing in the Iowa Caucus which opened the contest, and, despite an encouraging rally in New Hampshire, thanks in part to an emotional television performance, her early strategy of winning big up front and using the resulting momentum to bounce her opponents from the race had been foiled. Obama's superior ground organisation had delivered him a steady trickle of smaller state delegates before February's largest-ever Super Tuesday, and once the polls had closed that evening, the two remaining competitors, following the departure of John Edwards, were in deadlock.

Facing an uphill fight across the populous states to be contested over the next few days, Clinton had one last hope: a favourable resolution of the dispute surrounding January's primaries in Florida and Michigan. Owing to a breach of party rules on when the polls could be held (the states having moved them to the front of the campaign in an attempt to bolster the prestige and significance of the contests), the Democratic Party leadership had ruled, and the candidates been assured, that these races would count for nothing; they would be 'beauty contests' and nothing more. However, in declining to follow her opponents in removing their names from the

Michigan ballot in accordance with the party's requests, and enjoying a significant demographic advantage in Florida, Clinton had managed to win rich victories in both states, giving her a notional lead of some 120 delegates in all.

Although she had not protested the ruling stripping those delegates of their convention voting rights at the time, having won the contests Clinton knew that the prize for securing a reversal of the decision to invalidate the results would be an invaluable counter-strike, propelling the momentum back in her direction. She had been making noises since immediately after the contests about asking the Democratic National Convention's remaining delegates to seat their Floridian and Michigander colleagues voluntarily; in public, her case was that since the party's electoral hopes would depend in large measure upon its performance in those states, any failure to do so would risk demotivating their Democrats, putting the White House in jeopardy. The Obama campaign had responded with bemused ridicule, maintaining that her interventions demonstrated that Clinton would 'do or say anything to win an election'. Speculation over her intentions was rife among the more conspiracy-oriented posters on the Democrat-leaning blogs, and even from some quarters in the mainstream press. Nobody was under any illusions that for Clinton to force the issue while it might still affect the outcome of the contest would be tantamount to pressing the nuclear button.

Against that backdrop, on the night of 9 February – just as Obama was sweeping the board in Nebraska, Washington, Louisiana and the Virgin Islands – the Clintons convened that infamous, fateful late-night conference with the three key Democratic Party leaders: Democratic National Committee Chairman Howard Dean, Senate Majority Leader Harry Reid and Speaker of the House and Convention Chair-designate Nancy Pelosi. Details of the discussions remain murky, and to this day it is not known whether husband or wife had prompted the initiative. Nevertheless, it was quickly alleged that the Clintons had threatened, in the event of Obama's nomination, an angry public repudiation of the party and even an endorsement of Republican nominee Senator John McCain; they demanded that the disputed delegates be reinstated immediately. The meeting is said to have lasted for several stormy hours, but as dawn began to break the leadership evidently reached the conclusion that the couple could not be swayed, and that the sort of intervention they were threatening would torpedo the party's hopes for a general election victory. It must, they judged, be avoided at any cost. Following a day of reports of frantic comings and goings between the key players of both campaigns and the remainder of the party leadership at the Democratic headquarters in Washington DC, the very next evening, to near-universal astonishment, it was announced with the Maine returns that the Michigan and Florida delegates *would* be seated at the National Convention as elected, their voting rights intact.

Just how this could have happened remains the subject of fierce debate. As a matter of strict technicality, the decision to overturn its previous ruling was the Democratic National Committee's to make, but the immediate resignation of Convention Co-Chair Mayor Shirley Franklin – the first black female mayor of a large city in the South – and the narrow avoidance of similar action by her colleague Governor Kathleen Sebelius of Kansas, who had endorsed Obama a week before Super Tuesday, showed that the agreement was hardly unanimous. As to which of the three leaders had been the first or most ready to concede, again no hard evidence has emerged.

During his tenure as Committee chair, Howard Dean had sought to re-model the party to implement what he termed a 'fifty-state strategy', declaring no areas off limits to campaigning regardless of their historic support. Most commentators had reckoned Obama the candidate with the greater chance of implementing this approach, but Dean may have believed that a public breach with the Clintons would render it impossible. Previously he had referred the issue to a Credentials Committee over which he had no direct control, a move some interpreted as an exercise in back-covering, but the courts would later rule that he had no power to surrender his own right of initiative. Pelosi had been unusually circumspect in her public remarks on the contest thus far, other than her repeated assurances that the nomination would be determined by primary voters and caucus-goers, not by super-delegates – a reasoning she would later cite as justification for overturning what she began to call, in the Clintonian parlance, the 'disenfranchisement' of those from the disputed states. Reid had said and done perhaps the least of the three, giving the impression that his sole concern was to wrap up the nomination process as soon as possible so as to free the party to turn its attention on the Republicans. Whatever their private feelings, the three contrived to present a front of unity.

Not to be silenced, in public the Obama campaign immediately and strenuously remonstrated against the notion that a set of rules to which all candidates had agreed could be changed after the fact to the benefit of one of them. With a notable absence of its customary subtlety, the team leaked rumours of the Clintons' conference with the leadership to the press, and immediately launched a legal action to force the decision to be overturned. (The case of Obama v. Democratic National Committee was ultimately resolved in the defendants' favour after the nomination had already been decided.) Within the party hierarchy, too, its complaints fell on deaf ears; leading Democrats, terrified that the spectre of disunity could more easily be raised by the establishment's ultimate power couple than by the freshman senator from Illinois, closed ranks around the leadership.

The grassroots activists the Obama team had cultivated would not be so easily cowed. From mid-day on 11 February, young rank-and-file campaigners staged angry street protests in the nation's capital. Rioting broke out at Dupont Circle; the local branch of Books-A-Million was ransacked, and a makeshift bonfire lit in the road outside, its substantial inventory of copies of Hillary Clinton's *Living History* and her husband's *My Life* serving for fuel. Thirteen arrests were made. Yet in spite of the campaign's strenuous urging to sit tight, get out the vote and, as the subject of its urgent email to donors and supporters read, 'Don't let them steal your Presidency', the impromptu direct action served only to distract Obama's supporters from the following day's crucial Potomac primaries in Virginia, Maryland and the District of Columbia. Far from their intended purpose of encapsulating the national anger at Clinton's tactics, these acts served only to push older white Democrats, remembering the race riots of the past and fearful of escalation close to their homes, firmly towards Clinton. On the night of the 12th the District, the scene of most of the violence, still returned a narrow Obama victory, thanks mainly to a strong turnout among its majority black residential population, but Virginia was a virtual tie, and Maryland went to Clinton by a factor of roughly three to two. The un-elected 'super delegates', sensing the political wind and under pressure from the party leadership, began to break for Clinton, and in a matter of days it was apparent that the breeze had become a gale; the nomination process, shambolic though it had become, was concluded in Hillary Clinton's favour.

Despite general concern about the procedural chicanery that had led to this moment, America's women, by and large, were overjoyed with the result. Here at last was the opportunity to elect the country's first female president, someone with gravity, experience, brand recognition and – most importantly of all – her name at the top of a major party ticket. African-Americans, by contrast, deserted the Democratic Party in droves. Although tempers had ceased boiling into violence, their resentment simmered, and many resolved to sit out the election completely. For them, the key question of the cycle had already been answered. America was not ready for a black President; the party machines would simply not allow it.

Meanwhile, in the opposing camp, Senator John McCain was neatly tidying up his victory in the Republican primaries. By this point his sole remaining opponent was the former Arkansas governor and Baptist minister Mike Huckabee, who only days earlier had invoked the language of miracles in preaching to the CPAC conference of his intention to remain in the contest until the very end. It was speculated that he might, at any rate, have been able to afford to hang on until the 'second Super Tuesday' primaries in Texas, Ohio, Rhode Island and Vermont early in March, but in light of the Democratic meltdown even this arch-idealist could see the benefit to his party of giving it an undisputed candidate to unite around. Accordingly, on 19 February he took the opportunity presented by his defeats in Wisconsin and Washington to concede defeat, and hand his endorsement over to the Arizona senator.

McCain had, quite naturally, confined his remarks on the Democrats' travails to a general appeal for calm, but his stern looks and conciliatory tone must have masked a certain measure of glee as he watched his opponents turn their guns upon each other, and their chief supporters raise the white flag. On clinching the nomination he quickly moved to select as his running mate the former Massachusetts governor, renowned financial trouble-shooter and once-acrimonious primary opponent, Willard Mitt Romney. Though outlasted in the electoral calendar by Huckabee, Romney was nevertheless the runner-up according to the number of contests and delegates won, and after dropping out of the race at CPAC, just as Huckabee was pledging to continue, he had gone on to present McCain with a valued St Valentine's Day gift in the form of his endorsement and delegates.

Questions were asked as to whether a moderate Mormon – even one who had succeeded in picking up an endorsement from the arch-conservative populist Ann Coulter – could energise the evangelicals among the party base, who had so decisively rejected him at the Republicans' Iowa Caucus. Some among that constituency, curiously enough, had begun agitating for a half-term Alaska governor by the name of Sarah Palin, a suggestion that was quickly laughed off as an obscure feint toward the female vote in the event of an Obama nomination. Such distractions aside, McCain had made a safe if uninspiring choice, sacrificing the temptations of an immediate polling bounce in favour of a partner with the stamina to accompany him through a gruelling presidential race. More important still, as events would bear out, Romney had a reputation as a 'fixer', having been brought in as the Chief Executive of a Salt Lake City Winter Olympics organising committee that had been beset by a corruption scandal and financial shortfall, restoring the event to profitability and repute. In the event, the combination of Romney's polished handsomeness and an imposing résumé untainted by the miasma of a distrusted federal politics, added an accomplished attractiveness to the ticket while forestalling any concern over his readiness to take on the presidency should age catch up with McCain.

Clinton, by contrast, fumbled her selection of a running mate. Many Democrats hoped that she would bring Obama on to a unity ticket, but her advisers reckoned that even in the unlikely event of his accepting her invitation, his presence in the subservient role would present too awkward an image to effect any meaningful reconciliation. When her first choice, Ted Strickland, privately declined the nomination to focus on his duties as governor of Ohio, the compromise choice was the 35-year Senate veteran and also-ran primary contender, Joe Biden. As Chairman of the Senate Committee on Foreign Relations, Biden bolstered Clinton's own already formidable international credentials, and as a likeable populist he went some way to securing those parts of the base that had been demotivated by the seemingly dynastic nature of the Clinton nomination. More significantly, however, his tenure left the Democrats vulnerable to the charge that, running contrary to the anti-establishment mood that had taken hold on the country, they had selected two ultimate Washington insiders. Despite the undoubted novelty of Clinton's gender, the ticket appeared to lack youth or dynamism. Although the power of Obama's central theme of 'change' had led Clinton belatedly to frame herself as the candidate with the necessary experience to bring change about, this proved to be a slogan too far. 'Change we can believe in', it was not.

After a rather muted and formulaic Democratic National Convention, Clinton found herself already indebted to her personal fortune owing to unplanned profligacy during the primary phase, and also as a result of poor financial planning – she had relied heavily upon a fairly small group of high-dollar donors, but recent changes to campaign finance laws had significantly restricted the permitted sizes of individual donations. Her efforts to counter this constriction by establishing a network of fundraisers, termed 'HillRaisers', had been undermined by a 2007 scandal involving one of the team having turned out to be a fugitive from charges of fraud, and the scheme had on the whole proved far less lucrative than Obama's wider public appeals for whatever smaller sums his supporters could afford. As a result, Clinton quickly moved to join Senator McCain in accepting public finance for her campaign – a reversal of the position she had taken during the primaries, but not one to which voters had any reason to object. This eased the pressure on her team by circumventing the need for further fundraising but, by restricting her total expenditure from then until the election to little more than $84 million, guaranteed that what might otherwise have been one of the most expensive presidential campaigns in history was, in real terms, relatively cheap.

Neither candidate enjoyed any significant funding advantage, ironically scotching Howard Dean's ambitions for the Democratic fifty-state strategy that may have prompted him to agree to Clinton's demands in the first place. Financial constraints also forestalled any great expansion in the party's volunteer-based 'ground game', which had paid Obama such profitable dividends in the early caucuses. Instead, throughout the spring and summer both contenders fell back upon the tried and tested method of using mailings, television ads and stump speeches to shore up support in the states their parties had carried comfortably in the previous election, and to fight over the battlegrounds of New Hampshire, Pennsylvania, Ohio, Florida and Colorado. Democrats had at one stage entertained hopes of an upset in Virginia, which had given the party its two most recent Governors and featured the popular Mark Warner on the ballot for the Senate, but the migration of young professionals on the federal payroll into the state's northern DC suburbs could not compensate for the dampened enthusiasm of the black population; retaining Republican support in the southern heartlands, McCain quickly assumed an unassailable lead. Nevertheless, the dismal approval ratings of President Bush combined with the energy of former President Clinton's campaigning, which often recalled the economic salad days of his presidency, saw the polls running as even as they had before the last election.

Neither candidate, after all, enjoyed any great strategic advantage over the leading issues on which the election was fought. Hillary Clinton's long Washington tenure, combined with her vice-presidential selection, precluded any success in recapturing the passions excited by Obama's 'change' message. Representing the opposite party to the scorned incumbent certainly went in her favour, but McCain had begun to build his campaign around the milder but, broadly speaking, more associatively positive theme of 'reform', and the contrast between the candidates was not great enough to tip the scale far against him.

Similarly, the matter of the war in Iraq proved complicated for the Democrats. Obama had been able to portray himself as a down-the-line opponent of the venture, having claimed, without serious contradiction, to have disagreed with it from the beginning. McCain, on the other hand, was an unambiguous supporter, having voted for the war and then later supported President Bush's controversial 'surge' strategy of deploying over 20,000 additional troops in early 2007, which by this point was generally recognised to have paid dividends in the field. Clinton, however, was in the tricky situation of having voted in the Senate to authorise the war, but later opposed its most successful strategic manoeuvre. Given the slump in public support for the continuing US presence in Iraq, Clinton's professed goal of withdrawing troops by the end of her first term as President, particularly when contrasted with McCain's unwise flippancy toward the notion of American troops remaining there for as long as fifty or a hundred years, was always going to be appealing to a majority. Yet lacking recourse to the defence that she had opposed the war since before its beginning left her vulnerable to McCain's charges that, in opposing the surge, she had shown insufficient strategic insight or wisdom for one aspiring to the role of Commander-in-Chief.

Similarly, despite their experience both candidates had significant downsides, and each faced the usual array of minor scandals and missteps that seemingly afflict all presidential campaigns. McCain, once seen as a staunchly independent thinker, happy to speak out against the excesses of the Republican establishment – the 'maverick' label often appended to his name, with his supporters' eager encouragement – suffered from his close association with Bush over the past seven years, the Democrats making much of his boast in a 2003 television interview to have voted with the President over 90 per cent of the time. Clinton, on the other hand, had to contend with the fallout from a March speech on the subject of Iraq and foreign policy, when she claimed that a 1996 trip to Bosnia had forced her to flee across the airbase tarmac under sniper fire. CBS news footage revealed nothing unusual about the arrival, which included a calm stroll with her daughter, a warm greeting from political leaders and even a poetry reading from a local schoolgirl. Though she dismissed the incident as 'a minor blip', Clinton found herself at the centre of pointed questions from the McCain campaign about her credibility as well as her credentials.

Also damaging was her close association with her husband's failed attempt at reforming the country's healthcare system, back in 1993. Derided as 'HillaryCare', thanks to her having been placed at the head of a task force charged with drawing it up, the plan had attracted criticism from a swathe of interests for its bureaucracy, tendency to place mandates on the behaviour of states and citizens, and cost to taxpayers. Healthcare reform was a major plank of her 2008 campaign, and the Republicans met with success by portraying her proposals as a reheating of that earlier doomed effort, even luring the actors who had portrayed Harry and Louise, the stars of a devastating pair of political ads credited with helping derail it, to return from their subsequent leftward drift to rail against Clinton's candidacy over the dinner table.

The healthcare issue was problematic too for the Republicans, with Romney having introduced a plan in Massachusetts that Obama had previously cited as an inspiration for his own proposed model. Whenever this point was raised, however, they simply responded that the appropriate level of government for resolving these issues was the state, and that the federal government ought to restrict its role to freeing citizens to purchase insurance from wherever in the nation they chose, and enacting whatever local initiatives they wished. Independently of the McCain campaign, politically demotivated right-wing voters began to organise spontaneously against the Clinton policy, rallying around the slogan that citizens were 'taxed enough already' and evoking the imagery of the Founding Fathers and the Boston Tea Party. The populist combination of appeals to patriotism and the nation's founding ideology proved potent. Keen not to miss an opportunity, on the stump McCain quickly began to adopt elements drawn from the rhetoric of these latter-day 'tea partiers', and after a swift sequence of face-to-face meetings with its most promising emerging leaders the nascent movement was quickly subsumed within the wider Republican Party, not to be heard from since.

The common theme all this activity demonstrated was that for the bulk of the campaign, Clinton was just not quite different enough from her opponent, or from the much-derided 'old politics' of the past and present, to break the deadlock, grasp the popular imagination and pull away into the lead. Then, on 14 September, came the event that changed it all.

Although the so-called 'credit crunch' had never been far from the political agenda, the fallout from the collapse of the investment banking firm Lehman Brothers immediately propelled the state of the US economy back on to the front pages. At first it appeared that this further crushing blow to the economic legacy of the Bush presidency would benefit the Democrats. Clinton was quick to organise a press conference, tearing into the past years' financial deregulation which, she maintained, had allowed banks to lend based on far too optimistic a set of assumptions about future asset prices, and now threatened to destabilise the entire banking sector. The gutsy, if not quite so historically sound, performance won plaudits across the airwaves, and in its immediate aftermath the insta-polls suggested that Clinton's campaign might be on the cusp of a breakthrough. After initially appearing slow to react, the following day the Republican team announced an audacious and unprecedented response. They purchased ten minutes of primetime television across five major networks two nights thereafter, when the ticket, in a joint appearance, would make a live address to the nation on the state of the economy.

After a day and a half of tight-lipped silence in the campaign and tense speculation by political observers, at 7pm Eastern Standard Time on 17 September, an estimated 33.6 million Americans tuned in to witness what has since been hailed as the turning point in the Republican campaign. Sombrely dressed in dark suits, starched white shirts and near-funereal ties, the pair sat together in an empty television studio adorned only by a single large American flag. Romney took the lead, offering a frank, almost apologetic, assessment of the behaviour of his former colleagues in the world of high finance. He denounced the personal greed of the malefactors, but explained that the policies Senator Clinton had been excoriating were nothing more than a continuation of the agenda pursued throughout the 1990s by her own husband, levelling an unstated, but unsubtle, charge of hypocrisy. 'But these financiers,' he concluded, 'I know these people. I used to work with them, to be one of them. That's why I know how to pick up the pieces – just like I did in Salt Lake City.'

That message, a clever and finely-honed pivot back to the Republicans' key assets – their combination of both international and economic experience – was compelling. Critically, too, it succeeded in baiting President Bill Clinton into interrupting his heavy campaign schedule to make an ill-tempered defence of his own presidency, in which his wife was forced to join. This response allowed the Republicans – led again on the issue by Romney – immediately to accuse their opponents of being stuck in the past, of re-fighting old battles instead of working to win the day's. Their attack was lent potency by recollections of Clinton's earlier attempts to invoke nostalgia for her husband's presidency, whose long-term record Romney, benefiting from an unusually sympathetic hearing from the new-found Cassandras of the press, had successfully undermined in the popular imagination. The Republican team deftly avoided similar accusations of anachronism by studiously focusing from that point onwards on solutions to the economic woes. Declining to offer any further rebuttal, they effectively closed the debate, providing political historians with an instance of the expression 'I'm getting on with the job' actually being effective.

Just as he had hoped, the media quickly took up the narrative that the Republican ticket was winning the financial crisis, and McCain was delighted with the performance of his running mate. Disregarding warnings from his inner circle that he risked being overshadowed, he quietly leaked a reiteration of a rumour that had begun to circulate at the turn of the year that, if elected, he intended to serve for only four years, before handing over the fortunes of the Republican Party to a younger successor. The press response was most favourable, and internal polling showed that the overall party advantage to be won from revealing to an electorate still harbouring lingering concerns over the candidate's age the private vow he had already offered his family – to seek only four years in the White House – far outweighed any damage to his personal credibility. Accordingly, in a joint press conference with Romney he confirmed the story in public, positioning himself to become the first US President since Lyndon Johnson to seek no second term. It would, of course, have been impolitic for him to have responded directly to the *Washington Times* correspondent's inevitable question of who he intended to see follow him, but the impish grin and the hearty clap on Romney's back left no doubt: the election of the country's oldest President would leave no question over the succession, under any circumstances.

When the story broke that the Bush administration, led by Treasury Secretary Henry 'Hank' Paulson, was planning a massive, controversial government bailout of the country's banks, the Clinton campaign settled on one last, quixotic gamble. On 24 September, Clinton announced that she was suspending her presidential campaign to go back to Washington and, as Senator from New York, work on the bailout full time. McCain was initially tempted to join her, but was persuaded by Romney instead to make the case that the American public would be better served by a full, public discussion by its presidential candidates about how to move forward. Instead, on the following day he joined Clinton, President Bush and congressional leaders at a White House summit, keeping in close touch with his running mate and taking care to avoid missteps. Clinton, meanwhile, had implied a wish to postpone the first candidates' debate, scheduled for the day after that in Mississippi, prompting rumours of designs on displacing the single Vice Presidential debate to spare the gaffe-prone Biden from potential embarrassment. Bowing to media pressure (and dark words about empty chairs), she did eventually resolve to appear, but was ridiculed mercilessly by McCain for the campaign suspension, and for her reversal of positions on the debate. Clinton stood her ground, pledging her commitment to head immediately back to Washington and remain there 'until Congress passes this bill'. When, the following Monday, the Emergency Economic Stabilisation Act of 2008 was rejected by 228 votes to 205, with one abstention, on the floor of the House of Representatives, it was clear that Clinton had failed, and having already spent most of a week away from the campaign trail she could see no alternative to going back on her pledge. The passage of the revised bill on 3 October, with no further involvement from Clinton aside from her own Senate vote, only compounded the embarrassment.

The move had backfired spectacularly, and columnists competed to explain it. Parallels were conjectured with prior instances of her indecisiveness; the Iraq war issue was trotted out, as were her shifting stances on issues such as illegal immigration, the North American Free Trade Agreement and the possibility of negotiation with Iran. Through a series of unattributable press briefings the team sought to place the blame squarely on her campaign manager, Patti Solis Doyle, who was publicly fired. Yet this attempt to draw a line under the episode only heightened the sense of desperation. It also proved alienating to yet another minority constituency, Hispanics, who had held up Solis Doyle as something of a heroine as the first Latina ever to manage a presidential campaign. Without their support and enthusiasm, the campaign's remaining hopes in their demographic strongholds of Nevada, Florida and Colorado were dashed. From this point onwards, despite two spirited performances in the remaining debates, Clinton's hard-fought battle for the presidency began to slip inexorably from her grasp.

And so, as a bright, cold dawn broke across America on 4 November, the proceeding of the day's business appeared to most observers to mirror their recollections of 2004: close, but no less inevitable. Despite near-universal hatred of the incumbent, the Republican Party seemed bound for a third presidential term. Gender, in the event, had not been an issue. It was not that America was not ready for a female President; it was simply that America did not want this one, not this time.

The Democrats had not, of course, given up hope, and for weeks previously their surrogates had been shopped across the airwaves to declare, with forced cheerfulness, that nothing was decided (true) and that the polls were narrowing (false). That morning they were also pinning hopes on a variant of the so-called 'Bradley effect', a theory that swathes of white women, having told pollsters that they would vote for the more financially reputable and socially acceptable Republican ticket, would in the privacy of the polling booth instead plump for one of their own. As most commentators predicted, however, any such effect was insignificant. By nightfall, once the results had started to arrive it became clear that while margins had indeed tightened, the electoral map would look little changed from four years previously; only Iowa and New Mexico, which had turned slowly but irresistibly blue over the past four years, showed a different result. With 274 electoral college votes to 266, John McCain – narrowly, but no less certainly – had won.

From around midnight Eastern Standard Time, 5am GMT, as a deflated Clinton and an elated McCain addressed the nation and the world in turn, the years seemingly fell from the Republican to pile directly upon the Democrat. The mood of the American people was one of neither delight nor particular optimism, but merely a grim satisfaction in having gritted their teeth and done the best they could under the weight of circumstance. The country had its oldest President, and a Vice President who had emerged even more powerful than his divisive predecessor.

But the enduring image that will remain indelibly burned into the minds of those who look back on that election is of another man. For once eschewing his regular nine o'clock bedtime, he too had stayed up to watch the results come in, and as the Republicans' victory was announced an employee informed him that a small crowd of onlookers had gathered outside his house, should he wish to acknowledge them. Populist instincts undimmed by prior misfortunes, he readily agreed.

The photograph that made the front pages of late editions across the globe showed President George W. Bush bestriding the White House balcony in triumph, his right hand aloft, his thumb tucked into his palm, and his four fingers splayed.

Four more years.

Chapter 18

What if Harris and Marris had won in 2010?

Matt Cole

'Prime Minister Miliband'

Dawn was breaking over Wolverhampton Civic Hall on 7 May 2010 as the most agonisingly close and repeatedly recounted result of the general election was declared. Exultant cheers went up from exhausted Labour supporters as the Returning Officer confirmed that their candidate, Rob Marris, had held Wolverhampton South West by 12 votes. The cheers reflected relief that Marris, the understated but shrewd and serious MP who had been named backbencher of the year by *House Magazine* three years earlier ('for his rigorous and independent scrutiny of all front benches'), had been rewarded for his conscientiousness; but they also marked excitement at what looked increasingly like the last and deepest nail in the coffin of David Cameron's ambitions to be Prime Minister.

Elsewhere in the West Midlands, Labour had narrowly held on to Warwickshire North; in the North, Stockton South and Lancaster had resisted strong Tory challenges; and even in the South East the Conservatives had missed targets such as Thurrock, Hendon and Broxtowe. Labour had also held two seats in the face of a Liberal Democrat challenge, but they in reply had won five against Labour, gaining Ashfield, Sheffield Central and Edinburgh South and ousting former immigration minister Phil Woolas at Oldham East, while retaining Chesterfield where left-leaning Liberal Democrat Paul Holmes was MP. Another 'social' Liberal Democrat, Evan Harris, had kept his seat at Oxford West & Abingdon from a strong Tory challenge, as had four others, from Camborne to Harrogate.

The last-minute tiny shift in votes which brought about this result could in some cases be attributed to local factors; but the national press had also reported very credible leaks from the Conservative campaign during the last forty-eight hours that – contrary to David Cameron's pro-testations – they planned to restrict entitlement to child benefit, to remove altogether the cap on university tuition fees and to reorganise the NHS fundamentally. Some leading Labour figures had also let it be known that Gordon Brown was ready to step down as Prime Minister to facilitate a Lib Dem–Labour coalition, in the hope that this would secure a few more tactical votes from Lib Dems in places like Wolverhampton.

Whatever its cause, the significance of this small last-minute shift was clear: Cameron's claim to govern was fatally undermined. True, his Conservatives had won the largest share of the vote – larger, in fact, than Labour had won in 2005 – but they had failed to reach the target of 300 Commons seats which Cameron had told his team was the starting point for considering governing alone. In addition to their defeats in conventional marginal contests, the Conservatives had been pipped at the post in Wyre Forest by Independent MP Dr Richard Taylor after Liberal Democrat candidate Neville Farmer had advised those intending to vote for him to back Taylor to beat the Tories. With a vacancy at the Vale of York, where the contest had been suspended due to a candidate's death, Cameron was left with only 289 MPs; Labour had 266 and the Liberal Democrats 65. Neither of the two larger parties could hope to govern alone; only the Liberal Democrats, with a slightly enlarged vote and parliamentary group, could bridge the gap to a parliamentary majority; and though Labour had fewer seats than the Conservatives, most of the thirty 'others', such as the Scottish and Welsh nationalists, the lone Green MP and Dr Taylor, were at least less likely to obstruct a Lib Dem–Labour administration than a Tory-led one. As coalition negotiations began, the field of play was evenly balanced.

~

This is *almost* exactly what happened in May 2010. Just as the system used for elections to the House of Commons gives millions of voters no impact on the result, it loads a tiny number with enormous importance. The movement of rather less than 3,000 votes cast for the Conservatives in 2010 (a proportion smaller than one hundredth of one per cent of the total) to their main rivals in the right sixteen places would have produced this dramatically different scenario.[1] As few as 458 Conservative voters in seven marginal constituencies could have created a bare Lib-Dem–Labour majority in the Commons if they had voted differently.[2] All the seats reported as lost by the Conservatives above were in reality won by them, but in only one case by more than a thousand votes, and in all cases they could now be lost to the Tories' main challenger on a swing of less than one per cent.

Since the poll ratings of the parties during the 2010 election oscillated by 17 points for the Liberal Democrats, 10 for the Conservatives and 5 for Labour, and all three experienced movements of two or three per cent within 24 hours at different points, a shift of less than one per cent in a handful of constituencies is wholly plausible. The result of the May 2010 election was thus a matter of timing and chance, and the outcome sketched above alters not only the strengths of the parties, but some of the players in the discussions.

So what would have happened if Evan Harris and Rob Marris had won?

~

The negotiations for a coalition

The situation was in the first instance what had been anticipated, and Liberal Democrat leader Nick Clegg had prepared for it by pledging that his first approach in a balanced parliament would be to the party which had won the largest share of the votes and seats. His own party understood and supported this, though some like Harris and Holmes, and party heavyweights such as Lord Ashdown, Menzies Campbell and Vince Cable, were close to the Labour leadership or feared the embrace of the Tories. Ashdown even said that although the arithmetic meant that initial negotiations had to be with the Conservatives, the Liberal Democrats' heart was in a relationship with Labour; both Menzies Campbell and future Chief Secretary to the Treasury Danny Alexander said they thought a deal with Labour 'natural' for the Lib Dems.[3]

Some were worried that Clegg himself and some of his *Orange Book* lieutenants such as David Laws[4] were too ideologically close to the free-market Tories to be able to keep enough distance and hold their nerve in the negotiations. Generally, it was fair to assume that Lib Dem MPs were reassured that Labour's late recovery had ensured that the Conservatives were not the only show in town. All were grateful, some hopeful, that if negotiations with the Conservatives broke down, there would be the alternative of a majority government with Labour.

The Conservatives were in a mood of collective frustration, resentment and determination. Frustration at their failure to gain control of the Commons despite a clear victory at the polls; resentment – greater in some than in others – that Cameron's 'modernisation', with its gestures towards environmentalism, representation for gays, women and ethnic minorities, and the posturing cosmetic modernity of the leader's tieless shirt and Converse trainers, had not gained its promised goal of power; but determination that their party and its principles would not be swept aside in this freak election outcome at a time of great need for the country. Misgivings about the effectiveness of Cameron's rebranding of the Conservatives, and about his performance in the leadership debates, were already being expressed, even by supportive figures such as party benefactor Lord Ashcroft. One senior backbencher told the press that Cameron had 'pissed this election away'.[5]

The Conservatives' failure to win the next fifteen or twenty seats they had targeted deprived their leader of that number of young, pro-modernisation backbenchers; only one of the next seventeen who might have been elected was a former MP, and five were women, including thirty-one-year-old human rights activist Nicola Blackwood, who lost to Evan Harris. At Wolverhampton, Paul Uppal had missed the chance to be the Asian who won back Enoch Powell's old seat for the Conservatives. Because some of Cameron's new-image candidates had failed, his critics were more dominant on the Tory benches, both in numbers and in spirit of vindication. The argument for waiting for another election while the Lib Dems and Labour fell out – as Stanley Baldwin had done in 1924 – was more appealing to these Conservatives than the prospect of making concessions to the upstart Liberal Democrats. Some even talked about trying to govern alone, like Harold Wilson in 1974, if the stalemate went on; former Party Chairman Norman Fowler discovered that 'a surprising number of senior Conservatives took (and still take) this view'.[6]

Labour, like the Conservatives, was divided between cooperators and sceptics. Peter Mandelson, Andrew Adonis, Alastair Campbell and some others around Gordon Brown were eager to work with the Liberal Democrats. They saw this as an opportunity to revive 'the Project', Tony Blair's approach of cooperation over policy with the Liberal Democrats which had flourished in the early years of his premiership. From the start of the negotiations, these figures were in touch with Ashdown, Menzies Campbell and other Lib Dems to urge a Lib-Lab deal. Brown himself, desperate to remain in Downing Street to oversee the completion of Britain's economic recovery, contacted Vince Cable directly to put his case and arranged a meeting between Cable and Alistair Darling, still Chancellor, to discuss common ground on economic policy. He had invited Liberal Democrats into his first cabinet in 2007, and promised a referendum on the introduction of the alternative vote during the election campaign in anticipation of the situation in which he now found himself.

There was, however, a sizeable and significant body of diehard tribal Labourites who would not countenance any deal with the Liberal Democrats, and whose indignation at the idea of negotiations was only strengthened by their meeting with the Tories first. 'Can we trust the Liberal Democrats?' asked David Blunkett: 'they're behaving like every harlot in history'. Diane Abbott summoned the folk memory of 1931, warning that coalition with the Liberal Democrats 'could destroy Labour for good',[7] and John Reid went on air to claim that large sections of the Labour Party would not support a deal with the Lib Dems and that the idea was 'potentially disastrously wrong' for the party.[8] Even more pluralist and flexible Labour figures such as Jon Cruddas let it be known that they would not vote for some non-negotiable Lib Dem objectives; Cruddas also insisted that the whole Labour movement should be engaged in any negotiations.[9]

This division of opinion was reflected in the Labour negotiating team in a way in which it was not in the Conservative line-up, which was composed of Cameron loyalists who had discussed the possibility of coalition with their leader before the election. Gordon Brown sent Lords Mandelson and Adonis to try and build a coalition with the Lib Dems, but they were joined by Harriet Harman and Ed Balls, who were both sceptical about a deal. The Labour team had done no preparatory work and arrived without any documentary proposals, 'flying blind' as Mandelson later put it.[10] Whereas Andrew Stunell had been planning for these negotiations over months with the rest of the Lib Dem negotiators,[11] he found Labour's team 'disdainful and dismissive of what we might bring to the table', offering only 'business as usual which would probably have taken us to somewhere like Greece in the next twelve months'.[12] As a veteran of local government group leadership and negotiations with other parties, realism and party discipline on both sides were at a premium for Stunell.

The Tory team knew they had to behave positively and flexibly, and even impressed Simon Hughes and Lord Ashdown with their readiness to make concessions. Though Conservative doubters were fearful of the Liberal Democrats' enhanced leverage with Labour waiting in the wings, they were not involved in the negotiations. Aware that they were selling in a buyers' market, and that Harris, Holmes and others were pressing Clegg to get more concessions, the Conservative leadership went even further than they had planned, making an explicit commitment to a principally elected Lords and sounding accommodating about their likely response to the Browne Report on higher education funding. They also granted the Liberal Democrats a sixth cabinet seat by making Steve Webb Secretary of State for Work and Pensions, to the disappointment of Iain Duncan Smith (who, as a junior minister, became Webb's 'watcher') and his Thatcherite allies. Cameron's fateful Monday night meeting with the backbench 1922 Committee heard some misgivings, but even those such as the 'No Turning

Back' group of MPs who were most likely to oppose a deal kept their counsel in a way which suggested that a few more concessions would not have triggered rebellion. If the Rubicon-crossing promise of a referendum on AV did not even provoke sceptical Tory MPs to demand a vote, let alone spark a rebellion, not much else would. They had decided to give their leader latitude and judge him afterwards. As Churchill found of his position as Conservative leader:

> The loyalties which centre upon number one are enormous. If he trips he must be sustained. If he makes mistakes they must be covered. If he sleeps he must not be wantonly disturbed. If he is no good, he must be pole-axed.[13]

In this scenario, the subsequent talks between the Lib Dems and Labour were not altered by the theoretical possibility of a Lib Dem–Labour overall Parliamentary majority of twelve: half that number of Labour MPs had already been in front of cameras or in print denouncing such a deal, and they surely represented a larger number of their more discreet colleagues; in 2006 Jon Cruddas had been nominated for Labour's Deputy Leadership by no fewer than 49 MPs. Peter Mandelson learned from Gordon Brown's staff that both the cabinet and the Parliamentary Labour Party were split three ways over the possibility of working with the Lib Dems: those for, those wholly against, and those who saw it working under certain conditions, notably Brown's departure.[14]

As the negotiations on both sides continued, Gordon Brown eventually announced his intention to step down, but his uneasiness – being 'a bit Gordon-ish' as Mandelson put it – in engaging with Clegg or with his own party, and the resistance of some of Labour's backbenchers and even its negotiating team to a deal, meant that despite their 'most favoured' status with most Lib Dems, Labour's team was always one step off the pace in a rapidly-developing game which the civil service, the markets and the press wanted to see brought to a conclusion within days. Further strains were introduced by the Liberal Democrat team, emboldened by the flexibility of the Tories, increasing their demands to Labour for deficit reduction targets.

Moreover, Labour had lost the election; it had been rejected by the electorate and had won a smaller share of the vote than the Conservatives. Labour was too tired, too tarnished and in parts too tribal to talk. Another nine backbenchers did not alter those conditions. Lord Adonis later accused the Liberal Democrats of using parliamentary numbers as an alibi for a decision they had already made to go in with the Conservatives.[15] He was right that the numbers did not matter, but the real reason for the Conservatives' success was not the ideological preference of the Lib Dems, but the political culture of Labour.

The deciding factors in determining who formed the government of 2010 were not numbers alone or even ideological preference, but leadership, unity and flexibility. Though numbers made a Lib Dem-Labour deal possible, and ideology made it attractive to many, the Tories – as they usually had in the past – outstripped Labour on the latter three counts far enough to leave such an outcome very unlikely and even more unworkable. To this the Conservatives added a greater claim to legitimacy, which Clegg had recognised by negotiating with them first. The Liberal Democrats had secured a better deal than would have been the case with Labour out of the game; the Tory right was accordingly somewhat more anxious about Cameron's strategy and ready to intervene; but the initial form of the government was largely the same. It was only over the course of the Parliament that these greater tensions would produce a dramatically different outcome.

The course of the government
The Liberal Democrats enjoyed a slightly greater level of influence over events for the next two years than might have been the case if Labour had not recovered and the Tories had won over 300 seats. Higher education fees rose, but a determined rearguard action by the six Lib Dems in the cabinet kept the maximum to £6,000 a year. The tax threshold was raised to £10,000 a year, and the pupil premium introduced, as priorities within the first year, and some cuts in public services proposed by George Osborne and leaked to the press were forestalled. These concessions were a source of

increasing frustration to Conservative critics of the Coalition, like David Davis, Bernard Jenkin and Edward Leigh. No one, however, dared speak the reason that they were being given to the Lib Dems: the spectre of the Lib-Lab government that never was – but which conceivably still could be. Labour had chosen its new Leader, Ed Miliband, by a narrow margin, and was careful to leave the door open to negotiations with the Liberal Democrats in a future hung parliament.[16] For all the protestations of the Coalition's guaranteed five-year life – and they sounded at times like protesting too much – the British constitution had no hard and fast rules. Only the rules of conviction, strategy and self-interest would keep the Coalition together in the end.

It was the AV referendum which triggered a change of mood. Cameron's high-profile involvement in the 'No' campaign with its direct personal criticism of Nick Clegg and his 'broken promises' triggered fury among the Lib Dems, from Chris Huhne's outburst at cabinet to leading non-ministers such as Simon Hughes and backbenchers like Adrian Sanders:

> We have irrevocably damaged our public image. We now face the brutal realisation that we have fractured our core vote, lost a generation of young voters and alienated thousands of tactical voters in seats where it makes the difference between electoral success or failure. The message on the doorstep before the election was often 'I support another party, but you seem to have more integrity and do more for local people so you have my vote'. Now it is 'I used to vote for you, you still work hard for your local area, but you are discredited and lied just like the rest of them'. We need the leadership to start acting like the leadership of an independent political party that just happens to be in coalition, not the leadership of a coalition that seems to forget it has an independent political party to take into consideration.[17]

The contrastingly warm relationship cultivated with Ed Miliband by Vince Cable and others was evident at their meeting on the platform of Methodist Central Hall;[18] Lib Dem ministers were briefing the press that the civil service was excluding them from decision-making, and Nick Clegg said

openly that 'Whitehall has not adjusted' to coalition government'.[19] The
bitter blow of the local election results and the overwhelming 'No' vote in
May 2011 prompted Lib Dem MPs to rethink, and Evan Harris had already
taken to the airwaves to describe the Coalition as 'not a happy marriage
– it never was', but rather 'a pragmatic deal' with 'a party with whom we
agree on a few things, and disagree on many'.[20] Vince Cable condemned the
Tories as 'ruthless, calculating and very tribal.'[21] Scottish Lib Dem Leader
Tavish Scott, whose group in the Scottish Parliament had lost twelve of its
seventeen seats, resigned with a critical flourish:

> There's just no doubt that since last May we have been up against
> it because of the formation of a UK government where the Liberal
> Democrats were seen to be propping up the Conservatives. And that's,
> I think, in Scotland, a pretty disastrous and toxic mix in politics. It's for
> the party now to decide how to move forward.[22]

The rest of this account is almost wholly hypothetical, except where refer-
enced; but it reflects visible pressures and the balance between the parties
which would have been different had Harris and Marris won.

~

At a two-day meeting the following month the issues were thrashed out
among the Lib Dem MPs, and the significance of the previous year's election began to become evident. In the plenary assessment of the state of the
coalition, Clegg was quickly at bay, surrounded by anxious and angry colleagues. Former teacher Paul Holmes had been hit hard in Chesterfield by
tuition fees and the withdrawal of the Education Maintenance Allowance.
Simon Hughes, who had visited the constituency in February to emphasise
that he regarded Holmes as a friend, and to share publicly in his regret at
the effect of the measures,[23] felt ill at ease as the bitterness of backbenchers
towards the arrangement he had loyally defended poured out. He remained
uncharacteristically silent. Evan Harris attacked the health reforms; Vince
Cable bemoaned the failure of the banks to respond to the need for restraint
in executive pay and to make more loans to small businesses; and dozens of

MPs reported the painful losses of experienced and capable members suffered by council groups in their constituencies as a result of the coalition. There were also fears about the redrawing of constituency boundaries, which it transpired were likely to unseat more Liberal Democrat MPs than had been anticipated; some MPs had a keen interest revisiting those changes.[24]

Over two days Lib Dem MPs crafted a new set of demands: wholesale revision of the health reforms; legislation to create a House of Lords mostly elected using PR before the end of the Parliament; a generous replacement of the EMA and a tightening of the regulation of higher education fees; and the imposition of new taxes on the financial sector, where bonuses had returned to the excesses of the pre-recession period. 'And when Cameron says no?' asked Clegg indignantly of his critics at a final meeting. 'Then you tell him he can't count on our votes', snapped veteran MP Mike Hancock. 'We can't play fast and loose like this', Clegg insisted angrily: 'the public won't trust us to govern again'. Some MPs could not contain snorts of ironic derision. 'A lot of trust went with the tuition fees pledge', replied a former leader who had voted against the rise in fees.[25] 'But we can't abandon the coalition agreement', Clegg retorted, his tone growing testy. 'It would look like we were going in with Labour.' There was a weighty, silent pause. 'So what?' called out a voice from the back of the room.

The meeting between the Prime Minister and Deputy Prime Minister which followed was courteous and business-like, and brief. Clegg set out the Lib Dems' objectives for the rest of the Parliament; he tried to spike the Prime Minister's guns by acknowledging that some were aims which had not been included in the original coalition agreement, but argued that no government anticipates all the challenges and opportunities it will face over a whole Parliament, and emphasised that all the issues raised were within the scope of legitimate discussion within the terms of the original agreement. Clegg stressed that acceptance of the terms would strengthen a coalition which was performing vital work on the economy but which was suffering – particularly in his own part of it – damaging electoral decline which was sapping its morale. He ended by appealing to Cameron, as clearly as he could in a meeting minuted by civil servants, to shore up his own – Clegg's – position in his party. 'There are elements in my own party who feel we are paying too high a price to protect your colleagues from criticism. Give me the evidence to prove them wrong.' The Prime Minister was non-committal and from outside appearances unaffected by the meeting. But he sensed the undertone of desperation in Clegg's voice. 'I cannot speak for my colleagues', he cautioned; 'but I will speak *to* them'.

The next meeting of the 1922 Committee would be for Cameron a decisive one. He had a close enough relationship with Nick Clegg to know that the Lib Dem leader's appeal had been genuine; he had therefore concluded that only further concessions would hold the lid on Lib Dem dissent. None of the changes the Lib Dems wanted were beyond the Tory pale, after all, and there was a long-term cynical view that the longer the coalition went on, the weaker the Lib Dems became. Perhaps their nuisance role in British politics over the previous two generations could finally be ended by killing them with kindness. Above all, however, Cameron wanted to avoid the fate of Austen Chamberlain, the Conservative leader ousted in 1922 because he wanted to continue working with Lloyd George when most Conservative MPs listened to Stanley Baldwin's warnings that the Liberal Prime Minister was a 'dynamic force' who would destroy the Tories as he had destroyed his own party. The Prime Minister of 2011 was determined to keep faith with his own MPs while taking them as far as he felt he could down the road of concession to their coalition partners.

That was to be a short journey. Cameron's MPs were every bit as fractious as Clegg's. Andrew Lansley feared humiliation if his health reforms, prepared over years, were unpicked in the way that Cameron was urging, and although the Conservative leader was ready to make another major U-turn on this, his already bruised and indignant right wing was not, given the concessions already made in other areas. At least twenty other promising backbenchers felt evicted from the offices for which they had served in the shadow administration by Lib Dem unknowns, and even the courteous Iain Duncan Smith increasingly resented working under Steve Webb, who did not share all of his radicalism on welfare reform. Vince

Cable was regarded as having stretched the principle of collective responsibility beyond the bounds of decency.

However, it was around reform of the Lords that resistance to further concession hardened and grew, drawing in the Conservative peers, many of whom had very reluctantly given in to their Whips' pleas to vote through the AV referendum only to find its defeat by the public now jeopardised their own existence. 'Are we going to tear up the constitution – and the coalition agreement – to buy off a third party with declining support?' asked one backbencher; 'What will they come asking for next year? PR in local elections? Half the Cabinet? A timeshare at No 10?' Cameron felt himself being ridiculed. 'It seems that the less popular the Liberal Democrats become, the more we have to give them', carped another critic. 'Is that the "new politics"?' The Liberal Democrats had their Fixed Term Parliament Bill in train and should be grateful for it. The meeting was clear: it would support the Conservative leader in standing up to the bullying of his coalition partners. No significant new concessions; it was time for the Liberal Democrats to take a reality pill, and the Prime Minister was despatched to administer it.

The summer session of Parliament drifted on as the positions of the coalition parties were stated and re-stated to one another, becoming progressively hardened. Rumours were widespread of deteriorating relationships between Lib Dem and Conservative ministers, and when Andrew Lansley's largely unchanged Health Reform Bill reached its second reading, enough Lib Dem MPs joined forces with Labour to cause a narrow government defeat. Conservative whips were incensed to find Lib Dem ministers taking tea on the Commons terrace, unwilling to respond to the division bell. If not yet in meltdown, the coalition had clearly left its 'Rose Garden' phase far behind.

At this point Ed Miliband decided to play his hand. Having carefully distinguished between, on one hand, Nick Clegg – whom he described as 'betraying Liberal values' – and on the other Clegg's colleagues with whom Miliband had shared a platform in the AV campaign, the Labour leader opened informal discussions with Lib Dem dissidents. Two by-election gains for Labour had already modified the balance of Parliament, and a third looked likely to go the Opposition's way as well, leaving the parties' strengths in the Commons at Con 287, Lab 269, Lib Dem 65. In opposition, the Blairite Old Guard of Blunkett and Reid had lost profile and momentum. It had become received wisdom in the Labour leadership that 'it's fun to bate the Lib Dems, but it's better to beat the Conservatives'.[26]

Miliband chose the same method to fly his kite that his brother had chosen to challenge Gordon Brown three years earlier: an article in *The Guardian* during the slow news season.[27] Published in the first week of August, it argued that the time had come for Lib Dems to break with the Tories, and that if necessary they should look to their leadership. He offered the opportunity to work with him and the Labour shadow cabinet on areas of common policy – Lords reform, a Speaker's Conference to establish consensus on electoral reform at all levels, an easing of public expenditure cuts, an attack on the excesses of the banks and the regulation of the press. Miliband taunted Clegg and Cameron that 'a number of senior Liberal Democrats have already indicated privately that they are ready to co-ordinate action to protect the principles and services we all value'.

The Deputy Prime Minister was in Spain staying with his wife's family when David Cameron contacted him to discuss Miliband's article. Even over a mobile phone, Clegg could hear Cameron's concerned tone. Which Lib Dems had been talking to Miliband? Why didn't Clegg know about this, or if he did, why hadn't he stopped it? Cameron insisted abruptly that Clegg issue a thoroughgoing rejection of Miliband and a commitment to continue the coalition to the end of its term. Cameron had even emailed a prepared text for Clegg to use, though he advised 'it's better if it comes from you alone for public consumption, of course'. Clegg disliked being bounced in this way while on holiday – Cameron could hear Clegg's wife Miriam calling him as they spoke – and was mindful of the longer-term consequences of his response. It was obvious that Miliband could be a partner in government in the future, and Clegg wanted to be capable of benefiting from that offer. Instinctively, Clegg also knew that a robust dismissal of Miliband would strengthen the hand of those who were already questioning his leadership within the Liberal Democrats. To the Prime Minister's frustration, Clegg equivocated: 'I'm on holiday, you know, David …' The Prime Minister asserted that there were no holidays for cabinet ministers, merely other places to work. 'Look, I won't jump at Miliband's call or yours', Clegg countered. 'I'll put out a press release saying I'm on holiday'.

As he emerged from reclaiming his baggage at the airport (having followed the Prime Minister's example and travelled economy class as a gesture towards the hardships being suffered by the public) Clegg was besieged by the press pack and TV cameras. What would he do about the Lib Dem ministers who had responded warmly to Miliband's offer? Had he heard rumours that two Lib Dem ministers, including a cabinet member, were considering resignation? Why had he not responded immediately to Miliband's statement? Was there a challenge looming to his leadership at the coming Lib Dem conference? Again the Deputy Prime Minister kept his counsel; a sardonic 'yes, I've had a great holiday, thanks', was the best he could offer.

David Cameron decided to take control of events. In an interview with the *Daily Mail*, he announced that any minister failing to commit himself to support government policy for the full term would be expected to relinquish office, and that their place would not necessarily be taken by another member of their party. He hinted darkly that any failure by the Lib Dems to support the government would precipitate a general election, 'a situation none of us, least of all the Lib Dems under current circumstances, want to see'. Vince Cable had already told Clegg that he would not sign any open-ended commitment to policy, and Clegg himself resented what he saw as a breach of the dual control of cabinet composition which the coalition entailed. The rewards of partnership – in terms of policy and office – were drying up, and the party conference was approaching. Moreover, the press and the Palace of Westminster were alive with stories of putative leadership challenges from Tim Farron, Chris Huhne and a number of lesser backbench stalking-horses – all fervently denied by those concerned, of course.

The last time the Lib Dems had met at Birmingham's International Conference Centre had been the spring conference of 2010, at which Nick Clegg had asserted that he would not be a kingmaker in the wake of that year's general election. In truth he had been unwillingly doing just that ever since. In September 2011 Clegg took to the podium to explain a new situation. The hall was hushed with expectation, but no one outside his closest circle of advisers and colleagues expected – from Clegg, at any rate – the bombshell which followed. 'I have spoken at length with the Prime Minister', he confided, 'but to no effect':

'David Cameron is a man of integrity and great ability, but he cannot do other than his party will let him – and they will not let him share government in the way he promised and wants. His colleagues have accused us of breaking promises because we came to compromises with them; they have watched us bear the burden of their unpopular policies and then refused to listen to our ideas; and now they – and he – threaten us with exclusion from office. But office is not theirs to give. It belongs to Parliament, and Parliament may take it from them. I have begun discussions with the Leader of the Opposition about the possibility of working jointly to find a new, common approach to the nation's problems which will be our agenda when Parliament reassembles.'

He reassured his audience:

'There will be no vote of confidence put in the House immediately, but nor will there be any majority for the Tories' partisan legislation. Liberal Democrat ministers will resign office as soon as is practical. In these circumstances, following the passage of the Fixed Term Parliaments Act[28] earlier this year, there can be no dissolution of Parliament, and so I invite Mr Cameron to step down and allow the new agenda to be put into effect by a new team of ministers which enjoys the support of the majority of Members of Parliament. That administration may include Liberal Democrats; it may even include Conservatives; but it cannot realistically be led by Mr Cameron – and therefore it must be formed by the Leader of the Opposition.'

The speech sent shock waves with the same pace and distance as the ones which had followed Cameron's offer to form a coalition, and Gordon Brown's commitment to resign, eighteen months earlier. When the dust had settled from those convulsions in 2010, the unspoken assumption had been that the price of failure was too high for either side of the coalition to bear, and that in any case there was no alternative outcome. But events had shown that nothing is beyond price, and alternatives always exist for those prepared to risk the cost. The spectre of the government that never was, which only existed because of Labour's late recovery the previous year, returned to life.

Predictably, the Conservatives were incandescent at what they saw as a constitutional outrage – in the Parliament after an unelected Prime Minister had taken office, an unelected government would come to power. Some talked of resisting it in the way the Lords had rejected Lloyd George's 'People's Budget' in 1909; Professor David Starkey toured television studios denouncing the impropriety of Clegg's proposal. However, it was pointed out that there were historical precedents for a change in government, in 1931 and 1977, and that in recent times executives had changed composition in mid-term in Wales (in 2000) and the Republic of Ireland (in 1994).

Cameron began – as he had over Scottish independence after the election of the SNP majority government earlier in the year – by sounding a defiant note and promising to stay put in Downing Street. But it was the grey suits of his own party who told him his coalition strategy was a busted flush: it was time, in Churchill's phrase, for Cameron to be pole-axed. It was time for Prime Minister Miliband to have a go.

Notes

1 A total of 2,875 Conservative votes in the following constituencies would, if cast for their leading opponent, have produced this result: Warwickshire North, Thurrock, Hendon, Cardiff North, Sherwood, Stockton South, Broxtowe, Lancaster & Fleetwood, Amber Valley, Waveney, Wolverhampton South West (all to Labour); Camborne & Redruth; Oxford West & Abingdon, Truro & Falmouth, Newton Abbot, Harrogate & Knaresborough – the only seat with a real majority of over a thousand, at 1,039 (all to the Lib Dems).

2 Warwickshire North, Thurrock, Hendon, Cardiff North, Sherwood, Oxford West & Abingdon and Camborne & Redruth.

3 Ashdown made this remark about the real negotiations in an interview with Nick Robinson as part of *Five Days that Changed Britain* (BBC TV, 29 July 2010); Alexander

and Campbell are quoted saying this in Peter Mandelson, *The Third Man: Life at the Heart of New Labour* (Harper Press, 2010) p. 547.

4   *The Orange Book: Reclaiming Liberalism* (Profile Books, 2004) was co-edited by Laws with a contribution from Clegg, and was widely (if exaggeratedly) identified with a greater acceptance of privatisation and a reduction in the role of the state.

5   See Michael Ashcroft, *Minority Verdict: the Conservative Party, the Voters and the 2010 General Election* (Biteback, September 2010). This view was also reflected more bluntly in Michael Brown, 'Failure of Cameron's pet candidates will strengthen his opponents' hand', *The Independent*, 8 May 2010, where the Tory backbencher's remark is quoted; Simon Heffer, 'General Election 2010: David Cameron has had this coming to him', *Daily Telegraph*, 8 May 2010; and reported in Benedict Brogan, 'Hung parliament: Cameron's PR coup to wrong-foot Labour', *Daily Telegraph*, 10 May 2010, and Norman Fowler, *A Political Suicide* (Politico's, 2010), p. 210.

6   Norman Fowler, *A Political Suicide* (Politico's, 2010), p. 212.

7   *The Guardian*, 11 May 2010.

8   BBC News, 10 May 2010.

9   A. Boulton and J. Jones, *Hung Together: The 2010 Election and the Coalition Government* (Simon & Schuster, 2010) pp. 230-31. On 11 May 2010 Cruddas told the Socialist Unity website (http://www.socialistunity.com/?p=5841) that 'any negotiations must be conducted in full consultation with the PLP, NEC and affiliated trade unions'.

10 *Five Days that Changed Britain*.

11 *Stockport Express*, 14 May 2010.

12 Liberal Democrat Christian Forum Magazine, Autumn 2010.

13 Quoted in Sir Nigel Fisher, *The Tory Leaders* (Weidenfeld & Nicolson, 1977), p. 3. Churchill originally wrote this in *The Second World War* (Cassell & Co., 1948–54).

14 Mandelson, *The Third Man,* p. 549.

15 *Five Days that Changed Britain*.

16 Ed Miliband, 'Dear Lib Dem voter', *The Guardian*, 23 August 2010. It is most unlikely that the changed number of Labour MPs assumed here would have altered the outcome of the Labour leadership contest of 2010, close though it was. David Miliband would have needed only six more MPs' support to edge ahead of his brother, but though the seats restored to Labour by the hypothetical result described here would have brought back three definite supporters of David (Charles Clarke, Nick Palmer and Dari Taylor), another three (Phil Woolas, Gloria de Piero and Ian Murray) would have lost to the Lib Dems. Ed on the other hand would have lost Sheffield Central's Paul Blomfield, but he would have gained back Bob Blizzard at Waveney and Andrew Dismore at Hendon, increasing his margin of victory to seven MPs. Since only eight others who would have been restored to Parliament were undeclared, and some of these have very close

constituency party, family or union links to Ed, then it is reasonable to presume, *ceteris paribus*, that Ed would still have won.

17 *Liberator*, April 2011.

18 'Vince Cable: vote yes and end Tories' domination', *The Guardian*, 24 April 2011.

19 See front-page report by Sam Coates in *The Times*, 26 April 2011, as well as an interview with Nick Clegg in *Dispatches: A Year at No 10* (Channel Four, broadcast 9 May 2011).

20 BBC Radio Five Live interview, 7 May 2011.

21 BBC News website, 7 May 2011.

22 *The Herald*, 7 May 2011.

23 *Chesterfield Post*, 24 February 2011.

24 A projection for Democratic Audit by Lewis Baston (*The Guardian* 6 June 2011) showed, on the basis of a theoretical model, that the Liberal Democrats were likely to lose a larger proportion (nearly a quarter) of their seats than either of the other main parties.

25 Both Charles Kennedy and Sir Menzies Campbell voted against the raising of tuition fees in the Commons.

26 This observation was made to Andrew Rawnsley by Shadow Foreign Secretary Douglas Alexander on *Dispatches: A Year at No 10*.

27 David Miliband wrote an article in *The Guardian*, 29 July 2008, ('Against All Odds we can still win, on a platform for change') calling for a change of direction by the Labour Government in which he was Foreign Secretary under Prime Minister Gordon Brown.

28 The Fixed-term Parliaments Act means that a general election can be held only when Parliament has reached its five-year term, when two thirds of MPs have voted for an election, or when the Commons has passed a vote of 'no confidence' in the government. Even should the latter occur, the Act allows the formation of a new administration if the Commons expresses its confidence in the government again within two weeks.

Chapter 19

What if Nick Clegg had opted for 'confidence and supply' rather than full coalition in 2010?

David Mills[1]

I know many of you think that all politicians are just the same. I hope I've tried to show you that that just isn't true. Whether it is on the questions from Alan on care, Jacqueline on crime, Helen on politics, Joel on schooling, Robert on the deficit, I believe we can answer all of those questions, I believe we can rise to all of those challenges if we say 'no' to the old parties and 'yes' to something new and something different.

Nick Clegg, in his closing statement at the first leaders' debate, 16 April 2010.

On 11 May 2010, instead of saying 'no' to the old parties, Nick Clegg chose to say 'yes' to a full coalition with the Conservatives. By doing so, he put his party into government for the first time in seventy years, but he also committed his party to breaking its pledge on student funding and reversing its stance on the pace and timing of deficit reduction – two absolutely central elements of his party's election programme.

Just over a year after the election, the Liberal Democrats are in serious trouble. They failed to win the referendum on the alternative vote, with Nick Clegg's personal unpopularity contributing to the defeat. At the local elections in May, the party suffered its worst results for thirty years – losing nine of the twenty councils they held, including Sheffield, Bristol, Hull and Stockport, and 695 councillors. In the Scottish Parliamentary elections held on the same day, their popular vote was cut in half, and their Parliamentary team reduced from 17 to 5. Nationally, the party's poll ratings hover around 10 per cent, less than half of the share of the vote they won on the manifesto on which they fought the 2010 election. In an admittedly crowded field, Nick Clegg is arguably the most unpopular and derided politician in Britain.

Of course, the Lib Dems have got some positive results out of being in government – the commitment to raise the personal income tax allowance for lower paid workers is probably the biggest gain that Lib Dem supporters of the coalition can claim, alongside the bonus of simply being in power for the first time in decades. But by ceding their position on tuition fees and supporting essentially Conservative positions on in-year cuts and, more importantly, the pace of deficit reduction, the Liberal Democrats have paid a heavy price, and in the years to come many Lib Dem candidates may have good reason to rue the decision to enter full coalition with the Tories. The loss of the party's deposit in the Inverclyde by-election in June 2011, where their candidate won just 2.2 per cent of the vote, could be the first of many such occasions.

A coalition with Labour was never on the cards: the numbers weren't there, powerful Labour figures were opposed to coalition, the party was exhausted and Gordon Brown had run out of road as Prime Minister and party leader. But there was another option on the table – one which Clegg and his closest advisers looked at, and which he discussed with Cameron. That option was a 'confidence and supply' agreement with the Conservatives – a deal which was offered to the Liberal Democrats by William Hague on Monday 10 May 2010.[2]

Many well-informed political journalists considered a full coalition as a less likely outcome than some form of confidence and supply, even two days before it was formed;[3] David Cameron's old politics tutor at Oxford, Professor Vernon Bogdanor, felt able to state in the *Daily Telegraph*: 'Perhaps more likely than a Lib-Con coalition would be a "confidence and supply" agreement, like the Lib-Lab Pact of 1977–78'.[4]

Confidence and supply would have meant the Lib Dems reaching an accommodation with a Conservative minority government on confidence votes and permitting other pieces of legislation to pass. In practice, this would probably have meant supporting a mini-Budget, perhaps some minor spending reductions, a Queen's Speech – and possibly a spending review, though this need not necessarily have meant actively voting *for* them; the Liberal Democrats could have abstained on these and retained a free vote on everything else, as the Conservatives would have retained a solid majority over Labour and the other parties combined.

Nick Clegg could have opted for this arrangement on the basis that the coalition deal was not a good one for his party, and did not offer him enough on important issues such as deficit reduction, electoral reform or student finance. Indeed, it meant him implementing policies which were the opposite of some of the most important and defining positions on which his party had just fought the general election. Instead, he could still have exerted a measure of influence on other policies on a case-by-case basis, and his party would have retained the right to abstain or vote against the Conservatives on other measures.

Deficit reduction

The most pressing and politically sensitive issue facing the new government would have been that of deficit reduction.

Before the election, the Conservatives had warned of the dangers of an unclear result, and the impact it would have on the cost of borrowing.. But the Liberal Democrat position was quite different. In a television interview with Andrew Marr just before the election was called, Vince Cable, then the party's Shadow Chancellor, said that: 'all the evidence from other countries in the Western world is that governments comprising different parties *or minority governments* [emphasis added] have a better record in practice of managing economic crises than one party – often with a very narrow popular mandate'.[5]

Yet after the election, the Lib Dems shifted their position on the timing of deficit reduction, citing the risk of increased concerns in the international bond markets about the UK's fiscal position. Nick Clegg ascribes his conversion to the need for immediate action to eliminate the deficit to the gravity of the financial crisis which was affecting Greece around the time of the general election. Here is not the place to investigate the full circumstances in which he and other senior Liberal Democrats shifted their position on the deficit – though it is worth noting that they did so at a point which enabled them to conclude a full coalition with the only party in a position to offer one – nor to debate what the precise quantum of action on fiscal consolidation was required to prevent a loss of market confidence in the UK government's fiscal stance.

Yet with the Liberal Democrats promising to enable a spending review to take place, and using its position to influence it, a Conservative minority government would have had some cover against negative market reaction. Labour's position on deficit reduction could also have developed in ways which would have reduced the possibility of the financial markets seeing a Labour victory at a second election as a significant source of risk.

One can assume that there would have been a mini-Budget of sorts, and a confidence and supply arrangement would have meant that the Liberal Democrats would have had to abstain, at the very least, to enable it to pass. However, that is not to say that the Liberal Democrats could not have pressed for some elements of their plans to be included, or removed – for instance, the increase in personal allowances for low-paid workers.

It is possible that some small and fairly symbolic spending cuts could have been passed which would have attracted the support of Liberal Democrats – perhaps to some elements of regional and central government bureaucracy. The Conservatives and Liberal Democrats might also have been able to cooperate on process matters – for instance, the Lib Dems could have supported George Osborne's proposals for an Office for Budget Responsibility, a measure which could have been presented as a nod towards greater fiscal stringency.

The key event of the minority government's first six months would have been the spending review of autumn 2010. While the Treasury could possibly have conducted one faster than that, given the opportunity, the need to consult with the Liberal Democrats would have meant that it would still have taken place in the autumn. With a possible second election in the offing, Cameron and Osborne might have taken rather more care to make the cuts seem proportionate and careful, with a package emerging aiming at eliminating the deficit somewhat less quickly than was actually agreed in the coalition's spending review.

This Tory spending review would have put the Liberal Democrats under huge pressure. Backing a Conservative spending review, or even just permitting it to pass, would have opened the Liberal Democrats to some of the attacks which they have faced as a full coalition partner. There would have been accusations that the party had got nothing concrete from the Conservatives in return, and in terms of a lack of ministerial posts, the charge would have had some substance. But that argument fails to recognise the other side of the ledger: what the Liberal Democrats surrendered to the Conservatives by joining a full coalition, namely their independence and distinctiveness on the question of fiscal consolidation, and to some degree on economic matters in general, which has led to them having to bear the full weight of the unpopularity of the government's economic policies, with an extra dose for appearing to have abandoned their principles for power.

By offering 'confidence and supply' only, the Lib Dems would still have had room to stake out a principled and distinctive position between the government and a Labour Party whose position on deficit reduction would have been developing. Rather than rubber-stamping a Conservative spending review, as they effectively did as part of the coalition, the Lib Dems could have argued for a clearer, faster path to fiscal balance than Labour, but one with more regard to the potential impact on growth and public services than the Conservatives'. They might still have been able to wring some concessions out of the new Chancellor, George Osborne, for instance on tax reforms for the low paid, to prove that they could have an impact on policy, an important consideration for the election which would have followed shortly after.

The Conservatives

A minority government would have showed very clearly what the coalition agreement initially obscured, for David Cameron had failed to win the election, and had failed to convince the British public that his party had genuinely changed.

Cameron would probably have come under even more pressure from his own right wing than he did when he secured the full coalition, though any grumbling would have been slightly assuaged by the fact that he would have been able to distribute rather more ministerial jobs to his Tory colleagues as the Prime Minister of a minority government, with no Lib Dem MPs queuing up to accept them. But his leadership would probably not have been under immediate threat – he would, after all, have performed far better than Michael Howard or William Hague in the previous two elections. He would also have been spared the need to whip his MPs to support a referendum on the alternative vote.

As Prime Minister, David Cameron would have wanted to demonstrate that even without the ability to implement much of a programme, the Conservatives knew how to conduct themselves in government. The lack of Liberal Democrats alongside him on the government front bench would not have deterred him from trying to win the support of liberal-minded swing voters – in fact, it might even have made that task more urgent, with a second election in the offing.

One can assume that he would have tried to take the credit for enacting some Liberal Democrat proposals, such as the increase in tax thresholds for low-paid workers, to demonstrate that while the Liberal Democrats talked about such thing, only a 'liberal Conservative' Prime Minister like him was able to put them into practice. But his priority would have been to run as orderly a government as possible while preparing for a second election and bolstering the Conservatives' twin credentials of being fiscally responsible and socially moderate.

The effect on Labour
The potential effects on Labour of the Lib Dems opting for confidence and supply are particularly intriguing.

The conclusion of the full coalition deal convinced Labour that it could take a little time over choosing its next leader, as at that point the next general election seemed a long way off. In the months immediately following the election, when the party's leadership election timetable was set, the coalition seemed robust, and many senior Labour figures assumed that it would last for a long time, if not the full five years.

In contrast, the shadow of a second general election would have loomed over a minority Conservative government almost from the start. This would have increased pressure on Labour to conclude its leadership election earlier. In these circumstances, the former Foreign Secretary David Miliband might have held on to the lead in a contest in which he was always regarded as the front-runner, as Labour MPs in particular opted for a leader who had had more experience at the very top of government and who needed a little less introduction to the electorate.

David Miliband had been as semi-detached from the Brown years as any senior member of the cabinet, and his election as leader, coupled with the imminence of another general election, could have strengthened those who wanted a quick reckoning with the lessons of the party's recent past and the construction of an economic message that took more account of media and popular concerns about the deficit.

Labour MPs would still have attacked Liberal Democrats for supporting a Conservative government – some of this is inevitable in an adversarial political system like ours, where cooperation between parties is still the exception. Yet more intelligent Labour figures would have recognised the sacrifice that the Liberal Democrats had made in turning down the poisoned chalice of a coalition with the Conservatives, and the party would have been able to plan for and explore a potential future partnership with the Liberal Democrats much more thoroughly than it had before the 2010 election.

The impact on the Liberal Democrats

After finding himself in a position where Parliamentary arithmetic made a Con-Lib coalition possible, some elements within Nick Clegg's party would have seen 'confidence and supply' as an anti-climax. For instance, one can imagine that the so-called '*Orange Book*' Lib Dems such as David Laws and Danny Alexander might have raised their voices in favour of a closer relationship with the Conservatives. But this would have been balanced by senior figures from the party's left wing – Charles Kennedy, Paddy Ashdown, Simon Hughes and Shirley Williams – and by many of the party's councillors, not to mention Lib Dems in Scotland and Wales who would have been peering nervously towards the elections in their countries in 2011.

To satisfy his own party and the media, Clegg would have had to have presented confidence and supply as a positive decision, foregoing the trappings of power in order to exercise influence from outside government, while working to advance the party's programme in anticipation of another election in the near future.

There would, of course, have been downsides. No Liberal Democrats would have been able to experience being a minister, and the unique political perspective that brings, not to mention the gravitas and lustre which it can lend a politician (though the extent to which this will confer a tangible political advantage to the current batch of Liberal Democrat ministers in the years to come remains to be seen).

The media, and particularly the lobby, might have been baffled; they would have reacted with incredulity to a party leader who had passed up the chance to sit round the cabinet table after his party had been out of power for so long, and after being offered a 'big, open and honest' chance to do so by the leader of the largest party.

Labour would still have accused the Lib Dems of being tacit supporters of the Conservatives and would have taunted Lib Dem MPs for failing to vote down Tory measures in the Commons and for being the facilitators of a minority Tory government.

Staying out of government would also have been a gamble that first past the post would deliver another propitious outcome next time round. After all, the first election of 1974, which delivered a hung parliament, was followed ten months later by one in which the Labour Party won a narrow majority.

In short, there were plenty of arguments against it. It would have taken nerve. Yet this only tells half of the story.

The Lib Dems could have responded to Labour criticism by pointing to the fact that they had refused the trappings of power, ministerial salaries and prestigious titles and offices, preferring to retain their independence. Above all, they would have avoided the most corrosive charge – that they had changed their minds on two central issues of policy in order to facilitate their entry into government.

After a period in which politicians had seemed all too keen to cling on to the trappings and benefits of power, the public could have reacted quite differently. As the leading Lib Dem blogger Mark Pack wrote in November 2010, in his review of David Laws' account of the coalition negotiations and his brief spell in cabinet, confidence and supply – an outcome which he concedes as the only other possible outcome from the 2010 general election result and the only 'what if?' question worth asking about the post-election events – would have meant no AV referendum.[6]

With the benefit of hindsight, we can now see that the very offer which made coalition possible – Cameron's pledge to hold a referendum on AV – delivered nothing for the Lib Dems (not least because electoral reform could only pass with the support of Labour voters, who proved unwilling to look beyond Clegg's alliance with Cameron). Confidence and supply could have given the Liberal Democrats, who favour proportional representation, the space to agree on a process for progress on electoral reform with Labour. Of course, opposition to reform would have remained strong in parts of the Labour Party. but the debate could have taken place with less rancour and bitterness.

Even the parallel of the elections of 1974 can also be read in more than one way. Jeremy Thorpe saw his party's share of the vote hold up very well in October 1974 – falling back just one per cent from the 19.3 per cent share his party won in the February general election to 18.3 per cent. Starting from a similar level of support in 2010, there is no reason why the Liberal Democrats could not have looked to the next election with at least some confidence that they would be able to hold what they had won in May 2010, putting them in with a very good chance of once more holding the balance of power.

The central dilemma which the Lib Dems faced after the 2010 general election is best summed up by the former Lib Dem MP David Howarth. Howarth believes that Lib Dem MPs and their leadership did not give enough thought to confidence and supply, and overlooked the fact that, linked to fixed-term parliaments, it could have provided a measure of political stability without costing the Liberal Democrats quite so much in terms of unpopularity. He writes of a 'trade-off between influence and popularity, a trade-off in which coalition leans towards influence and confidence and supply towards popularity ... Coalition does mean more influence to shape decisions than confidence and supply, but it is far worse in terms of blame. That is precisely why the choice is so difficult: it is a choice between policy and politics.'[7]

This is true up to a point – but it is worth remembering that whatever influence on policy that the Liberal Democrats bought by entering into full coalition must be measured against the 'influence' of the Conservatives on their positions – of which student fees is just the most infamous.

Hindsight (a tool not available to Howarth, whose piece was written before the AV referendum was lost) enables another judgement to be made. The Lib Dem leadership seemed to believe that in any calculation of the trade-off between the unpopularity of being in coalition with the Tories and the influence of being in government, the prize of a referendum on AV was a sufficient bonus to tip the scales in favour of coalition. This was the political judgement which Nick Clegg made in May 2010 and it is one for which his party is already paying a heavy price in terms of lost support.

A second election

As a *Times* leader stated on 8 May 2010, confidence and supply 'would make another election almost inevitable within a year or so'.[8]

By spring 2011, David Cameron would have been Prime Minister for almost a year and would have had the chance to put through a mini-Budget, a Queen's Speech (albeit one lacking much in the way of substance) and a spending review. But the lack of an overall majority and the need to negotiate with the Lib Dems on every single Commons vote – plus the nagging fear of going down in history as a political failure – would have made him keen to seek a full mandate.

Cameron would have gone into a second election with the added prestige of being Prime Minister, yet he would have been on the back foot, having been forced to show his hand first on public spending cuts. The ensuing election could have been a referendum on whether his party's mix of spending cuts and tax increases were the correct way to tackle the deficit.

Ranged against him would have been a Labour Party led by David Miliband who, as its new leader, would have had the authority to enforce a clearer line on deficit reduction – one providing somewhat more granularity than that produced by his close supporter Alistair Darling for the 2010 election, when he was Gordon Brown's Chancellor. Armed with 'Darling II', drawn up by Darling in opposition as Shadow Chancellor, David Miliband could have claimed, with some plausibility, that Labour had moved on from the last election and offered a safe pathway back to a balanced budget. Such a development in Labour's position would also have gone some way to calming market fears about the return of a recalcitrant, 'deficit-denying' Labour government being returned at the election – always a caricature and now unthinkable.

Vince Cable would have pressed home a nuanced Liberal Democrat critique of the Conservative spending review ('harsher than we would have liked, though we did force them to make it somewhat fairer'), Labour's record in government and Labour's current stance. He might have pointed to the lack of realistic policies for generating economic growth and building Britain's skills base in the Conservatives' plans, and the relative opacity of Labour's, while warning of the dangers of a one-party government being in charge of deficit reduction.

The Liberal Democrats would have had to face accusations that a vote for them was a wasted vote. But in return, Clegg and Cable would also have been able to claim that, by offering support on a confidence and supply basis, the Liberal Democrats had done all they could to ensure economic stability without betraying their principles – and had made a difference to some policies in the process.

The election of May 2011

Turnout might have remained fairly static – voters turned off by a second election in a year would have been matched by those energised to campaign and vote by the closeness of the previous election. Voting could have been subtly different to that of 2010 – but subtle difference can be enough to produce a very different result.

The Conservatives would have had more money to spend than the other two parties. Yet by going into office, their deficit reduction plans would have become more concrete in the minds of the electorate. Voters who had wanted to see the deficit reduced but were worried about the impact of cuts on their own lives and those of the most vulnerable would have had an early opportunity to register their concern. As a result, the Conservatives share of the vote might have fallen back by a shade over 2 per cent, to, say, 34.8 per cent. This would have cost the Tories some 40 seats, leaving them on just 267. Almost all of these lost seats would have been those which had been held so fleetingly by new Conservative MPs such as Ben Gummer, Anna Soubry and Louise Bagshawe.[9]

Labour could scarcely have fought the 2010 election with a less popular leader, and still they won 29 per cent of the vote. In 2011, they would have had a new leader, and it is hard to see how he would have performed any worse as a campaigner than his predecessor. Running against the Conservatives' cuts, while being more open about the need for a balance between deficit reduction, economic growth and public services, Labour could have put on an extra 3.2 points, taking them to 32.2 per cent. Thanks to the vagaries of the electoral system, this would have won them an extra 36 seats, putting the party on 294 MPs, including those representing Hastings & Rye, Stroud and Wolverhampton South West – all seats which the party lost in 2010, having held them since 1997.

Across the country, a decisive number of tactical voting Liberal Democrats could have backed Labour candidates, especially after the Labour leader David Miliband had made clear that electoral reform would have to follow if no single party won an overall majority for a second election in a row. Similarly, many Labour voters would have felt able to vote for Liberal Democrats where it helped to defeat a Conservative, as the Lib Dems would have made clear their distaste for elements of the Conservative Party's deficit reduction strategy. This churn of votes could have left the Liberal Democrats with an extra 0.7 per cent of the vote, putting them on 24.3 per cent, enough to deliver a net gain of four seats, taking them to 61 MPs, with Camborne & Redruth, and Oxford West & Abingdon returning to the Lib Dem fold.

The result would have proven that Britain's first-past-the-post electoral system was well and truly broken. Not only would it have failed to produce a majority for one party for the second time in succession, but it would have meant that the party with a clear advantage in terms of seats – Labour – was significantly behind the Conservatives in votes cast. Such a result could even have triggered a reassessment by some Conservatives of the advantages of sticking with first past the post.

It would also have presented Nick Clegg with a clear path forwards. David Cameron would have lost seats and votes from a year before, and the numbers would barely have been there for a stable Lib-Con coalition. Combined, the two parties would have had a majority of just eight seats. Yet a Lib-Lab government would have had a solid majority of 60, and Labour and the Lib Dems could have found common ground on many issues – not least the need for urgent electoral reform. In these circumstances, even sceptical Labour MPs could have been persuaded of the benefits of ditching first past the post.

A coalition government

On the afternoon of Wednesday 23 May 2011, the new Prime Minister David Miliband sat in his office in No. 10. He was still slightly stunned at how quickly he had gone from being an out-of-favour Foreign Secretary to Prime Minister, with a record-breakingly short stint as Leader of the Opposition in between.

Sure, he'd had to endure some cracks from the new Business Secretary Ed Balls about 'caving in to Clegg', but after seeing the Lib Dem leader walk away from coalition talks with David Cameron a year before, he had been determined to conclude a deal that would last. Offering Vince Cable the position of Chancellor was a no-brainer, as was appointing the popular former Treasury minister John Healey as his Labour 'minder' in the role of Chief Secretary. Reworking the spending review in a way which reassured the markets but put greater emphasis on growth and protected more public services was not going to be an easy task. But at least they now had the reasonable expectation of four years in government to get the job done.

Nick Clegg had accepted the post of Deputy Prime Minister with a brief to run the coalition's constitutional reform programme – including a two-stage referendum on whether to keep first past the post, and then a referendum between AV and PR to follow if it was rejected, an innovation from New Zealand. This was what had clinched the coalition deal for Clegg – Miliband was simply able to go one better than Cameron had a year before, and offer the Lib Dems a shot at their Holy Grail, PR for Westminster elections. Of course, some resistance to electoral reform persisted among Labour MPs, and the party in the country, but Miliband reckoned that for most of them, the chance to destroy the Tories would be too good to pass up. Both party leaders were relaxed about winning the first round against what they hoped would be a demoralised Tory-led 'Keep FPTP' campaign and a broad coalition of reformers drawn from both government parties.

Elsewhere, Paddy Ashdown became Defence Secretary in the Lords, David Laws took Education – a major spending department, seen as one of the biggest prizes in the coalition deal. Chris Huhne went to Energy, Simon Hughes became Transport Secretary, Sarah Teather went to Culture and Danny Alexander to Scotland. Alistair Darling had graciously agreed to become Foreign Secretary – a move he had resisted when Gordon Brown had tried it two years before. With Ed Balls at Business, Jim Murphy at the Home Office, Douglas Alexander at Work and Pensions, Yvette Cooper at Local Government, Liam Byrne at Health and Andy Burnham as Party Chair, no one could accuse his government of lacking experience or weight.

The new Prime Minister had more than enough proper work to get on with, but his mind drifted to the more personal task at hand – organising a stag party for his brother Ed, now Environment Secretary. That awkward period when they had both challenged for the party leadership were long behind them now – and fortunately, David's victory, while clear, had been close enough to enable both brothers to emerge with pride and mutual respect intact.

A few hundred yards away, Nick Clegg was being applauded into work by staff at the Cabinet Office. It had been quite a day for ovations. Earlier, he'd been carried into Cowley Street by a crowd of activists, and welcomed by party grandees including Ming Campbell, Simon Hughes, Charles Kennedy and Shirley Williams.[10] With Liberal Democrat red lines on student funding written into the Lib-Lab coalition agreement, and the real prospect of getting PR, or at least AV, Clegg was the toast of both his party and the media for the masterful way in which he had played a difficult hand over the previous twelve months. Someone asked him to sign the cover of that week's edition of *The Economist*, which depicted Clegg as a puppeteer, pulling David Miliband's strings, with the headline: 'The Masterful Mr Clegg'.

Later, sitting behind his new desk, Clegg mused on how tempting it had been to go into government with the Tories in 2010. There had been good arguments either way, and his top team had gone backwards and forwards on it. But the deal just didn't feel right, and as one of his savvier aides had said to him, after he'd finished the last, difficult conversation with a crestfallen Cameron: 'Look, it's been seventy years – we didn't wait this long just to make a bad deal. Our time will come sooner than you think.' And so it had. Nick Clegg's decision to reject David Cameron's 'big, open, comprehensive offer' back in May 2010 had been vindicated.

Meanwhile, the Tory leader sat alone in the kitchen of his Notting Hill home, surrounded by unpacked boxes. Tomorrow, he had to meet the executive of the 1922 Committee, chaired by the Altrincham & Sale West MP Graham Brady, and he was not looking forward to it.

Notes

1   I am grateful for Duncan Brack's comments on earlier drafts of this chapter.
2   According to David Laws' account in his book, *22 Days in May* (Biteback, 2010), p. 122.

3 FT blog, 9 May 2010, 'The shape of a Lib-Con deal: three templates': 'A full coalition … The least likely option'. The piece went on to describe 'enhanced confidence and supply' and 'minimal confidence and supply', both presumably more likely, either singly or in combination, than 'full coalition'. Available at http://tinyurl.com/3utsj4y

4 *Daily Telegraph* 9 May 2010, 'General Election 2010: Voters of Britain have elected an unviable parliament'. Professor Bogdanor went on to explain why he felt that a coalition was impossible, and why even 'confidence and supply' would be difficult: 'The Conservatives believe that the deficit should be dealt with immediately, and propose an emergency budget within 50 days. The Lib Dems agree with Labour that cuts should be delayed until the recovery is assured.'

5 Andrew Marr Show, 7 March 2010 – transcript available at http://tinyurl.com/3c6c9x8

6 Mark Pack, review of David Laws, *22 Days In May*, on Amazon.co.uk – available here at http://www.amazon.co.uk/review/R6HRKLP73NAI2

7 David Howarth, 'A coalition is born', *Journal of Liberal History* 70 (spring 2011), pp. 41–42.

8 *The Times* 8 May 2010, 'Yes We Can'.

9 All electoral calculations based on outcomes from Electoral Calculus (http://www.electoralcalculus.co.uk/).

10 Shirley Williams supported confidence and supply between the May 2010 election and the formation of the coalition: *The Guardian*, 8 May 2010, 'Shirley Williams warns Nick Clegg against coalition with the Conservatives' – 'Speaking to *The Guardian*, she said she would prefer the Lib Dems to agree to vote through key Tory bills rather than become coalition partners. Asked if she thought an alliance was a good idea, she said: "No. Instead I think it would be better for us to offer them 'confidence and supply' and let them govern as a minority government, coupled with cross-party work in two areas: we need swift cross-party action to bring down the deficit, and action on political reform".'

Chapter 20

What if Pope Benedict had been assassinated on his visit to Britain in 2010?

Andy Mayer

Creak … knock … creak, creak … knock … creak … knock … creak, creak … knock …

A note, half-weighted by granite, flutters in the Monahagn breeze. As the corner lifts in the wind, the words 'I'm sorry, it didn't help' can be read. The rest is indistinct; smeared and stained.

Unsmudged, the sentiment contained would be clear: a small private tragedy; a life unfulfilled; banal, futile, without hope.

To the boy who finds the note, the words mean little. Not that he got to read much, the source of the creaking noise, a cadaverous metronome, causing him to loosen his grip on the scrap of paper.

To the Gardaí tasked with securing the scene, the words are sad – pitiful, even; but nothing out of the ordinary.

To the man to whom the note is addressed and eventually handed, they contain a darker insight. 'Did you cut him down yourself?' he asks.

A mumble and a nod from the officer can be translated as an affirmative.

'I thank you for that; he was never one for making a scene. He would have hated all this fuss.'

The officer's body language shows every sign of him finding this conversation rather more difficult than his earlier task – holding the legs, while a colleague cut the rope. He can still hear the sawing and thump; the squeak of the metal on wood, over and over. Listening to this stranger over that racket is proving hard.

Sensing his discomfort, the man holds out his hand. 'You leave this with me now; our revenge will be the laughter of our children.'[1]

The odd remark snaps the constable briefly out of his daze; however, puzzlement quickly gives way to incomprehension.

'Too young', thinks the man as he walks away, fumbling for his car keys. Leaving his brother's remains to the care of this confused sentry. The man's self-control is impressive; bonhomie calculated, nonchalant walk rehearsed, the anger pulsing in his veins, entirely concealed. There is work to be done.

He pushes the note in his pocket, starts the engine, and heads to the airport.

~

Half a year later another man, this time in overalls, is also leaving for work.

Danny is good at his job. Danny even likes it … most days. It's not the challenge – servicing photocopiers is something he learned quickly on the company apprenticeship scheme. He had spent his childhood surrounded by bits of old wire in his dad's workshop. He had made his pocket money upgrading early BBC computers for the local college students. Danny was a natural with machines.

What he did like was the gratitude. For the busy researchers and secretaries – particularly the secretaries – whose boredom he occasionally attempts to relieve, he is an essential service. People would miss him.

He likes the hours as well. It gives him time to do his course at Birkbeck.[2] Next week they're studying 'God and Evil'. Not that he needs much convincing. Ever since he picked up a copy of *The Blind Watchmaker*,[3] left on a machine he was servicing around the time of the Education Reform Act,[4] he'd been an avid consumer of writing by other non-believers. That his older, 'more successful', brother, 'who ran a whole Post Office depot', as his mother would remind him – frequently – was a bit of a God-botherer had nothing to do with it. He was sure on that point.

However, the satisfaction he felt the first Christmas he was able to describe in detail why there was no credible evidence Jesus Christ even lived,[5] let alone was related, in some way, to an entity no more plausible than a Flying Spaghetti Monster,[6] was indescribable vengeance for a hundred childhood humiliations. That Number One Son, exhausted of argument, spluttering and waving his arms about, had spilt turkey gravy all over himself, turning the colour of cranberry jelly in the process, was an image recorded – and on loop-replay – in the private cinema facility of the memory palace he had constructed after reading *Tricks of the Mind*.[7] All the best brains were on his side of the debate; he was sure on that point as well.

He was looking forward to the protests next week, and had something quite special planned.

~

On the evening of 17 September 2010, Pope Benedict – the sixteenth to take that name – finished his speech in Westminster Hall. Flanked by the Speakers of both Houses, he walked down the stairs, crossing the ground where Guy Fawkes and Charles I had both been tried for treason, and towards the exit to New Palace Yard.

It was then that a figure, who could have only come from inside the Parliamentary Estate, pushed through the security cordon flanking the path to the Popemobile, and detonated a device arranged around his person and concealed beneath his jacket.

The presence of the cordon and stone gateway contained some of the damage, shielding those still in the hall. However the bomber obliterated himself and the protection officers in close proximity, and mortally wounded several others, including the Pope, who was pronounced dead some thirty minutes later across the river at St Thomas's Hospital.

Also killed in the blast were the Commons Speaker, John Bercow, and Black Rod, Sir Freddie Viggers. Many were seriously wounded, including Lords Speaker, Baroness Hayman, the Archbishop of Canterbury, Rowan Williams, and journalist Polly Toynbee, her writing arm shattered by shrapnel flying deep into the hall.

The assailant's timing, and the unwitting bravery of the fallen, spared many more, including current and former leaders of the nation. Deputy Prime Minister Nick Clegg, Lady Thatcher, Tony Blair and Gordon Brown were all sitting within feet of the Pope during his speech.

Prime Minister David Cameron, attending to his father's funeral,[8] was absent. Within an hour of the incident, Cameron gave an impromptu speech from his parents' family home. Later comparisons were made with Blair's 'Diana moment',[9] also in the first year of a new administration. Both Prime Ministers were natural orators with an empathic grasp of the nation's mood.

'There are families across Britain and the world grieving today: not just for those murdered, but in confusion and anger at what it might mean. I buried my father today. Others will be burying their parents in the coming days. The Catholic community will be burying a man who was father and leader to millions.'

'This act of terrorism, in the heart of our democracy, is shocking and unacceptable. We do not know, at this time, who has done this, or why. It is only clear that the assassin, in his coward's death, has denied us a full explanation.'

'We will find out. And if this is part of a wider conspiracy, we will find and punish those responsible. We will review security and take whatever steps are necessary. This should never be allowed to happen again.'

Nick Clegg, dazed by the blast, but otherwise unhurt, echoed the remarks. His dust-covered jacket and hair, against a backdrop of the grieving in Parliament Square, contrasted with the unruffled Prime Minister, provided many with their abiding image of that day.

~

In the immediate aftermath of the blast, among small protest groups in Whitehall, there was panic, confusion, and some arrests.

Some, further from the blast, misinterpreted police attempts to remove them. As shouts of 'There's been a bomb', and 'The Pope is dead' began to penetrate, a drunken minority started cheering. This prompted scuffles, and urgent pleas from the more sensible to shut up.

Most had gone home within the hour. But the *Daily Mail* front page showed a young girl, somewhat the worse for wear, in a tight-fitting 'Atheists have morals' tee-shirt leaping, apparently in joy (though actually to avoid tripping over dropped placards), set against the ambulance flotilla pouring from the hall.

The 'Protest the Pope' campaign[10] cancelled their major rally planned for Saturday, just yards from the bomb site. They issued a statement condemning the attack and called for calm.

Within 24 hours those calls would intensify.

~

Forensics, sorting through the debris discovered the charred remains of the Parliamentary pass of one Danny Poundstone.

Danny had no business being in Westminster Hall that evening. He was a contract photocopier engineer who had worked on the Parliamentary Estate for years. He had unusually come to work that day without his van: in for servicing, he had said.

A search of his flat uncovered a treasure trove of wires and mechanical collateral, shelves of atheist literature, and detailed maps of the Papal visit. A call to a Sunday tabloid, the usual exchange of money around the back of New Scotland Yard, and on the 19th the headline 'Police investigate atheist fanatic' painted a credible picture of a delusional loner obsessed with the Pontiff.

Colour was added by a family member, an older brother: 'When I became a Christian, Danny became very angry. He used to hector me at family gatherings and try to convince me I was wrong. He was lovely as a kid, but became so angry, so very angry, since he started reading that stuff. I only hope we can find it in our hearts to forgive him for this appalling atrocity.'

Richard Dawkins, author of many of the books in Danny's flat, was enraged by the headlines, particularly those creating links between the influence of his writing and the event. Acting against the advice of the police, he responded vigorously to media requests, and dismissed the suggestion of an atheist gunpowder plot. 'We're humanists, we love human life. That someone with some humanist views, if these reports are correct, has acted in this way, shows they have not understood that. Some of these commentators have been waiting all their adult lives to make this kind of spurious link. It sickens me and is profoundly dangerous.'

His tone only inflamed the media. 'Pontius Prof washes his hands' said *The Sun* editorial the following day. A student from Danny's course claimed that Danny used to talk about Dawkins like some kind of messiah. 'He used to wave *The God Delusion*[11] at me and scream: "just read it, read it, you fool". Quite a scary guy.'

When leaked DNA tests confirmed Danny's hair on a recovered fragment of boiler suit, there could be no doubt. Here was a hate-fuelled zealot, with engineering skills, who had pulled off the crime of the decade by exploiting his privileged access to Parliament.

~

The method of execution used was a jacket lined with Pentaerythritol tetranitrate (PETN),[12] a hard-to-detect high explosive that burns at over 4000°C. Investigators discovered traces in empty toner cartridges disposed of in bins near a machine on which Danny had been working in the afternoon.

The spares had been delivered a few days earlier that week. They had escaped detection despite Parliament's sophisticated scanning equipment, upgraded many times since the INLA murdered Airey Neave with a car bomb in 1979[13] and in response to 9/11. When a copycat plot involving printer cartridges was uncovered on Yemeni cargo planes in England and Dubai only a month later[14] it was intelligence, not technology, that had foiled the bombers.

Danny must have accessed the supply store on the pretext of fixing a fault, removed the explosives from the cartridges, used them to line a jacket and belt he had brought in with his tool bag, and found a place to hide, or wander around, until the conclusion of the speech. No suspicious materials had come in with him that day, just a bag full of tools wrapped in cloth that turned out to be the jacket and belt.

Security remembered that he had explained a change of clothes he brought with him as being intended for a party in Victoria after work. Another had noted that he hadn't swiped out of the building after knocking-off time, but had thought little of it. He'd worked late previously on a number of occasions.

Not all elements in the plot fitted so well. No one could work out from where he had sourced the material. Outside Yemen and other failed states, PETN was not an off-the-shelf purchase. The material used was professional, not the lucky result of a home experiment. Even his helpful brother couldn't provide any insight as to when he might have learned to handle advanced munitions. 'It's the only project in his life he ever completed', he muttered off camera.

Other items in Danny's flat included protest gear for the day after the explosion. An 'Abstinence makes the Church grow fondlers' board looked as though it had been particularly lovingly crafted, alongside a more rudimentary pink mitre made from folded paper with something impolite about condoms. It was not obvious why he had bothered.

A myriad of other DNA traces were found in the hall. The quantity identified as Danny alone was tiny, but only his mother was still protesting his innocence. The public were convinced.

~

Just how convinced was in evidence when the first bricks were thrown through the windows of One Gower Street, the headquarters of the British Humanist Association (BHA). The green door was sprayed red with indelible paint, and police narrowly averted the firebombing of Conway Hall in Red Lion Square, the site of a comprehensive humanist library.

For Dawkins these acts only encouraged him to increase his activism. A prepared speech, a response to the Pope's 'aggressive secularist' remarks scheduled for the 18th,[15] was instead delivered by YouTube, labelled in defence of free speech. 'I can just imagine the discussions in the corridors of Vatican power: how are we going to distract them from buggering boys? Why don't we blame them for Hitlerism?' Followed by an analysis of the evidence for Hitler's Catholicism.

It was deemed particularly inflammatory. SO15, the British counter-terrorism command, detected the video link being posted to the discussion forums of many known fascist groups. The Dawkins residence was put under special protection watch.

~

Parliament was recalled on 20 September for a special session, an all-day debate and statement by the Prime Minister, chaired by Acting Speaker Nigel Evans.[16] It was a dignified affair, more given to condemnation of the act, and touching personal speeches, than politics.

What little policy did intrude, principally from Conservative back-benchers and former Labour ministers, concerned their worries about the government's mooted reforms to control orders. This, they said, with the debris still being cleared from the hall, was no time to be relaxing vigilance in the war on terrorism. Following the debate, a Royal Commission on Parliamentary Security, to be co-chaired by Sir Menzies Campbell, Lord Howard[17] and Lord Reid,[18], was announced. The cross-party nature of the group attracted widespread praise.

Within the debate, however, the press particularly noted the command-ing and statesmanlike performance of former Labour Foreign Secretary David Miliband. He and the other four Labour leadership candidates, having suspended campaigning over the weekend, had agreed to give one speech each during the debate. David Miliband's calm authority and sense of proportion shone through in his remarks. Calling for unity, investiga-tion, and firm action against those responsible, he sounded like a leader.

His brother Ed, who many considered a serious challenger, was more empathic. He spoke passionately and compassionately in support of the victims, but his nasal twang and more stilted delivery gave the words less conviction. Only one of the brothers looked like a potential Prime Minister.

No one could entirely recall what any of the other three said, bar a lingering sense of irritation and impatience after Ed Balls had sat down.

No one was then surprised when on 25 September, as a prelude to a som-bre Labour Party conference in Manchester, David Miliband took his place as the new leader of the Labour Party, albeit on the thinnest of margins, of 0.5 per cent[19] over his brother, who had narrowly won the union vote, but not those of the parliamentarians or party members.

Ed Miliband, despite his disappointment, graciously accepted David's victory, and his later offer of the Shadow Chancellorship. He agreed that despite his relative economic inexperience, with Alistair Darling in a mentoring role as Shadow Chief Secretary to the Treasury, he would provide a calmer voice than the obvious alternative, Ed Balls, who was to unleash his attack skills in the Home Affairs portfolio.

The Liberal Democrats, meanwhile, saw their own conference in Liverpool turned into a ghost town. Leading figures made brief appearances and the full assembly only appeared on the Tuesday for Nick Clegg's postponed leadership speech. Dignified, sombre, and calling for national unity, it was well received. Clegg noted briefly the troubling events at Gower Street, and reflected on his own family circumstances, a Catholic-atheist marriage; how it was helping him understand the public mood, and giving him the strength 'to pull together, in the way we all must, to prevent this awful event being exploited by extremists'.

'And I will say one more thing. In these times, it would be the easiest thing in the world for us to make concessions to reactionaries on civil liberties. This we will not do. The erosion of our civil liberties under the last Government is what many of you came into politics to oppose. We will not let you down.'

~

Two days after his death, the Pope's body had been flown home to the Vatican, setting in chain a series of formal, if hastily arranged, events over four days – the Rite of Visitation. His Requiem Mass and Rite of Interment took place on the 23rd. The event secured a global audience of 2.5 billion people,[20] and was attended by both the Prime Minister and his Deputy.

Despite the shock of the assassination, the Vatican machine, orchestrated by Tarcisio Bertone,[21] the Carmalengo, acted with calm efficiency and attention to ritual.

The ceremony was altered in one small way. The explosion had separated the Pontiff from his signet, the Ring of the Fisherman, a symbol of papal authority, and in earlier times his seal. The destruction of the ring had always been the first formal act of the Carmalengo following death: historically, a method of preventing forged orders in the name of the Pope. The half molten lump of metal that was returned on the 21st needed little further destruction. It had turned up only after being surgically removed from one of the security officer victims, having cost them their right leg.

The Novemdiales, nine days of official mourning, followed the funeral. After that the Dean of the College of Cardinals led over 120 leading members of the church into conclave in the Sistine Chapel. Four days later, after a rumoured eleven ballots, white smoke replaced black, and the man who had entered as Cardinal Marc Ouellet, previously prefect of the Congregation of Bishops, and before that archbishop of Quebec, emerged as Pope Benedict XVII.

It was a name designed to calm nerves and celebrate continuity. He promised to heal the church from the 'egregious wounds it had suffered from without and within' – a choice of words deemed interesting, promoting much speculation as to which way this Pope would bend on reform.

The timing, along with the start of the Commonwealth Games, served to entirely distract attention from the Conservative Party conference in Birmingham, which was otherwise remarkable mostly for debates over child benefit and welfare reform. The fringe was lively, with talk of conspiracy theories and militant atheism. Lord Gummer, speaking from the floor of the Conservative Christian Fellowship reception,[22] received a particularly loud cheer when calling for recognition that the Conservatives 'were, are, and always will be a Christian party, as resolute in our faith as we are against the bigots who seek to destroy faith with the unreason of violence'.

The British Humanist Association reception at the same time was a small affair. Staff manning their floor stand, facing angry abuse (mostly about Dawkins) from activists for much of the day, had little energy left for socialising. The usual assortment of hacks and candidates seeking support for various internal party posts were staying away. ConservativeHome sardonically reported the alleged words of the BHA Chief Executive that 'at least we felt safer inside the security cordon with you lot than out there with the public. It's the first time I've felt relatively comfortable stuck in a room with a bunch of Tories.'

~

The resumption of Parliament on 11 October was not the main item of news that day, nor was the opening of the inquest into the 7/7 bombings in 2005. The release of the Browne report into student finance, on the 12th, calling for unlimited fees and welcomed by Business Secretary Vince Cable as 'fair and affordable', passed with less comment than many had expected.

At 09:33 on the 11th, a DHL delivery van pulled up in a leafy Oxford street. A young man in a hurry, very late on his rounds, got out, pulled a package from the rear, and sprinted to his destination, a nearby residence. He rang the doorbell. It was opened by a women in her late fifties, with, he noted, a 'fading aristocratic beauty' and 'enormous smile'.

It was the smile he remembered most. As he was handing over the parcel, they were both startled by the sound of pounding footsteps and shouting, muffled through the hedgerow, of '... OP!' Panicking, the lady pulled sharply on the package, falling backwards on a rug and into the house, kicking the door shut as she fell. The delivery courier fell forward with her momentum, but arms around his legs then cut the ground from under him, pushing him to one side.

He would observe later that this act probably saved his life, as the door exploded into shrapnel and the letter box whistled over his descending frame. The police officer dislodging him was not so lucky, disfigured for life with a face full of splinters.

Mrs Dawkins – Lalla Ward,[23] an actress who had captured the hearts of a million geeks in the early 1980s as Doctor Who's Time Lord assistant Romana – was even less fortunate. Caught in the full force of a blast in the corridor of her hallway, she was killed instantly.

Richard Dawkins, the intended target, was left without the dignity of a private grief. Tabloid reporters swarmed over Oxford for days demanding interviews. For once the Oxford Professor for the Public Understanding of Science had nothing he wanted to say.

His pain, however, proved something of a catharsis in the public mood. People were revolted by the act. Thousands turned out to pay a silent tribute to Ward, some in Whovian costume, lining the streets around an otherwise family funeral. Small badges with Ward's face and the slogan 'not in my name' became commonplace. References to aggressive secularism in the popular media declined sharply.

~

The start of the rescue of miners trapped 700 metres underground in a mine in Copiapó in Chile the next day, a worldwide story since August, lifted some spirits. The contrast of hope and despair, the sense of inspiration in human ingenuity, peppered David Miliband's first Prime Minister's Questions as Leader of the Opposition – against his brother's advice to focus on benefit cuts.

Home Secretary Theresa May's statement on the Oxford parcel bomb added an investigation to the remit of the tripartite inquiry on the Papal assassination. At a speech at a school in Chesterfield on the 15th, principally concerning the Liberal Democrats' success in persuading the coalition government to agree a spending boost for poorer pupils, Nick Clegg tacked on some pertinent comments. He compared what was happening in response to the papal assassination with a virus in society. Using Dawkin's own analogy of the 'meme' in *The Selfish Gene*,[24] he stated:

'Hatred, prejudice, and violence have no place in British society. What happened on 17 September was an expression of all three. What it has been alleged was done in the name of atheism has generated a meme of hatred, causing fear, injury and now loss of life. This must stop.

'The United Nations today announced the elimination of a little known virus, rinderpest.[25] A threat to cattle, this is only the second virus in human history to be utterly destroyed by people – civil society and governments acting together, not just in one country, but across the planet.

'That gives me great hope that we can kill the virus of hate caused by this outrage: by tackling it inside ourselves, as well as through civic action and policing; by cooperating, and recognising the difference between the act of an extremist, and the ideas they claim to represent.

'This attack is not the first time different points of view have clashed violently. But it can be the last. We must now pull together, confront this bigotry for what it is, and move on.'

~

The speech was supported in particular by the Prime Minister and leader of the Opposition. An undercover reporter however, part of a *Guardian* team seeking the honest views of different members of the coalition in their constituencies,[26] caught the unguarded remarks of Andrew Rosindell, Conservative MP for Romford, and Chair of the All-Party Parliamentary Group on the Holy See:

'Going soft, isn't he [Clegg]? What is this "I'd like to teach the world to sing" Lib Dem bullshit? We should find those responsible and string them up' – remarks for which, although condemned by his leader, he was unapologetic.

Conservative commentators were divided. Some, like blogger Iain Dale, condemned his language and *The Guardian*'s subterfuge in equal measure. Others, like ConservativeHome, noted that it reminded people there was still a real Conservative Party, one more in touch with the sentiments of ordinary people than Cameron's inner-circle love-in with Nick Clegg, one worth listening to on matters of national security and criminal justice.

Tim Farron MP, standing for the post of President of the Liberal Democrats, spoke for many party members when he said: 'If anyone still doubts why it is important we are in this coalition to moderate the excesses of the Conservative Party, they should spend some time with Andrew Rosindell and a hidden microphone.'

~

On Monday 18 October the government released its National Security Strategy, 'A Strong Britain in an Age of Uncertainty', the new annual strategy of the National Security Council. It was followed a day later by the

Strategic Defence and Security Review, focused on the armed forces. Few were surprised by the focus on 'acts of terrorism' threatening the UK in both, nor the promised increase in spending on intelligence at the expense of MoD bureaucracy. Much of this in any case related to the pre-crisis coalition agreement and the desire of both parties to improve accountability, limit waste, and roll back some of the last Labour government's assault on civil liberties.

Low-level grumbling on that latter point, largely from Conservative backbenchers, was ignored. Was an 8 per cent cut in defence spending really wise, they asked, when terrorists could get a bomb into Parliament?

What did cause surprise was the discovery, later that week, of Danny Poundstone's body.

~

Shortly after George Osborne's delivery of the Comprehensive Spending Review, a police officer, responding to a complaint of a strange smell near woods in Kennington Park in south London, uncovered a shallow grave. Within twenty-four hours[27] the Forensic Science Service confirmed a match with the unfortunate photocopier engineer.

Labour's hope of a week of coverage on the coalition's 'savage cuts' agenda was blown off the airways. A confident Nick Clegg dismissed out of hand a report of the Institute of Fiscal Studies citing the CSR as 'unfair'[28] before launching an angry and personal attack on the commentators who had rushed to demonise Poundstone – and atheists in general – as murderers and extremists.

Menzies Campbell, commenting on the early work of the tripartite Commission, noted that they had concerns about the quality of the early forensics work at the bomb site, and indicated he had asked the Home Secretary for an urgent review. In the midst of that review, on the 29th, the discovery of the second Yemeni PETN device set off a wave of speculation about links to Al-Qaeda.

Paddy Ashdown and Patrick Mercer appeared on *Newsnight* debating control orders[29] and whether they would have prevented either attack. The growing split between the front and back-benches of the Conservatives on the matter was reported in several dailies, while the Liberal Democrats remained united in their desire to scrap the measure.

A week later Conservative backbenchers were particularly emboldened by the performance of the Republicans in the US mid-term elections, recapturing the lower house and making significant advances in the Senate.[30] They noted the influence of the mixed libertarian / ultra-conservative Tea Party movement and a general trend away from consensus towards bipartisanship. Did the UK Conservatives really need the Liberal Democrats?

~

November 10 was the day of a major NUS march against the Browne report. Westminster was locked down under temporary measures to reroute protests, an early decision of the Tripartite Commission. Anarchists, militants and the usual assortment of the starry-eyed swept up in the protest mood still attempted to reach Parliament and the party headquarters, but they were easily deflected by the strong and effective police presence, deploying 'kettles' around Vauxhall Bridge, Victoria Station and Trafalgar Square.

What limited damage was done – some idiot throwing a fire extinguisher into the Thames[31] being a highlight – received scant attention. It was a sideshow compared to the day's main story, the findings of the forensics review. The investigation had revealed that among the samples taken that day only one did not match records of known guests and staff. Furthermore, it was the DNA of a known criminal with links to terrorism. Further still, the suspect bore a marked physical resemblance to the unfortunate Poundstone.

Mark Harte, who had grown up in the 1970s on the Falls Road in Belfast, had been arrested in Craigavon, in County Armagh and imprisoned in the late 1980s in the Maze, convicted of gun-running for the Provisional IRA. Bright and technically gifted, he was suspected of other crimes, but nothing had ever stuck. He had been released under the terms of the Good Friday Agreement in 2001.

After that he had moved to the Republic, and settled down to life as an appliance engineer, using skills acquired in prison. Little had been heard of him since. He was certainly not linked to the dissident groups suspected of continuing the armed struggle.[32] His motive was entirely unclear.

Although Martin McGuiness and Gerry Adams of Sinn Fein moved swiftly to distance the Republican movement from the act, coming across quite as baffled and shocked as most other Catholics, the reaction from Unionists was nevertheless predictable. As Tom Elliot, the UUP leader and MLA for Fermanagh & South Tyrone, stated in an ill-tempered public meeting: 'The scum[33] of Sinn Fein/IRA have reaped what they have sown, cutting off the head of their own serpent.'

Such remarks were short-lived, most moderates calling for calm while investigations were ongoing. It was in any case unclear whether some Unionists were angry or delighted by the irony. Newsnight cancelled a special report[34] into the actions of dissident groups on 11 November for fear of inflaming tensions. Several Republicans had already issued statements condemning Harte as either a government spy or a turncoat, largely to derision from all sides.

~

On 15th November, links were made by the *Irish Independent* to a short piece in the *Monaghan Gazette* from March. It noted the suicide of an Aidan Harte, Mark's brother, who had been found by a local delivery boy, having hanged himself.

Aidan Harte had appeared in the media a week or so earlier, part of a delegation of victims and relatives seeking an explanation from the Primate of Ireland, Sean Brady,[35] for his role in the cover-up of their abuse, in the 1970s, by the convicted 'Falls Road' paedophile, Father Brendan Smyth.[36] Smyth had been convicted in 1994 and died in 1997. But it emerged later that Brady had taken witness statements from two victims of Smyth in his role as secretary to the Bishop of Kilmore in 1975. Rather than pass their complaints to the RUC, he had hushed it up. The revelation of this negligence did not prompt his resignation; in fact he stated that he would only resign if 'asked to do so by the Pope'.[37] No such instruction was issued. Pope Benedict instead preferred a letter to all Catholics in Ireland on 19 March[38] calling for 'a path of healing, renewal and reparation'.

Aidan had been a troubled man since his childhood, involved in drugs and alcohol abuse, and unable to hold down a job or form close personal relationships. He had attempted suicide several times before and had only confessed his troubling secret to his few friends and family eighteen months before his death.

For Mark, Aidan's death had been a cause of deep anger and guilt. His brother's many insecurities had seen them drift apart since their teenage years. Mark in part had found the camaraderie of the IRA a substitute for the fraternal love he could not feel at home. Aidan had rarely visited him in prison and Mark had not been surprised.

Finally understanding why it was that Aidan had shut himself off from the world, Mark wanted justice. He wanted to turn back the clock. He wanted to make those still left alive pay for those wasted years. Brady's decision all those years ago to let the abuse continue had exposed Aidan to danger, and denied him his innocence. The Cardinal's arrogance when exposed, and the failure of the Papacy to remove him, is what Mark believed had finished his brother's will to fight on.

Aidan's suicide ended Mark's belief in doing anything but fight. He would become the weapon of his brother's revenge. He would make his own church understand the wrath of a vengeful God.

~

Mark, as the authorities suspected, had been something more than a gun-runner in his youth. His skills had been picked up and his training in a variety of bomb-making techniques was quite extensive. Contacts made with various dealers led him to a former Libyan contact now living in Yemen, who updated him on the possibilities of using and sourcing PETN.

The Parliament bomb plot was a rehash of a dozen schemes invented in the 1980s and refined in the chapel of the Maze during Mass, one of the best colleges for bomb-makers outside Afghanistan. The location was selected mainly on the grounds of the Papal visit, but also with a nod to the possibility of one in the eye for the old enemy.

Mark could not conceive of a delivery mechanism that would both guarantee success and see him survive, so he chose a method unusual for his cause,[39] but ideal for one who had abandoned it. Poundstone was chosen on profession and appearance after a week's surveillance of those entering and leaving the Estate. Once targeted he didn't stand a chance. A bullet in the back of the head the night before the operation, delivered by 'a great Irish lad who'd bought him enough whiskey to get senseless', ended his dreams. His atheism was not thought a decisive factor.

These facts were, at least, the conclusions of the detectives, pulling together what they could from phone records, sketches and rambling diaries uncovered in a storage unit used by the assassin.

The implications of the truth, that the leader of the Catholic communion had been murdered by a Catholic in revenge for the sins of the Church he led, were profound. The BHA demanded a public apology from various newspapers. Danny Poundstone's reputation was restored and the Press Complaints Commission took the unusual step of funding a memorial plaque for him and Lalla Ward at Conway Hall.

The brother who had done so much to trash Danny's reputation was not invited for the family Christmas that year, or any after that. His church forgave him, but not his wife, who left him later that year. He did not remarry. His Post Office depot was closed, unusually without protest from local Liberal Democrats.

The conclusion stiffened the unity and resolve of the Liberal Democrats on civil liberties, just as it deepened divisions within the Conservatives. For the former it strengthened their stance that intelligence, not control, was the key to security — a view given some sympathy by the Prime Minister, Justice Secretary Ken Clarke, and other Conservative modernisers. For traditionalists it showed that Northern Ireland remained a threat, security levels were inadequate, and there should be tougher sanctions. A solution to the issue of control orders mooted for January dragged on well into March and was eventually resolved by a free vote in the House, where the Liberal Democrats were the only united party and on the winning side for full abolition.

The tripartite commission made some recommendations for the improvement of security in the House, including yet another upgrade of scanners, and this in turn informed a review of airport cargo security that was implemented six months before the London Olympics of 2012.

Noting the risks of wider dissent in the coalition, and growing student unease, Cameron, Clegg and Cable agreed in December 2010 that it would be prudent to put the Browne Commission conclusions to a wider review, including consultation within the Liberal Democrats. The graduate tax compromise that was eventually implemented in 2013, while not popular, did at least have enough similarities to the NUS's own proposals that the reaction was more mooted than it might have been had the Deputy Prime Minister ridden roughshod over his 'solemn pledge' in 2010 not to raise the cap on tuition fees.

~

Going into the local elections in 2011, both coalition partners expected something of a rocky ride. The global implications of the bombing had allowed David Miliband to show all his qualities, and while it was too soon for the public to forgive Labour entirely for the credit crunch, they went to the polls with high hopes of gains. Miliband had shrewdly judged that Labour's best hopes of regaining power rested on dividing the coalition, while keeping the door of cooperation open. He therefore directed campaigners to focus on wooing disaffected Liberal Democrats while reserving their strongest attacks for the Conservatives. Feelers were extended through various think-tanks. He and Lord Steel launched the Progressive Alliance, an independent campaign vehicle for future cooperation on the centre-left, starting with a major Lib-Lab campaign to win the referendum on the alternative vote. The narrative of two Davids and a new Alliance attracted much attention.

It was the Conservatives, then, who went into the 2011 elections most divided. The 800 council seats they lost had been expected, but was still a bitter blow. Many backbenchers then publicly attacked Cameron when on the Friday Britain's old electoral system was ditched by a margin of just 1.5 per cent.[40]

The Liberal Democrats lost 300 councillors, but felt that it could have been far worse,[41] and Nick Clegg emerged from the referendum campaign the leader of a united party. Labour's night was marred only in Scotland where the relative failings of local leadership allowed the SNP to achieve a small overall majority. However, Labour romped home in Wales and with 1,350 gains in the council elections reversed their losses from 2007. With AV won, with the full backing of their leader, they were able to claim themselves well on the road to recovery.

In Rome, Pope Benedict XVII had reacted to the revelation of a link between his predecessor's demise and the abuse scandal calmly. He had kept his own counsel in the light of his own brother's conviction for abuse of minors in 2008.[42] But as a Cardinal in Quebec he had previously apologised for the way in which the Canadian Church had promoted 'anti-Semitism, racism, indifference to First Nations and discrimination against women and homosexuals.' His apology on behalf of the whole Church of Rome, echoing his predecessor, was equally sincere,[43] and within it contained the promise to create a wide-ranging Pontifical Commission to review whether any practices of the church had contributed to the scandal.

When several Anglican Bishops and priests joined the Catholic Church in November and January of 2010–11, the attention given to the accommodation of their wives was noted by many.

~

Pontifical Commissions are not rapid decision-making bodies. Their recommendations are not always accepted. However, in November 2015, Prime Minister Miliband and his Foreign Minister Nick Clegg welcomed the following statement by the Pope:

> There comes a time in the progress of our communion to pause and reflect on whether the rules we apply to ourselves are appropriate for the time in which we live.

For the first thousand years of this Church we accepted the rights of priest to marry and raise children. Over the next thousand we did not. This was a rule, not dogma; we have, for example, always welcomed the married who come to us having started out in a different tradition.

I do, then, accept the findings of the Commission and hope that the sacrament of marriage, a part of natural law inspired by our Lord at the wedding feast in Cana, will grant our priesthood the same grace as it grants their congregations.

It was a small change; but an important one. It was perhaps enough for the preservation of the next thousand years of Catholicism; or perhaps too little.

Near a barn in Monaghan a butterfly passed on the morning breeze. A little fluttering, and then all was calm.

Notes

1   A famous Bobby Sands quote; http://en.wikipedia.org/wiki/Bobby_Sands
2   In this instance, an introduction to anthropology and religion; http://www.bbk.ac.uk/study/ce/religiousstudies/courses/
3   A 1986 book on evolutionary biology by Richard Dawkins; http://en.wikipedia.org/wiki/The_Blind_Watchmaker
4   The Education Reform Act 1998.
5   R. G. Price, *The Case Against Historical Christ* (2007); http://rationalrevolution.net/articles/jesus_myth_history.htm
6   A popular American campaign highlighting the possible absurdity of arguments from faith and authority; http://www.venganza.org/
7   Hypnotist, and famous former Christian, Derren Brown's guide to memory (2006); http://www.amazon.co.uk/Tricks-Mind-Derren-Brown/dp/1905026269
8   Ian Cameron died on 8 September 2010. His funeral service was on the 17th; http://www.bbc.co.uk/news/uk-politics-11227525, http://www.dailymail.co.uk/news/article-1312966/David-Cameron-takes-baby-Florence-fathers-funeral.html
9   'People's Princess' speech, 31 August 1997; http://www.youtube.com/watch?v=XssMtfxY5ao
10 http://www.protest-the-pope.org.uk/
11 Richard Dawkins, *The God Delusion* (2006); http://en.wikipedia.org/wiki/The_God_Delusion

12 First manufactured in 1912, and used for terrorist purposes in 1983; http://en.wikipedia.org/wiki/Pentaerythritol_tetranitrate

13 30 March 1979; http://en.wikipedia.org/wiki/Airey_Neave

14 30 October 2010; http://www.telegraph.co.uk/news/uknews/terrorism-in-the-uk/8099344/Yemen-bomb-plot-key-questions-raised.html

15 Which can be seen at http://www.youtube.com/watch?v=q_0kFU7IfPM

16 Who would have replaced Bercow from his position as Chair of the Ways and Means Committee; http://en.wikipedia.org/wiki/Nigel_Evans

17 http://en.wikipedia.org/wiki/Michael_Howard,

18 http://en.wikipedia.org/wiki/John_Reid,_Baron_Reid_of_Cardowan

19 As opposed to the actual result, a 1.3 per cent margin for Ed Miliband.

20 It is thought that 2 billion watched the funeral of his predecessor John Paul II in 2005.

21 The administrator of revenues and properties in the Holy See who has special responsibilities during a change of Pope; http://en.wikipedia.org/wiki/Camerlengo_of_the_Holy_Roman_Church, http:/en.wikipedia.org/wiki/Funeral_of_Pope_John_Paul_II#Rite_of_Visitation

22 19:30, Tuesday October 5th.

23 http://en.wikipedia.org/wiki/Lalla_Ward

24 Richard Dawkins, 1976.

25 The disease is characterised by fever, oral erosions, diarrhoea, lymphoid necrosis, and high mortality; http://en.wikipedia.org/wiki/Rinderpest

26 This never happened but was done by the *Daily Telegraph* to Liberal Democrat ministers around the same time.

27 Eight hours appears possible in an emergency; three to five days is more normal; http://www.forensic.gov.uk/html/services/analytical-solutions/dna/

28 A report that significantly cooled the relationship between the party and the IFS.

29 Originally Campbell and Patrick Mercer; http://news.bbc.co.uk/1/hi/programmes/newsnight/9150106.stm

30 Going from 60 Democrats and 40 Republicans to 53 and 47, respectively.

31 As opposed to dropping it on police officers.

32 A particularly vicious attempt made on 5 November by Óglaigh na hÉireann injured three officers; http://www.u.tv/News/Device-could-have-killed-or-maimed-Baggott/59893223-dbe9-4caf-b6b8-5cc33a29c61c

33 A comment actually made on 8 May 2011 after being heckled at an election count; he later apologised; http://www.bbc.co.uk/news/uk-northern-ireland-13323749

34 Broadcast planned for 11 November 2010; http://www.bbc.co.uk/blogs/newsnight/fromthewebteam/2010/11/thursday_11_november_2010.html

35 It emerged in March 2010 that Brady had participated in an internal church legal process in 1975 that had required victims of Brendan Smyth to remain silent about their abuse; http://en.wikipedia.org/wiki/Seán_Brady

36 In 1994 Brendan Smyth was convicted of dozens of offences against children over a forty-year period; http://news.bbc.co.uk/1/hi/northern_ireland/8567868.stm

37 He refused to resign on 10 March 2010; http://news.bbc.co.uk/1/hi/northern_ireland/8567144.stm

38 Full letter at http://www.vatican.va/holy_father/benedict_xvi/letters/2010/documents/hf_ben-xvi_let_20100319_church-ireland_en.html

39 The IRA did not use suicide bombers. Bombers occasionally blew themselves up, but as a result of incompetence, not intent.

40 As opposed to the actual No vote of 68 per cent, a margin of 36 per cent.

41 In the real election the Liberal Democrats lost nearly 700, Labour gained 800, the Conservatives gained 80, and others lost 200.

42 Sixty-three year old Paul Ouellet pleaded guilty to two counts of sexual assault against minors in December 2009; http://www.cbc.ca/news/canada/montreal/story/2009/12/18/quebec-cardinal-brother-sex-assault-ad.html

43 A letter of apology to the victims of abuse in Ireland was issued on 20 March 2010; http://news.bbc.co.uk/1/hi/world/europe/8578064.stm

Chapter 21

What if Ken Livingstone had won the 2012 London mayoral election?

Mark Munro

'Fighting the Cuts': Ken Livingstone's Third Term

The eyes of the world were on London. That evening three billion people were expected to tune into the opening ceremony of the 2012 Olympic Games. In the mean time, an estimated 20,000 journalists had time to kill and an angle to find. Ken Livingstone knew it better than anybody.

Since becoming mayor for the second time, just two months before, he had played the press like a fiddle. He was the most senior and the most powerful Labour politician in the land, and the media were listening.

The top floor of City Hall has a view of London that is hard to beat, with a 360-degree panorama of the capital that takes in almost every landmark. Except today. Normally only dedicated political hacks attended the mayor's press conferences, but now they were joined by journalists from around the world, crammed in, confused and obscuring every part of the view, except for a small sliver on the easterly side where a podium stood.

Ten minutes late, Livingstone arrived, beaming like a Cheshire cat.

'Good morning everyone.

'Today is a genuinely great day for London. So, welcome, all of you who don't have the privilege of living here, because what you will see in this city is something I don't believe you can find anywhere else on the planet.

'But as the Mayor of London, it is my duty to represent the men and women of this city, and that means speaking the truth, no matter how unpalatable or uncomfortable it may be for the people who hear it.

'The truth is that London is on the brink of catastrophe. The cuts agenda being forced through by this government is bringing pain and suffering to the ordinary families who live here – ordinary families who have seen their standard of living fall at a faster rate than at any time since the great depression, or quite possibly, even earlier.

'Now, I stand before you as one of the people who helped bring the Olympics to London. But I was always clear that I had no interest in sport or in the spectacle that millions of people will be tuning in to watch. Rather, my interest was in seeing billions of pounds invested in London, and the regeneration of one of the most deprived areas in the developed world. And it is with that in mind that I am speaking to you today. Because while the games have brought in money and investment, the current government with its agenda of cuts have launched an assault on the very people who I supported the Games in order to help.

'Just a few hundred metres from the Olympic stadium tonight, children will be going to bed hungry because this government has cut their parents' tax credits. Families of six, seven, eight or even more will settle down for the night in two-bedroom flats in the knowledge that there is no hope of them finding a suitable-size home, thanks to this government's slashing of the money for new affordable housing. And even more will turn off the television, having seen this government of millionaires spend the money that could have supported ordinary families spent on a spectacle that gives politicians the chance to flaunt themselves on the world stage, but leaves the people with nothing.

'So I urge you, when you report back to wherever it is that you come from, leave the artificial paradise of the Olympic Park and visit the surrounding parts of the city. Go to Bow, and to Canning Town, and to Barking. Report on the real London and the cost of this extravaganza being paid for in the misery of the desperate. Thank you.'

With that, Livingstone turned and left the room. His job was done.

Short of ideas of their own, the world's media did exactly what Ken had asked of them. There were eight hours before the start of the opening ceremony and that was more than enough. The Thai news anchors, Detroit sports hacks, Parisian supplement-writers and everyone in between all had their angle. Every part of East London that could still be called working class was swamped by journalists trying to stand up Livingstone's story. The traffic slowed. Chicken shops had to close as desperate journalists tried to find the under-class Livingstone had described. The bemused stewards on the Olympic site's media village, told to prepare for the busiest day of their lives, were left twiddling their thumbs.

The reaction from No. 10 was initially to do nothing. By mid-afternoon CNN were asking whether the silence from Downing Street signified the contempt that the coalition government held ordinary people in. By 5pm, Olympic President Jacques Rogge was quoted as saying that he: 'didn't know 100 per cent' whether the Games would still start that evening. Something had to be done.

Deliberately caught by the press pack on his way to the opening ceremony, Prime Minister David Cameron told journalists that it was a 'silly outburst, the sort of thing we have all come to expect from Ken'. The foreign networks, he said, probably didn't realise that people in the UK wouldn't take Livingstone's attempt to upstage the Olympics seriously.

It was too late. Around the world that night, in every language, presenters lowered their voices to mark a more serious tone and took a moment to tell their viewers the plight of London's suffering and the impact of coalition spending plans.

Not for the first time in the history of the Olympics, politics had taken centre stage.

~

The election campaign had been hard fought and bloody.

London found the entire thing rather tiresome, and wholly uninspiring. Voters stayed away in their droves. Luckily for Mr Livingstone, the ones who could be bothered to turn out tended to be the ones who were slightly more fed up with his opponent. Ken returned to City Hall with more votes than Boris, but with fewer than he had managed himself in 2008. That, however, was enough.

The first few weeks of his mayoralty had been a whirlwind of activity as he unstitched much of what Boris had done, replacing it with a cross between a carbon copy of the mayoralty circa 2007 and the wildest days of the GLC.

The congestion charge system would be modified so that people driving the biggest cars would have to pay £25 to enter the zone. Anyone in a 4x4 would pay £100. Ken's advice was simple: 'Get a new car'.

Most importantly to Livingstone, City Hall was to be turned into the front line in the battle against the government and against the cuts. Plans were made for a giant, free-to-attend, open-air music festival in Hyde Park in defence of public services. Named 'Defiance' and paid for by the taxpayer, the budget for this event was coincidentally the same as the increased revenues from the congestion charge in the first year.

Indeed, each of the Royal Parks, all of which had recently come under City Hall's control, was to become the host to a memorial garden for those who lost their lives as a result of government inaction. Each was to be named after a famous free-market thinker or economist. Ken's reasoning was that: 'We're forever remembering people who died because the government sent them to war, but what about the elderly who freeze to death because the government or council have sacked the only person who used to check they were all right? Weren't they sacrificed too?'

All this, however, would take time and Livingstone knew he needed to make an early impact. At the end of his first week, Ken unveiled the first plank of his plan to battle the government. The grass outside City Hall became home to the 'cuts counter'. Standing 20 metres tall, it was nearly half the height of the Great Glass Gonad itself. The new glass and steel scissor-shaped structure was Richard Rogers-designed and nothing if not striking. Four enormous screens rotated around the middle of it, twenty-four hours a day, counting not just London's jobless, but every police officer, tube driver, youth programme, environmental measure and everything else that had actually been cut by Livingstone since entering office. The message was clear: it was the government that was to blame. They had cut off his money.

Building such a machine at such short notice had been costly. The cheapest price GLA officers were quoted was £8 million, but Ken opted for a more expensive 'green' version, replete with solar panels and a wind turbine. Even then it burned nearly £1,000 of electricity every day.

That was the tip of the iceberg. Every tube station was kitted up to carry the same message on signs that greeted every passenger. On the platforms, digital displays designed originally to tell 'customers' information about the next train were re-programmed to update them on the size of the shrinking state as well.

It was a measure designed to piss off the government, and it worked. An expensive legal case was prepared, destined for the High Court, accusing Livingstone of misuse of public money. This merely gave him more publicity and while the case dragged on, the counters kept creeping up.

~

Away from the drama in City Hall, Boris Johnson wasted no time. Through love and persuasion his younger brother Jo showed his older sibling more courtesy than has sometimes been the case in modern politics and resigned as the MP for Orpington. In a short, high-profile, but largely uneventful by-election the former mayor was elected to Parliament to represent the outer London seat.

Despite constant invitations from the media to blame Downing Street, the coalition or the cuts for his defeat, Mr Johnson stayed fully on-message. The defeat was his own; magnanimity and grace was the aim. The reward was a fast track into government.

But he had made enemies at the highest level while mayor, and their punishment for his indiscretions was simple. The brash, publicity-hungry Boris Johnson was given a role of mind-crushing tedium of interest to few. Boris was to be the new Parliamentary Under-Secretary of State at the Department of Communities and Local Government, with special responsibility for decentralisation and localism. The job, it was supposed, was one where the only chance of success was meticulous attention to detail, technocratic finesse and the mastery of a brief which, his enemies assumed, would be far beyond him. Most of all, it gave no opportunity to rock the boat.

At least that's what they thought.

~

Livingstone, in the meantime, was having the time of his life. The food parcels for London's destitute from Venezuelan President Hugo Chavez were carefully orchestrated to make the most of the post-Olympic climate. When North Korea sent them too it was the icing on the cake.

But he had a serious problem – the public didn't like any of it. 'THE MAN WHO RUINED THE OLYMPICS' was what *The Sun* had screeched on its front cover the day after Ken's now-famous intervention, and the public seemed to agree. No less than 75 per cent of the population agreed that Ken had 'damaged' Britain with his outburst (at least according to the opinion polls) and there were calls in the right-wing press not just for Ken's removal but also for the abolition of the GLA itself. No body that gave that type of platform to that type of man, they said, could really be justified.

This delighted Livingstone. A veteran of the GLC's battle for survival in the 1980s, the mayor knew that nothing had ever helped his reputation as much. Ken and his advisers reasoned that little could be better than a Conservative campaign to get rid of City Hall. Ken would cast himself as the saviour of London, fighting for a voice for ordinary men and women against a government opposed to democracy and frightened of the elected representative of the people.

It was decided. The government would be goaded into trying to abolish City Hall.

Livingstone didn't believe that Cameron, Clegg or Osborne had the bottle to go through with it. A victorious campaign, won in the name of London, the people and democracy itself would not only make him a shoo-in for 2016, but deal the body blow to the government that his Parliamentary comrades seemed incapable of delivering.

His strategy was clear. Antagonising Tories was something which he had always had a gift for.

Along with the millions being spent on anti-government propaganda, Ken decided that a few more court cases would be helpful. The publicity would be enormous. The trick was finding issues where the mayor would be seen as being on the side of the people, while the government was cast on the side of a mendacious economic philosophy.

The simplest idea would be to call for a judicial review of the government's finance settlement for London. But while this might allow for a head-on collision and an argument on his terms, legally there wouldn't be a leg to stand on. Few people would understand it and even fewer care. Plus, when he lost the case, he might appear to the only half-interested as having lost the argument over the cuts. Instead, he decided to lay a trap.

Powers given to City Hall in the last days of Boris Johnson allowed the GLA to build houses, old-fashioned council houses. Although there wasn't any money to do it, Ken decided to utilise this new authority beyond to its full potential – and beyond.

In early September, with some of the country's grandest political correspondents squeezed into a two-bedroom flat on the top floor of a Tower Hamlets tower block, the mayor announced the largest programme of house-building in London since the end of the Second World War. The capital was to become home to half a million GLA council houses, for over a million residents in East London. The money, he said, was to be borrowed from the bond markets against the future rents that these new homes would bring in. He called it 'the solution to London's housing crisis and the blueprint for London's future'. His enemies called them 'Ken's Folly', or 'Livingstone's Lithuania', and predicted a Soviet-style slum where only the most desperate would be housed in identikit concrete apartment blocks. The word that most warmed the mayor's heart was 'treason'.

The house-building drive may or may not have been morally or aesthetically right, but it was most definitely illegal. Ken had no right to borrow the money and, despite the high-profile launch, had made no real attempt get it. Indeed, he never expected a single house ever to be constructed. The aim was provocation.

The government reacted furiously. Who did this man think he was? What was he up to? He would have to be put in his place. As the minister most familiar with the workings of City Hall, it was Boris Johnson who was despatched to attack. Just past 8am in the morning, he told BBC Radio 4's *Today Programme*:

'I find it absolutely inconceivable that having spent money with an extravagance not witnessed in a leader since Caligula made his horse a Senator, Mr Livingstone cannot accept that there is no money left. It beggars belief that in the name of nothing more than his own vanity he is trying to borrow money we can't afford, despite the eye-popping debt he and his chums in the Labour Party left us with. And finally, let me just remark, if I may, that some say that a sign of madness is to not learn from one's mistakes and to repeat them again and again. I think I will leave it up to your listeners to make what they will of that.'

By lunchtime, Livingstone had announced his intention to borrow yet more money from the bond markets, this time in order to build holiday homes for working-class Londoners to enjoy subsidised weekends by the sea.

Before dinnertime, legal proceedings against him had begun.

~

Livingstone had become not just the biggest story in London, but in national politics as well. The actions of the mayor dominated Prime Minister's questions. Ed Miliband had tried to say as little as possible, but it didn't work.

Did he or did he not back Livingstone? David Cameron taunted him. 'He can't even control his own party. But then again, maybe he doesn't want to? Maybe he approves of a mayor who spends millions of pounds the country can't afford on vanity schemes? I don't know what the Right Honourable gentleman thinks, but personally I don't believe I can think of anything that better sums up the Labour Party or how we got into this mess than the current Mayor of London.'

He sat down to rapturous applause. The Labour leader was lost for words. Humiliated, he needed to be seen to do something. He rang Livingstone.

'Err, look Ken, this is just ridiculous. You have to stop it. As leader of the Labour Party I have to insist you stop this council house thing.'

'Let me tell you now that I have absolutely no intention of doing so and there's nothing you can do to change my mind. I mean, do you seriously think that they're going to win this? Because, they won't. I am proposing to build London out of a crisis. There are half a million people on council-house waiting lists in London, nearly a million in overcrowded conditions. I'm offering a solution where we can stop that at no cost to the taxpayer, because it will be paid for by the rent these new homes will bring in. These idiots think they're going to win an argument by saying that people shouldn't have a decent place to live and they would rather the misery continued than watch a left-wing policy go through. If you can't see that, no wonder Cameron makes you look like a bloody plonker every week.'

'Look, the party needs a credible alternative and it doesn't help when you're throwing money away on pop concerts and unwinnable court cases, but at the same time complaining about the cuts. These stunts have got to stop, Ken.'

'Or what exactly?'

'Or else ... I'll be bloody cross.'

~

London had no legal basis on which to declare independence from the UK – but then again, Livingstone reasoned, neither did Scotland.

He timed his referendum on the question of whether the capital should abandon the country it governed to happen on the same day, in early 2014, as the vote north of the border. The new independent city state would keep the Queen, but become a member of the Commonwealth like Canada or

Australia, outside the United Kingdom. Freed from supporting the less affluent parts of the country, it could afford lower taxes and higher spending. The great buildings of Whitehall would be turned into hotels and galleries. Parliament would become a refuge for battered women. While the constitution of the new state was agreed Livingstone would take over as president temporarily, with a promise to concede power when the appropriate moment came.

Without doubt it was the most audacious move he had ever attempted. Even if he lost, Livingstone reasoned that those on both sides of the debate would have spent months drilling home the message that the rest of the country depended on London, its money and its influence. The case for not cutting investment in the engine of the British economy would surely be won.

Much to Livingstone's surprise, in the rest of the country the idea was popular. A slim majority of people thought they would do better without London's magnetic pull sucking in investment, jobs and the educated – not to mention the smug swagger of the self-satisfied metropolitans. Losing the capital's one million Muslims and large black population was also a consideration to some.

But in the 33 boroughs that would actually get to vote on the issue, the cause was considerably less popular. The £20 million spent on holding the plebiscite was money, Londoners seethed, that would otherwise have been used to pay for police on their streets and to maintain their roads. Their cash was being thrown at another 'vanity scheme'.

More to the point, while the government said that it would abide by the result of the vote on Scottish independence, in London they made no such promise. Livingstone's referendum would be ignored, meaning that the enterprise was guaranteed to be a waste of money.

As far as the government was concerned, this was now a life-or-death struggle. It was war – and if it was the only means of getting rid of Livingstone, the GLA would have to be collateral damage.

The first member of the government to finally say it was none other than Boris Johnson. In an article for the *Telegraph*, the former mayor wrote:

No right-thinking person can seriously now believe that allowing King Newt to turn the seat of our great capital's government into nothing more than a monstrous megaphone of malice should be allowed to continue. His own desire is no less than a one-man state. A dictatorship, trampling on the wishes of this ancient and free city. Nobody, I doubt even Mrs Livingstone, wants to live in a Ken-ocracy. He must desist or we will stop him. Mr Livingstone may well be Mr Leaving-soon.

~

And so it came to pass.

Ken did not believe a word of his old adversary's rhetoric, but not for the first time he underestimated him. It would be Johnson's job at the Department of Communities and Local Government to preside over the GLA's abolition and design the new constitution for London.

It would be too ridiculous, Livingstone assumed, for a man who had been mayor a little less than two years before to abolish the post completely in an act of political revenge; and Johnson would have neither the attention to detail nor the heart to reduce his old friends and colleagues to long and lonely afternoons at the nearest Jobcentre Plus. But the mayor was wrong. It was exactly what Boris decided to do.

The battle was lost. For the second time, Ken Livingstone presided over the abolition of London's regional government, and once again it was to be the only capital in Western Europe not to govern its own affairs. The GLA had nine months to wind itself up, before the London Localism Authority – a newly created quango –took control of its remaining assets. London Underground – already technically a limited company – would be privatised, as would any remaining state-owned transport infrastructure. The police would be run by a directly elected commissioner, as would the fire service. In the name of localism, any remaining planning and housing jobs would be devolved to local authorities.

As far as Ken was concerned, he had nine months to give away as much of City Hall's money as was possible before the government could get their hands on it.

He started with the big stuff. Nearly half a billion pounds of assets held by the Mayoral Development Corporation was given away to councils. As it happened, and entirely by coincidence, all the recipients were Labour boroughs with a strong bias towards those whose leaders had supported Ken in his campaign to become the Labour candidate for mayor.

Derelict land owned by Transport for London was given away to housing associations, despite protests that it would make future expansion of the transport system impossible.

Computers used in City Hall and other agencies were given away, with strict instructions that hard drives should not be deleted. Information, after all, is power. Power in these cases went straight into the hands of those who would continue the fight. TfL's machines went to transport unions, hell-bent on fighting plans for privatisation. Machines blessed with information on policing went to the Justice for Smiley Culture Campaign and Victims of Police Brutality.

In the GLA's last weeks, the sight of lorries being loaded up with desks, chairs, telephones, water coolers, carpets and even the ovens from the City Hall kitchen became standard fare. The recipients were the usual suspects, now joined by anyone who said they had room for equipment and a worthy cause – Class War, Free Quebec and the Movement Against the Monarchy.

The last night of the GLA's existence was 13 March 2014. In Jubilee Gardens on London's South Bank thousands gathered to watch the likes of Billy Bragg, Paul Weller and Speech Debelle sing out the last hours of London government.

In front of the assembled activists and music lovers, Ken took to the stage just minutes before midnight.

'If you want to know why Cameron and Johnson are doing this, you need look no further. You are the reason. It is because you care enough to come. It is because you, the ordinary people of London, are showing that there is an alternative to their dogma and division. You are the alternative. The future of our city, of our country relies on you.'

The crowd whooped and cheered before breaking into a rendition of 'We'll Meet Again'.

On the stroke of midnight, heavy-set staff from the new London Localism Authority descended en masse. The exciting, flattering stage lighting was turned off and replaced by an overwhelming floodlight. It transformed the stage into nothing more than a large plank of wood with some people on it – and expensive equipment, now being taken away by the stocky men and women in high-visibility coats. The crowd booed. Plastic glasses were thrown. Chants of 'Tories out' rang out through the night.

Still standing in the middle of the stage amid the chaos, Ken Livingstone tried to take it all in. It was too much. A single defiant tear rolled down his face. He knew this was the end, not just of the GLA, but also his political life. No local party would have him as their MP. A life of occasional political punditry and restaurant reviews for gloating right-wing editors (who delighted at the one-time symbol of the left indulging in possibly the most decadent and useless of jobs) was all that would be left for him. For Livingstone that was no life at all.

Watching the whole thing on television, Boris Johnson was delighted. His career in government had just begun.

Chapter 22

What if Boris Johnson becomes Prime Minister in 2016?

Sam Macrory

Oxfordshire, 2019

Sweat dripping from his brow, the middle-aged man with the unconvincingly covered bald spot jogged slowly up the driveway towards his front door. Gasping for breath, he stopped to glance at his watch – and winced. He seemed to be getting slower by the week. Then again, the regular jogs through the Oxfordshire countryside kept him feeling healthy, and relatively happy.

Kicking off his well-worn running shoes, he padded through his tastefully furnished home towards the kitchen. No messages on the answer phone from anyone important – as usual. Turning to the mock art deco fridge, he dug out a carton of ginseng-infused water, poured a glass and then lit up a cigarette – a soothing habit which he no longer worried about hiding. Switching on the television, he impatiently flicked through the channels until he reached UK Fox, the twenty-four-hour rolling news channel which had dominated the airwaves since its controversial launch eighteen months before.

He strained his eyes in an effort to make out the images in front of him. A crowd had gathered on what looked like an unpromising pile of earth, with cameramen desperately clambering over each other for the best possible angle to film whatever it was they were watching. Their attention was focused on a rotund figure in a fluorescent safety jacket who was recklessly waving a garden spade around his head, apparently to the delight of his audience. As the cameras zoomed closer, a familiar shock of blond hair could be spied escaping from beneath the hard hat on top of his head.

Back in the Oxfordshire kitchen, the man's hand gripped his glass tensely. He didn't need the caption on the bottom of the screen to tell him what was happening: 'Prime Minister celebrates as work commences on "Boris Island" Airport'. The cameras zoomed closer, revealing the grinning face of Boris Johnson, Prime Minister of the United Kingdom of Great Britain and Northern Ireland for the last four years.

Struggling to make his excitable gabbling heard over the cheering crowd, the Prime Minister bellowed: 'This is an historic day. Pat your neighbour on the back. Shake their hand! Plan your holidays! This will be a new airport for a new Britain. The Thames Estuary will never be the same again, and neither will Britain! New jobs! New transport! A chance for all of us to pull together for our ... great British society.'

Staring into the Fox camera, the Prime Minister seemed to be locking eyes with the man in the Oxfordshire kitchen. The glass narrowly missed the TV screen as it smashed against the wall. Collapsing into the nearest chair, David Cameron asked himself, as he did every hour of every day: 'How on earth have things come to this?'

Eight years earlier

As 2011 drew to a close, David Cameron stood in the same Oxfordshire kitchen and waited for his guests – Elisabeth and Matthew, Andy and Eloise, and Bono and Ali – to arrive. The Christmas holidays could not have come quickly enough he thought, as he stared out across the snow-covered lawn. The feud over NHS reform – and it was bloody annoying the way Nick claimed to have saved it! – had drained him, Ken Clarke's radio interviews had frayed his nerves, and, as every admiral and general kept telling anyone who would listen, British involvement in Libya was proving to be uncomfortably expensive. Then there was that rather awkward thing with Andy and the phones – no invitation for Rebekah this year. The backbenchers were hounding him, the Lib Dems were harassing him, and the next three years of this wretched coalition seemed to stretch out interminably. Still, he thought to himself, he was the Prime Minister! And only forty-five years old! This was the mere adolescence of his premiership! The ungrateful bastards would soon remember what he'd achieved: over-throwing the Labour government, gaining huge local election victories, bringing in tougher sentencing powers, and, of course, dealing with any plans for electoral reform for a generation. The alternative vote was dead, the constituencies were being redrawn, and the Conservative Party, with Prime Minister Cameron at the helm, should be looking forward to a long stretch in power. His mood considerably lifted, Cameron smiled – 2012 was going to be a good year.

~

The bomb went off at 8:57 a.m. on Wednesday 9 May, a few hundred yards from Stratford tube station. Striking the heart of the Olympic village, the message was clear: whoever planted the bomb could do it again, at any time – perhaps when the Olympic Stadium was packed, as it would be in just three months' time.

With incredible good fortune, however, it appeared that the timing and location of the bomb had been botched. David Cameron was in Germany, invited by the German Chancellor Angela Merkel to make the second speech of his 'multiculturalism' series, so Nick Clegg – the day started with a series of 'Don't Forget!' tabloid headlines – was in charge. After digesting the news, the Deputy Prime Minister sensed the chance to flex some muscle. Boris Johnson, the recently re-elected mayor of London, had been dominating the airwaves, redirecting his early morning run to make his way across to East London and condemn the attacks. In response, Clegg quickly summoned a meeting of COBRA – one for the rolling news cameras, he thought – and began to prepare for what he hoped would be an easy opportunity to dominate that afternoon's Prime Minister's questions. Initial briefings were encouraging: no loss of life had been reported. This was a near miss rather than a catastrophe.

Then the call from MI6 was put through. Clegg's facial features fell back to their familiar setting of tired and grey. 'You're absolutely certain? I see.

Thank you.' The phone went down. Norman Lamb, his political adviser, and James McGrory, Clegg's press secretary, looked concerned.

'Not good. Not good at all,' Clegg told the anxious-looking pair. 'Well, obviously. But nobody was killed', Lamb replied with an optimistic lilt.

'That's not the problem,' Clegg replied, wearily. 'Until yesterday, the suspected bomber was being held – without charge – on suspicion of involvement in a terrorist plot.' A puzzled McGrory asked why the bomber was on the streets. 'Yesterday was his fourteenth day. By law, the police couldn't hold him any longer. He was released, and then met up immediately with the cell that had plotted the attack', Clegg replied, planting his head in his hands. 'We changed that law. That was our law.' No one said anything in return. The implications were clear. Life was about to get very difficult for the Liberal Democrats.

~

PMQs were a nightmare for Clegg, as Tory and Labour MPs alike accused him of putting British people at risk with his soft approach to terror.

That afternoon David Cameron, who had flown back from Germany, announced emergency plans to increase to ninety the number of days that a suspect could be held without charge. Given the public mood and the frenzied response of the right-wing press, the protests of Liberal Democrat MPs – and a rather half-hearted David Davis – were easily drowned out. That evening, in a ferocious behind-closed-doors exchange, Clegg tried to convince his MPs that he had been wrong: they should now back the new anti-terror legislation and demonstrate that they could be taken seriously as a party of power. His MPs stared back incredulously – the Rubicon of coalition compromise seemed to grow wider still. Warning of the irreversible effects of the 'poison of power', Charles Kennedy was the first MP to walk out of Committee Room 11, while Sir Menzies Campbell, after a short speech on the sad death of Liberal principles, followed suit. Vince Cable just looked glummer than ever. Clegg was confident however – if he could steer his party through the tuition fees row, then surely they would come round on an issue of national security?

He was badly wrong. Just three Liberal Democrat MPs supported the measures: Clegg himself, Danny Alexander, and David Laws. By voting no, every other Liberal Democrat minister had effectively left the government.

Later that evening, Sarah Teather, the young MP who had once been so decisive in the downfall of Charles Kennedy, was sitting in the Newsnight studio, telling Jeremy Paxman why Clegg had lost the support of his party. From the safety of the 10 Downing Street kitchen, the Deputy Prime Minister watched with a concerned David Cameron. 'That's that. It's over', Clegg declared, staring vacantly at the TV.

'Come on – there must be a way through this? We could speed up the timetable for Lords reform. I know, why don't we get David Laws into the cabinet? Nick, if you walk away, then you leave me horribly exposed,' Cameron pleaded.

'I'm sorry Dave. We did our best. "Events, dear boy", isn't that what your hero Harold said?' Clegg replied, as he stood up to leave.

'Let's talk this through in the morning – it isn't over', Cameron shouted after him, but Clegg had already shut the door. Sam had prepared a spare room so that he could avoid the media throng on his journey home to Putney, but Clegg knew he wouldn't sleep. He was already running through the wording of a resignation statement in his head.

Twelve months later

After Clegg stepped down, David Cameron initially embraced the opportunity to head up a minority government. His backbenchers were thrilled by the new arrangement, with the 1922 Committee holding a 'Not for Turning Again' reception on the Commons terrace, and a string of promotions to fill the Liberal Democrat vacancies triggering a second honeymoon for Cameron as he wooed the disaffected in his party. Andrew Tyrie succeeded Alexander as Chief Secretary to the Treasury, Bernard Jenkin took over the constitutional affairs brief, and Grant Shapps replaced Chris Huhne as Energy Secretary. All spoke a rather different language to that of their coalition predecessors, and so now did Cameron, with his talk of the 'Big Conservative Society', warnings of the growing 'European menace', and speeches on the need to be 'tough on crime – but tougher on criminals'.

Cabinet government, ministers declared, worked far more success-fully without the need to kowtow to the demands of a minor party, and after a summer of back-slapping, that October's party conference, hastily rearranged to be symbolically held in the nostalgia-packed Blackpool Winter Gardens, took place against a back drop of Union Jack-waving triumphalism. 'At last – it's our party ... back again', a cheering Norman Tebbit was overheard mumbling, while a misty-eyed Tim Montgomerie, whose ConservativeHome website did its best to claim credit for reshaping the government's new direction, dominated the airwaves.

The traditional vision of Conservatism mapped out in Cameron's conference closing speech met with loud cheers, but the Prime Minister left Blackpool feeling hollow. The party was pushing itself in a direction which was, he believed, ultimately unsustainable, and on the train home to London his mood plummeted. He hadn't spoken to Nick in weeks, while his strategy adviser Steve Hilton was spending ever more time 'working from home'. Ken Clarke, who appeared to have slept his way through Cameron's speech, seemed utterly detached, while Nick Boles, a one-time Notting Hill set associate, was stirring up disquiet among disgruntled modernisers.

Cameron's mood was not misjudged. By December, the government had suffered humiliating back-to-back Commons defeats, as hastily pub-lished bills to make fox-hunting legal and set in motion a programme for nuclear weapons renewal – red meat for the Tory right – failed to make progress. Tim Farron, the new leader of the Liberal Democrats follow-ing his defeat of Chris Huhne and Simon Hughes, had little difficulty persuading his MPs to vote against the Conservative Party, with former Lib Dem ministers jeered by Tory MPs as they filed through the no lobby. The impossible mathematics of minority government began to bite, slowly gnawing away at the electorate's faith in the Prime Minister. When a crisp and snow-free winter provided no excuse for the appalling economic figures of the last quarter, a harsh truth was made unavoidable at the start of 2013: Britain was sliding towards a double-dip recession. The increasingly ragged Chancellor George Osborne refused to bow to demands to switch to a 'Plan B' to fix the economy, however, and once Andy Murray fell in the second round of Wimbledon the newspapers turned their attention on the under-pressure occupant of 10 Downing Street.

'For God's sake. I gave him his sodding TV deal – this is ridiculous', shouted Cameron on sighting a particularly uncompromising *Sun*. On the front page was pictured a mallard, with a top hat and full Bullingdon Club tails photo-shopped on its feathered frame. 'Quack off! Lame-duck Prime Minister must go', ran the headline.

A string of poorly attended Cameron Direct events failed to mask the obvious: it was now clear that Cameron's government was effectively unable to legislate. The modernisers were disaffected and the right – Defence Secretary Liam Fox to the fore – were grumbling. The reputation of Ed Balls, the Shadow Chancellor, was steadily rising as the economy refused to pick up, and even Farron's Liberal Democrats had seen some of their core support return. As Parliament returned that September, and with the fixed-term parliaments unexpectedly bogged down in legal complications, Cameron was left with no choice but to call a general election.

Standing on a ticket of 'no more compromise,' the Tory leader embraced the campaign with gusto. The early public backing of Tony Blair – now envoy to Tripolitania, the western part of the former Libya, ruled by Saif Gaddafi – was mildly awkward, but he was pleased that Nick Clegg, not contesting his Sheffield Hallam seat, was helping out behind the scenes. The television debates were confusing. Tim Farron agreed with Labour leader Ed Miliband, and Ed agreed with Tim too, but Tim also wanted to claim credit for much of what Dave was bragging about, none of which Ed wanted to praise at all. Dave just looked horribly isolated.

Away from the TV studios, the rush for selection had witnessed some of the most unsavoury sights in recent years. The worryingly rapid reordering of Parliamentary constituencies had seen 650 seats reduced to 600, an ugly equation which saw sitting MPs given little time to reapply for seats and fight for the right to keep their jobs. In South London three seats turned to two, with Chuka Umunna forced to intervene as Harriet Harman's and Tessa Jowell's verbal spat threatened to turn physical, while up in Stoke a teary-eyed Tristram Hunt found his political career prematurely ended as his seat vanished from the Parliamentary map.

The result shocked politicians and pundits alike. Labour secured 293 seats, the Tories 261, and the Lib Dems 37. Chris Huhne's Eastleigh seat fell to the Tories, two UKIP MPs, from Essex and Kent, entered Parliament, while the Greens gained two more MPs, in Norwich and Oxford, to join Caroline Lucas at Westminster. Incredibly, there was no clear winner, so despite Liberal Democrat losses a second hung Parliament once again saw their leader play the part of kingmaker.

The thought of another round of coalition talks left Cameron feeling exhausted. 'I'm not doing this again. I can't. I mean, do they really want another referendum?' he wondered. However, after Tim Farron and his negotiating team of Steve Webb, Norman Lamb, and Duncan Hames had spent three days scuttling between their Labour and Tory equivalents, a referendum on the alternative vote is exactly what Cameron offered.

However, the stakes were now higher. With that promise in his pocket, Farron forced Miliband and his deal-making unit of Ed Balls, Sadiq Khan, and Chuka Umunna to raise Labour's bid. A switch to the additional member system (AMS) was offered without a referendum, and a deal between the Liberal Democrats and Labour was hastily drawn up. David Cameron, having failed twice to secure a majority for his party, was now officially the least successful Tory leader in history, in electoral terms, but as a man used to winning, he was not prepared to accept failure. The Saturday evening, with the dustsheets not yet removed, he summoned his closest allies to his old North Kensington home and began plotting for his survival.

~

At the BBC's Millbank studios the following morning, Tom Bradby – who had succeed Andrew Marr earlier in the year – was preparing for his regular Sunday morning show. Post-election analysis would dominate the programme, but an upbeat interview with the Mayor of London should provide some light relief. After all, it really had been an astonishing year for Boris Johnson. After successfully distancing himself from the more unpopular policies of the coalition government, Boris had comfortably beaten Ken Livingstone in the previous May's mayoral election. The London Olympics followed, and after Boris' defiant stand against terrorism an entirely glitch-free Games took place, with the British athletics team amassing a record medal haul. Spectators had made their way across London on Boris Bikes – number 50,000 was cycled hands-free into the stadium by Boris himself – and the new Routemaster bus was a hit with London commuters, all of whom travelled for free for the duration of the Games. Ever the showman, Boris ensured his place on the front pages as he embraced the Duke and Duchess of Cambridge on closing night at the Olympic Stadium, with photographs catching Cameron looking on awkwardly.

With his poll ratings soaring, Boris had every reason to look forward to the next three years. So, he told Bradby, did London. But that wasn't all Bradby wanted to discuss. 'It has been a terrible few months for your party. What will you be doing to help?' he asked. Without hesitation, Boris answered: 'The answer, of course, Tom, is whatever I can. I'm a Conservative mayor and a member of the Conservative Party. I love my party, and I want it to be in government.' Naturally, Bradby then asked the question which Boris had straight-batted away many times. 'And could you be the man to lead it there?' Apparently off the cuff, Boris replied: 'As I said, Tom, I'll do whatever I can. Whatever my party asks me to do, however my country needs me, I am merely a humble servant.' Watching, Guto Harri, Boris' press chief, mouthed one word: 'Perfect.'

~

Just one week later, on the back of a series of pleas from Tory associations and MPs, Boris resigned as Mayor of London. 'For the good of my country,' he declared, 'It is time to leave City Hall and return to Westminster.' Conveniently enough, the general election count in Sheffield Hallam had been declared null after pro-PR campaigners had set fire to a pile of ballot boxes. The courts demanded a recount, and to add to Boris' good fortune the Tory candidate stood aside to create a vacancy. 'Don't worry, Dad. This will work out well for both of us', Boris told his father, Stanley, who had sacrificed his long-held dreams of becoming an MP.

As Cameron began to panic, his ever-loyal spinner Gabby Bertin busily spread tales of Boris's colourful private life, but nothing seemed to stick. In homage to Alan Clark, Boris told hustings meetings that he had 'whole cupboards of them' when asked about the skeletons in his private life. 'I've said this before: there will be the odd indiscretion, but then who can't say that? We've all done things which we wished we probably hadn't.'

The threat to Cameron was clear. Boris, a former schoolmate and Bullingdon Club drinking partner of the ex-Prime Minister, knew far too much. As for Boris' colourful CV, the blue-rinsers in the party loved him for it. A bit of back-to-basics mischief was to be forgiven, and anyway, his long-suffering wife Marina was always by his side. He narrowly edged out Chris Huhne – still denying newspaper reports of alleged speeding offences – to victory in Sheffield, and just twenty-four hours later the Boris bandwagon rolled into Westminster. He didn't wait to catch his breath.

'I'm often accused of not being serious. Well, I've never been more serious about anything', he announced as he arrived on the steps to Parliament. 'Some people write down their dreams on the back of envelopes. Well, I'd decided in the womb before I could, er, write. How we failed – twice – to beat a discredited Labour Party is beyond me. Do we want to win? If the answer is yes, and I jolly well hope it is, then it is time to think again about the journey we must take to get us to that green and pleasant land.'

The phone banks were firmly in place and the support had been primed: that evening fifteen Conservative MPs published a letter calling on Cameron to resign, including backbench rebel leader Mark Pritchard, Boris' brother Jo, Theresa Villiers – still smarting at failing to make cabinet under Cameron – and Iain Duncan Smith, whose welfare reforms had been repeatedly undermined by former Chancellor George Osborne. Boris led the news bulletins and dominated the next day's papers: 'The Boris Factor!'

shouted *The Sun*. 'Time to get serious', announced the *Telegraph*. 'Better late than never', declared the *Mail*. Guto had been busy.

~

'What on earth are you doing? You're tearing the party apart. You had a perfectly good job. Don't do this to me!' Cameron was screaming into his mobile phone, Bertin looking on nervously. 'Yes, you bloody well are. This is about you, your ego, and getting one over me. Just stop it.' He resisted throwing the phone at the door – but only just – and turned to his worried-looking aide. 'What? What are you looking at?' he shouted at Bertin. 'This isn't about me. I *am* thinking about the bloody party.' He looked close to tears.

But as the grassroots membership flocked to Boris, and the majority of the party's MPs followed suit, Cameron was left with no choice but to call a leadership contest. The voting was worse than he could have expected, with Cameron forced to drop out after the first round, leaving Boris to romp to victory against the unpopular pair of George Osborne and Liam Fox. At that year's delayed Conservative Party conference, Boris was unveiled as the party's new leader. Walking on to the stage to the strains of the Beatles' 'Here Comes the Sun' – Boris's 'fantastically optimistic' choice on *Desert Island Discs* seven years previously – he sent delegates into wild delight as he declared: 'Mr Miliband – we're coming for you. Mr Fallen, er, Farron – watch your step. The Conservative Party is back and ready for business.'

~.

Over the next few years, Boris successfully dominated the media, outwitted the earnest Miliband at PMQs, and prompted a rapid rise in party membership. His reserves of energy surprised many pundits, but those who knew him best recognised the same youthful Boris who would smash his siblings at table tennis and repeatedly top the family general knowledge contests.

Miliband and his team were at a loss. Class warfare didn't work – Boris felt no shame in talking about his happy days at Eton – and any attempts to paint the Conservative leader as a philandering cad were met with a shrug of the shoulders. And if Boris ever strayed into un-politically correct territory then he seemed to have little problem laughing it off. The non-political classes loved him; the Tories felt indebted to him; and his opponents were driven to despair. Ed Miliband was unable to make himself heard, while Boris' apparent inability to remember Tim Farron's name had the desired – humiliating – effect.

David Cameron, meanwhile, had slipped from view. Bloggers joked that he was now living in isolation with Gordon Brown, who despite his re-election in Kirkcaldy in 2013 was still rarely spotted in the Commons. But the truth was that Cameron was in a state of shock: he simply could not accept that his old rival had beaten him. But Boris didn't give his predecessor a moment's thought. All eyes were set firmly on the next election.

~

It came quicker than he had expected. By the start of 2016 Ed Miliband was in a precarious position. His inability to break through Boris' wall of sound had caused considerable disquiet in party ranks. The Labour Party was increasingly split as the Prime Minister's feuds with his brother David Miliband, the Home Secretary, were played out via anonymous briefings. Boris, meanwhile, had lost his clownish reputation. Osborne, Michael Gove, and Fox were all denied roles in his shadow cabinet, with a well-timed visit from his old friend Arnold Schwarzenegger, reputation restored after the success of Terminator IV, leading to the inevitable headlines in the tabloids. Boris seemed to be taking the reverse journey of a number of his predecessors as Tory leader – the buffoon was now respected for his seriousness.

Worse still for the government, the international situation had dragged Miliband horribly away from his party. The great uprisings of 2011 had seen unrest spread across the Arab world and the Middle East, and by 2016 Iran was on the brink of war with Israel. US President Romney, desperate for re-election, was pushing for military intervention. Not on speaking terms with France's President Le Pen since calling time on the

UK's three-year-long involvement in the no-fly zone over the former Libya, Miliband had led his government into near-global isolation, with foreign leaders far more interested in spending time with the charismatic new Tory leader. In a desperate bid – his 'Falklands moment', suggested some commentators – to regain some international standing, Miliband declared his support for Romney. Fifteen years since they had gathered to register their opposition to the invasion of Iraq, the anti-war marchers reassembled on the streets of London, holding aloft placards of the late anti-war campaigner Brian Haw. Deputy Prime Minister Farron was quick to resign, and Ed Miliband, having learned from Cameron's inability to lead a minority government, wasted no time in calling a general election.

~

The campaign, of course, was dominated by one man. Boris, preaching a return to 'good old-fashioned Conservatism', flamboyantly dominated the television debates as Farron and Miliband unconvincingly argued the toss over the Lib-Lab coalition's failings. The cameras loved him and the right-wing press cheered him has he cycled his way across the UK, soapbox never far behind.

His shadow team, containing the likes of Ken Clarke, Iain Duncan Smith, Rory Stewart, Margot James, and his uncompromising Chief Whip Mike Penning, provided an impressive mixture of youth and experience, and while his policies were light – national Boris Bike roll-out, nationwide crime-mapping, the revival of Green Line buses, and the creation of a wave of so-called 'Boris' Grammars – the media were hardly exacting in their scrutiny. Boris-mania had gripped the country, and there was nothing anyone could do to stop it. Farron's Lib Dems were increasingly divided at Westminster, while Miliband and Miliband were barely able to share a platform together. Boris seemed to be the only candidate leading a party which was pulling in the same direction.

To the evident bamboozlement of the psephologists, the 2016 election was also the first contested under AMS, as the 2014 Electoral Reform Act had easily passed after Farron and Miliband had presented a united Yes front. Boris had seemed strangely calm during the TV debates, telling interviewers 'that he would play the ball, not the man' – a nice line which saw that clip of his famous popular footballing cameo replayed endlessly on the rolling news channels. The result saw a tentative re-ordering of the political landscape. Parliament now had 12 UKIP MPs, 7 Greens and, depressingly, 2 BNP members. Boris, however, had secured a 53-seat majority, defying predictions that nothing but first-past-the-post would suit the Tories. Second-choice votes fell almost unanimously for the Tory leader. 'Tory? Well, of course. But not in some ghastly tribal way. I'm British, I just happen to be a politician. That's the main thing, isn't it?' Boris had famously declared on the *Today* programme as the election approached. His party flinched, but the opinion polls soared. London's doughnut, the ring of suburbs which had flocked to him in the 2008 mayoral elections, filled out nicely across the central boroughs, while a record number of Labour constituencies showed their anger at Miliband's foreign policy by noting their support for Boris, a man who every house in Britain was aware of. The country's most recognisable politician had reaped the benefit of a system in which everyone could vote more than once.

Following a visit to Buckingham Palace and a meeting with the recently crowned King George VII, Boris skipped down Downing Street in front of the waiting media. 'Floreat Patria', Boris declared, modifying his old school motto, with his triumphant victory cheer picked up by an ITN microphone as he bounded through the front door of No. 10. For some reason Gordon Brown, the recently appointed Greenspan chair of economics at Harvard, had still refused to submit a photo for the famous Downing Street stairwell gallery, but Boris didn't care. He had done it. A Conservative Prime Minister with a majority government, the first in nearly twenty years. Life had always been rather interesting, he thought, but this was something else.

~

Cabinet appointments followed. Clarke became party chairman, IDS was handed the Home Office, while his old schoolmate Rory Stewart was made Foreign Secretary despite some last-minute lobbying from Sir Malcolm Rifkind. Philip Hammond was made Chancellor, Zac Goldsmith was handed the energy brief, Margot James was fast-tracked to Business Secretary, and Jo Johnson, Boris' younger brother, was promoted to Chief Secretary to the Treasury. A series of policy announcements followed. Lords reform, which had progressed no further than the abolition of a further forty-two hereditary peers under the Lib-Lab government, was thrown out, work on the controversial High Speed 2 rail project was stalled as Boris ploughed resources into speeding up the completion of Crossrail, a promise for 'all of Britain to fly where they want to' was issued, and a referendum on the UK's membership of the EU was casually talked up. Boris then exerted his authority in the most extraordinary of ways, declaring that to 'be elected is to be given the power to decide', after King George had called for the construction of a Poundbury in every county. Boris's chiding somehow managed to be deferential, playful, and authoritative all at once, and across the board, the remaining newspapers – 2015 had seen the closure of both *The Independent* and *The People*, with *The Guardian* becoming an entirely online operation – declared their admiration.

The Lib Dems, shell-shocked after securing just 40 seats under the new system, endured their most fractious autumn conference in living memory, with a split between the party's left and right wings ending a torrid week. Farron remained in charge of the Liberal Democrats, while David Laws and Danny Alexander left the conference vowing to establish the New Liberals as Britain's realistic alternative. From his position as EU Commissioner for Trade, Nick Clegg expressed his support for the latter.

The Labour Party, meanwhile, was far from happy. David Miliband had been elected to lead under the slogan of 'New Labour – the Only Way', but Lord Prescott had been aggressively beating a drum for a Real Labour Party to represent honest working people. Ed Balls, left out of a job after the abolition of Labour's shadow cabinet elections, was notably supportive.

So along with the four Irish parties, Plaid Cymru, and the SNP, as well as Liverpool Wavertree's Socialist Labour MP Ricky Tomlinson, the Palace of Westminster was now officially home to fourteen parties, all jostling for attention.

~

Some Tory MPs, however, were not so comfortable with Boris' nationwide appeal, and on May Day 2018, Penning broke the news to him. Three senior government figures had resigned: Ken Clarke, Caroline Spelman, who had been reinstated as Environment Secretary by Boris after her 2012 resignation over the sensational badger-culling U-turn, and Stephen Dorrell, the Tory Health Secretary – then spokesman – since Andrew Lansley's stress-related retirement from front-line politics in late 2012.

For the past three months the Conservative Party had been at war with itself over the issue of Europe. Egged on by the old Maastricht rebel Iain Duncan Smith, and further supported by the influential junior ministers Chris Heaton-Harris, Andrea Leadsom, and Mark Pritchard, Boris had got dragged into the tedious legalities of how to hold an in/out referendum on the EU. The party was not as supportive as he might have hoped, with 77-year-old Father of the House Clarke continuing to make persuasive speeches in support of the EU and rumours of splits in the cabinet eagerly seized on by a media looking for a way around Boris' dominant personality. The triple walk-out came as little surprise, with poverty guru Michael Heseltine, nearing his ninth decade, praising their boldness, and Sir David Cameron, in California for the latest leg of his lucrative global lecture tour with Tony Blair, declaring himself 'intrigued'. Anything to knock Boris of his perch must be good, though, he privately thought, as he headed off for a set of doubles with Tony, Silvio, and Cliff.

Boris laughed off the resignations as 'irrelevant piffle – just three people who are out of touch with the country', and moved quickly to replace the grumbling trio.

Perhaps it was five years of media adulation. Maybe he had been encouraged by the splits among his rival parties. Could his majority have left him feeling invulnerable? It was, according to *The Times*, the 'the most embarrassing reshuffle in history', while *The Sun*, with a woefully politically incorrect picture of Boris in President Mobutu-style headwear, announced the reign of 'Tin Pot Boris'.

Stanley Johnson, Lord Johnson of Exmoor, had been named as the new Environment Secretary. At 77, he was the oldest man ever to be appointed to the cabinet for the first time, the great Sheffield Crucible Pact paying off at last. Just as unexpected was the elevation of Kit Malthouse, Boris' former mayoral deputy and now MP for Witney, to the policing brief, while Ray Lewis, MP for Hammersmith and another former City Hall colleague, was handed a job in the Cabinet Office. His opponents screamed cronyism – 'Who next? Darius Guppy?' snarled Danny Finkelstein in *The Times* – while the London-focused leader's circle left many in the party deeply concerned. Boris declared himself uninterested. 'I was elected to save this country, whose people share my vision, and that is what I am doing – with the best possible people I can work with.'

But alarm bells in the party were set ringing. With Boris's local government reforms passing slowly through Parliament, 57 Tory MPs, the majority of whom represented rural constituencies, were led by the restless – and jobless – Liam Fox into an informal voting bloc with the Commons' UKIP MPs. Though agreeing with Boris's European plans, they were in opposition to his proposed council tax reforms which, following a deal with Mayor of London Lord Coe, were designed to favour a capital 'still paying the price for hosting this country's perfect Olympics'. Noting the shift in influence, the 23 members of the Liberal Democrats quickly stitched up a cooperative pact with Caroline Lucas' growing Green Party. David Laws' New Liberal grouping, the last rump of Nick Clegg's coalitionists, now effectively operated as Westminster's fifth largest party.

~

A week before Christmas, Boris and Guto were reclining in the Prime Ministerial den with plates of bangers and mash and Dijon mustard and a bottle of red wine. 'Don't worry about Liam and those UKIP loons. He'll come back – they always do. The party needs me more than I need them',

Boris declared through a mouthful of food. 'But the time seems right, wouldn't you agree?'

Guto nodded. 'Jobs, money, national pride, and named after you. Not bad. Incidentally, the latest polling has you as pretty much every non-Tory supporter's second choice – again.'

Boris smiled. 'Good-o! Need to win an election? Appear on TV a lot then slap your ugly mug on every election pamphlet and the undecided or the uninterested tick the box. This additional member thing is bloody brilliant.'

Guto chuckled, and replied: 'And when the election comes around, just build an airport, eh? Now, let's get to work on that press conference.'

He set off to break the good news to Lord Branson of Kidlington, the new transport envoy. 'Guto, hold on', Boris shouted. 'Will you sort a meeting with Rachel while you're at it? I never really agreed with the need for a women's minister, but she's been nagging me for ages. Seems a harmless enough thing for her to do once we get the second term sorted out. And shall we take a look at this voting systems green paper again? There might be something that will do me even better than this current arrangement, and this really is such terrific fun. I'm only 54 after all – and up for another decade of this …'.